The Human Tradition in Colonial Latin America

The Human Tradition around the World
Series Editors: William H. Beezley and Colin M. MacLachlan

The Human Tradition in Modern Brazil edited by Peter M. Beattie

The Human Tradition in Latin America edited by William H. Beezley and Judith Ewell

The Human Tradition in Modern Latin America edited by William H. Beezley and Judith Ewell

The Human Tradition in Modern Europe, 1750 to the Present edited by Cora Granata and Cheryl A. Koos

The Human Tradition in Premodern China edited by Kenneth J. Hammond

The Human Tradition in Modern China edited by Kenneth J. Hammond and Kristin Stapleton

The Human Tradition in Modern Russia edited by William B. Husband

The Human Tradition in Modern Britain edited by Caroline Litzenberger and Eileen Groth Lyon

The Human Tradition in the Black Atlantic, 1500–2000 edited by Beatriz G. Mamigonian and Karen Racine

The Human Tradition in Mexico edited by Jeffrey M. Pilcher

The Human Tradition in the Atlantic World, 1500–1850 edited by Karen Racine and Beatriz G. Mamigonian

The Human Tradition in Modern France edited by K. Steven Vincent and Alison Klairmont-Lingo

The Human Tradition in Modern Japan by Anne Walthall

The Human Tradition in Imperial Russia edited by Christine D. Worobec

The Human Tradition in Colonial Latin America

Second Edition

Edited by
Kenneth J. Andrien

ROWMAN & LITTLEFIELD PUBLISHERS, INC.
Lanham • Boulder • New York • Toronto • Plymouth, UK

Published by Rowman & Littlefield Publishers, Inc.
A wholly owned subsidiary of The Rowman & Littlefield Publishing Group, Inc.
4501 Forbes Boulevard, Suite 200, Lanham, Maryland 20706
www.rowman.com

10 Thornbury Road, Plymouth PL6 7PP, United Kingdom

British Library Cataloguing in Publication Information Available

Library of Congress Cataloging-in-Publication Data
The human tradition in colonial Latin America / edited by Kenneth J. Andrien.—Second edition.
pages cm. — (The human tradition around the world)
Includes index.
ISBN 978-1-4422-1298-5 (cloth : alk. paper)—ISBN 978-1-4422-1299-2 (pbk. : alk. paper)—ISBN 978-1-4422-1300-5 (electronic)
1. Latin America—History—To 1830—Biography. 2. Social conflict—Latin America—History. 3. Latin America—Social conditions. 4. Latin America—Biography. I. Andrien, Kenneth J., 1951–
F1412.H76 2013
980'.01—dc23
2013008122

Printed in the United States of America

:

I believe in aristocracy, though—if that is the right word, and if a demo-crat may use it. Not an aristocracy of power, based upon rank and influ-ence, but an aristocracy of the sensitive, the considerate and the plucky. Its members are to be found in all nations and classes, and all through the ages, and there is a secret understanding between them when they meet. They represent the true human tradition, the one permanent victory of our queer race over cruelty and chaos. Thousands of them perish in obscurity, a few are great names. They are sensitive for others as well as for themselves, they are considerate without being fussy, their pluck is not swankiness but the power to endure, and they can take a joke.
—E. M. Forster, *Two Cheers for Democracy* (1951)

Contents

Acknowledgments   ix

Introduction   1
    Kenneth J. Andrien

**Part I: New World Beginnings and Efforts to Create a Colonial
Social Order, 1492–1610**   7

1   Gaspar Antonio Chi: Bridging the Conquest of Yucatán   13
    Matthew Restall

2   Don Melchior Caruarayco: A *Kuraka* of Cajamarca in
   Sixteenth-Century Peru   33
    Susan E. Ramírez

3   Doña Isabel Sisa: A Sixteenth-Century Indian Woman
   Resisting Gender Inequalities   47
    Ana María Presta

4   Domingos Fernandes Nobre: "Tomacauna," a Go-Between
   in Sixteenth-Century Brazil   63
    Alida C. Metcalf

5   The Mysterious Catalina: Indian or Spaniard?   77
    Noble David Cook

Part II: The Mature Colonial Order, 1610–1740   97

6   Ursula de Jesús: A Seventeenth-Century Afro-Peruvian
   Mystic   101
    Nancy E. van Deusen

7   Agustina Ruiz: Sexuality and Religiosity in Colonial Mexico   117
    Zeb Tortorici

8   Zumbi of Palmares: Challenging the Portuguese Colonial
   Order   133
    Mary Karasch

9   Diego de Ocaña: Holy Wanderer   151
    Kenneth Mills

10 Felipe Guaman Poma de Ayala: Native Writer and Litigant
   in Early Colonial Peru   173
    Rolena Adorno

11 Ana de Vega: Seventeenth-Century Afro-Mexican Healer 199
Joan Bristol

Part III: Reform, Resistance, and Rebellion, 1740–1825 **215**

12 Pedro de Ayarza: The Purchase of Whiteness 221
Ann Twinam

13 Victorina Loza: Quiteña Merchant in the Second Half of the
Eighteenth Century 239
Christiana Borchart de Moreno

14 José Antonio da Silva: Marriage and Concubinage in
Colonial Brazil 257
Muriel S. Nazzari

15 Juan Barbarín: The 1795 French Conspiracy in Buenos Aires 269
Lyman L. Johnson

16 Agustín Agualongo and the Royalist Cause in the Wars of
Independence 289
Marcela Echeverri

17 Angela Batallas: A Fight for Freedom in Guayaquil 305
Camilla Townsend

Index 321
About the Editor and Contributors 339

Acknowledgments

This book has emerged from my experiences both as a research scholar and as a teacher. While administrators in higher education often explain that scholarship and classroom teaching reinforce each other, too often they do not. Preparing and teaching a class, grading papers, and spending time with students often takes hours away from conducting research and writing. In the case of this volume, however, that synergism between scholarship and teaching did occur. For many years I have listened to my colleagues in various restaurants, bars, and cafés in Spain, Latin America, and the United States recount fascinating stories about the life histories of individuals, which they had uncovered during their archival research. During my time teaching at Ohio State University and at Southern Methodist University, my own students also have found the real lives of historical figures one of the most interesting aspects of history classes. As a result, I have called on my colleagues to contribute some of the more "colorful" stories of ordinary people in colonial Latin America to this volume. I sincerely hope that students at SMU and elsewhere will find them an interesting and useful way to understand the past.

In the process of editing this second edition of *The Human Tradition in Colonial Latin America*, I have accumulated many debts. Most of all, I thank Susan McEachern of Rowman & Littlefield, who gave me the opportunity to undertake the project and waited most patiently for me to conclude it. I would like to thank the many students who took my classes at Ohio State and SMU; the joys and occasional frustrations of teaching those courses have inspired this book. As always, my wife, Anne, and our children, Jonathan and Elizabeth, have given me the love and emotional support that sustained my efforts. Indeed, I am dedicating this book to Jonathan and Elizabeth because being a father and watching my own children's efforts to learn about the past have taught me invaluable lessons, which I hope will make me a more sensitive, caring teacher. I trust that they will also make this collection a better and more useful book.

Introduction

Kenneth J. Andrien

A major challenge in teaching colonial Latin American history is convey-
ing to students how major historical events influenced the daily life experiences of common people. All of the essays in this volume address this
problem by providing life histories, which show real people in colonial
Spanish and Portuguese America adjusting to the large, impersonal historical forces that helped shape their lives. These personal stories seldom
deal with momentous historical events, yet each one offers a glimpse into
important aspects of everyday life in colonial Latin America. After all,
history is never only the affairs of kings, noblemen, and generals; it is also
about more ordinary men and women who cope with daily challenges.
At the same time, each of the personal histories contained in this book
illustrates a recurring theme in Spanish and Portuguese colonial societies:
the enduring social tensions that emerged when the political, social, religious, and economic ideals of the crown and the Roman Catholic Church
conflicted with the often messy day-to-day realities of colonial life. These
societal tensions could arise from squabbles over a wide range of disparate issues—gender roles, sexuality, racial and ethnic identities, or religious orthodoxy. Some could be resolved, while others reflected deep
sources of discontent that exploded into violence and rebellion. In all
cases, these daily "lived" experiences of people in colonial Latin America
reveal how men and women dealt with the contradictions between elite
notions of order and stability and the more disorderly and uncertain
realities of everyday life.

ORDER AND DISORDER

Spanish and Portuguese settlers in the New World (then called the Indies) shared many basic assumptions about social stratification, religious
orthodoxy, and entrepreneurship. The conquistadors and those who followed them wanted to establish a new colonial order that guaranteed
their own preeminence and also maintained political, social, economic,
cultural, and religious ties to their homelands in the Iberian Peninsula.
These new colonial societies would be rigidly hierarchical, with only limited social mobility, particularly for Amerindians, people of mixed racial

ancestry, and persons of African descent. Church officials decided to incorporate the large Amerindian population into the social order by converting them to the "true faith." After all, the Iberian invaders had justified their overthrow of indigenous polities and subsequent colonization projects by vowing to reap a bountiful harvest of indigenous souls for the Catholic faith—a new crusade. And finally, the settlers went to the Americas to get rich. Most came from the middle classes in Spain and Portugal and had only limited prospects of rising in wealth and status at home. The New World offered rich deposits of gold and silver, abundant land, and many exotic products not available in Europe. As Bernal Díaz del Castillo, a Spanish conquistador in Mexico, explained, the invaders acted "in the service of God and of His Majesty, and to give light to those in darkness, and to acquire that gold which most men covet."[1]

To these Spanish and Portuguese settlers, social status, honor, and wealth were assigned at birth; human efforts to change them threatened God's natural order. As a result, for most elites, social mobility signaled disorder—not a valuable way to ensure that society rewarded merit. In Spain, for example, gaining admission to a university, holding a government job, or entering the clergy required proof of "purity of the blood" (*limpieza de sangre*)—that is, an ancestry untainted by blood ties to Judaism, Islam, or social inferiors. Sumptuary legislation (laws limiting the consumption of luxury items) forbade commoners from carrying swords or from dressing above their social station in silks or other expensive materials. Honorific titles such as "don" and "doña" conveyed honor, status, and real privileges: freedom from judicial torture, certain exemptions from taxation, and the right to wear a sword. Iberian towns usually were constructed according to a grid pattern, with a central plaza surrounded by the church, municipal government buildings, the houses of some prominent citizens, and perhaps a monastery or convent. Where citizens resided in the city also reflected their social class and standing. In short, social hierarchies remained deeply rooted in the Iberian mentality.

Religion had become a key ingredient in enforcing unity in the Iberian Peninsula, particularly in the Spanish kingdoms. While Portugal was a relatively united polity, Spain was a loose dynastic union of the crowns of Castile and Aragon (until the eighteenth century), with separate currencies, systems of taxation, laws, customs, and several commonly spoken languages. During most of the medieval period, Jews suffered from bigotry but also continued to exercise their faith, as Christians and Moors (Muslims) competed for control of the peninsula during the seven-hundred-year Reconquista. Given this heritage, Iberia remained a political and cultural polyglot, forcing the kings of both Spain and Portugal to rely on the Catholic Church as a key unifying institution. As a result, with the fall of the last Muslim kingdom of Granada in 1492, King Ferdinand and Queen Isabel of Spain reinforced the Church's power by ending the long era of religious coexistence and expelling all Jews who did not accept conversion to Christianity. After consolidating control in formerly Moorish regions, the Spanish crown issued a similar edict in 1502, ordering the expulsion of any Muslims who refused conversion to Catholicism.[2] From its foundation in 1480, the task of enforcing religious orthodoxy in their kingdoms fell to the Holy Office of the Inquisition, a Church council designed to police the purity of the faith. The intermittent seven hundred years of warfare during the Reconquista had convinced Iberians that whenever different faiths existed side by side, disorder, conflict, and bloodshed inevitably followed.

Despite these shared ideals, most Spanish and Portuguese settlers found it difficult to impose European political, social, economic, and religious hierarchies in the New World. Resources were more open and difficult to control and maintain. Land became more readily available, particularly after European epidemic diseases decimated indigenous populations. Even the large deposits of gold and silver could be mined by anyone with both luck and an entrepreneurial spirit, regardless of a person's social class upon arriving in the New World. The invasion, conquest, and settlement of the Americas was essentially a middle-class enterprise; the wealthy had little incentive to risk their lives and fortunes, and the poor lacked the money to pay for passage to the Indies. Over time, men of new wealth and status claimed the title of "don," whether or not their birthright justified it. Sumptuary laws were more difficult to enforce. Spanish and Portuguese officials in the Indies, for example, continually railed against the lowborn and even slaves who dressed above their station in silks and satins. Even religious unity proved troublesome. Although the crown ordered the foundation of the Holy Office of the Inquisition in both Mexico City and Lima in 1569, it had no jurisdiction over Amerindians. At first, conversion efforts proceeded smoothly, but later it became clear that many indigenous communities still clung to their traditional religious beliefs, often merging them with Christianity in ways that horrified some members of the Church hierarchy. In short, the Spanish and Portuguese overseas possessions were truly a "New World" that mixed European, Amerindian, and African societal values.

European colonizers' attempts to control the large Amerindian population and the growing numbers of African slave laborers hardly created the more "orderly" societies of Iberia. In the Spanish Indies, for example, authorities attempted to enforce a legal separation of the races, establishing a corporate status for Amerindians, the Republica de Indios. The indigenous peoples had to pay a head tax, serve periodic terms of forced labor, and remain in Spanish-style towns (called *reducciones* in Peru). The failure of this policy of separation became apparent with the rise of a racially diverse population. Clerical and state authorities struggled to impose order by establishing categories for every possible mixture, as this partial list from New Spain demonstrates:

1. Spaniard and Indian beget *mestizo*
2. Mestizo and Spanish woman beget *castizo*
3. Castizo woman and Spaniard beget Spaniard
4. Spanish woman and Negro beget mulatto
5. Spaniard and mulatto woman beget *morisco*
6. Morisco woman and Spaniard beget *albino*
7. Spaniard and albino woman beget *torna atrás*
8. Indian and torna atrás beget *lobo*.[3]

Establishing fixed, orderly social categories for the infinite number of racial combinations was clearly a futile exercise.

Over time the Spanish and Portuguese possessions in the Americas developed more stable, diverse economies, but signs of instability and disorder persisted. In the vast Spanish possessions in North and South America, European settlers established a network of regional markets initially based on the extraction of gold and silver deposits, which they exchanged for European imports. By the seventeenth century, however, these market exchanges expanded as several other viable economic activities emerged: agro-pastoral enterprises, manufacturing, and artisan production. In Portuguese Brazil, settlers initially bartered with Amerindian groups for brazilwood, a tree that yielded a red dye used by European textile producers. The success of coastal sugar cultivation, particularly in the northeastern provinces of Bahia and Pernambuco, laid the foundation for a prosperous colonial economy tied to Europe, the principal market for Brazilian sugar. The discovery of gold in the interior provinces of Minas Gerais, Mato Grosso, and Goiás also prompted a move to settle these remote frontier zones. Nevertheless, the expansion of colonial economies provided both pitfalls and opportunities for European settlers, not the more stable socioeconomic order that theoretically prevailed in their homelands. Wealth could be made and squandered in a single generation, and social controls over access to wealth and status often proved difficult to enforce. Conquistador families, for example, began by amassing considerable wealth, but subsequent generations often squandered these fortunes. Conversely, a poor mulatto in the gold-mining zones of Minas Gerais might make a fortune that eclipsed the assets of a successful coastal sugar planter.

By the seventeenth century, social hierarchies and religious orthodoxy became more entrenched in the Spanish and Portuguese possessions. Colonial elites maintained control over society by inculcating the belief that all social classes and both sexes were connected in a hierarchical pattern ordained by God, with each member of society having certain responsibilities and rights. According to the Italian Marxist Antonio Gramsci, this represented a form of cultural "hegemony," which involved some level of acceptance by members of society.[4] It also united people more effectively than brute force. Widespread belief that inequality represented the "natural order" allowed elites to dominate the lower classes and men to dominate women. The power of the Catholic Church also gave this hegemonic social ideal greater legitimacy by linking prevailing social attitudes to the "will of God." Ordinary people often internalized these values of European cultural superiority and the subordination of women to men.[5]

Despite the overall prevalence of this colonial worldview, individuals and groups contested inequalities and attempted to negotiate a better position for themselves. Sometimes, these everyday forms of resistance turned violent, and full-scale revolts against the colonial order erupted, such as the rebellion of Túpac Amaru in 1781. Nonetheless, full-blown rebellions were rare, and individuals most often resisted or contested their status in more limited, personal ways—by practicing indigenous religious rituals, resisting an employer's sexual advances, or promoting new ideas that challenged the prevailing order. In this sense, establishing a hegemonic social order was a process rather than an unchanging set of outcomes, as ordinary people resisted and worked to forge a society that gave them a better life, with greater freedom and independence.[6]

THE HUMAN TRADITION

The lives of the men and women that fill this volume epitomize what E. M. Forster has called the "true human tradition." According to Forster, such ordinary people represent "not an aristocracy of power, based upon rank and influence, but an aristocracy of the sensitive, the considerate, the plucky."[7] Their stories often challenged the prevailing colonial social, economic, and religious order. These biographies are not a representative sample of larger historical trends but instead give a single profile that opens a window onto colonial society. These people did not always accept the hegemonic colonial order but viewed life from the borders or margins of society, which gave them a different perspective about the prevailing societal norms.[8] As a result, their lives demonstrate graphically how social tensions and disorder emerged when individuals attempted to cope with the demands of the values of colonial society as well as with the challenges of everyday life.

The life stories presented in this volume span the chronological divisions of the colonial era in Spanish America and Brazil. The selections in part I illustrate the conflicting attitudes over efforts to create the new colonial social order. The selections in part II deal with the struggles of a diverse group of individuals who attempted to cope with prevailing hegemonic colonial social values. Part III presents the attitudes and realities of individuals dealing with the changes prompted by imperial reforms, rebellions against the colonial regime, and the turbulent wars of independence. Although very different from each other, the lives depicted here demonstrate the continual social tensions that emerged when ordinary people, in large and small ways, attempted to carve out a place for themselves despite the constraints that society imposed on them. From the turbulent years following the Spanish invasion in the sixteenth century to the long, slow-motion collapse of the colonial order between 1808 and 1825, these individuals dealt with life's many challenges, using a wide variety of strategies that ranged from reaching an accommodation with the hegemonic social order to violent rebellion. While their histories may not always be noble or dramatic, they afford insights into the lives of ordinary people, the true human tradition in colonial Latin America.

NOTES

1. Bernal Díaz del Castillo, *The Conquest of New Spain*, trans. J. M. Cohen (London, 1963), 9.

2. J. H. Elliott, *Imperial Spain, 1469–1716* (New York, 1963), 46–52.

3. Magnus Morner, *Race Mixture in Colonial Latin America* (Boston, 1967), 58.

4. Antonio Gramsci, *Selections from the Prison Notebooks of Antonio Gramsci*, ed. and trans. Quinto Hoare and Geoffrey Nowell Smith (New York, 1971), 12–13, 416–19.

5. David G. Sweet and Gary B. Nash, eds., *Struggle and Survival in Colonial America* (Berkeley, 1981), 6.

6. Peter Guardino, *The Time of Liberty: Popular Political Culture in Oaxaca, 1750–1850* (Durham, 2005), 7–9.

7. E. M. Forster, *Two Cheers for Democracy* (New York, 1951), 26.

8. Walter B. Mignolo, *Local Histories/Global Designs: Coloniality, Subaltern Knowledges, and Border Thinking* (Princeton, NJ, 2000), passim.

Part I

New World Beginnings and Efforts to Create a Colonial Social Order, 1492–1610

Following the first voyage of Christopher Columbus in 1492, the Spanish American empire expanded dramatically during the sixteenth century. Spanish colonists fanned out from a few isolated Caribbean outposts to include Mexico, as the armies of Hernán Cortés and his followers overthrew the Aztec empire and later moved southward to annex the Maya domains in southern Mexico and Central America. By 1533 equally spectacular victories by Francisco Pizarro in the Andes brought down the Inca empire (Tawantinsuyu), giving the Castilians control over vast human and mineral resources in South America. The conquistadors tried to ensure their wealth and status by making grants of *encomienda*, which allowed them to collect taxes and labor services from a defined group of indigenous towns in return for military protection and religious instruction. These grants gave the holders of an encomienda (called *encomenderos*) social status and economic power—a source of capital and labor that could be used to buy property, engage in mining, or pursue a wide range of commercial activities. By midcentury, however, squabbles among the fractious conquistadors had undermined the encomienda system, along with the omnipresent epidemics that dramatically reduced the Amerindian population in the wealthy central areas of the Spanish Indies. Moreover, crown authorities wanted to limit the political and economic power of the unruly encomenderos, while many Churchmen wanted to gain complete control over converting the indigenous peoples.

Over time the power of the Spanish conquistadors waned as crown bureaucrats, Churchmen, and other settlers from Castile came to rule, convert, and populate the newly acquired lands and to benefit from its fabled riches. The crown established an extensive bureaucracy to rule in the Indies, headed by one viceroy in each of the two major political units, New Spain and Peru. The Madrid government also established a network of high courts (*audiencias*) to hear civil and criminal cases, and the justices worked with the viceroys to enforce legislation sent from Spain and also to issue any laws needed to handle local matters (see maps 1 and 2). To limit the local powers of the encomenderos, authorities in Spain also created a network of rural magistrates (*corregidores de indios*) to regulate contact between Spanish settlers and Amerindians, to collect the head tax or tribute, and to assign *corvée* (forced) labor service. Magistrates (*corregidores de españoles*) also served in most important municipalities to hear court cases and to regulate local affairs in conjunction with the city council (*cabildo*). Colonial commerce was also strictly regulated through Spain's Atlantic port of Seville and a series of licensed ports in the Indies. From 1561 all trade went in legally sanctioned convoys dispatched from Seville to designated locations, where trade fairs (at Veracruz, Cartagena, and Portobelo) were held to exchange European wares for colonial products. The Church also took firm control of the evangelization of the Amerindians in the viceroyalties. At first the religious orders played a leading role, but then members of the secular clergy established parishes under the overall supervision of a series of bishoprics (seven in New Spain and eight in Peru). In short, by the first decade of the seventeenth century, the turbulent early years of the Spanish invasion and conquest of the New World gave way to a more stable colonial political and religious order.

The Portuguese exploration and settlement of Brazil proceeded more slowly, as the crown concentrated its resources on expanding trade links in the Far East and later in Africa. After the initial explorations of Pedro Alvares Cabral in 1500, small coastal settlements slowly appeared by the 1530s and engaged in a profitable trade with the local Tupi-Guarani peoples for brazilwood. Within a few decades this barter system began to break down as many Amerindian groups began to balk at cutting dyewoods for the Europeans. The economic success of Portuguese Brazil was not ensured until profitable sugar plantations emerged in the northeast, around Olinda and Salvador da Bahia, by the second half of the sixteenth century. This only intensified the demand for labor, which the Portuguese met by enslaving Amerindians to work in the cane fields. Nevertheless, the Portuguese had founded stable coastal colonies; the only successful inland settlement was established at São Paulo in 1565.

Map 1. The Viceroyalty of New Spain in the sixteenth and seventeenth centuries.

Map 2. The Viceroyalty of Peru and the Viceroyalty of Brazil (inset) in the sixteenth and seventeenth centuries.

In both Spanish America and Brazil, the era of conquest and pillage had receded, but many troublesome problems emerged as Europeans, Amerindians, imported African slaves, and people of mixed racial ancestry all struggled to find a place in the new colonial order. Many of the stories in part I deal with the efforts of indigenous people to accommodate themselves to this often unstable society. The Maya nobleman Gaspar Antonio Chi belonged to the Xiu clan, who had allied themselves with the Spaniards against competing Maya groups. Chi received his education from the Franciscans, serving as a translator for the order and for local political leaders, and he used his position as an intermediary between the Spaniards and the Maya to advance his own career and the interests of the Xiu. The northern Andean ethnic leader Melchior Caruarayco attempted with less success to meet Spanish demands for taxes and labor while still carrying out traditional leadership tasks—providing for the sick, poor, and disadvantaged of his community. Some indigenous leaders, such as Caruarayco, lost the respect of their people. Too often they failed to protect their communities from excessive Spanish demands. Over time, however, many Andeans learned to manipulate colonial law to their own advantage. The legal struggles between doña Isabel Sisa and her husband, don Domingo Itquilla, over the disposition of their joint assets illustrate just how skillful indigenous people had become in using the Castilian legal code to advance their own agendas.

Questions about racial and ethnic identities also disrupted the colonial social order in the formative years of the sixteenth century. In Brazil, people of mixed indigenous and Portuguese ancestry often served as go-betweens, mediating between the Portuguese coastal settlements and the Amerindians of the wilderness interior. Domingos Fernandes Nobre, known by his indigenous kinsmen and followers as Tomacauna, was a successful slave trader whose unorthodox lifestyle and religious practices led local officials in Bahia to denounce him before the Inquisition in 1591. Although he escaped the most severe forms of punishment, Fernandes Nobre's life demonstrates the tensions between European notions of social hierarchy and the actual wilderness society in Brazil's interior. In a similar fashion, the controversy surrounding the racial identity of the servant girl Catalina in the Caribbean port of Havana offers insights into the problems of assigning fixed, unambiguous identities in the racially mixed world of the Spanish Indies. Each life story, in its own way, illustrates the ambiguities, difficulties, and tensions that arose in attempting to impose European ideas about social order in the more disorderly environment of the New World.

ONE

Gaspar Antonio Chi

Bridging the Conquest of Yucatán

Matthew Restall

Long after the Spanish conquest of the Yucatán Peninsula, many crucial aspects of Maya civilization endured. It took three invasions, spanning a period of twenty years, before conquistadors led by the Franciscos de Montejo (father, son, and nephew) were able to settle a colony. The third campaign was successful largely because the Spaniards brought tens of thousands of native warriors from central and southern Mexico to fight the Maya. Even then, the new colony only comprised the peninsula's northwest regions.

There the Montejos founded the colonial capital of Mérida on the Maya city of Tihó, divided the surrounding Maya towns and villages into grants of enco-mienda, *and established Franciscan missions. The Maya responded with a complex mixture of cooperation and resistance, as they attempted to control these changes and incorporate them into their own social, cultural, and religious framework. Maya society continued to revolve around two central institutions: the* cah *(plural* cahob*), a community with a defined geographical territory; and the* chibal *(plural* chibalob*), a patrilineal descent group identified by a common surname. Class divisions also endured within the cahob, as some chibalob maintained prominent political and social roles from the pre-Conquest era onward. On the other hand, political battles revolved around local municipal councils imposed by the Spaniards. Over time, various Maya elite factions continued to vie for control of important municipal offices that regulated local affairs within the cah as well as relations with outsiders, especially the Spaniards and their African slaves.*

Preexisting political divisions often set the context for Maya accommodation or resistance to the Spaniards. Thus some prominent chibalob, hoping to retain status during and after the Conquest wars, all at the expense of their rivals, made common cause with the invaders. The Xiu (pronounced SHOE), for example, eventually came to adopt such a position. As a result, the lives of many important sixteenth-century Xiu noblemen, such as Gaspar Antonio Chi (pronounced CHEE), were closely intertwined with those of the European invaders. After the assassination of his father by the rival Cocom chibal, the family of Gaspar Antonio Chi wanted to have him schooled in the ways of the Europeans and put the young nobleman under the care of the Franciscans. The friars were a powerful political and religious force in the early years of Spanish rule, and they taught the young Maya lord Latin and Castilian and saw to his instruction in Roman Catholicism. For their part, the Spanish political and religious leaders in Yucatán enthusiastically embraced young, well-connected Maya boys such as Chi, who could help to forge alliances with influential chibalob. Such connections would promote the spread of Roman Catholicism among the Maya and consolidate Spanish power in Yucatán. The first generation of Spanish rule in any region of the empire usually involved such strategic alliances.

This selection on Gaspar Antonio Chi begins with his birth in 1530, moving through the stages of his life—and Yucatán's turbulent history—until the eve of the venerable nobleman's death in 1610. Chi was not just a witness to the foreign invasions and the transformation of his homeland into a province of the Spanish Empire; he experienced those changes from the inside, participating in them as a translator and a notary for the leading Spanish bishops and administrators in the Yucatán Peninsula. Chi even served the two powerful rivals for leadership among the Franciscans in the sixteenth century, fray Francisco Toral and firebrand fray Diego de Landa. When these two men vied for control over the evangelization process, Chi wisely withdrew from the whirlwind of Spanish politics to serve as a local leader of the Tizimin cah, far from the capital at Mérida. Later he moved closer to the center of Spanish power while still remaining largely in the Maya world, taking up the post of notary and community leader (governor, or batab) *in his hometown of Mani. Throughout his adulthood, Chi used his position between the Spaniards and the Maya to advance his own career and the interests of his chibal, the Xiu. The life of Chi literally spanned two ages, linking what he described as an era of prosperity and abundance before the Spanish invasion with the years of disease, tumult, and religious discord that followed it. Although Chi became closely associated with the Spanish legal system and Christian evangelization, he remained deeply rooted in his heritage as both a Xiu and a nobleman of the old Maya order.*

Gaspar Antonio Chi was a Maya nobleman whose eighty-year life spanned the most turbulent and remarkable decades in the history of the Yucatán Peninsula (in what is today southwest Mexico). Chi was born before the Spanish invasion of Yucatán and died early in the seventeenth century when a Spanish colony had been firmly established, one that had employed Chi himself for much of his life. His longevity and career give us invaluable insights into the ways in which the Conquest affected native noblemen in the Americas and, equally important, the ways in which the native elite contributed to the course of the Conquest and the construction of the colony. In this chapter I shall trace Chi's life from birth to death, from the precolonial period to the Conquest era and into midcolonial times. Chi's high status and identity in old age is something of a riddle. But by exploring who Chi became and how he got there, we can begin to solve that riddle—and thereby also see what Yucatán became and how it got there.

DAWN (1530–1535)

Chi's dawning years were the twilight of pre-Conquest Yucatán. In 1530, the year of his birth, Yucatán was virtually free of Spaniards. By the time he was five, there was not a Spaniard for hundreds of miles from his hometown of Mani, where he lived with his father, the priest and nobleman Ah Kulel Chi, and his mother, Ix Kukil Xiu, of the region's ruling dynasty.

Not that the peninsula had avoided all contact with the foreigners. Spaniards were shipwrecked on its coasts in 1511, and perhaps even before then. Expeditions from Cuba in 1517 and 1518 landed at various points on the long Yucatec coast and engaged Maya warriors in brief but bloody battles. In 1519 the soon-to-be-famous Hernán Cortés landed at Cozumel and six years later passed along the peninsula's base. Then, for over two years in the late 1520s a full-scale campaign of conquest was undertaken in Yucatán by the family and allies of Francisco de Montejo. But it failed, as did a second campaign, begun in 1529 and abandoned after five years. In 1535, Chi's father, Ah Kulel, might have reasonably assumed, as he watched his young son playing on the family patio, that the threat of foreign invasion had finally passed. Ah Kulel might have imagined that his boy would grow up in a world much like that of his own youth.

Ah Kulel could not have anticipated his own death just a year later, or the third invasion of Spaniards a few years after that, or their subsequent permanent settlement. He could hardly have foreseen that the priests who would educate his son would not be *ah kinob* like Ah Kulel, but foreigners who would teach him a new faith, foreign tongues, and a strange new way of writing. He could not possibly have imagined all that his son would witness and record on paper. Had Ah Kulel been able to envision how violently the Maya world would be altered as his son grew from childhood to old age, he would have been terrified.

Yet had he been able to witness, seventy-five years later, his great-great-grandson's baptism in Mérida's cathedral, his reaction would have been more positive. For surely, despite the strangeness of that initiation, in a vast and unfamiliar temple, into Yucatán's brave new world, Ah Kulel's heart would have been warmed and his mind reassured by the persistence of family life—the life of *his* family.

YOUTH (1536–1560)

But Ah Kulel Chi lived to see none of this. In 1536, when his son was only six, he was brutally murdered. As a prominent priest, scribe, and government officer in Mani, Ah Kulel was a member (if not the head) of an embassy and pilgrimage from Mani to Chichen Itzá. To reach the sacred site, where rites were to be performed to bring rain to end a drought, the group of Xiu and related lords had to cross the territory of their Cocom enemies. In view of the peaceful nature of their mission, they were granted safe passage by Nachi Cocom. But the Cocom ruler had laid a trap, ordering the pilgrims massacred at the village of Otzmal (figure 1.1). The event would live in infamy; as the annals of one Xiu town, Oxkutzcab, declared, "May it be remembered!"[1]

Chi certainly remembered. Forty-five years after the event, he described it in writing. Chi was asked by several *encomenderos* (conquistadors holding encomienda grants) to help them complete questionnaires on their districts required by the king. In one report, Chi narrated:

> The province of Mani was always at war with that of Sotuta—[particularly] with a lord of the ancients of the land named Nachi Cocom—because of an ancient enmity which the said Cocom had against the Xiu. . . . Thus after the initial invasion of the first conquerors, whom the lords of Mani received in peace, without any resistance, giving obedience to His Majesty, the aforementioned Nachi Cocom treacherously killed more than forty lords of the said province of Mani, who were passing through his province on a pilgrimage, unarmed and under safe passage—beheading and putting out the eyes of Ah Kulel Chi, who was the most senior of them.[2]

Later, describing his father's mutilation in his own petitions to the king, Chi claimed that "they also cut out his tongue."[3] Indeed, Chi made his father's murder central to his argument that his life from the earliest age had consisted of service and sacrifice for the sake of the king of Spain and his representatives. According to Chi, the motive for the Otzmal massacre was the Cocom desire to punish the Xiu for appeasing the Spaniards during the second unsuccessful Montejo invasion of the early 1530s. In support of this view, Chi was able to enlist the testimony of some twenty Spaniards that this was common knowledge.

Chi's childhood and adolescence were therefore lived against the backdrop of civil war, famine and epidemic disease, and a bloody war of invasion and conquest. The Otzmal massacre set off a series of hostilities

Figure 1.1. The memorial shield of the Otzmal massacre. *Source:* **Drawing by Matthew Restall from the seventeenth-century copy by Diego López de Cogolludo, itself possibly made from an original drawing by Gaspar Antonio Chi.**

between Xiu and Cocom. The drought that had necessitated the pilgrimage to Chichen Itzá persisted. Disease brought by earlier Spanish expeditions continued to ravage the Maya population. And then a few years after Ah Kulel Chi's death, the Montejos returned in greater force, with a massive multiracial invasion force of Spaniards, Africans, Nahuas, and other Mesoamericans. There were no battles in the streets of Mani. But Chi would have seen the men of the town leaving to fight the invaders, and he would have heard gruesome tales of war from the few who returned. As Chi entered adolescence, foreigners appeared in town, word came of the new capital city being built to the northeast, and war continued to flare up to the east and south. Throughout these years of Chi's youth, there was no peace in Yucatán.

Then the first Franciscan friars arrived in Mani, and the changes surrounding Chi suddenly impacted him directly and permanently. First, he was baptized and given a new name. The orphaned Maya nobleman, who had spent his youth mourning his father, acquired several new fathers in the faith—the Franciscan *padres*. But he also became explicitly linked to the father figure of civil rule, as his full name became Gaspar Antonio de Herrera Chi, after his godmother doña Beatriz de Herrera, the wife of Yucatán's conquistador and governor, don Francisco de Montejo. At the same time, Montejo became godfather to the lord of Mani, the Xiu ruler, who was baptized don Francisco de Montejo Xiu—a moniker that neatly symbolized the continuities and changes of local politics in the 1540s.

Second, Chi went to college. In 1547—as Chi turned seventeen—the friars began the construction of the convent church in Mani and also set up a small school (figure 1.2). The Xiu lords fully collaborated in the project. In fact, when the Franciscans chose the nearby town of Oxkutzcab as the site for the new convent and school, irate Maya nobles were stopped from burning it down only because a local boy told the friars of the plot (the boy was not Chi, but his first months of instruction by the Franciscans probably took place in Oxkutzcab). Those nobles—twenty-six in total, many related to Chi—were condemned as conspirators and in turn saved from being burned at the stake in Mérida only by the pleas of Luis de Villalpando, the head Franciscan in Mani. The alleged plotters were pardoned, the baptisms proceeded, and the convent and school moved to Mani.

Based on a model established in Mérida a few years earlier (and in Mexico City a couple of decades before that), the school's purpose was for Franciscans to educate the sons of local nobles, native boys who

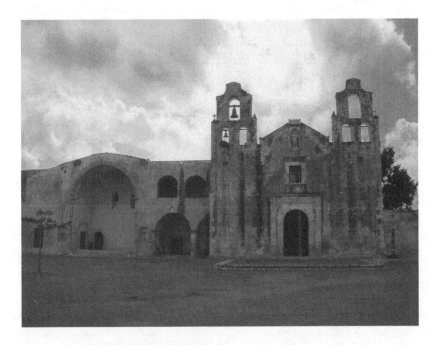

Figure 1.2.   The sixteenth-century monastic church complex at Mani, Yucatán.
Source: **Photograph by Amara Solari.**

would go on to be assistants, interpreters, and agents for the friars. As Diego de Landa later put it, "These children, once they had been instructed, took care to inform the friars of any idolatries and drunkenness and to destroy any idols, even if they belonged to their parents." Landa claimed that parents soon got over their initial opposition to Franciscan schools such as the one in Mani, and they began sending their boys to live and study there while continuing to visit them and "bring them food." In turn, the friars "learned to read and write in the language of the Indians, which was so reduced to an art [that is, a grammar book] that it could be studied like Latin."[4]

Latin, in fact, was one of the languages that the young Chi soon learned in Mani, along with Spanish and Nahuatl. The Franciscan chronicler Diego López de Cogolludo, writing forty years after Chi's death, stated that "he knew Latin grammar very well."[5] Sánchez de Aguilar, who in the seventeenth century became dean of Mérida cathedral and a chronicler of the spiritual conquest of Yucatán, spent part of his childhood in Tizimin, where his elder brother was encomendero. There he got to know Chi—"everybody in that era knew him," the Spaniard later wrote—as he was the town's schoolmaster and choirmaster in the 1570s. Chi "knew grammar reasonably well," reminisced Sánchez de Aguilar, "and in my childhood it was he who placed its art in my hands. . . . He was as *ladino* as any Spaniard, sang plainsong [*canto llano*] and sang to the organ with great skill, and could play the keyboards. I knew him as organist of this holy church and later as Interpreter General to the governor."[6] According to Chi, in his own words:

> I was the first native to learn the Castilian and Latin languages; and being of great ability and understanding, performed great services for God and Your Majesty in order to bring about the conversion of the natives of this province, which is of much concern to Your Majesty; and, as requested by the said friars [*religiosos*], translated and wrote sermons in the Indians' language in order to preach to them . . . the word of God and the Christian doctrine . . . and was always at the service of the friars, teaching them the language and interpreting for them.[7]

Chi must certainly have been a star pupil in the small school in Mani, where he studied, began writing, and remained based for most of the 1550s. He almost immediately would have learned of the energetic and already somewhat controversial Diego de Landa; and, as a shining example of the efficacy of Franciscan policies, Chi would also have come to Landa's attention. We don't know exactly when the two men met, but it must have been early; and while Landa was only seven years older, he was to become something of a mentor and patron to the bright Maya nobleman. Chi does not seem to have worked full-time with Landa until 1561, but their paths crossed repeatedly in the 1550s. Spanish colonists later saw the two as having been so closely associated that Dr. Pedro Sánchez de Aguilar could claim with exaggeration that Chi "was raised from childhood by the lord bishop don Diego de Landa."[8]

During Chi's twenties, Landa was based in Izamal, where from 1553 to 1561 an impressive convent was constructed on the base of one vast Maya pyramid, adjacent to a sibling pyramid (figure 1.3). The church was a monument to Landa's ambitions (and later denounced as such by his rival, Toral)—ambitions that frequently took him to Mérida and other parts of the colony. Similarly, Chi's budding career as a notary of rare skill and learning often took him out of Mani. In 1557 he served as interpreter and chief notary to the Spanish judge commissioned to ratify the Xiu land boundaries, both within the Xiu domain centered on Mani and between it and the Cocom region of Sotuta. Chi participated in the summit at the spectacular ancient site of Uxmal, in the great border walk that followed the summit, and in the writing of the treaty. Spanish officials intended the event as an imposition of the *pax colonial* on the feuding Xiu and Cocom chibalob; for their part, the two dynasties saw it as a way to consolidate their respective territorial and political authority. That clash and collusion of interests was precisely how colonial Yucatán was forged.

The 1557 treaty contains the first example of Chi's signature. The treaty is also the earliest surviving example of the Maya language written alphabetically. It is thus a landmark, as it were, in both Chi's professional

Figure 1.3. The sixteenth-century monastic church complex, built on top of an ancient Maya pyramidal platform, at Izamal, Yucatán. *Source:* Drawing by Matthew Restall.

life and the early development of the colony, the two being as intertwined as the Spanish and Maya cultures represented in the treaty and its written records. This was not the first time, of course, that Chi had written his name or that Maya had been written alphabetically. Indeed, it is Chi's fully developed professional skills as well as the full-fledged nature of alphabetic Maya in these documents that indicate the effectiveness of Maya-Franciscan educational collaboration in the decade before 1557.

That the collaboration served Maya purposes as much as Franciscan ones is illustrated by Chi and other native notaries using literacy in contexts such as the 1557 treaty; as Sánchez de Aguilar would later write, Chi "defended the Indians in their lawsuits and presented or composed their petitions for them."[9] It was also about this time that Chi probably created an extraordinary drawing known to us as the Xiu family tree (figure 1.4). It depicts members of the Xiu lineage descended from a pre-Conquest dynastic founder and includes Chi himself and his mother, Ix Kukil Xiu. Its iconography mixes Christian, Maya, and native central Mexican elements in a way that reflects the unique Franciscan-Maya context of Chi's education. Yet the tree was not drawn for Franciscans. It was created, rather, for Chi's Xiu relatives and descendants, who jealously guarded it for centuries.

MATURITY (1561–1578)

One of the conquistadors whom Chi had helped in 1581 with his royal questionnaire, Pedro de Santillana, gratefully acknowledged Chi's role in a succinct hagiography:

> Usually called Gaspar Antonio among the Spaniards, his age is fifty years, a little more or less, and he is a man of many abilities, a scholar, a *ladino* [Hispanized, cultured] well versed in the Castilian language, the Mexican [Nahuatl] and Maya language [*mayathan*], which is his mother tongue. And he is a person who knows well all the local peculiarities . . . as he was born in this country and was taken as companion of the bishops here, which were fray Francisco Toral, glory be to his memory, and fray Diego de Landa, glory be to his memory, as they thought him a truthful man. And through him they learned about the peculiarities and customs that the natives used to have, and still have at present. And as a man of character these bishops relied upon the things that were investigated and understood, in the language of this country, by this Gaspar Antonio.[10]

The conquistador's ready association of Chi with the colony's first two bishops, Toral and Landa, evokes the significant roles that these two Franciscans played in Chi's life in his twenties, thirties, and forties. But it barely begins to convey the complexity of the relationships between the three of them, particularly the bitter rivalry between the obsessively driv-

Figure 1.4. The Xiu family tree, possibly drawn by Gaspar Antonio Chi (with family members added on the left, in the seventeenth century, by don Juan Xiu). *Source:* **Reproduced courtesy of the Tozzer Library, Harvard University.**

en and often irascible Landa and the mild-mannered Toral. Both men may have trusted Chi as "a man of character" and "a truthful man." But because they did not view each other in this light, Chi found himself caught between them, an uncomfortable position from which he sought escape. For over a decade, from the mid-1560s to the late 1570s, Chi pursued a career outside of Mérida and the immediate circle of the Franciscans. Although Toral was bishop until his death in 1571 and Landa, appointed as his replacement, returned from Spain in 1573, Chi worked for neither of them during these years.

Instead, around 1565, he took up a post as choirmaster and schoolteacher in a Maya community, a role that was in a sense as close as a colonial Maya man could legally get to the position of a traditional Maya priest—the *ah kin* that Chi's father had been. The community was Tizimin, a cah with few Spanish residents far from Mérida and on the northeast margins of the colony. One imagines that here Chi found refuge from the Spanish world in which he had spent almost two decades of his young adulthood.

In 1572 he moved back into the center of things, but still very much within the Maya world, taking up the post of batab of his hometown; Mani's continued importance as a regional capital made its governorship one of the highest-ranking Maya offices in colonial Yucatán. Although he was only batab for a year or two, he had succeeded in taking up the political legacy of his maternal ancestry, and it was in Mani that he remained for most of the 1570s, enjoying his status as a former batab and a high-ranking notary. When he moved to Mérida in the late 1570s as interpreter general, he did not go to work directly for the bishop. Moreover, Landa was ailing; not long (possibly months) after Chi's return in 1578, the bishop was dead.

Why, if Chi was so close to the bishops, did he escape their employ and pursue a career in Maya politics? Part of the answer no doubt lies in the understandable (and, arguably, universal) desires to pursue a career in one's father's footsteps and to regain contact with one's native roots and family. But part of the answer surely also lies in Chi's experience of the turbulent early 1560s. In 1561, Chi had recently turned thirty, had married not long before, and by now was probably a father. He and his new family were living in Mérida, where Landa, already famous throughout the colony as a Franciscan firebrand, moved that year to take up his new appointment as *provincial*, or head of this religious order in the province. Chi seems to have begun working for the provincial as notary, interpreter, and assistant almost immediately. His tasks were relatively routine, but that would all change the following spring. In retrospect, Chi's first year as Landa's assistant in Mérida must have seemed mercifully mundane.

In May 1562, Pedro de Ciudad Rodrigo, the Franciscan friar in charge of the monastery in Chi's hometown of Mani, received reports of the practice of "idolatry" in a sacred cave on the edge of town. Finding "idols" or non-Christian religious images in the cave, Ciudad Rodrigo initiated a sequence of events that would be repeated many times in this and other colonies of Spanish America: prominent locals were interrogated, some were tortured, confessions were made, and the transgressors were lectured, fined, and ritually humiliated in the town plaza. However, what made these events unique in Yucatán, and to some extent in Spanish America, was that in this case they were merely the beginning. Having read a full report of the matter, Landa decided to travel to Mani and investigate further. He took Chi with him.

Landa's investigation immediately took the form of a large-scale version of Ciudad Rodrigo's, with not dozens but hundreds, and then thousands, of Mayas arrested, jailed, and systematically tortured. Landa started in Mani and then moved north to Sotuta. He targeted women as well as men. Many were permanently maimed, some committed suicide, and some 5 percent of the 4,500 victims died under torture. Even for the sixteenth century, this extraordinary campaign of extirpation was an excessively violent expression of colonialist frustration.

It culminated in the Mani plaza on July 12, 1562, at the ritual of public punishment and humiliation called an *auto-da-fé*. The Franciscans sentenced the condemned to having their heads shaved or to wearing the yellow red-crossed robes of shame called *sanbenitos*. Others were made to pay heavy fines, or to serve a Spaniard for up to ten years, or to suffer further torture (and possibly death) in the form of two hundred lashes. The representative of colonial government, the *alcalde mayor* (mayor) Diego de Quijada, repeated the sentences, which were then read out in Maya by a native interpreter to the gathering of condemned Mayas and their families. The interpreter was Gaspar Antonio Chi.

The assembled Mayas thus learned of their fate from the lips of one of their own—a Chi-Xiu nobleman from Mani, to whom many of them were related. It was surely difficult for Chi to participate in this Conquest ritual in this way—and to witness the brutal floggings and burning of religious images and objects that immediately followed his reading of the sentences. That much is suggested by the fact that when the procedure was repeated in Sotuta the following month, Chi was not present as interpreter. The arrests, tortures, suicides, and killings continued for weeks as the campaign spread through the Sotuta region and into neighboring Hocaba and Homun. But Chi was back in Mérida. He was there in late August when the colony's first bishop, Francisco Toral, arrived in the city and immediately summoned Landa to account for his actions.

Chi must have been relieved. He had watched his mentor wreak havoc on his hometown and neighboring communities for three months, learned how many of his relatives had been tortured to death, and found himself a party to a horrific ceremony of humiliation. He had also witnessed or learned of Landa's mass burning of "a great number of books in their letters [hieroglyphs],"[11] an act of vandalism that must have shocked a learned and literate Maya such as Chi. To be sure, he was the product of a Franciscan education, but his father had been one of the priests and scribes who had written and kept hieroglyphic manuscripts. The destruction of pre-Conquest Maya literature underscored the fact that, although Chi in many ways symbolized the continuity into colonial times of the Maya tradition of literacy, he and other native notaries would write only in the alphabet borrowed from the invaders as well as in the genres and formats set by them.

If Chi's absence at the August 1562 auto-da-fé in Sotuta can be taken as a sign of his feelings about Landa's campaign against "idolatry," further indication of his discomfort lies in the fact that shortly after Toral's arrival in Mérida, Chi began working for the new bishop. Toral knew Nahuatl and Popoloca but not Yucatec Maya, so he greatly needed a skilled interpreter such as Chi; for Chi, the job was a prestigious one. But Toral and Landa had almost immediately become bitter enemies, and Chi knew only too well the violent forms that Landa's disappointment and retribution could take.

Despite these risks, Chi accepted the position. Perhaps he viewed his new tasks as some kind of recompense for his work in the summer of 1562, for he now set about drawing up documents for Toral: a summons to Landa to justify certain aspects of his campaign, the translations of new Maya testimony asserting that earlier confessions had been false and forced under threat of torture, and the papers releasing still-imprisoned Mayas—including the lord of Mani, don Francisco de Montejo Xiu, who later wrote a bitter letter about "the great persecution" to the king of Spain.[12] The ubiquity of Chi's signature on the records of this power struggle between the two Franciscans reflects his role as an eyewitness to the battle for the soul of the new colony. The conflict was not solely over control but was about competing visions of the nature of native culture and the entire grand scheme of colonization.

If Chi's experience of the summer of 1562 turned him sour on Landa's vision of Yucatán's future, he was not alone. Spanish colonists and Maya leaders alike breathed collective sighs of relief as Toral continued to pursue his investigation into Landa's activities through the autumn of 1562, inexorably tipping the balance of power in the bishop's favor and, in January 1563, prompting Landa's sudden return to Spain. There, Landa spent the next decade defending his record of service in Yucatán. For years he had been assembling his observations and those of Spanish and Maya informants in a great compilation or *Recopilación*, and in the late 1560s parts of it were reworked and presented in his defense. The *Recopilación* is long lost, but fragments were later copied and survived as the *Relación de las cosas de Yucatán*, or *Account of the Things of Yucatán*. It is part narrative of Yucatec history and part ethnography of the Maya.

There can be little doubt that Chi contributed to the *Relación*. The two men worked closely together when Landa was making notes on Maya matters, and some passages in the *Relación* are very similar to Chi's own writings. Yet the only Maya informant given credit is the man whom Chi believed responsible for his father's murder, as Landa well knew—Nachi Cocom. Chi is not mentioned at all. In the end, the retribution that one imagines Chi feared from Landa uncharacteristically took the form of silence. [13]

SENIOR YEARS (1578–1610)

In 1578, the year of Bishop Landa's death, Chi was recently settled in the capital of Mérida. He was now the much-respected, known-to-all, highest-ranking translator in the colony, the interpreter general. He would hold the post for decades, during which his handwriting and signature, the latter an elegant rendering of his Christian names sandwiched between a pair of tightly styled rubrics, are frequently found on the written records of colonial business. We know, therefore, what cases Chi read and contributed to, and we can imagine how he reacted to some of them and how he perceived the colonial Yucatec world.

For example, in 1577, Yucatán received its copies of the above-mentioned set of royal questionnaires sent from Spain as part of an ambitious campaign to gather detailed information on all the colonies of the empire. Every encomendero was to answer all fifty questions; few did so, and in Yucatán at least a dozen sought out Gaspar Antonio Chi for assistance in responding to the two questions on pre-Conquest native religion, politics, and economics. Chi appears to have written replies for these Spaniards in 1579 and 1581 and to have done so with some relish. Rather than translating the words of others, he was here given a chance to express his own views.

Chi wrote wistfully of Yucatán before the Conquest as a land of great prosperity and abundance, governed well and densely populated. He lamented the decline of that population and, rather pointedly, blamed the loss not only on "the war of the conquest with the Spaniards" but also on misguided colonial policies of resettlement and the banning of native drinks (replaced by the pernicious wine of the Spaniards). He wrote, too, of the feud that had so touched his own life and of the death of his father, Ah Kulel Chi, recording for posterity his own understanding of the murder at Otzmal. The Cocom are condemned, the Xiu defended. As in another version of his account of Yucatán's past, written for the king in 1582 at the request of the provincial governor, Chi unabashedly promotes the Xiu dynasty as lords of "this province of Yucatán." [14] Thus even though many of his answers to the royal questionnaires were anonymous, his partisanship is clear. Nevertheless, he was surely telling it the way he saw it: the Xiu legacy was a supremely noble one. His father had died for the cause of the Xiu policy of peace and accommodation toward the Spaniards, a cause to which Chi himself had dedicated his life.

Another example of Chi's work as interpreter general dates from the dawn of the next century but also evokes the troubled years of his childhood. In the summer of 1600, Yucatán's Spanish governor, in response to a minor land dispute among Maya communities to the colony's east, ordered three cahob to submit land titles. Chi wrote a translation of the order into Maya and signed his name to it before it was sent out from Mérida. The following month, he translated into Spanish the splendid record of a territorial treaty made in 1545, one of the first documents written in Maya with an alphabet adapted from Spanish; Chi's 1600 copy (the only to survive) was then confirmed by a half-dozen cahob and dozens of Maya *batabob* (governors) and nobles from the region. As "Interpreter General of the high court of this government for the king our lord,"[15] Gaspar Antonio was simply doing his job. But in doing so, he was a witness to (and a recorded participant in) the adaptation of the Maya nobility to the demands and opportunities of the new colonial system—its legal culture of writing, its self-interested concern for local political stability, and its willingness to allow (or failure to observe) various forms of continuity.

There was, however, a personal twist to the case for Chi. For the dominant role in the 1545 land treaty had been played by Nachi Cocom. As ruler of the Sotuta region, Cocom had survived the Spanish invasion, was confirmed in office as don Juan Cocom, and won the friendship of Chi's own sometime mentor, Landa—all despite his resistance to Spanish demands into the late 1540s (he is still styled as Nachi Cocom in the 1545 treaty), a resistance motivated in part by the early Xiu collaboration with the invaders. The Cocom chibal suffered Landa's violent investigation as much as did the Xiu in the summer of 1562 (Nachi Cocom himself was condemned posthumously as an idolater). But that may have been of little comfort to Chi. The resurfacing of Cocom's name in 1600 must have brought back painful memories.

A third example of Chi's work dates from the start of this long final phase of his career. In 1578 he translated into Spanish the testimony of a Maya woman claiming to have been sexually abused by a Spanish priest named Andrés Mexia. In this instance, Chi sat with the woman and the priest and orally translated her replies to his questions; a Spanish notary wrote down Chi's translations, to which Chi signed his name. As Church officials under Bishop Landa built a case against Mexia during 1578, Chi translated other testimony, both oral and written, including shocking and well-substantiated accusations of rape.[16] Unfortunately, while the case records the voices of Maya parishioners, the outraged responses of the bishop and other Spaniards, and Mexia's own protestations, we can only imagine Chi's reactions. What appalled him more: Mexia's cynical exploitation of his priestly position to abuse and violate his parishioners, or the fact that he got away with it for so long? On the other hand, perhaps Chi's reaction was tempered by the fact that he had seen worse manifestations of the dark side of colonial relations; he had even witnessed them firsthand.

Arguably, Chi was a key contributor to the development and maintenance of the colony and its legal system in Yucatán. He may even have viewed himself in that light. Certainly he claimed as much in a brief autobiography that formed part of a petition to the king of Spain sent in 1580 and again, in revised form, in 1593. This petition was drawn up in a genre of letter that Spaniards called a *probanza de mérito*, or proof of merit, one that conventionally accompanied requests for royal rewards and pensions.

The king recognized the cogency of Chi's claims, albeit belatedly and not in the form of the coveted annual pension. Instead, he granted him lump-sum payments of 200 pesos in 1593 and 1599 (the latter probably in response to a third petition). These grants were a recognition, at long last, of "the many merits and services performed, for which," as Chi wrote in 1580, "he had received neither remuneration nor help nor support, despite being poor and in need and weighed down by debt and the costs of keeping his wife and children and family, and being a noble and virtuous person, a good Christian of good repute." By 1593, Chi had served the colony still further, and his burdens had increased, too, for now he wrote, "An ulcer on his leg caused him much pain and necessitated him going about on horseback." [17]

TWILIGHT (1610)

At the ripe old age of eighty, Chi completed what may have been his last professional deed: he acted as interpreter and notary during the trial of the so-called rebels of Tekax—the Maya men accused of inciting a riot and leading a revolt in that town during the February carnival of 1610. The intended target of the rioters had been the town's batab, don Pedro Xiu—a kinsman of Chi's. It must have been with a certain partisan satisfaction that Chi recorded on paper the damning testimony about—and official condemnation of—don Pedro's rival, don Fernando Uz, and his allies. [18]

Yet it was not the Xiu dynasty that Chi represented, but rather the Spanish provincial authorities—colonists who had sought to manipulate political factionalism among the noble families of Tekax in the years before 1610 and then condemned its riotous expression as "rebellious." As Chi well knew, in the years after the final Spanish invasion, the Maya elite received confirmation of social status and local political office; men like Chi were allowed to serve as batabob of the cahob—governors of their own towns. But as the century drew to a close, the growing Spanish community increasingly asserted its claim to monopolies on regional authority and political (and religious) violence, including the right to interfere with politics in the cahob should it serve Spanish interests. Chi was intimately acquainted with this pattern of colonial assertion; indeed, he had worked for its architects on and off for half a century. His identity as an important instrument of the colonial Spanish legal system was thus as deeply rooted as his identity as a Xiu and a Maya nobleman.

Chi participated in another event in 1610 that also can be seen as symbolic of the changes that had accompanied his life's passage as well as of the hybrid nature of his own identity. In the spring of that year, he stood by the baptismal font in the cathedral of Mérida to witness the christening of his great-grandson. Perhaps he sensed, as the baby was given Chi's own name of Gaspar Antonio, that the baptism would presage his own death before the baby would take his first steps and with that passing would die the last member of his family to remember the age before the Conquest—the violent years when Spaniards first marched along the forested trails of Chi's Maya ancestors.

The Yucatán into which Gaspar Antonio Chi was laid to rest was a very different world from the one into which he had been born eighty years earlier, or even the one in which he had striven with considerable success to build a career. His great-grandson's baptism was a symbol of such change. In addition to Chi's Christian names, the boy was also given the surname of his Spanish father, del Castillo. Thus the permanence of the Spanish presence in Yucatán was reflected not only in the baptismal ceremony and the building and city in which it took place, but also in the very blood of Chi's descendants.

QUESTIONS FOR DISCUSSION

1. How does Chi's life and career help explain how the Spanish Conquest was possible, and how does it illustrate the mechanisms whereby Spaniards established colonies in the Americas?
2. Could Spaniards have established colonies in places such as Yucatán without native interpreters?
3. Could one argue that Chi betrayed his own people? If not, why not, and how might one take issue with the terminology of the question?
4. Despite the dramatic changes in Yucatán between 1530 and 1610, were there also continuities? In what ways was Chi's adult life similar to the life he might have led had the Spaniards not invaded the peninsula in the sixteenth century?
5. What roles did the Franciscans and other religious officials play in the Spanish Conquest and colonization in the Americas, and how are such roles illustrated and reflected in Chi's biography?

NOTES

1. Taken from my translation of the annals in Restall, *Maya Conquistador* (Boston, 1998), 81.
2. Translation from Restall, *Maya Conquistador*, 149.
3. Archivo General de las Indias, Seville (hereafter AGI), *México* 105, 4b, f.2.
4. My translation from Diego de Landa, *Relación de las cosas de Yucatán* [1566] (Mexico City, 1959), 31–32.
5. Fray Diego López de Cogolludo, *Historia de la provincia de Yucathan* [1654] (Madrid, 1688), 238 (Book 4, Chapter IV).
6. Pedro Sánchez de Aguilar, *Informe contra Idolorum Cultores del Obispado de Yucatán* [1639] (Madrid, 1892), reprinted in *El Alma Encantada: Anales del Museo Nacional de México* (Mexico City, 1987); quote my translation from p. 96.
7. AGI, *México* 105, 4a, f.3 et al.
8. Sánchez de Aguilar, *Informe*, 96.
9. Ibid.
10. *Relaciones de Yucatán*, 2 vols. (Madrid, 1898; Mexico City, 1983), 1:251.
11. Quote by Landa himself, who adds that the book burning "greatly amazed them [the Mayas] and caused them much pain"; my translation from Landa, *Relación*, 105.
12. From my translation of the whole letter in *Maya Conquistador*, 165–68.
13. There is an element of speculation here simply because—as described above— the *Relación* as we know it was not written as a book by Landa; it is thus possible that passages in his lost *Recopilación* mentioned Chi but were not copied into what became the *Relación*. See Matthew Restall and John F. Chuchiak, "A Reevaluation of the Authenticity of Fray Diego de Landa's *Relación de las cosas de Yucatán*," *Ethnohistory* 49, no. 1 (2001).
14. Chi's original 1582 *relación* went to Spain, was preserved in the AGI, and is reproduced in Alfred Tozzer, *Landa's Relación de las cosas de Yucatán* (Cambridge, 1941), Appendix C; a copy stayed in Mérida and was acquired by López de Cogolludo, who worked it into his *Historia* of 1654 (Book 4, Chapters 3–4), 233–38.
15. Ralph L. Roys, *The Titles of Ebtun* (Washington, DC, 1933), 432; the Appendix contains the entire treaty record.
16. Archivo General de la Nación, Mexico City, *Inquisición* 69, 5.
17. AGI, *México* 105, 4a/b (quotes my translations from 4a, f.3 and 4b, f.5).
18. AGI, *Escribanía* 305a.

SUGGESTED READINGS

In addition to the primary sources cited in the notes, two previous Chi biographies contributed much to this chapter—a brief summary in my *Maya Conquistador* (Boston, 1998) that focuses on Chi's *relaciones* contributions, and a far more substantial and pioneering scholarly account by Frances Karttunen in *Between Worlds: Interpreters, Guides, and Survivors* (New Brunswick, 1994), which also places Chi in the context of other native interpreters, most notably La Malinche and Guaman Poma.

For more on the conquest of Yucatán and on Diego de Landa, see *Maya Conquistador* and Inga Clendinnen's *Ambivalent Conquests: Maya and Spaniard in Yucatán, 1517–1570* (Cambridge, 1987). John F. Chuchiak has also published over a dozen articles on Conquest-era Yucatan, including "Forgotten Allies: The Origins and Role of Native Mesoamerican Auxiliaries and Indios Conquistadores in the Conquest of Yucatán,

1526–1550," in *Indian Conquistadors: Native Militaries in the Conquest of Mesoamerica*, edited by Michel Oudijk and Laura Matthew, 122–97 (Norman, 2007), and "In Servitio Dei: Fray Diego de Landa, the Franciscan Order, and the Return of the Extirpation of Idolatry in the Colonial Diocese of Yucatán, 1573–1579," in *The Americas* 61, no. 4 (April 2005): 611–45. Also of interest is Landa's *Relación de las cosas de Yucatán*, of which the Alfred Tozzer edition is the most useful (Cambridge, 1941), although one by William Gates (New York, 1978) is the easiest to find. On the Mexia case, see my "The Telling of Tales: Six Yucatec Maya Communities and Their Spanish Priest," in *Colonial Lives: Documents on Latin American History, 1550–1850*, edited by Geoffrey Spurling and Richard Boyer (New York, 2000). On the Mayas after the Conquest, see my *The Maya World: Yucatec Culture and Society, 1550–1850* (Stanford, 1997) and William F. Hanks, *Converting Words: Maya in the Age of the Cross* (Berkeley, 2010). On other aspects of colonial Yucatec history, see the books and articles of Grant D. Jones and Robert W. Patch.

TWO

Don Melchior Caruarayco

A Kuraka of Cajamarca in Sixteenth-Century Peru

Susan E. Ramírez

Although the victorious armies of Tawantinsuyu spread the official imperial religion, more localized Andean religious practices endured alongside these state cults of the Inca. The Andean peoples believed that the sacred permeated every aspect of their world and deeply influenced everyday life. Inanimate natural objects such as mountains or trees represented or evoked divine ancestors, known as huacas, *who had founded extended human kinship groupings or lineages called* ayllu. *Within these communities, traditional leaders (*kurakas*) traced their ancestry back to these divine personages and served as an essential link between the huacas and the more mundane world of the ayllu. Powerful kurakas served as political leaders, but they also performed a multiplicity of important tasks—assigning labor, confirming land usage, mediating community disputes, and punishing lawbreakers. These Andean lords even dispatched community members to live on and cultivate lands at different ecological levels, providing the ayllus with a range of goods (in the absence of formal market exchanges) that they could not secure where they lived. By linking divine powers with everyday events in the material world, the kurakas allowed Andean men and women to forge a profound spiritual link to their gods, who protected them from human enemies and arbitrary forces of nature.*

After the Spanish invasion and conquest of the Inca empire, the political, social, and religious roles of the kurakas began to change in fundamental ways. The conquistadors divided the Andean ethnicities among themselves into enco- miendas, *which forced the kurakas to serve as intermediaries between the Span- iards and their kinsmen. Kurakas now allocated the tax and labor burdens de-*

manded by Spanish encomenderos *instead of exercising these powers in the name of local divinities. Later in the sixteenth century, crown bureaucrats (cor-*regidores de indios*) replaced the encomenderos in administering these tax and labor assignments, as the crown slowly began to ease from power the fractious conquistadors to gain greater political control over the Andean peoples. Nevertheless, too often kurakas had to deal with the exploitative demands of the Spaniards, who were interested only in draining human and material wealth from indigenous communities at a time when devastating epidemics spread throughout the Andean cordillera. These demands severely undermined the moral and political authority of the kurakas while at the same time Roman Catholic priests undercut their religious powers by spreading Christianity and suppressing Andean religious rites.*

Don Melchior Caruarayco, a leading kuraka of the Cajamarca region (northern Peru), lived in this turbulent post-Conquest era. He came from an ancient line, yet his traditional powers slowly eroded under Spanish rule. Nevertheless, as his last will and testament indicates, don Melchior still retained many Andean notions of wealth and power, measuring his fortune by the numbers of his retainers. With Spanish rule, however, came new laws and customs, which emboldened rival claimants to ethnic leadership in Cajamarca. They finally managed to unseat the venerable don Melchior. Indeed, the life and travails of don Melchior were in many ways typical of the traditional kurakas, who found it harder and harder to meet escalating Spanish demands for tribute and labor. These ethnic lords were often forced either to exploit their kinsmen or to meet these quotas by depleting their personal resources. Like other lords, called dueños de indios, *don Melchior began to lose the respect of his own people for failing to protect them from Spanish depredations. These leaders also found it harder to fulfill traditional religious obligations and Andean notions of reciprocity—providing feasts and other largesse to validate their power, status, and authority in the community. Indeed, these old-style kurakas were slowly replaced, often by handpicked cronies of local Spanish overlords who had no traditional claim to community leadership.*

Before the Spanish invasion, the Andean peoples believed that the sacred penetrated every aspect of their world, profoundly influencing daily life experiences. The sun and the moon, the stars, and planets were all considered gods and ancestors who had given birth to human lineages. Moreover, divine power could manifest itself in mountains, streams, trees, boulders, and even mundane objects such as small stones. Places evoked stories of the origin of lineages where the founder first emerged or settled, of a past hero who turned to stone and became immortal, and of ancestor-gods and their forces who fought and won important battles. Indigenous leaders called *kurakas* (or caciques by the Spaniards) traced their lineage back to these forefathers and led lives surrounded by public ritual. Within Andean communities, these chiefs represented more than just political leaders; they served as the living personification of divine forces. The kuraka was also responsible for the well-being of his people—coordinating work parties, redistributing crops from community fields (to care for the orphans, the widows, and the poor), and even dispatching community members to distant places to gain access to important products at different ecological levels. Products gained from these colonists formed a portion of the goods that the kuraka dispensed among his people, since in Andean societies there were no markets, merchants, or money. Ethnic leaders also resolved disputes within the community or with outsiders, even meting out punishment when necessary, but the wise leader used this power sparingly. After all, the chief's status was measured by the number of his followers—the larger the population of faithful devotees, the higher a headman's position among his neighbors and peers. Thus, the chief was a central figure, serving as mediator between the living and the dead as well as between mere mortals and the gods and as benefactor to all his loyal followers. These relationships gave nobles and peasants alike a sense of their common history, celebrated and taught in annual rituals and festivals. Such religious occasions also reinforced the social and ideological ties that kept local society cooperating, functioning, and viable.

These social and religious relationships changed dramatically in 1532 when the Spanish invaders arrived in the Andes. Some native leaders were not totally surprised and unprepared for the appearance of the Spaniards. Even before their boats anchored off the western shores of South America, there were signs that the gods were displeased with native leaders and society. During the reign of Guayna Capac, the last Inca king to rule a united empire that extended from what today is Chile to Colombia and inland into Bolivia and Argentina, omens appeared that foretold impending doom. A great condor, which might have a wingspan of ten feet or so, was attacked by less powerful and smaller hawks. It fell dead in the plaza of the ceremonial center, called the City of the Sun after the main Inca deity. Other sky signs indicated that blood would spill. Guayna Capac dreamed about a plague during which thousands of his people would perish. He himself died of a strange disease (c. 1524–1526) a few years before the Spanish arrival. Neither of the persons he designated as his successors was favored in divinations meant to find out whom the sun god chose to be the next king. In this context of disease and impending gloom, a civil war between two half brothers (Atahualpa and Huascar) broke out to see whom the gods would favor on the field of battle. A victory would mark one brother as the next king. In this conjuncture of events, the Spaniards sailed into view and began their own war of conquest against the massive Inca empire (called Tawantinsuyu), capturing the Inca king in less than one year.

After the Spanish invasion, local kurakas served as mediators between their communities and their new European overlords, who were entrusted by the Spanish crown to supervise and indoctrinate them in return for labor services and tribute. The Spaniards called these chiefs caciques, using a term that they imported from the Caribbean. To survive colonial exploitation and abuse, the kurakas quickly learned to protect their followers, maintain their community's socioeconomic order, and celebrate religious rituals. At the same time, a kuraka had to meet Spanish labor and tribute levies. This task involved assigning men as bearers (in places where the numbers of llamas, horses, and mules were insufficient to transport needed supplies) and women as cooks and laundresses. The kuraka also delegated ever larger numbers of his followers to produce food, to spin and weave tribute cloth, to pan for gold in local rivers, or to dig for silver ore in highland mines. Thus, the kuraka became a go-between, linking native society and the emerging Spanish colonial order. In playing this uncertain and difficult role, the kuraka had to please the Spaniards, a task that often meant organizing, manipulating, cajoling, and even exploiting his own people.

The kuraka don Melchior Caruarayco found himself thrust into this rapidly changing era of invasion, conquest, and social upheaval. Indeed, his life story epitomizes how the local native social organization was turned upside down, or what the Andean peoples in the provinces termed a *pachacuti*, a transcendental inversion of their world. In the first generation after the initial encounter with the Europeans, native religious and political structures were discredited and simplified, thus reducing the number of indigenous authorities. Moreover, Andeans continued to sicken from European epidemic diseases and die in alarming numbers. Some native peoples left their communities to serve the Spaniards, thinking that the Christian god was more powerful than their own or trying to evade mounting tribute exactions. Others fled into remote areas to escape the Spaniards' demands for goods and labor and their wrath when quotas were not met. In the process, many commoners lost respect for their native authorities as it became more evident that their ancestral gods either were not powerful enough to protect them against the Christians or had abandoned them. Worse, when the natives tried to worship their own gods and feed them to give the lineage renewed strength, they were condemned by omnipresent Roman Catholic priests. It seemed to many Andeans that the Spanish god and the Christian saints only helped the Europeans. Nonetheless, the Andeans often found ways to continue worshipping their ancestral deities in clandestine religious ceremonies. These traditional religious practices became one means, short of open rebellion, to resist the unreasonable demands of their Spanish overlords.

DON MELCHIOR CARUARAYCO

Descended from a long line of native leaders, don Melchior Caruarayco and his ancestors had been headmen of a large group in the sierras of northern Peru. Oral tradition records their title, *Guzmango Capac*—Guzmango being the name of the ethnic group or polity, while Capac signified a divine ruler whose forefathers displayed a special force, energy, and wisdom in ruling. By the time the Spaniards began to ask about their history, the polity's residents (called Cajamarquinos today) could remember the names of only two brothers who had served as Guzmango Capac under the Incas. The first was called Concacax, who was followed by Cosatongo.

After Concacax died, his son, Chuptongo, was sent south to serve the emperor, Túpac Inca Yupanqui. There he received an education at court and, as a young adult, became the tutor of one of Inca Yupanqui's sons, Guayna Capac. Oral history records that "he gained great fame and reputation in all the kingdom for his quality and admirable customs." It was also said that Guayna Capac respected Chuptongo as he would a father. Eventually, Túpac Inca Yupanqui named Chuptongo a governor of the empire. When Guayna Capac succeeded his father, Chuptongo accompanied the new sovereign to Quito. After years of service, he asked Guayna Capac to allow him to return to his native people. His wish was granted; and, as a sign of his esteem, Guayna Capac made him a gift of one hundred women, one of the highest rewards possible in the Inca empire. In this way, Chuptongo established his house and lineage in the old town of Guzmango, fathered many children, and served as paramount lord until his death.

The struggle for the throne between the two half brothers Huascar and Atahualpa, sons of Guayna Capac, also divided the sons of Chuptongo. During the civil war that broke out after Guayna Capac's death, Caruatongo, the oldest of Chuptongo's sons, sided with the northern forces of Atahualpa, while another son, Caruarayco, allied with Huascar, who led the forces from the south. Caruatongo, who was privileged enough to have been carried into the plaza of Cajamarca on a litter, a sure sign of the Inca's favor, died there on November 16, 1532, when Francisco Pizarro and his followers ambushed and killed many of the emperor's retainers and captured the Inca, Atahualpa.

Although Caruatongo left an heir (named Alonso Chuplingón, after his Christian baptism), his brother, Caruarayco, succeeded him as headman following local customs. Pizarro himself recognized Caruarayco and confirmed his right to assume the authority of his father. Caruarayco took the name Felipe at his baptism, becoming the first Christian kuraka of Cajamarca. He remained a steadfast ally of the Spaniards during his lifetime, helping to convince the lords of the Chachapoyas people to submit to Spanish rule. Felipe Caruarayco was paramount lord of the people of Guzmango, in the province of Cajamarca, under the authority of the Spaniard Melchior Verdugo. Pizarro had awarded Verdugo an encomienda in the region in 1535. Documentation from that year described Felipe as the *cacique principal* of the province of Cajamarca and lord of

Chuquimango, one of seven large lineages or *guarangas* (an administrative unit of one thousand households) that made up the polity. By 1543, however, Felipe was old and sick. His son, don Melchior Caruarayco, whom he favored to succeed him, was still too young to rule, so two relatives were designated as interim governors or regents: don Diego Zublián and don Pedro Angasnapon. Zublián kept this position until his death in 1560, and then don Pedro appropriated for himself the title "cacique principal of the seven guarangas of Cajamarca," remaining in office until his death two years later. After his death, the people of Cajamarca asked the *corregidor*, don Pedro Juáres de Illanez, to name don Melchior as their kuraka. After soliciting information from community elders, Illanez named him "natural lord and cacique principal of the seven guarangas of Cajamarca."

As the paramount Andean lord of Cajamarca, don Melchior was responsible for the guaranga of Guzmango and two more *parcialidades* (lineages or other groupings of a larger community): Colquemarca (later Espiritu Santo de Chuquimango) and Malcaden (later San Lorenzo de Malcadan). This charge involved approximately five thousand adult males, under various lesser caciques; and, counting their families, the total population that he ruled approached fifty thousand. Most of these mountain people, who lived dispersed in more than five hundred small settlements, subsisted by farming and by herding llamas. Their tribute responsibilities included rotating labor service at the nearby silver mines of Chilete.

During one of his many long trips down from the highlands to visit the nearest Spanish city, Trujillo, don Melchior was stricken by a serious illness. He prudently dictated his last will and testament before the local Spanish notary, Juan de Mata, on June 20, 1565. Coming as he did from a relatively remote area where very few Spaniards resided, his will reflects traditional Andean conceptions of society and values before they were fundamentally and forever changed. This is evident in the care he took to list all of his retainers. He claimed ten potters in the place or hamlet of Cajamarca, a mayordomo or overseer from the parcialidad of Lord Santiago, a retainer from the parcialidad of don Francisco Angasnapon, and a beekeeper who lived near a river. In the town of Chulaquys, his followers included a lesser lord (*mandoncillo*) with jurisdiction over seven native families. At the mines of Chilete, he listed twenty workers who served him. Don Melchior also claimed six servants with no specific residence and at least twenty-four corn farmers and twenty-two pages in the town of Contumasá. Nine different subjects cared for his chili peppers and corn either in Cascas or near the town of Junba (now Santa Ana de Cimba). He also listed the towns of Gironbi and Guaento, whose inhabitants guarded his coca and chili peppers; Cunchamalca, whose householders took care of his corn; and another town, called Churcan de Cayanbi. Finally, he mentioned two towns that he was disputing with a native lord whose

Christian name was don Pedro. In total, don Melchior claimed jurisdiction over a minimum of 102 followers and six towns, including the two in dispute.

This preoccupation of don Melchior with listing all of his retainers shows how strong Andean traditions remained in the Cajamarca region, even thirty years after the Spanish invasion. Among the indigenous peoples, numbers of followers denoted tangible wealth and power. An Andean chronicler, Felipe Guamán Poma de Ayala, wrote that lords "will gain rank if the numbers [of their subjects] multiply according to the law of the dominion over Indians. And, if their numbers decline, they too lose [status]." This concept of status was the same one held in the Inca system. The *hatun curaca* or *huno apo*, lord of ten thousand households, ranked higher than a *guaranga curaca*, the lord of one thousand. The latter dominated the lord of one hundred Indians, a *pachaca camachicoc*, who in turn was superior to the overseers (*mandones* and mandoncillos) with responsibility for as few as five households. Don Melchior, as a chief of seven guarangas, had jurisdiction over other lesser lords, who themselves ruled individual lineages.

In several clauses of his testament, don Melchior reflected his concern for the poor and disadvantaged among his subjects, leaving them food and other items. He left a total of fifteen fanegas (each approximately 1.5 bushels) of chili peppers, five fanegas of peanuts, twenty fanegas of corn, ten fanegas of potatoes, eight fanegas of yuca, three goats, and one *oveja* (a Castilian sheep or an Andean llama?) to the needy in Cajamarca, Contumasá, Chilete, and Cascas. The will also listed a number of items, all of them of Andean origin. They included five houses in Cajamarca, Guzmango, or Chilete, and fifteen planted pieces of land, noted as *chac[a]ras y tierras* (planted fields and ground). Land, like the air don Melchior breathed, was an open resource, available to anyone willing to work it while it remained fertile. The cacique did not claim ownership of these fields; he owned only the plants, which presumably had been sown by his retainers with seed that he had provided them. Other notable objects were all ceremonial items: the litter in which the Inca and presumably he himself was carried, a trumpet, and four large *cocos*, or ceremonial serving vessels, for drinking *chicha* (maize beer used in Andean religious ceremonies). Don Melchior listed only two items of European provenance: two mares. From his testament, it seems that people, more than material possessions, were the source of status and power.

Don Melchior did not die from the sickness that afflicted him in Trujillo but recovered to face many other challenges during his tenure in office. He returned to Cajamarca, the territory occupied by the people of the kingdom of Guzmango, to coordinate the activities of some five thousand tribute payers (males, aged eighteen to fifty) and heads of household and a total population that was dying off rapidly but which still totaled between twenty-five thousand and thirty thousand individuals (see table

2.1). This population continued to pay the tribute required first by the encomendero, Melchior Verdugo, and then after his death in 1567 by his widow, doña Jordana Mexia. Although tribute assessments had been reduced over the years to reflect the precipitous decline of the indigenous population, they remained onerous and burdensome. Native shepherds guarded Verdugo's large herds of animals; other Cajamarquinos made cloth; many also served his household. Verdugo, notoriously cruel, ruled with an iron hand. The memory of his hunting dogs, which had once ripped apart the son of the lord of Bambamarca when his father had failed to meet his quota of gold, remained fresh in the minds of residents of Cajamarca.

Dr. Gregorio González de Cuenca, a supreme court judge in the Spanish capital of Lima, visited the Cajamarquinos during the tenure of don Melchior to conduct a census of the indigenous tributaries. Cuenca counted 3,823 married and 1,346 single men eligible for tribute service. During this census, don Melchior negotiated new tribute allocations with Cuenca to reflect the declining Andean population. Cajamarquinos at midcentury delivered annually hundreds of lengths of fine woven cloth; thousands of fanegas of corn; baskets of chili peppers, chickens, and game birds; unnumbered pairs of sandals; and innumerable llamas, besides providing unpaid personal services. After 1567, however, each married male head of household was required to deliver 2.5 *pesos de plata corriente* (three *patacones*, or pieces of eight [reales]), one fanega of corn, and one chicken. Some of these goods could be delivered in silver. Thus,

Table 2.1. Population of Cajamarca, 1570s

Guarangas	Pachacas*	Population
Bambamarca	9	3,511
Pomamarca	7	2,246
Chondal	4	5,207
Caxamarca	10	2,497
Guzmango	6	5,631
Chuquimango	4	2,435
Mitimaes	4	1,697
Parcialidades		
Colquemarca	4	2,219
Malcaden	4	2,395
Total		27,838

Source: María del Pilar Remy Simatovic and María Rostworowski de Diez Canseco, *Las visitas a Cajamarca, 1571–72/1578*. Lima: Instituto de Estudios Peruanos, 1992, Appendix 1.
* Units of 100 Indians

the Cajamarquinos paid 14,780 pesos de plata corriente (17,605 patacones and 5 reales), 3,823 birds, and 2,584 fanegas of corn in 1567.

As the population continued its decline, don Melchior still had to deliver the same amount of tribute as if all the persons counted by Cuenca were still alive or living in their natal communities. Either he could track down everyone who had left the polity to make them contribute what they owed or make those who remained each pay more to make up the deficit. If these two strategies failed, don Melchior then was obliged to make up the difference from his own resources, which he found increasingly difficult to do.

Don Melchior also had to adapt to profound religious changes brought about by the colonizers' introduction of Christianity. The Franciscans had established a monastery in the area in 1549. They and the Augustinians, who lived nearby in Guamachuco, insisted on baptizing the indigenous peoples and giving them Christian names. They also curtailed both the worship of Catequil, a famed local deity and oracle, and the ancestors of the Cajamarquinos. Andeans did not understand why they should forgo worshipping powerful spirits who had granted them fertility and life-giving rain for generations and who could talk and answer the questions of their devotees. How could these forces be replaced with a single god who had died far away and who did not speak? The coming of the missionaries also meant abandoning the practice of polygyny and adopting the notion of legitimate and illegitimate offspring.[1] Ancestor cults survived underground, however, with the connivance of don Melchior and other lords, but superficial repudiation of ancestor worship undermined the ancient mechanisms related to succession, whereby community leadership passed to brothers of the same generation. Instead, European ideas about primogeniture gained currency in the Andean provinces, and positions of power passed directly to the oldest (and usually male) child.

As Andeans began to realize that Spaniards neither understood nor respected traditional succession practices, many claimants came forward to challenge don Melchior's charge and mandate. Two cousins, don Sancho and don Cristóbal Xulcapoma, declared that they had rights to the position of kuraka and brought their claim to the Spanish magistrate, Juan de Fuentes. He ruled in favor of don Melchior's claim, but the cousins then appealed the ruling to Dr. Cuenca. At this point, more alternative candidates came forward to present their claims. It was clear that the Spaniards did not respect native succession rights. In pre-Hispanic times, the general pattern was for one brother to succeed another, and only after the death of all able sons of one generation did leadership pass to a son of the next generation. After having heard testimony by the interested parties, Dr. Cuenca settled the dispute by naming Alonso Chuplingón, a son of Caruatongo, as lord. At the investiture, all the other lords accepted Chuplingón, making gestures of veneration to him once he had been seated on the *duho* (stool of office): "Each one of the said nobles came up to the said don Alonso Chuplingón who was seated on the said stool [and] they worshipped him in recognition of and as a sign of [his status] as cacique and natural lord." All participated except don Melchior, who remained at a distance, obstinate and convinced that his legitimate, ancestor-given rights had been usurped in 1568.

Don Melchior was not the only headman to face such difficulties. In the late 1560s and early 1570s, there were various indications that the old-style kurakas, called *dueños de indios*,[2] were dying off and not being replaced by individuals who were respected and feared like those of the past. It became harder for these new kurakas to mobilize labor and convince their Andean followers to obey. Therefore, the colonial state, which relied on their assistance and mediation, began to recognize them officially, issuing written titles to the positions they held and granting them privileges to bolster their faltering image. When royal officials traveled through the area, they gave the lords coveted licenses to ride horses with saddle and bridle, to own *arcabuces* (matchlock guns), to be carried on a litter, to wear Spanish clothing, and to have trumpets. But these privileges did little to maintain the general esteem that kurakas of old had enjoyed.

The absurdity of installing Alonso Chuplingón soon became obvious, even to Spanish authorities. He was described as "an incapable Indian because of his innate rudeness and little intelligence." As a result, a regent or governor, Juan Bautista, assumed his responsibilities. When Bautista died soon thereafter, the corregidor, Diego de Salazar, named a new governor, don Pablo Malcaden, even though he was a lord of a guaranga and not of the Guzmango lineage. Once again, Spanish authorities allowed ethnic leadership to pass to an illegitimate candidate who in pre-Hispanic times might not have been considered.

Despite lacking any legitimacy, don Pablo Malcaden served as governor after the death of Alonso Chuplingón, who died without children. There was a general consensus that the lordship should revert to a Caruarayco. Since don Pablo had outlived don Melchior, he declared Luis Caruarayco, the son of don Melchior, his successor as kuraka. In the end, Luis won back the title and position of kuraka of the people of Cajamarca, but only after a court case involving another pretender, Sebastián Ninalingón (of questionable parentage and a distant relative of Alonso Chuplingón). Viceroy Conde de Chinchon installed Luis Caruarayco as cacique principal in 1635.

EPILOGUE: THE TRANSITION FROM ANDEAN TO SPANISH VALUES

These struggles over local power illustrate how Andean values, practices, customs, and beliefs were subverted and changed under the Spaniards during the first half century of colonial rule. Indigenous concepts of legitimacy were based on the supernatural powers and special ties to the ancestor gods, which the Conquest had undermined. As ethnic leaders and their people converted (at least outwardly) to Catholicism, accepted baptism, and took Christian names, divination rituals and native religion in general were prohibited and usually driven underground. Although many lords continued to pray and sacrifice to the ancestors for wisdom to rule, other aspects of pre-Hispanic practices declined. Moreover, traditional ideas about legitimacy and succession also suffered by the imposition of Spanish ideas regarding primogeniture, which destroyed the custom of one generation of brothers ruling before their sons.

The imposition of Christianity brought many new rules and values, particularly monogamy. Don Melchior could not live as his ancestor, Chuptongo, taking one hundred wives. Instead, don Melchior remained legally married to only one woman, but, as he noted in his will, he had taken several mistresses and sired many illegitimate children. Old customs such as these were hard to eradicate. The imposition of Catholicism also began to destroy the basis of an individual's identity. Before the Spanish invasion, individuals worshipped many gods—from the sun and the moon to notable ancestors. In this way, every person felt part of a divine kin network and an extended ethnic community. It was not until the seventeenth century, and in some places the eighteenth, that the natives began to identify themselves as Christians. Likewise, the term "Indian" was a new one for Andeans; they had, of course, never heard the term "*indio*" before the arrival of the Spaniards. Indigenous leaders lobbying in Lima for colonial reforms in the mid- and late seventeenth century were the first to use the term to underscore their demands to the Spanish authorities for change.

Some aspects of communal life survived, but only for a few more years. The redistributive economy continued to function, though weakened, as the colonists demanded more and more silver or gold as tribute instead of products and services. To get these metals, tribute payers had to work for the Spaniards to earn cash wages, to sell surpluses in the Spanish market, or to travel to the mines or rivers in search of specie. In fact, parallel and overlapping economic systems were operative for many years. Natives traded, exchanged, and gave gifts among themselves to obtain commodities that they could not produce or procure on their own. They used the market to obtain cash and European goods.

Change would become even more pronounced when Spanish authorities began to consolidate the scattered settlements of don Melchior's time

into only forty-three villages, called *reducciones*, to facilitate religious conversion, tribute collection, and overall Spanish control. These were later
further consolidated into only seventeen towns by the 1570s. The problem faced by don Melchior's successors was how to satisfy the Spaniards
without exploiting their own kin to the point that they would either
sicken and die or flee to areas of the Andes beyond Spanish reach. Others
chose to leave their communities and become the retainer of a Spanish
master, which could take them into the city and eventually merge them
and their descendants with the growing class of cultural and biological
half-breeds or *mestizos*. Any of these alternatives weakened native polities and drove some to the point of extinction.

QUESTIONS FOR DISCUSSION

1. Characterize a pre-Hispanic kuraka.
2. How did the roles of the kuraka change after the arrival of the
   Spanish?
3. How did the indigenous definition of the word "wealth" change
   after 1532?
4. In a society without writing, how could a person prolong his or her
   memory after death?
5. What were the consequences of the arrival of missionaries among
   the Cajamarquinos?

NOTES

1. According to European customs, a man could have only one wife, and any
offspring of that relationship were legitimate. Any other children sired with any other
women were illegitimate. Under Andean traditions, however, a man could have
multiple spouses, and any children that resulted from such unions were considered
legitimate, not just the offspring of the principal or first wife.

2. *Dueño de indio* means "owner of Indians" when translated literally. It is the
Spanish translation of the Quechua and Aymara words *marcavoc* and *llactyoc*. These
words better translate as "possessor of people." Such terms were not meant to indicate
slavery but rather refer to an administrator of people.

SUGGESTED READINGS

The best general work on the history of Cajamarca is a three-volume set
compiled by Fernando Silva Santisteban, Waldemar Espinoza Soriano,
and Rogger Ravines, entitled *Historia de Cajamarca* (Cajamarca: Instituto
Nacional de Cultura, 1986). Another work worthy of mention is José
Dammert Bellido, *Cajamarca en el siglo XVI* (Lima: Pontificia Universidad
Católica del Perú, 1997).

For information on the local kurakas and their lives, see Horacio Villanueva Urteaga, *Cajamarca: Apuntes para su historia* (Cuzco: Editorial Garcilaso, 1975, especially 1–22); and *Los caciques de Cajamarca: Estudio histórico y documentos* (Trujillo: Universidad Nacional de Trujillo, n.d.). For background on the social organization of Cajamarca and the practice of polygyny, see the articles by Espinoza Soriano, "La poliginia señorial en el Reino de Caxamarca, siglos XV y XVI," *Revista del Museo Nacional (Lima)* 42 (1977): 399–466, and my book, *The World Upside Down: Cross-Cultural Contact and Conflict in Sixteenth-Century Peru* (Stanford: Stanford University Press, 1996), chapter 4.

Finally, to compare don Melchior's will with others, see Ella Dunbar Temple's article on three wills written by heirs of the Incas, "Los testamentos inéditos de Paullu Inca, Don Carlos y Don Melchor Carlos Inca," *Documenta: Revista de la Sociedad Peruana de Historia (Lima)* 2 (1949–1950): 630–51, and my chapter, "Rich Man, Poor Man, Beggar Man, or Chief: Material Wealth as a Basis of Power in Sixteenth-Century Peru," in *Dead Giveaways: Indigenous Testaments of Colonial Mesoamerica and the Andes*, edited by Susan Kellogg and Matthew Restall, 215–48 (Salt Lake City: University of Utah Press, 1998).

THREE

Doña Isabel Sisa

A Sixteenth-Century Indian Woman Resisting Gender Inequalities

Ana María Presta

The expansion of Tawantinsuyu set in motion a series of subtle religious and cultural changes affecting gender relationships. According to many Andean traditions, the panoply of indigenous gods and goddesses was arranged in a hierarchy characterized by gender complementarity. Human men descended from the male-oriented gods, who oversaw traditionally male activities — hunting game, caring for flocks, or waging war. Likewise, females descended from roughly an equivalent number of goddesses, who cared for the traditional female activities on earth such as agricultural duties, rearing children, and weaving cloth, which held important ritual significance. Under the state religion of the Inca, however, the sun god (Inti) and his descendant, the emperor or Sapa Inca (meaning "unique or supreme ruler"), were clearly superior to their female counterparts. Moreover, men's work seems to have become more highly valued. The Inca state religion also began controlling gender relationships directly, demanding that Andean communities supply set numbers of young women, called aclla, *to serve the Sapa Inca — spinning and weaving, serving in local temples, and preparing food and maize beer for festivals. In this way the Inca turned the aclla into symbols of state power by removing the labor, sexual behavior, and reproductive functions of these women from the control of their* ayllu *and families.*

The Spanish invasion and conquest of Tawantinsuyu moved Andean society much further toward the patriarchal values that permeated the Castilian legal code, particularly those laws governing inheritance. Nonetheless, Andeans soon began struggling to interpret and then to manipulate these new laws for their own advantage in the first century after the Conquest. One fascinating legal imbroglio over inheritance laws emerged between a wealthy and powerful Andean cacique principal *in Santiago de Curi (near the provincial capital of La Plata, the seat of the Audiencia of Charcas, today's Sucre, Bolivia), don Domingo Itquilla, and his strong-willed indigenous wife, doña Isabel Sisa. According to Castilian law, a couple owned jointly any assets acquired during marriage, although the husband retained the right to manage all the couple's property during their lifetimes. When don Domingo wrote a last will and testament, he declared that certain lands had been left to him by his ancestors, and so he felt free to bequeath them without regard to his wife's wishes. As a woman, doña Isabel could not openly dispute her husband's claims, so she filed her own will, claiming that these assets were joint property that she wanted to leave to her son and heir, Juan de Acuña.*

During the legal proceedings over the inheritance, a series of scandalous revelations about the couple and their strategic maneuverings, illicit sexual relationships, and shady political and economic deals emerged. While he lived, don Domingo had the better of the legal battles, but soon after his death, the wily and resourceful doña Isabel prevailed through skillful litigation and her knowledge of Castilian law. The turning point came when she presented evidence that her husband had gained his post as cacique principal *not through inheritance, but because his ability to read and write in Castilian had made him indispensable both to the community and to the Spanish authorities. He was one of a new generation of caciques who had usurped power from traditional ethnic leaders such as don Melchior Caruarayco of Cajamarca (see chapter 2).*

During one of her customary trips through the rugged terrain between the small indigenous town of Santiago de Curi and the city of La Plata (now Sucre, the historical capital of Bolivia), doña Isabel Sisa fell from her horse. What provoked the accident remains unknown. Perhaps her horse was startled by thunder or lightning, both of which commonly occur during the Andean rainy season. Nevertheless, the fall happened on December 31, 1602. Upon her return home, doña Isabel, a true Catholic, suffering great pain and believing herself near death, summoned a notary to her bedside to take down her last will and testament.

Doña Isabel did not die from her accident, but this incident marked her first attempt to obtain her rightful share of the property accumulated during her marriage to a wealthy but domineering husband, don Domingo Itquilla. The ensuing battle between the couple over this estate subsequently revealed secrets, coverups, and scandals perpetuated by the desire of doña Isabel and her spouse to control wealth, power, and prestige. Because she married a member of the indigenous elite, doña Isabel enjoyed status, wealth, and power, but she was subordinate to her husband in a male-dominated society. Nevertheless, she proved to be a formidable foe in her battle to control her own destiny by skillfully using Castilian inheritance laws to resist the prevailing gender inequalities of society.

A last will and testament usually was a written text signed by the testator, if literate, and witnesses such as the attending priest and the notary. Although testaments varied in length, they usually began by identifying family members, kin, and the testator's social status. The will followed with provisions to pay for the burial, posthumous ceremonies and masses, and donations to charity, and then with lists of the material belongings, debts, heirs, and debtors of the testator. In this way, testaments were ordinary, mundane documents, but they also reflected the cultural universe of the times and shed light on collective and personal representations of the supernatural.

The custom of producing a last will spread to the Spanish colonies and was practiced extensively among all kinds of people regardless of class, race, ethnicity, and gender. In many cases, for those who belonged to either the Spanish or the Indian elite, wills were inventories of their lives where private and public activities had their distinct place and meaning. Decoding those activities and the hidden practices that remain embedded in these texts is a fruitful challenge, allowing indigenous life stories and patterns of sociocultural changes to emerge. In some cases, testaments are the itineraries of life written before the passage into death.

It is through a number of testaments that the private story, the public life, and the hidden past of doña Isabel Sisa slowly come into view. Her initial testament, and the two that follow it, tell a private story of desire, love, distrust, and resentment. Moreover, through her wills—along with those of her husband—it is possible to know more about how Spanish notions of wealth, status, and gender hierarchies influenced the lives of indigenous peoples in early colonial times. The Spaniards introduced new conceptions of property ownership and land tenure, enforced by a legal system designed to reproduce Castilian patterns of inheritance and the ideology of a society of estates, which established differential rights and privileges under the law and imposed rigid patriarchal structures, subordinating women to men. The story of doña Isabel also provides evidence about gender constraints, strategic liaisons, illicit relationships, and bitter claims sheltered from public view in order to protect the couple's wealth and status. Nevertheless, the story of secrets and lies evolved from the documents, demonstrating how property and inheritance formed the center of this woman's concerns when death seemed imminent. Doña Isabel's testaments portray in writing a determined woman who battled to secure her legacy for her son and designated heir, Juan de Acuña.

The first of the documents from the testament of doña Isabel followed the standard legal form by identifying her as the legitimate wife of don Domingo Itquilla, *gobernador* (governor) and cacique principal (ethnic lord) of Santiago de Curi. These titles demonstrated that don Domingo was recognized both by Spanish authorities and by members of his own community as paramount lord of the town.[1] She also asserted her belief in the Holy Trinity, naming the Queen of the Angels as her mediator and the angels as her lawyers; both were needed to guide her soul to the gates of heaven. After placing her soul in God's hands, doña Isabel requested that her earthly remains be buried in the local church, in the chapel that she and her husband were building. If the chapel remained unfinished when she died, then doña Isabel wanted to be buried beside the main altar, after several masses were said on behalf of her soul. She declared herself to be a member of the *cofradía* (religious brotherhood) of Our Lady of Guadalupe, and she wanted this sodality to sponsor masses for her soul, paid for from her assets. Next, she asked her executors to invest one hundred *pesos corrientes* (pesos of eight reales) to support the celebration of seven masses annually for her soul. Doña Isabel specified that she had no debts, although she claimed that the Indian community of Santiago de Curi owed her (and her husband) more than six hundred pesos corrientes from the money payable to the *corregidor* (Spanish rural magistrate) for their taxes. One Hernando Chuquichambi also owed the couple an additional sixty pesos corrientes. Moreover, doña Isabel made it clear that she had the right to receive half of the money owed to the couple.

Regarding her personal belongings, she left her granddaughter Juana de Acuña eighty pesos corrientes and bequeathed some dresses to her granddaughters. After these items, she emphatically declared everything else community property. Among these goods, she listed a house and a lot located within the city of La Plata; houses, lots, and orchards in Santiago de Curi; one hundred cows, eight pairs of oxen, twenty-five mares, two mules, and a horse. Household goods included a Chinese satin tapestry (purchased for 120 pesos corrientes), a cloth with the image of the Mother of God and a crucifix, some furniture, and "siete libros de leer viejos" (seven old reading books). Also listed were 750 pesos in cash, forty *cargas* (one hundred pounds) of wheat, five cargas of potatoes and two of maize sown in their fields, an unspecified quantity of stored wheat, corn, and potatoes, eighty cargas of dry wheat to be given to their Indians, twenty-eight pesos corrientes owed to doña Isabel and don Domingo (by Juan de Tudela and his wife for ten cargas of wheat), and agricultural tools. She included personal belongings—an *axu* (woman's outfit), a *lliqlla* (wide shawl), a pair of Castilian velvet sleeves embroidered with gold, and four new cotton shirts from Rouen. Finally, since she had benefited from the labor of the Indians of Santiago de Curi, she left the elderly and poor of that community a pair of oxen. Moreover, she named her husband, don Domingo, and her son, Juan de Acuña, as executors. She addressed Juan de Acuña as her "legitimate" son and sole heir. The husband and the son (as executors), the notary, and two witnesses signed the testament. One did so in her name, since doña Isabel was illiterate.[2]

One day later, while alone, doña Isabel asked the notary to add a codicil to her original testament. According to doña Isabel, her husband had forced her to dictate her testament in his presence, and she had accepted "because he is her husband and to avoid afflictions and because she is afraid of him."[3] Behind this admission were colonial notions of patriarchy, male domination, the weak social position of women, and even the threat of domestic violence. Determined to overcome her fears, however, doña Isabel asserted that there were some items she needed to add.[4] She stated that her husband had refused to give her half of the last harvest of wheat and maize, worth one thousand pesos corrientes. Moreover, she declared that he had taken another three thousand pesos corrientes that she had earned by selling *coca* (coca leaves) and *chicha* (maize beer). Although his wife had demonstrated her ability to earn money and transact business, don Domingo assumed the legal inferiority of women and their incapacity to administer assets, given the innate mental deficiency of the female sex (*imbecilitus sexus*). Castilian law allowed husbands and fathers to manage the assets of their wives and children. Thus, legalized gender prejudice denied doña Isabel the right to enjoy, administer, or invest her earnings.

Despite this legal support for patriarchy, Spanish law also provided that upon the death of one spouse, the other was entitled to half of the assets accumulated during the marriage. After the death of her husband, a wife had the right to get back her dowry, any other property that she had owned before the marriage, and one-half of the *gananciales* (community property) gained in common with her husband during their marriage. Since doña Isabel brought no dowry, she claimed that her earnings came from marketing goods and the property acquired during the marriage. She also claimed that don Domingo had not allowed her to include among their community property their *chacra* (small farm), called Chilcane, and their cattle ranch. Consequently, she named her "son," Juan de Acuña, the heir to her community property, including Chilcane and the ranch. Was doña Isabel really so near death when she dictated her will, or did she use her injury as an excuse to demand her share of valuable community property? Her first will and codicil may well have been a strategy to overcome gender constraints and contest her husband's will, which was dated two years before hers. It also served to remind her husband about her legal rights to their community property.

Don Domingo Itquilla had hired a notary to write his first will and testament on June 23, 1601, in La Plata.[5] Following convention, the cacique stated that he was the son of don Martín Chinori Guarachi and doña Ana Anama, former lords of Santiago de Curi. He declared his belief in the Holy Trinity and asked to be buried in the church of his hometown in the presence of the local priest and the members of the Brotherhood of Our Lady of Copacabana. He also requested masses on his behalf to be celebrated in Santiago de Curi as well as at the four monasteries and cathedral in La Plata. Don Domingo designated for the statue of the Virgin of Copacabana in the church of Santiago de Curi a new cloak made of Chinese satin and embroidered with gold thread. He also left money to be applied to the canonization of Saint Isidore. After recognizing his debts to his Indians and others, don Domingo declared among his personal assets the chacra of Chilcane, which he "had inherited from his parents" before marrying doña Isabel. He also mentioned other properties and belongings that his wife had declared as communal property. Furthermore, he stated that thirty years ago he had married doña Isabel Sisa, who had neither brought a dowry nor given him heirs. Consequently, he named her as the sole heir to their remaining community property. Moreover, he left his "nephew," don Domingo Hamamani, the estate of Chilcane and the *cacicazgo* (chieftaincy) of Santiago de Curi. Additionally, don Domingo demanded that his nephew look after, support, and marry the child named doña María Chocoboto, daughter of the deceased don Domingo Andaca, as a condition of inheritance. Surprisingly, after this clause don Domingo asserted that he had no children, either with his legitimate wife or with another woman.[6] Finally, he named don Juan Prica, *segunda persona* (second in command) of affairs in Santiago de Curi, and his "nephew," don Domingo Hamamani, as his executors.

It seems clear that instead of going to court to resolve their disputes over communal property, the partners had chosen to use their wills to litigate the property rights. Doña Isabel prepared her wills and codicils as a strategy of defense under Spanish law, acting as the plaintiff. Accordingly, her husband, the defendant, promptly understood the game and responded in the same way. Thus, a confrontation of "wills" began between doña Isabel and don Domingo. These legal actions avoided any long, tedious, and costly lawsuits over the disputed communal property and kept the battle in the domestic sphere once the pact of silence between husband and wife had been broken. While both spouses added more information in each new will, don Domingo introduced contradictions in his version of events that would eventually lead to his defeat in court.

All of these changes in the testaments involved efforts by both spouses to name their legitimate heirs, but, in so doing, they began to leave a number of questions unanswered about their kin relationship. Thus, new names and questions about kinship appeared in the wills. A "legitimate son" was soon thereafter addressed as a "son" in doña Isabel's statement, and in the last will of don Domingo the heirs to the alleged personal property were a "nephew" and a "child." At first glance, these puzzling contradictions seem difficult to resolve. For example, was don Domingo the father of doña Isabel's "legitimate" son? If so, why did he assert that he had no children? If not, was she married before? Why did don Domingo award his office to a nephew whose kinship was not clearly established in his will? Why did he show concern over looking after a child who had no ties of kinship to him? And how could caring for this child be a condition for having his nephew and heir inherit the most important office within an Indian community? The answers slowly emerge from a careful reading of the testaments themselves.

For six years doña Isabel kept silent, leaving aside her quest for community property and inheritance rights. Perhaps the spouses had reached some understanding or just decided to put off a family feud. Nevertheless, don Domingo produced two more wills between 1606 and 1608, and the clauses dealing with his personal information, burial plans, charity works, and donations remained the same as the one written in 1606. As before, he persisted in declaring that he had inherited the estate of Chilcane in addition to two previously unmentioned properties, Vilcaparo and Otavi, from his parents and grandparents. In keeping with Castilian law, don Domingo, like many other indigenous property owners, based his rights both on inheritance and genealogy. Since his genealogical proof of ownership did not extend beyond his grandparents, however, don Domingo stated that he also had formal written, legal titles to the chacras.

After mentioning other assets and people who owed him money, the cacique stated that he had married doña Isabel Sisa, a "palla" (noble woman) from Cuzco, thirty-four years earlier. According to don Domingo, when the couple had married they had no assets, with the exception of the estates of Chilcane, Vilcaparo, and Otavi, the properties bequeathed by his parents and grandparents. Accordingly, doña Isabel had the right to inherit half of everything acquired during their marriage: household belongings, houses, orchards, livestock, and harvests. Although don Domingo declared that he had no legitimate children, at this time he recognized "dos hijos bastardos" (two bastard sons) born after his marriage to doña Isabel: don Alonso and don Diego Itquilla, who both lived in his town. Don Domingo appointed Martín de Olmedo, a Spanish *vecino* (citizen) of La Plata and his "nephews" don Domingo Hamamani and Domingo Itquilla as his executors. Finally, he named his illegitimate children as heirs to his remaining assets.

According to Castilian law, parental assets passed to legitimate heirs, regardless of sex. One-fifth of this property could be given freely to any favored heir. From the remaining four-fifths, the testator could dispose of one-third, the *mejora* or supplementary bequest, to endow an heir. Demonstrating some knowledge of the law, don Domingo donated to his elder son, don Alonso, the supplementary bequest of one-third and the one-fifth of free disposition. Nothing was stated about the succession to the cacicazgo of Santiago de Curi, but don Domingo declared his previous testament invalid.[7]

When don Domingo ordered his last will and testament in 1608, he was ill in his house at Santiago de Curi. After repeating the clauses found in the earlier versions of his will about details of his burial, masses to be said on his soul's behalf, and charitable works to be done in his name, don Domingo again declared that the properties of Chilcane, Vilcaparo, and Otavi were his personal belongings, inherited from his parents. He

enumerated the debts that his executors should collect from several patrons, including his Indians and Domingo Hamamani, a native from Toropalca. Don Domingo took this opportunity to refer to Domingo Hamamani as an Indian, who allegedly claimed to be his relative and owed him
one hundred *fanegas* (1.5 bushels) of maize, twenty cows, two pairs of
oxen, fifty sheep, and fifty cargas of wheat. Did don Domingo Itquilla's
illness make him unable to remember that he had named Hamamani as
"don," his "nephew," and his successor to the government of Santiago de
Curi?[8] In truth, Hamamani was apparently a client of the cacique, serving merely as a tool in his dispute with doña Isabel. For some unknown
reason, he was no longer useful to accomplish this initial role assigned to
him by don Domingo. Finally, don Domingo requested his executors to
pay two hundred pesos to a "moza montañesa" (a young *mestizo* woman)
who worked for a rich Spaniard in La Plata. Could she have been one of
the elderly cacique's mistresses or perhaps even the mother of one of his
illegitimate children? After those odd clauses, don Domingo described a
series of debts owed to several individuals from La Plata and Santiago de
Curi. It is possible that the cacique was a moneylender because his will
mentioned that he had custody of money for several people, and these
funds should be returned by his executors after his death.

Don Domingo insisted again that doña Isabel had brought no assets to
the union, reiterating that he alone owned the estates of Chilcane, Vilcaparo, and Otavi, which he had inherited from his ancestors. By declaring
these assets as property owned before the marriage, don Domingo tried
to show that his wife had no claim over them, leaving him free to donate
them to any heir of his choice. Subsequently, don Domingo stated that he
had two illegitimate sons, don Alonso, a five-year-old born to Luisa, an
Indian from Santiago de Curi who was no longer in town, and don Diego,
a three-year-old who lived with his mother, the Indian Barbola, in the
neighboring town of Guata. Don Alonso, the elder, was raised at don
Domingo's home by his legitimate wife, doña Isabel. Consequently, don
Domingo bequeathed legacies to these two illegitimate sons, naming don
Alonso his successor to the cacicazgo of Santiago de Curi and the heir to
the one-fifth and one-third of his remaining assets.[9] Until don Alonso
came of age, don Domingo's nephew—an Indian of his same name—
would remain in charge of the government and his assets. In an attempt
to maintain control even after his death, don Domingo declared that if his
elder child died, his office and belongings should pass to the younger
son. However, his lands remained his greatest obsession. He demanded
that his heirs never sell them, because they had to remain in the family
"until the end of the world" ("que las dichas mis chacras no se vendan
hasta el fin del mundo"). The executors of this last will were doña Isabel
Sisa, her son Juan de Acuña, one don Diego Aricoma, and the nephew of
don Domingo of the same name, whom he had also designated as
governor until his elder son reached the age of majority.[10]

This last will finally made public the seamy personal affairs of don Domingo, including the names of his mistresses and illegitimate children. The offspring of his illicit liaisons were children of status who, like their father, enjoyed the title "don." In the absence of one child's mother, doña Isabel, his legitimate wife, was even raising the very youngster who was supposed to succeed her husband as cacique and as the owner of lands that she claimed as her own.

The office of cacique allowed don Domingo to take advantage of business opportunities while enjoying respect, status, and prosperity. Money-lending gave him the chance to add cash to his enterprises. The absence of a banking system during colonial times generated a market for people who made significant profits from lending money at interest. As the local lord, don Domingo received the tribute of his Indians (in specie and in kind), which gave him access to cash. Moreover, because of his prestige within the region, he enjoyed the confidence of a wide range of locals who were willing to allow him to invest their savings. As a result, the last statement of don Domingo left legacies to his heirs, satisfied the demands of creditors and business associates, and named executors to carry out his plans to control the patrimony that he had amassed so skillfully over his lifetime.

Despite this carefully designed scheme, the persistence of doña Isabel to realize her own goals checked and then undermined his efforts, both by unmasking his lies and deceptions and by using Spanish law to her advantage. According to Castilian law, as a married woman, doña Isabel could own property that her husband could only administer but never own. Nevertheless, the system of communal property, guaranteed by the same legal provisions, stated that assets acquired during a couple's married life—interest, salaries, real estate, rents, or any kind of investment—were jointly owned. Upon the death of one of the spouses, the profits from their joint enterprises were communal property, which could be divided among the surviving spouse and the remaining legitimate heirs without regard to how much money each partner brought to the union or invested during the marriage. Don Domingo and doña Isabel were aware of the law, and both tried to turn it to their own advantage. If the estates of Chilcane, Vilcaparo, and Otavi, for example, were, as don Domingo asserted, his own possessions, inherited from his parents, and if his wife brought no dowry to the marriage, then there was no substantial community property to bequeath. On the contrary, if (as doña Isabel had declared) the chacras were common assets accrued during their long marriage, then she had a right to them regardless of whether or not she had brought any dowry to the marriage. Both spouses were fighting for their assets, but only one could win the bitter, gendered battle of "wills."

Don Domingo Itquilla, cacique of Santiago de Curi, apparently died soon after dictating his final testament in 1608. Months later, in 1609, doña Isabel, now a widow, asked a notary to write another will. Widowhood was a status that gave women a certain autonomy and freedom from male subordination. Now, no censorship, tutelage, or mistreatment could stop doña Isabel from undermining many provisions of her late husband's wills.

Doña Isabel pressed her case vigorously by presenting herself as a woman of noble blood and as a dedicated wife. She professed to be a palla from Cusco and the legitimate daughter of don Hernando Tupa and Juana Carua. As a respectful and loving wife, she asked to be buried in the church of Santiago de Curi in the grave of don Domingo and beside him. She requested that Mass be celebrated during her funeral and that fellows of the Brotherhood of Our Lady of Copacabana accompany the body. Doña Isabel left money to pay for more masses and to buy candles and white wax for the altar of the church as well as for her grave. Her executors were to provide Juan de Acuña, her "natural" son, his wife Magdalena Gutiérrez, and their daughters Juana, Angelina, and Mariana de Acuña with mourning clothes for her funeral. According to a provision from her husband's last will, doña Isabel redirected the investment of 180 pesos corrientes to her granddaughters Juana and Angelina. By playing the dutiful wife instead of offending the memory of her deceased husband or calling him a liar, doña Isabel did much to advance her claims for their disputed property.

The widow then undermined her husband's last will by casting doubt on his testimony on the "venta y composición de tierras" (sale and verifications of land ownership) that had taken place in the district during the 1590s. According to both documents, she asserted that don Domingo had stressed before the notaries who signed his wills and the judge who confirmed his land ownership that "the lands *we* possessed" had been inherited from his parents and grandparents, all natives of Santiago de Curi. Nevertheless, doña Isabel boldly countered that don Domingo and his relatives were not natives of Santiago de Curi but came from Toropalca, a town near Potosí. She wisely set her claim in the center of a debate that was taking place in the Southern Andes at the end of the sixteenth century over the large-scale migration of indigenous people from their natal communities. What did doña Isabel expect to gain by disclosing that her husband was not a native of the town where he had held the office of cacique? If his family had migrated to Santiago de Curi, was he merely a migrant or "foreigner" (*forastero*), not a respected ethnic leader with long-standing kinship ties in the town? Moreover, if don Domingo were a lowly forastero, could he enjoy hereditary rights to the prestigious office of cacique principal?

Migration was a deeply rooted practice in the Southern Andes, an extremely harsh environment that offered remarkable climatic variations, even at short distances up or down the mountainsides. Permanent, cyclical migration from different ecosystems characterized the life of diverse Andean ethnic groups. Kinship, reciprocity, and redistribution were the principles that bound together the inhabitants of the highlands and low-lands and regulated their permanent exchange of labor and produce in the absence of a market economy. Depending on their needs and the geographical constraints, Andean peoples lived in dispersed settlements scattered across different altitudes and climates. This way of living, how-ever, was totally alien to the Spaniards, who usually spent their lives in the same town or village where they were born. In the Andes, however, peoples from the high plateau dispatched kinsmen to found settlements in the valleys and lowlands to gain access to resources such as maize, chili, wood, cotton, and coca leaves, which complemented those in their highland natal settlements. Many natives of Toropalca, for example, had lived in the valley of Curi before the Spaniards' arrival. Curi was a pe-ripheral settlement where peoples from different ethnic groups in the highlands became *mitmakuna* (permanent colonists from other regions) to contribute to their own group's self-sufficiency. After the Conquest, how-ever, new European ideas about private property, land ownership, and citizenship linked to territorial origin were introduced into the Andean world, causing considerable confusion and numerous disputes over land ownership and what constituted legitimate kinship ties.

Before the 1570s, some ethnic groups from the highlands took advan-tage of the confusion generated by pre- and post-Conquest customs of property ownership to seize lands worked by their own colonists in the lowlands. This confusion was compounded during the last thirty years of the sixteenth century, when Spanish authorities tried to resolve such dis-putes between highland and lowland groups. Between 1572 and 1575, for example, the fifth viceroy of Peru, don Francisco de Toledo, conducted a *visita general* (general inspection) and a *reducción general* (resettlement program). He wanted to take a census of the indigenous population, organize the *mita* (cyclical forced labor draft) to provide a steady stream of workers for the mining center of Potosí, and concentrate the dispersed Andean settlements in *reducciones* (Spanish-style villages) to collect the head tax or tribute more effectively.

Toledo's survey allowed highlanders the opportunity to develop new strategies for maintaining access to their landholdings in the lowlands. Artificial divisions introduced by the Spaniards differentiated between the "natives" of a town and those who were merely colonists or recent migrants, who had originated in another community at a different eco-logical level. The colonists would be registered in highland or valley settlements as "natives" or in both towns by virtue of their dual resi-dence. Thus, the disclosure that don Domingo was a native of Toropalca living in Santiago de Curi makes sense in an Andean world where kin-ship, descent, and ethnicity did not require only one residence. Pre-Con-quest Andean ideas about "citizenship" were rooted in ethnicity rather than place of birth. Relying on traditional Andean beliefs, don Domingo stressed kinship, status, and residence to advance his claims as both ca-

cique principal and the owner of lands in Santiago de Curi. Doña Isabel
(or her attorney) relied on Spanish law, however, to emphasize her husband's natal community (Toropalca) to undermine his case, leaving aside
the ethnic and kinship ties of don Domingo.

The second major move from the colonial administration to concentrate the scattered Amerindian population and gain land to be sold or
granted to the Spaniards was to compel those who occupied lands to
show their legal titles. Only those persons who could claim ancestral
occupation and were able to pay a set fee to confirm their holdings could
remain in possession of their lands. Don Domingo had obtained property
titles to the lands allegedly belonging to his ancestors, with the land
ownership confirmed during the general land survey of 1593–1595. Although doña Isabel was close to winning her battle for community property, her arguments were not strong enough to invalidate don Domingo's
will. Nevertheless, she persisted.

Just as don Domingo had declared in his last statement, doña Isabel
agreed that they had married in La Plata. However, she revealed that he
was then a "particular"—an ordinary Indian, a commoner, a taxpayer, a
status he had enjoyed before moving to Santiago de Curi, where "he
became skillful at knowing how to write without being a cacique principal from this town . . . to which we came and being and residing there
and letting the people be aware both notables and commoners that *he
knew how to read and write* and since there was no one in town who knew
how, they [the Indians from Santiago de Curi] said he was from their
ayllu [kin group] and a relative and requested him to be their cacique."[11]

As this testimony indicates, don Domingo was not a cacique by birth
but a commoner who had gained status by virtue of his literacy. Thus,
apparently neither descent nor residence made a difference in this case,
but both partners skillfully manipulated the concepts to support their
arguments. What matters here is that don Domingo, the alleged cacique
and landowner, had gained his office by being literate rather than by
virtue of his kinship and hereditary status. As an ordinary Indian, penniless like his wife when they married, don Domingo acquired his estates
during his marriage. For this reason, doña Isabel argued, Chilcane, Vilcaparo, and Otavi truly were the property of both spouses. According to the
resourceful doña Isabel, don Domingo was persuaded by "someone"
who knew how much he loved his sons to pass on to them assets that did
not rightfully belong to him.

Only after don Domingo had died could doña Isabel raise the veil that
had obscured the true story of the couple and their joint assets. While her
husband was alive, doña Isabel could not reveal the true story of how he
had gained community leadership despite his humble origins. As an ordinary Indian, don Domingo could not claim hereditary rights to ethnic
leadership or hope to gain large amounts of property. His attempt to gain
legitimacy by claiming lands supposedly inherited from his ancestors

eventually undermined his pretensions. After his death, nothing prevented doña Isabel from calling on Castilian laws of inheritance, which worked to her advantage because they gave wives equal rights to inherit their husbands' estates. She did not have to rely on rank or status to gain her inheritance. By admitting her husband's humble origins, doña Isabel gained her community property. Like her husband, she was also moved by the power of blood ties and love. She persisted in gaining her share of the joint property for her son's sake. After finally winning her long inheritance battle, doña Isabel thus named as her heir Juan de Acuña. As her testimony revealed, however, Acuña was a mestizo, fathered by Diego Vásquez, a Spaniard from Jerez de la Frontera, who had returned to the Iberian Peninsula long ago. By addressing her son as a mestizo, she guaranteed that he would not be subject to the indigenous head tax, after losing the tax exemption that he enjoyed as a member of the household of a local lord. This may explain why she addressed her son as "legitimate" in her initial testament.[12]

In the final version of her last will and testament, doña Isabel detailed once again her community property and personal belongings. Among her own assets, she listed a house and two peach orchards in Santiago de Curi, 388 cargas of maize harvested from Chilcane (sown after don Domingo had died), animals, tools, and six hundred pesos corrientes. She also included two outfits made of *cumbi* (finely woven cloth) with their axu, another axu embroidered in silver, one *vara* (one vara equals sixty-six inches) of blue *paño* (woolen cloth) and silver thread to sew an axu, three *ñañacas* (cloth used as a turban) made of *abasca* (ordinary domestic wool), and five pairs of *topos* (pins for clothing) with their silver pendants. Among her household goods, doña Isabel owned two pairs of *cocos* (ceremonial drinking vessels) and several silver vases.

The story of doña Isabel Sisa—an indefatigable indigenous woman— and her husband, the cacique of Santiago de Curi, fits the model of a new Andean elite that enjoyed political power through writing. As Joanne Rappaport puts it, "Only those who knew how to write, or who were able to communicate with scribes, either through Spanish or through an interpreter, could lay any claim to the reins of power."[13] Writing gave a commoner his chance to become a lord, and written communication through an interpreter gave doña Isabel the opportunity to defend her rights and enjoy the assets that belonged to her by virtue of her marriage.

The newly made lineage of Itquilla was short-lived. Status and office were curtailed by doña Isabel's claims to her property, providing a clear example of how wealth prevailed over other traditional values. Finally, testaments had an additional meaning in colonial Latin American history. They were instruments of self-promotion, manipulation, and lies that showed the rapid sociocultural changes in the lives of those who wanted to climb the social ladder.

QUESTIONS FOR DISCUSSION

1. Assuming that women were subordinated to men and their roles were limited throughout the colonial period, is it possible to describe strategies used to overcome male domination?
2. How do you describe the ambiguous role that the Spanish law played over women? Relate your answer to female status before the law, marriage, and inheritance.
3. How did doña Isabel Sisa interpret her legitimate rights to property, and what tools did she use to succeed in the long battle fought against her husband?
4. How did don Domingo Itquilla obtain legitimacy to hold the office of cacique?
5. It is true that the Spaniards brought to the Andes new concepts and practices such as property rights, citizenship, naturalization, and landownership that conflicted with the indigenous values of kinship, reciprocity, and redistribution. In the recent past, anthropologists and historians agreed in an abrupt collapse of indigenous culture and patterns of behavior. Do you agree or disagree with this statement? Why?

NOTES

1. "Cacique" is an imported Caribbean word for lord or chief, a title the Spaniards extended to address the Andean lords. *Cacique principal* means "principal lord" in Spanish. Although the name of an Andean ethnic leader is *kuraka* in Quechua or *mallku* in Aymara, I use the word "cacique" to address don Domingo Itquilla or his office since that was the word written on the documents.

2. Archivo Nacional de Bolivia, Escrituras Públicas (hereafter ANB, EP) 52, Francisco de Tovar notary–Santiago de Curi, December 31, 1602, 523–25.

3. "Por ser su marido y por evitar pesadumbres y por miedo del."

4. ANB, EP 52, Francisco de Tovar notary–Santiago de Curi, January 1, 1603, 526.

5. ANB, EP 32a, Diego Sánchez notary–La Plata, June 23, 1601, 448–52.

6. Ibid., 451.

7. ANB, EP 63, Juan Fernández de Castro notary–La Plata, July 19, 1606, 414–17.

8. ANB, EP 68, Andrés Gonzalez de Cavia notary–Santiago de Curi, May 31, 1608, 367–72.

9. Ibid., 370–71.

10. Ibid., 371.

11. ANB, EP 144, Diego de Adrada notary–Santiago de Curi, October 6, 1609, 715–19.

12. According to Castilian law, legitimate children were those born from a legitimate marriage. Legitimate birth gave heirs, regardless of sex, full rights to inherit equal shares from their parents' assets; however, the same law offered parents the chance to endow a preferred heir with additional assets. Naming an heir as legitimate meant to secure rights of inheritance to all the property and, in some cases, to offices and privileges held by one or both parents.

13. Joanne Rappaport, "Object and Alphabet: Andean Indians and Documents in the Colonial Period," in *Writing without Words: Alternative Literacies in Mesoamerica and the Andes*, ed. Elizabeth Hill Boone and Walter Mignolo (Durham, NC, 1994), 276.

SUGGESTED READINGS

The testamentary practices of Andean women can be seen in Elinor C. Burkett, "Indian Women and White Society: The Case of Sixteenth-Century Peru," in *Latin American Women: Historical Perspectives*, edited by Asunción Lavrín (Westport, CT, 1978); Frank Salomon, "Indian Women of Early Colonial Quito as Seen through Their Testaments," *The Americas* 44, no. 3 (January 1988); and Susan Kellogg and Matthew Restall, eds., *Dead Giveaways: Indigenous Testaments of Colonial Mesoamerica and the Andes* (Salt Lake City, 1998). Gender ideologies and hierarchies are developed by Irene Silverblatt in *Moon, Sun, and Witches: Gender Ideologies and Class in Inca and Colonial Peru* (Princeton, NJ, 1987). Female urban commercial practices are depicted by Ann Zulawski in "Social Differentiation, Gender, and Ethnicity: Urban Indian Women in Colonial Bolivia, 1640–1725," *Latin American Research Review* 25, no. 2 (1990).

Migration, labor, taxation, and patterns of indigenous control of resources can be seen in the outstanding works of Thierry Saignes, "The Ethnic Groups in the Valleys of Larecaja: From Descent to Residence," in *Anthropological History of Andean Polities*, edited by John V. Murra, Nathan Wachtel, and Jacques Revel (Cambridge, 1986).

For the Andean ambivalence toward the Spanish market economy, see Steve J. Stern's "The Variety and Ambiguity of Native Andean Intervention in European Colonial Markets," in *Ethnicity, Markets, and Migration in the Andes: At the Crossroads of History and Anthropology*, edited by Brooke Larson and Olivia Harris, with Enrique Tandeter (Durham, NC, 1995). The cultural impact of writing (including testaments) has been examined in Joanne Rappaport, "Object and Alphabet: Andean Indians and Documents in the Colonial Period," in *Writing without Words: Alternative Literacies in Mesoamerica and the Andes*, edited by Elizabeth Hill Boone and Walter Mignolo (Durham, NC, 1994); and Rappaport, *The Politics of Memory: Native Historical Interpretation in the Colombian Andes* (Durham, NC, 1998).

FOUR

Domingos Fernandes Nobre

"Tomacauna," a Go-Between in Sixteenth-Century Brazil

Alida C. Metcalf

The Portuguese settlement of Brazil followed a markedly different course than the Spanish pattern in Mexico and the Andes. The fleet of Pedro Álvares Cabral, en route to India, made the first recorded European landfall on the coast of Brazil in 1500, but the Portuguese crown chose to focus its attention on India instead. No immediate settlement followed Cabral's discovery. Rather, a small but profitable trade in brazilwood developed along the coast. Portuguese merchants as well as interloping French rivals fostered contacts with the indigenous Tupi-Guarani peoples who lived along the long coastline of Brazil. With these tribes, merchants exchanged European trading goods for brazilwood. Over time, this mutually beneficial bartering relationship broke down and the enslavement of Indians began. The first Portuguese settlers arrived at São Vicente, in southern Brazil, in 1532. Other important early settlements were Salvador da Bahia, located in the northeast, which became the capital in 1549, and, farther north, Olinda, the major settlement of Pernambuco. In central Brazil the French established a small Protestant colony at Rio de Janeiro in 1555, which was taken by the Portuguese in 1560.

*The success of sugar cultivation in the northeast, around Olinda and Salvador da Bahia, led to a growing demand for Amerindian slaves to work in the cane fields, producing escalating levels of conflict later in the sixteenth century. Gangs of Portuguese began penetrating the rugged wilderness interior (*sertão*) in search of Amerindian captives to sell as slaves for the coastal sugar plantations. The warlike indigenous peoples resisted these incursions, but ancient ri-*

valries between tribes made any type of unified response to repel the invaders difficult. Moreover, Portuguese slavers began learning indigenous languages, marrying Amerindian women, and taking part in tribal affairs. Mixed-blood offspring of these relationships (mamelucos) *often served as cultural mediators, living part-time in the interior among their Tupi-Guarani kinsmen and part-time in coastal Portuguese settlements. Over the years Portuguese and mameluco slave hunters cultivated their Amerindian allies to help them capture enemy groups, turning indigenous rivalries to their advantage and taking larger numbers of slaves for sale in the coastal settlements.*

One of the more famous of these mameluco go-betweens, who made his living by slave trading in the sertão, was Domingos Fernandes Nobre, known among his indigenous kinsmen and followers as Tomacauna. Like his fellow mameluco traders and slave hunters, Fernandes Nobre lived a dual life, moving freely between the Portuguese in the capital and the frontier world of the Tupi-Guarani. When in the interior, Fernandes Nobre became Tomacauna, tattooing his body in the indigenous style and taking part in local religious rituals of the syncretic Santidade cult. Although his ability to function in both the Portuguese and indigenous worlds made him both feared and successful as a slave trader, he eventually ran afoul of authorities along the coast.

In June 1591 a visiting inquisitor from Portugal's Holy Office of the Inquisition arrived in Bahia, and several of the city's citizens denounced Fernandes Nobre for his heretical participation in the Santidade cult. Although he defended himself and escaped the most severe discipline, this case demonstrates the tensions between the hierarchical Europeanized society developing on the coast and the individualistic and pluralistic society evolving in the wilderness. To the inquisitor, the tattooed Tomacauna with his questionable ethics and heretical religious beliefs was a barbarian, a threat to the "civilized" Portuguese colonists in Bahia. Although the sugar planters of the coast relied on mameluco go-betweens to provide slave labor, these individuals also represented European fears that overseas colonies stood on the verge of lapsing into "barbarism" and social disorder. Men such as Tomacauna were necessary to the economic prosperity of sixteenth-century Brazil, but their rugged individualism threatened to undermine the Catholic, family-oriented, and civilized world of Salvador da Bahia.

When an inquisitor from Portugal's Holy Office of the Inquisition arrived in Brazil's capital of Salvador da Bahia in June 1591, Domingos Fernandes Nobre was not in the city. Neither was he in the Recôncavo, the rich forestlands around the Bay of All Saints into which Portuguese settlers had carved their sugar plantations. Instead, Fernandes Nobre was deep in the *sertão*, the wilderness, living in a camp with nearly one hundred other men who had left the coastal settlements of Bahia and Pernambuco a year earlier to trade for Indian slaves. Such expeditions, known as *entradas*, had become essential to supply the incipient sugar plantations of the Portuguese colonies of Bahia and Pernambuco with laborers. Many *mamelucos*, men of mixed Indian and Portuguese parentage like Domingos Fernandes Nobre, had become slave traders who used their ability to move between the worlds of the Indian wilderness and the Portuguese coast in order to make their living. Therefore, while Fernandes Nobre and the other leaders of this expedition negotiated with the Indian chief, Arataca, the inquisitor made his entrance into the capital. Thus, the men in the sertão missed the pomp and ceremony that marked the inquisitor's arrival and subsequent transformation of the rhythms of daily life in Salvador.[1]

These mamelucos were go-betweens—men who lived both in the wilderness and in the coastal settlements. Because of their facility with Indian languages and customs and their willingness to use that knowledge for the benefit of the Portuguese colonists, they were essential in the development of the sugar economy in Bahia and Pernambuco. Go-betweens supplied the Indian slaves who labored on the first sugar plantations in Brazil. Yet, as the inquisitor's sojourn in Bahia and Pernambuco would make clear, the Portuguese were not entirely comfortable with their reliance on these men.

The first go-betweens in Brazil were Europeans who had been shipwrecked along the coast and who had survived by joining Indian tribes. One such man in the south was João Ramalho, who, when the Portuguese began their first permanent colony at São Vicente, was living as an Indian. Ramalho forged an alliance between the Portuguese and his tribe that allowed the new colony to survive. As the colony grew, Ramalho became increasingly powerful and began to supply the colonists with Indian slaves from enemy tribes. In Bahia, another go-between was Diogo Alvares Caramurú, who had also been shipwrecked in the early years of the sixteenth century. Like Ramalho, he had married into a local Indian tribe and had considerable influence among them. Caramurú also became an ally of the Portuguese when they attempted to establish colonies in Bahia. The mameluco descendants of Ramalho and Caramurú continued to live as go-betweens, often becoming involved in the Indian slave trade.[2]

The early settlers of Pernambuco and Bahia intended to profit from the new colony, and to do so they needed an economic focus. They chose sugar. Sugarcane had been grown successfully in other Portuguese colonies off the coast of Africa, such as the islands of São Tomé and Madeira, but its planting, cultivation, harvest, and milling required many laborers. Who would work in the fields and in the mills? The Portuguese had become slave traders along the coast of Africa in the sixteenth century, and planters in Brazil might have thought of obtaining African slaves. But the settlers in Brazil had little capital to finance slave trading across the Atlantic. They turned, therefore, to a more immediate source: the Indians. Later, after the disastrous decline in the Indian population, planters would indeed look to Africa for slaves. But in the sixteenth century, planters had little sense that the combination of disease and slavery would drastically reduce the Indian population. Instead, they viewed Indians as an unlimited resource of cheap labor whom they could enslave for their own profit.[3]

The Portuguese crown saw as its moral obligation the conversion and baptism of the Brazilian Indians into the Christian faith. To this end the crown designated the Society of Jesus (or Jesuits) to evangelize in Brazil, yet the economic interests of the settlers clashed with the moral obligations of the distant crown. Moreover, the Indians of Brazil were not the peaceful "noble savages" that early reports described. Rather, they lived in many different tribes, some of which practiced violent warfare. Cannibalism was sometimes the result of such wars. Even some of the Portuguese who became parties to intertribal warfare were put to death in cannibalistic ceremonies. Thus, while the crown did not want to see widespread Indian slavery in Brazil, by royal legislation it provided the loopholes that colonists used to enslave Indians freely. According to law, Indians who made war against the Portuguese or who practiced cannibalism could be taken legally as slaves.[4]

Indian slavery became commonplace in Bahia and Pernambuco after the 1560s. And so, when the inquisitor arrived in Bahia in 1591, the men with Domingos Fernandes Nobre were trading for slaves. In the sertão, the leaders of the entrada sent gifts and promises each morning to Arataca. The chief was an avowed enemy of the Portuguese, but because of the size of this particular entrada, the gifts promised each day, and the skill of the expedition's leaders, he kept the peace. In return for swords, pistols, gunpowder, and the repair of arms that the Indians already possessed, Arataca exchanged Indians. The leaders of the expedition carefully controlled these negotiations and insisted that the men trade with the Indians only through them. But the men soon learned that if they patterned themselves after Fernandes Nobre, they, too, could deal on their own with the Indians.[5]

His fame as a man of the wilderness was legendary in Bahia. Fernandes Nobre was a mameluco—his mother was Indian and his father Portuguese—and he drew on this dual identity to exploit the wilderness. He was as accustomed to living in the sertão among Indians as he was to living in the city among the Portuguese settlers. In the wilderness he was known by his Indian nickname, "Tomacauna." He spoke Indian languages, and parts of his body were tattooed in the Indian style to signify that he was a brave warrior. Seeing and perhaps admiring his example, some of the men on this expedition also spoke in the Indian dialect and tattooed their bodies to more convincingly offer arms to be traded for slaves.

While Fernandes Nobre negotiated in the wilderness, his wife saw or most certainly heard about the procession, Mass, sworn declarations of faith, and decrees of July 28, 1591, in honor of the inquisitor. To her it must have brought back memories, however sketchy, of her childhood in

Portugal, where the presence of the Holy Office and its procedures for ferreting out heretics were etched into the memories of local townspeople. On that Sunday in Salvador, the bishop of Bahia led a procession from the Church of Our Lady of Ajuda to the cathedral. The governor, judges, members of the city council, priests, and clerics solemnly accompanied the inquisitor, who was escorted under a canopy of golden cloth. Inside the cathedral, he sat on a red velvet chair beneath a crimson damask canopy in the main chapel. Mass was said in Latin, followed by a sermon preached in Portuguese by the provincial of the Jesuit mission. Then the archdeacon of the cathedral mounted the pulpit and read the edicts brought by the inquisitor from the king of Portugal. The notary of the inquisitor next stepped up to read, in Portuguese, a document of the late Pope Pius V in favor of the Holy Office and in opposition to those who dared to criticize it.

The inquisitor then moved to an altar in the middle of the chapel, which was richly adorned with a silver cross, four silver candlesticks, and two missals resting on damask cushions whose pages were held open by two silver crosses. One by one, the governor, judges, councilmen, and other officials approached the altar, knelt, placed both hands on the crosses on the missals, and swore to uphold the faith. In a loud voice the notary asked the congregation to promise to do so as well. At the end of the ceremony, the notary affixed these documents to the door of the cathedral along with one that stated that under pain of excommunication, all residents of the city and one league around it must denounce within thirty days anything they knew, or had seen, or had heard against the holy Catholic faith. He affixed another document to the church door stating that the inquisitor would grant thirty days of grace during which time those residents who confessed their faults would not lose their properties.[6]

The arrival of the inquisitor in Salvador brought to Brazil, for the first time, an institution well known in Portugal. The Portuguese Inquisition shared many similarities with the Spanish Inquisition, which had been brought to Spain by Ferdinand and Isabel in the fifteenth century. The Inquisition had as its mission the elimination of heresy from Catholicism. The Spanish inquisitors fixed their attention on the *conversos*, Jews who had converted to Christianity and who then had married into old and established Catholic families. Actively pursuing them, the inquisitors accused, tried, and punished thousands of conversos for crimes of heresy. When Ferdinand and Isabel expelled the Jews from Spain in 1492, many crossed the border into the kingdom of Portugal, where there was no Inquisition. But there, too, the Jews faced pressures. A decree of 1496 forced all Jews in Portugal to convert to Christianity and to be known thenceforth as New Christians. In 1546 the Portuguese Inquisition began, and the New Christians quickly became the major target. Many of them took refuge in Brazil. In 1580, when King Philip II of Spain took the crown of Portugal, the Portuguese Inquisition became even more influenced by the Spanish Inquisition. Because so many New Christians had settled in Brazil, the Inquisition authorized its first visit there in 1591. Brazil would never have a resident Holy Office, as did Mexico and Peru, but through occasional visits and the work of *familiares*, a privileged group of literate individuals who served the Inquisition, its presence was felt in the colony.[7]

With the arrival of the inquisitor in 1591, a new era in the history of the city of Salvador had thus begun. But the men of the wilderness were not there to see it. In Salvador and in the Recôncavo, many pondered the instructions brought by the inquisitor. Their thoughts may have turned first to the obvious heresies: secret Judaism, the reading of banned books, and covert Protestantism. Other crimes sought out by the inquisitor might have crowded into their thoughts: blasphemy, bigamy, bestiality, sodomy, and witchcraft. Only later, perhaps, did the go-betweens come to mind: the odd way that they moved back and forth between two worlds, stepping into and then casting off opposite identities at will.

When the men returned to the city of Salvador in December 1591, the period of thirty days of grace had ended. Unbeknown to Domingos Fernandes Nobre, four people had already denounced him. On August 7, a twenty-three-year-old mameluco accused him of worshipping an Indian idol in the wilderness seven years earlier. On August 21, a student in the Jesuit school denounced him for worshipping the same idol and participating in a heretical cult in the sertão of which the idol was a part. That same day, Paula d'Almeida gave an even fuller account of how Fernandes Nobre had knelt three times before the idol, rebaptized himself in the ritual of the cult, and offered fishhooks and knives to the cult's Indian leader. Then, on August 26, Diogo Dias, a mameluco farmer, gave a complete account of this sect, known as Santidade, or "holiness." Dias appeared before the inquisitor, who sat with his assistants and the leading clergy of Salvador da Bahia at an inquisitorial bench, or court, that questioned each person who presented him- or herself. Dias related that a number of Christian Indian slaves had fled from the Jesuit missions and from the estates of their masters into the wilderness. There, the members of the sect had built their own church with a baptismal font, an altar, a confessional, and an idol shaped like an Indian, which they called their god. Domingos Fernandes Nobre, Diogo Dias continued, was part of this movement for eight or nine months. Then, because the cult encouraged all the slaves to flee from their masters and because the masters feared that they would attack the city, the governor commissioned a company of men (of which Diogo Dias was a part) to apprehend the sect members and imprison its followers. But, according to Diogo Dias, Fernandes Nobre fled deep into the sertão and took the followers of the sect with him. From there, Fernandes Nobre took the Indians of the sect to the parish of

Jaguaripe in the Recôncavo, to the estate of his own patron, a Portuguese sugar planter.[8]

The Santidade sect appealed to the Indians as well as to the small but growing number of African slaves in Bahia. It was a millenarian sect, and, as is common in such movements, it predicted imminent divine intervention to save the faithful who suffered under the yoke of oppression. Influenced by indigenous traditions of renewal and revival together with the Christian teachings of the Jesuits, the believers retreated into the wilderness, where they built their own religious community. Mamelucos and free Indians were attracted to the rituals of the sect and to its baptisms, dancing, smoking of tobacco, and speaking in tongues. The sect appeared to validate those considered outcasts (such as slaves) or marginal (such as mamelucos) by the dominant Portuguese culture of Salvador. According to the standards of the Inquisition, it was clearly a heretical sect and one that required the punishment of any Christian who believed in it.[9]

On January 12, 1592, after the men from the expedition had returned to Bahia, the inquisitor granted another thirty days of grace, this time to the residents of the parishes of the Recôncavo, the agricultural hinterland of forests, sugar plantations, and small farms around the Bay of All Saints. Mamelucos tended to live in the Recôncavo as opposed to the city of Salvador because in the Recôncavo they worked for sugar planters or claimed small farms cut from the forest. Men whom Fernandes Nobre had known for most of his life, including some who had been with him on the most recent expedition to Chief Arataca, began to denounce him. A Portuguese carpenter who had been with Fernandes Nobre on the recent entrada claimed that the men had eaten meat on Catholic holy days, when meat was forbidden. Men such as Fernandes Nobre, he stated, had servants and slaves with them who easily could have obtained fish, beans, or fruit. A soldier who also had just returned from the same expedition stated that in the wilderness Fernandes Nobre told him that he had joined in the Santidade sect seven years ago out of fear that the Indians would kill him. Men who confessed their sins to the inquisitor also implicated Fernandes Nobre. One confessed to truly believing in the sect, while four others maintained that they "pretended" to believe in its teachings to fool its adherents. All of them implicated Domingos Fernandes Nobre as one who had bowed deferentially before the idol and told them to do the same.

On January 21, Isabel Beliaga, Domingos Fernandes Nobre's wife, went to the inquisitor to testify to what she knew. Isabel, forty years old and a native of northern Portugal, first denounced the habits of women she had known in Pernambuco. These women were New Christians, accused by Isabel of secretly practicing Judaism. Then she denounced her husband. Perhaps Isabel denounced him to protect herself, or perhaps she hoped to minimize his sins. She referred to her husband as Domingos Fernandes Tomacauna, thereby, perhaps inadvertently, reinforcing his dual identity. But she accused him only for the tattoos that his body bore. Isabel stated that she "had heard" that he tattooed himself to show Indians that he was brave and to escape certain death at their hands. She concluded by describing another man who she knew also tattooed himself. Isabel may have intended to show how modest her husband's sins were compared to those of the New Christians or how explicable they were, given the dangers that he faced in the wilderness.

Domingos Fernandes Nobre "Tomacauna" arrived home after most of the rest of the expedition. He returned to Bahia via the northern cities of Pernambuco, apparently during the middle of the grace period. He may not have heard his local priest read to the assembled parishioners the document sent by the inquisitor to every parish of the Recôncavo, but he certainly would have known of its being tacked onto the church door. For reasons that we shall never know, he decided to confess his faults to the inquisitor on February 11, the last day of grace granted to the residents of the Recôncavo. By that time, fourteen people had denounced him, and his name and his faults had come up in the confessions of eight more. Although every person who passed before the inquisitorial bench was required to swear to uphold the secrecy of the Holy Office, it is unrealistic to think that the inquisitor operated in total secrecy. Perhaps Fernandes Nobre feared for the fate of his soul as well as for the confiscation of his property if the inquisitor found him guilty of heresy.

This confession provides a fascinating glimpse into the life of a go-between. His dual identity was reflected in his Portuguese and Indian names. Born in Pernambuco and presumably baptized Domingos Fernandes Nobre, his father was a Portuguese stonemason, while his mother was a free Indian woman. From the time he was eighteen years old, he confessed that although he remained a Christian at heart, he lived more as an Indian than as a white man. He went into the wilderness on many expeditions, lasting for many months, either in search of gold or Indians. It was during such expeditions that he became Tomacauna: he tattooed his legs, arms, and buttocks with red *urucu* and black *genipapo* inks, tied feathers in his hair, and walked naked among the Indians. He explained to the inquisitor that he tattooed himself for the same reason that Indian men did—to show that they were brave warriors. He danced, sang, and shook the rattles in Indian ceremonies; he smoked tobacco and drank fermented palm wines. He accepted women given to him—sometimes as many as seven—and lived with them as wives, according to Indian custom. This he did, he told the inquisitor, so that the Indians would accept him as one of theirs, call him nephew, and treat him well. On his last expedition as well as on others, he had knowingly violated the law by trading arms to Indian nations known to be at war with the Portuguese. During all of the time he spent in the wilderness, he never abstained from eating meat on holy days, nor did he pray or commend himself to God.

Tomacauna described in detail his association with the Santidade religious sect. In his version of events, he had led a company of soldiers into the wilderness with the goal of imprisoning the followers of the sect. When he met up with its members, he doffed his hat and bowed to their idol in order, in his words, "to make them understand that he believed in their heresy." Then he and his men took part in a procession with the idol. Having won their confidence, Tomacauna sent this branch of the sect back to the Recôncavo, where, on the estate of his patron, they built a village and church. Tomacauna continued on deeper into the wilderness in search of the rest of the sect. In a place known simply as Tall Palms, Tomacauna met the leader, "the one they call Pope." Tomacauna greeted him on bent knee, then "wailed and lamented" in the Indian style. He danced, celebrated, sang, played their musical instruments, "drank the smoke," and allowed himself to be revered and adored as a saint. All of this, Fernandes Nobre maintained to the inquisitor, he did to deceive them and to bring them to the Recôncavo.

Following his confession, as was customary, Fernandes Nobre reappeared before the inquisitorial bench. When asked why he had joined in the ceremonies of the Santidade sect, he responded that while he knew perfectly well that they were wrong, he took part only because of his material interest in bringing the believers to the Recôncavo, where his patron hoped to make use of their labor. When told that he must confess if he had ever left the true faith—because he could be absolved only by the Inquisition—he replied that he had never left the holy Catholic faith. And when asked how many times he had not refrained from eating meat on holy days, he replied that there were many times, but, being such a large man, he was obliged to do so.

Tomacauna's confession reveals that he lived in a complex and ambiguous world with few moral absolutes. Although he claimed to have kept the holy Catholic faith in his heart, his behavior suggests that he adopted whichever religious practices best suited the occasion. Apparently, he learned from a young age to use his imposing physical presence and cunning mind to survive in dangerous situations. How much did he really reveal to the inquisitor? How trustworthy is his confession? Given what is known about him, it seems likely that Fernandes Nobre, with a convincing display of outward humility, told the inquisitor what he wanted to hear.

In fact, while the inquisitorial bench did not believe Fernandes Nobre's insistence that because of his great size he could not exist without meat, the inquisitor did show mercy. He reprimanded the go-between for his many errors but recommended leniency because he had confessed during the grace period. Various acts of penitence were required. Among them, Fernandes Nobre was to make an even fuller confession of his entire life and to continue confessing regularly for six months. During those six months, he was to receive special religious instruction from a priest and was to fast on five Wednesdays following Easter. The inquisitor also imposed one onerous punishment: Tomacauna was never to return to the wilderness. From now on, Tomacauna would again be simply Domingos Fernandes Nobre.

This sentence paralleled those received by other mamelucos found guilty of similar faults. Together they reflect the inquisitor's willingness to forgive their past behavior, yet he was not willing to let them return to the sertão, the place where they had made their living. In the eyes of the inquisitor, the mamelucos had to maintain their Portuguese heritage; they could not continue to slide back and forth between Indian and Portuguese identities.

Seen through the eyes of such a bastion of Portuguese culture as the inquisitor, the mameluco go-betweens were rude, uncivilized, and backsliding Christians. They set poor examples for others because they encouraged relativism and an extreme individualism. In their world, moral decisions were made based not on principles but on the immediate need. Go-betweens remained true only to themselves; loyalty to an Indian tribe or to the Portuguese colony depended on the situation. Such attitudes served the go-betweens well in the fluid and ambiguous world in which they lived, but they were diametrically opposed to the values of Portuguese colonization. For the crown and the Church, colonization had moral imperatives such as the evangelization of Indians, the propagation of a Portuguese culture in a new land, or the obedience of colonists to the officials of the crown and Church. As it turned out, the inquisitor could not prevent the go-betweens of the late sixteenth century from returning to the sertão. But, increasingly, they would be pressured to assimilate more fully into the Portuguese culture or else to retreat from the core of the colony and move with the frontier toward the wilderness.

The early Portuguese colony in Brazil depended on go-betweens, those men who could move easily between the very different Indian and Portuguese worlds. In the earliest days, the survival of colonists depended on good relations with neighboring Indians. Shipwrecked Portuguese go-betweens became essential first intermediaries. As the colonies became established, however, and as sugar emerged as the economic motor of Bahia and Pernambuco, the Portuguese depended on go-betweens not for good relations with neighboring tribes but for supplying the sugar plantations with Indian slaves. Mameluco slave traders such as Domingos Fernandes Nobre led expeditions into the wilderness to capture Indians, usually illegally, for the sugar planters. To take an expedition into the wilderness and return with hundreds of slaves required a special kind of leadership, cunning and treachery in dealings with Indian tribes, and a hardened attitude toward the future of the men, women, and children who would be reduced to slavery. Because of their own experiences, the mameluco go-betweens understood Indian life better than anyone else in the colony, but to make their own livings they chose to work on behalf of the sugar planters and to encourage the violence of slavery. The planters clearly recognized the contribution of the go-betweens to their success; indeed, many employed them on their own estates. But as the colony developed and became more Portuguese in its culture and outlook, the go-betweens, with their dual identities, embodied less and less of the ideals of the Christian Portuguese colonists.

First in Pernambuco, then later in Bahia, a disastrous decline in the Indian population forced sugar planters to search for other laborers. African slaves already outnumbered Indians on the sugar plantations in Pernambuco when the inquisitor finished his work in Bahia and began it anew in Pernambuco. By the seventeenth century, Bahian planters began to rely increasingly on African slaves. As the labor demands of the sugar plantations changed, the mameluco go-betweens had less to offer the planters. Indeed, the wilderness itself was rapidly disappearing beyond the cane fields. Only on the frontiers could go-betweens still cross from the Indian to the Portuguese world and live in the complex and contradictory ways suggested by the life of Domingos Fernandes Nobre "Tomacauna." In succeeding centuries, go-betweens paved the way for Portuguese, and later Brazilian, colonization of the wilderness to the north, south, and west. But they would not inherit the world they helped to create, nor would their distinctive lifestyle survive past the initial stages of colonization. Like the Indians they had exploited, the go-betweens found themselves cast aside by the advancing colonial culture.

QUESTIONS FOR DISCUSSION

1. How was the discovery and early settlement of Brazil different from that of Mexico and Peru?
2. What exactly is a go-between, and how do they influence the interactions between cultures?
3. How did Domingos Fernandes Nobre Tomacauna become a go-between, and why did he remain one?
4. Why was Domingos Fernandes Nobre Tomacauna denounced to the inquisitor, and how serious do you think the inquisitor found his faults?
5. Did these go-betweens have a moral conscience? Should we blame them for causing the enslavement of Indians?

NOTES

1. This dignitary came as a "visiting" inquisitor, meaning that his presence in Brazil was limited to a specific time. Brazil did not have its own formally established Holy Office of the Inquisition with a permanent, resident inquisitor, as did Mexico and Peru.

2. There are brief accounts of João Ramalho, Diogo Alvares Caramurú, and Domingos Fernandes Nobre "Tomacauna" in John Hemming, *Red Gold: The Conquest of the Brazilian Indians* (Cambridge, MA: Harvard University Press, 1978).

3. Stuart Schwartz, *Sugar Plantations in the Formation of Brazilian Society: Bahia, 1550–1835* (New York: Cambridge University Press, 1985), 28–72; Alexander Marchant, *From Barter to Slavery: The Economic Relations of Portuguese and Indians in the Settlement of Brazil, 1500–1580* (Baltimore: Johns Hopkins University Press, 1942). On the sixteenth-century Portuguese slave trade in Africa, see A. C. de C. M. Saunders, *A Social History of Black Slaves and Freedmen in Portugal, 1441–1555* (New York: Cambridge University Press, 1982).

4. Dauril Alden, *The Making of an Enterprise: The Society of Jesus in Portugal, Its Empire, and Beyond, 1540–1750* (Stanford: Stanford University Press, 1996), 474–501; Thomas Cohen, *The Fire of Tongues: António Vieira and the Missionary Church in Brazil and Portugal* (Stanford: Stanford University Press, 1998), 13–49. Famous accounts of cannibalism in sixteenth-century Brazil include: Neil L. Whitehead and Michael Harbsmeier, *Hans Staden's True History: An Account of Cannibal Captivity in Brazil* (Durham, NC: Duke University Press, 2008); and Jean de Léry, *History of a Voyage to the Land of Brazil, Otherwise Called America*, trans. Janet Whatley (Berkeley: University of California Press, 1990).

5. Trials of mamelucos, Inquisition Archive, Arquivo Nacional da Torre do Tombo, (hereafter ANTT), Lisbon, Portugal. For Portuguese readers, many of the confessions and denunciations have been published; see *Primeira Visitação do Santo Ofício às partes do Brasil pelo Licenciado Heitor Furtado de Mendonça: Confissões da Bahia 1591–1592* (Rio de Janeiro: F. Briguiet, 1935); and *Primeira Visitação do Santo Ofício às partes do Brasil pelo Licenciado Heitor Furtado de Mendonça: Denunciações da Bahia 1591–1593* (São Paulo: Paulo Prado, 1925).

6. This description of the ceremony marking the arrival of the visiting inquisitor is drawn directly from the documents written by the notary of the Inquisition. Portuguese readers may find it in *Confissões da Bahia*, 39–45.

7. On the Portuguese Inquisition, see Francisco Bethencourt, "Portugal: A Scrupulous Inquisition," in *Early Modern European Witchcraft: Centres and Peripheries*, ed. Bengt Ankarloo and Gustav Henningsen (Oxford: Clarendon Press, 1990), 403–22. An excellent starting point for the Spanish Inquisition is Norman Roth, *Conversos, Inquisition, and the Expulsion of the Jews from Spain* (Madison: University of Wisconsin Press, 1995).

8. Trial of Domingos Fernandes Nobre, ANTT. Portuguese readers may find his confession and the denunciations of him in *Confissões da Bahia* and *Denunciações da Bahia*.

9. On the Santidade sect of Bahia, see Alida C. Metcalf, "AHR Forum: Millenarian Slaves? The Santidade de Jaguaripe and Slave Resistance in the Americas," *American Historical Review* 104 (1999): 1531–59.

SUGGESTED READINGS

Understanding Brazil in the sixteenth century begins with recognizing that there was no war of conquest, as occurred in Mexico and Peru, but rather many encounters along the coast that gradually developed into small settlements; see Alida C. Metcalf, *Go-Betweens and the Colonization of Brazil: 1500–1600* (Austin, 2005). One of the most influential texts describing the encounter between Europeans and indigenous peoples was written by the German soldier Hans Staden, who, like Fernandes Nobre, was a go-between. A new English translation of Staden's account is *Hans Staden's True History: An Account of Cannibal Captivity in Brazil*, edited and translated by Neil Whitehead and Michael Harbsmeier (Durham, 2008), while Eve M. Duffy and Alida Metcalf situate Staden's story in the early Atlantic world in *The Return of Hans Staden: A Go-Between in the Atlantic World* (Baltimore, 2012). A modern translation of the French Protestant Jean de Léry's classic account of sixteenth-century indigenous life in the Guanabara Bay is *History of a Voyage to the Land of Brazil, Otherwise Called America*, translated by Janet Whatley (Berkeley, 1990). The early relations between Indians and Portuguese are explored by Warren Dean in *With Broadax and Firebrand: The Destruction of the Brazilian Atlantic Forest* (Berkeley, 1995), while the best discussion of the development of the sugar plantation remains *Sugar Plantations in the Formation of Brazilian Society: Bahia, 1550–1835* (New York, 1985), by Stuart Schwartz. The early Jesuit mission is of paramount importance for understanding sixteenth-century Brazil; see relevant sections of Dauril Alden's *The Making of an Enterprise: The Society of Jesus in Portugal, Its Empire, and Beyond, 1540–1750* (Stanford, 1996) and Thomas Cohen's *The Fire of Tongues: António Vieira and the Missionary Church in Brazil and Portugal* (Stanford, 1998). Unfortunately, little has been written in English on the Portuguese Inquisition and Brazil, but an excellent overview is Francisco Bethencourt's "Portugal: A Scrupulous Inquisition," in *Early Modern European Witchcraft: Centres and Peripheries*, edited by Bengt Ankarloo and Gustav Henningsen (Oxford, 1990). The confession of Domingos Fernandes Nobre has been translated by Sandra Lauderdale Graham and is available in *Colonial Latin America: A Documentary History*, edited by Kenneth Mills, William B. Taylor, and Sandra Lauderdale Graham (Wilmington, 2002), 236–41.

FIVE

The Mysterious Catalina

Indian or Spaniard?

Noble David Cook

The Spanish Caribbean in the early seventeenth century was far removed from the centers of Amerindian population, mineral wealth, and political power in the Spanish Indies, yet it was a strategic area, protecting the sea lanes to Mexico and the north coast of South America. The first Spanish settlements, originally established by Christopher Columbus and his successors, appeared in this region from the late fifteenth century. After the exploitation of some gold deposits, pearls, and other wasting assets, however, the centers of wealth and power shifted to the more populous provinces of Mexico and the Andes. The Amerindian population of the scattered Caribbean islands declined catastrophically within two generations, the victims of European epidemics coupled with the depredations caused by warfare and overwork. Spanish efforts to resettle the dispersed Amerindians into European-style towns both changed indigenous lifeways and helped to spread the deadly European diseases.

Spanish entrepreneurs had begun to import African slave labor and to experiment with a variety of export crops, notably sugar, tobacco, and cacao (particularly on the mainland of northern South America), but the region still receded into an economic backwater of the empire. Nevertheless, the fleets from Spain still sailed with European wares to exchange for Peruvian and Mexican silver. The riches conveyed in these fleets attracted Spain's enemies, particularly pirates and privateers who sought to prey on Spanish commerce and its more isolated Caribbean outposts. Strongholds such as Havana or Cartagena were usually able to resist the incursions of these pirates and became the lynchpin of Spain's defenses in the region. More isolated outposts — Puerto Rico, Portobelo (in Pana-

ma), or Florida—remained dangerously exposed to attack. It was a violent and often unstable world.

The controversies surrounding the enigmatic young servant girl, Catalina, took place in the city of Havana, where ships from Mexico and Peru, laden with silver, gold, and other American resources, rendezvoused for the return trip to Spain. While this fleet was taking on water and provisions, bureaucrats in Havana detained a prominent notary, Francisco de Ludeña, and his family for attempting to have an Amerindian (Catalina) accompany them to Spain, a practice expressly forbidden by crown law. Bureaucrats frequently tried to extract bribes or confiscate the goods of travelers returning to Spain to supplement their meager government salaries, but the case of this young servant girl proved particularly complicated and revealing about colonial ideas of caste and gender. Ludeña claimed that Catalina was a Spanish woman entrusted to his care, while his detractors used her lowly status as a servant, her appearance (dark skinned and short), and her lack of any education or refinement as proof that she was an Amerindian.

The controversy surrounding the case demonstrates the difficulty of maintaining clear, unambiguous categories of race, caste, and ethnicity in the volatile world of the Spanish Indies. Once away from orderly European social hierarchies, records could be easily falsified and a person could "pass" for someone of a higher or, in the case of Catalina, a lower social position. Indeed, the difficulty in determining the caste of people such as Catalina probably explains why settlers in the Indies became obsessed with questions of race, caste, and status throughout the colonial era. The case also demonstrates how biases, self-interest, and outright lies enter into the historical record, thus making it difficult for historians to extract the "truth" when attempting to reconstruct the past.

Colonial social labels such as Indian, *mestizo*, Spaniard, and black were markers of caste, an identity assigned at birth that largely remained fixed throughout a person's lifetime. Most Europeans thought that social position should remain unchanging, and in the Spanish Indies, for example, elites believed that an Amerindian tributary should remain one until death. Even ethnic lords who traced their ancestry to the Inca, Maya, or Aztec nobility or had accumulated great wealth could not become "European," regardless of whether they had adopted the dress, speech, or mannerisms of their colonial overlords. Likewise, someone of African ancestry would be given a label of color, whether slave or free. Sixteenth- and seventeenth-century colonial elites seemed obsessed by caste, much as their counterparts in Spain were preoccupied with demonstrating "purity of blood" (*limpieza de sangre*), proving that their ancestry was not "tainted" by the blood of *conversos* or *moriscos* (Jews or Muslims who had converted to Christianity). In Spanish America, the process of race mixture (*mestizaje*) was widespread, which always clouded issues of individual and collective identity.[1]

Despite Spanish efforts to establish fixed racial and ethnic categories, complications abounded in individual cases. Even a definition of what constituted "Indianness" in late sixteenth-century Spanish America could prove contentious and ambiguous. What characteristics set one person apart from others and placed him in a clearly defined category, "Indian"? What were the markers of caste, and how did contemporaries interpret them? These issues come into focus in a particularly contentious case in Havana in late 1605, when various witnesses volunteered testimony on "Catalina, a young Indian woman" who had allegedly arrived in the city from the port of Cartagena de Indias (in current-day Colombia). Their statements, extracted during legal hearings of the Casa de la Contratación (Board of Trade) and kept on file in the Archivo General de Indias, offer fascinating insights into the nature of societal stereotypes as well as the vexing problem of finding "truth" in documentary evidence.

Catalina, a seventeen-year-old servant girl, appeared in the record because her master, Francisco de Ludeña, a royal notary (*escribano del rey*) who had lived and worked in Cartagena de Indias for several years, was attempting to bring her along with his family to Spain. He understood that royal ordinances explicitly prohibited the transport of Amerindians to Europe. As a result, shortly after the fleet reached Havana, *alguacil* (constable) Francisco Báez of the port city denounced the royal notary and filed charges before the lieutenant general (*teniente general*) of the Island of Cuba, Licentiate Bernardo de Argüello. Báez complained that Ludeña transported with him "an *india* (Indian woman), native of Cartagena, such being prohibited."[2] The accusation was so serious that local authorities jailed Ludeña immediately and sequestered his property en route to Spain. His case is just one of dozens; officials in Havana frequently scrutinized to the last detail the papers of travelers to Spain. It was profitable for authorities in the port city to denounce and prosecute unsuspecting travelers, and it was certainly one way to supplement their meager salaries.

Báez quickly found witnesses willing to implicate Ludeña. The first was Juan Fernández Jaramillo, Havana's public executioner, who by occupation might be considered a reliable observer. He swore that he had known the notary and his family for about a decade in Cartagena de Indias. His testimony (December 6, 1605) was explicit: "She [Catalina] was very young, and [I] know that she is an Indian, native of the city of Cartagena . . . , because [I] saw her growing up from a young child, and she was always viewed and taken for an Indian." Fernández Jaramillo added that he "had seen them whip her as a black woman" in the house where she served. Others provided similar testimony. A week later, Báez presented Juan Delgado, a supervisor of the butcher shops in Cartagena, who also knew Ludeña and his family there. One time, Delgado had heard Ludeña exclaim: "Here comes my india, give her something." He said that Ludeña always sent the girl to buy items for the family's table.

Furthermore, during the five years he lived in Cartagena, he always heard the girl called an Indian. This last testimony, however, was undermined because Delgado himself was incarcerated at the time of his deposition.

The critical testimony against Ludeña had already been taken on December 7. On that day, the lieutenant general of the island ordered that a girl who "seems Indian" be examined to determine her status. Captain Gómez de Roxas, the "protector general of the Indians (*protector general de indios*) of the island" was present for the questioning.[3] The court took Catalina's sworn testimony in Spanish, however, because she spoke the language, making an interpreter unnecessary. She promised to tell the truth. When asked, "What is your name and status?" she replied that she was "an Indian, a native of Cartagena, and was named Catalina." She then testified that her parents were Anton de Mairena and Catalina Rodríguez, both natives of Cartagena, and that she was eighteen years old.

Catalina was then pressed about why she gave this testimony, when not long before she had sworn to the lieutenant general that she was from the kingdom of Castile. The judges then demanded: "Who counseled you to say this?" Catalina replied that her master, Francisco de Ludeña, had ordered her to say that she was from Guadaira and to deny that she was an Indian. She now swore that she was indeed an Indian. "That is the truth," she insisted. Queried about who brought her and in what ship, Catalina said that she came with Ludeña in the vessel of Captain Pedro Sánchez, part of the fleet presently anchored in the harbor and under the command of General don Francisco del Corral. Catalina was then asked how long she had served Ludeña and how much he paid her. When her parents died, she replied, she was still very young, and her sister María proposed that she serve Ludeña. "In all this time he has not given [me] anything more than clothing and footwear." When questioned when and how Ludeña decided to take her from Cartagena to Spain, she said that "while serving he persuaded her, saying that if she would come with him to the kingdom of Castile he would give her clothing and whatever else was necessary."

To verify her story, the officials asked Catalina to provide the names of people who might know her and be able to support her new testimony. She said that the shipmaster, Cristóbal Gómez, and a sailor named Jacomes as well as others on the boat knew of her identity. The girl seemed honest to the Havana officials, and, given the possibility of corroboration from other witnesses, they began civil proceedings against Francisco de Ludeña. Acting in Catalina's best interest, "Indian Protector" Gómez de Roxas secured an order from the lieutenant general to place "Catalina india in the house of Licentiate Suárez de Poago, and be put under the care of his wife, Ana María, until the matter can be investigated further."[4]

The alguacil, Francisco Báez, pressed the case against Ludeña. On January 30, 1606, he presented as a witness forty-seven-year-old Juan de Sequera, then residing in Havana. Sequera reported that he had seen the young Catalina in Cartagena in the service of Francisco de Ludeña and his wife. At times she "would go with a jug for water, coming from the garden of Governor don Pedro de Acuña, who had found her and brought her from the Xagueyes province."[5] Sequera further reported that he thought Catalina "had a carnal relationship with one Lucas Garcilán, a barber, who often absented himself from the service of the governor to spend time in the house of Catalina." Sequera also testified that Catalina was Indian because "it seems the said Catalina has the shape (*talle*) of an Indian, because her body demonstrates it." But he admitted not knowing her mother or father.

The following day, Báez secured the testimony of twenty-two-year-old Nicolás de Silva, who had seen Catalina three or four times in Cartagena de Indias. On board the ship to Havana he had observed Catalina serving Ludeña, "cooking and providing other services." But Silva was less certain of her Indianness: "I don't know if she is Indian or mestiza." In fact, he admitted that while in Cartagena, he "had always taken her for a mestiza."

A few days later, on February 9, Báez interrogated two forceful witnesses who claimed to be more certain of the girl's identity. Sixty-year-old Gerónimo de Valdes had worked for General Francisco del Corral and had also served in the house of the governor of Cartagena, don Pedro de Acuña, along with a companion, the barber Lucas Garcilán, Catalina's alleged lover. Valdes reported that whenever Lucas was missing from the household, it was said "he was with the Indian woman that the said Francisco de Ludeña had." The witness stated that he had seen the girl named Catalina serving Ludeña on the way from Cartagena to Havana, and when Valdes asked her if "she knew Lucas the barber, she had responded 'yes.'" He therefore thought that they were one and the same, and further he believed "it is very certain that she is by caste Indian (*de casta de india*), because by her looks one can easily see it."

The same day, Báez brought forth forty-year-old Havana resident Simón de Padilla, who had worked for Ludeña while in Cartagena. He had observed the young woman Catalina serving regularly in the household. Simón reported that many times he had heard Ludeña call to her, "Come here, india!" Since Ludeña and his wife always referred to Catalina in this way, Padilla also took her for an Indian. Furthermore, he stated, "by her looks she shows it and thus he knows [she is]."

Despite Catalina's confession that she was an Indian, the court sought additional proof of her caste. Another Indian woman, María Díaz of Santa Marta, testified before the alguacil on February 10 and corroborated Catalina's story. The witness was herself twenty years old and a servant of María Díaz, the wife of Luis González, a permanent resident (*vecino*) of

Havana. María testified that she had known Catalina in Cartagena and saw her serving a married man who lived near the Indian settlement of Xagueyes del Rey. According to María, she had often observed Catalina going to fetch water from a well in the house of Anton Nesado, a vecino of Cartagena. The woman whom Catalina served many times called her an "Indian . . . , and she frequently whipped her." María Díaz added, "I saw her dishonoring her, calling her 'Indian bitch' (*perra india*)." She concluded, "This is the same Catalina who at present is in this city and who has been shown to me."

Three days later, Francisco de Castilla, a thirty-two-year-old vecino living in the La Punta neighborhood of Havana, testified that about six years ago he had been in Cartagena and had seen Catalina treated by local people as an Indian, "a daughter of Indian parents." He saw her several times in Ludeña's residence and twice since she had arrived in Havana, so he was certain that it was the same person. As part of her service, she was ordered to bring water from the fountain "and other even lower things." Castilla said that he "had never heard anyone refer to her as a Spaniard or *mulata*, rather always as Indian." He elaborated further that by her "looks and bearing Catalina seems to be an Indian." Moreover, "she has the color of such, and wide short feet, as the other Indian women do." The markers of identity for Francisco de Castilla and the other Spanish witnesses were clear—phenotype, body structure, and outward appearance as well as the menial occupation of servant girl. No Spanish woman in the Indies could look or act as Catalina did; therefore, she must be Indian!

While Francisco Báez collected testimony against him, Francisco de Ludeña attacked the integrity of the public executioner, Fernández Jaramillo, forcing the alguacil to recall him to testify. Fernández Jaramillo swore again that his earlier testimony was the whole truth. He now recalled that on the day that Ludeña was jailed, he demanded to know: "Why have you denounced me for this Indian woman?" Fernández Jaramillo confided to the interrogator that he replied: "I have not denounced you. . . . The Indian girl had spoken to him [Ludeña] earlier, and he knew it." Ludeña then said to Fernández Jaramillo, "If you join me, then you will know her." The executioner next claimed that Ludeña offered a bribe: "Why not ask me for four or five pesos? . . . Don't be someone who would denounce me, we have established a close friendship after all." Without question, Ludeña was attempting to pay off the executioner and abort the legal proceedings. If Fernández Jaramillo's testimony was truthful, Ludeña's guilt was clearly implied by the offer of a bribe.

Ludeña and Fernández Jaramillo apparently conspired to manipulate the sexuality of the defenseless Catalina. The testimony of Juan de Sequera and Gerónimo de Valdes, establishing a physical relationship between the barber and the young girl, already attested to her carnal relationship with a European male. The sexual affair occurred with or without the knowledge and control of her master. If Fernández Jaramillo were telling the truth, however, Ludeña was offering not only four or five pesos but also Catalina's sexual services.[6]

The testimony taken by Báez apparently established Catalina's status as an Indian. There was only some hesitation on the part of a few witnesses who indicated that she might be a mestiza. Nevertheless, over the weeks the alguacil had assembled numerous witnesses attesting to the Indian identity of eighteen-year-old Catalina. Although her parentage could not be established, several said that she probably belonged to an ethnic group settled near Cartagena de Indias, the Xagueyes del Rey. She served her masters as an Indian woman would, doing menial tasks that would not be done by any respectable Spanish woman in the Indies. She carried water, brought food from the market, cooked it, and did a thousand other things expected of a female Indian servant. Furthermore, her masters called her an Indian in the presence of many witnesses. Their treatment of her was clearly exploitative; there were frequent whippings and cutting verbal abuse. Even an Indian woman testified that Catalina was Indian. Most important, Catalina herself provided the proof by her sworn statement. By all accounts she fit the stereotype, and the colonial elite who glanced at her in the street recognized her as Indian. Her stature, her demeanor, her dress, her short, stubby feet, and her skin color, as Francisco de Castilla indicated, demonstrated her essentially "Indian" nature.

Despite all of this evidence indicating Catalina's Indian identity, much of the documentation in such legal cases is filled with truth, half-truths, and even outright lies.[7] Francisco de Ludeña had been in the Indies for several years and was returning to Spain with his family and significant assets. During a decade of service overseas, most Spaniards made both friends and enemies. There were always astute officials in a port like Havana, where virtually all travelers spent a few days or weeks while the ships of the fleet returning to Spain were outfitted for the Atlantic passage. Cuban officials in Havana looked out for their own interests as well as the crown's, and any bureaucrat who denounced a civil crime could reap a handsome reward. It was into this type of environment that Ludeña sailed in the last days of December 1605. He had capital and plenty of enemies. His apparent attempt to transport an Indian servant girl back to Spain was the perfect pretext for ambitious officials in Havana to move against him.

Ludeña's initial defense was straightforward: he was innocent of the charges. He insisted that Catalina was a Spaniard. Her identity was clear, and he could prove it. Many years ago he had gone from Seville to nearby Alcalá de la Guadaira, serving with a judge under a commission from the Holy Office of Seville. There, he resided in the house of Rodrigo Caro, the notary of the local arm of the Inquisition. Caro and his wife doña Ysabel begged him, "for the love of God, please take on and raise the orphan girl

Catalina," who was poverty stricken. The couple was keeping her temporarily out of charity. Convinced by their pleas and that of the girl's older sister, Ludeña took Catalina into his household to be a companion for his son Gerónimo. In the ensuing years, Ludeña and his family took Catalina with them to the Canary Islands, Margarita in the Caribbean, Caracas in Venezuela, and finally Cartagena de Indias.[8]

As Ludeña prepared a comprehensive questionnaire for use in his defense, many loathsome character traits emerged, particularly his insensitivity and overall bigotry. In addition to background questions on the case, he asked the witnesses to discuss why Catalina now said that she was an Indian because she "has been pressured and threatened by some people for her to say it." He also stated that "she is so simple and ignorant that with any bit of fear that you put into her, she will say whatever you put in her mouth." Some of his questions reveal Ludeña's low opinion of Amerindians, whom he considered so worthless as servants that he never used them. Instead, he had several black men and women serving him and a black slave as a page. His son, Mateo de Ludeña Valdes, apparently shared his father's opinions. After marrying and settling in Cartagena, he kept more than "thirty head of slaves."

Ludeña did his best to collect witnesses who knew him in Havana; there was insufficient time to gather information from distant Cartagena, on the mainland coast. On January 4, he presented Ana Duarte, who had known his family seven years ago in the city of Santiago de León, Caracas; she later sailed on the same frigate with the Ludeña household to Cartagena. Duarte thought that Catalina was an "ignorant" Spaniard. The following day, another witness, Diego Enríquez, testified that he had stayed in the Ludeña house in Cartagena. During this visit, he asked Catalina about her background, and she told him that she was an orphan from Alcalá de la Guadaira, where she still had a sister and other relatives. He took her for "simple, ignorant, and of little knowledge." He further recalled that Ludeña had many slaves in Cartagena, and "ordinarily he took a young black page who followed along behind him through the city." Indians were not employed in the household. On January 7, Ysabel Gutiérrez, the wife of Diego Enríquez, testified that when the Ludeñas had moved to Cartagena, she often visited their household. She also had spoken to Catalina in Havana. Another household servant told Ysabel that "she [Catalina] was not thinking of anything other than returning with this witness to Spain, because all she wanted was to return to her homeland." Ysabel concurred that Catalina was "a simple girl of little understanding."

The same day, Ludeña summoned a fifty-eight-year-old soldier, Damián de Levia, stationed at the Morro fortress in Havana harbor, who claimed to remember Ludeña from the time of his service in the Canaries. Levia was in the port guard when Ludeña with his family and Catalina had first disembarked. He stated that he knew the whole household well because he frequently visited their house on business of Governor and Captain General don Luis de la Cueva. Two years later, Governor Cueva discharged his soldiers and returned to Spain, leading Levia to serve in Las Palmas, where he again met Ludeña. Levia later watched the notary and his family depart for America, taking Catalina with them. Before their departure, however, two of his fellow soldiers had told Levia that they had known Catalina's parents in Alcalá. Most important, while Catalina was being examined before the lieutenant general of Cuba, Levia asked her, "Why is it that you, a Spaniard, have said you are an Indian?" She replied that she did so "out of fear and consternation." He characterized her mental state in the same terms as Diego Enríquez: "simple, ignorant, and of little knowledge," reiterating the same labels used by Ludeña in the original testimony.

Ludeña also called several other witnesses, including a fifty-year-old Seville resident, Bartolomé Rodríguez, who provided on January 16 important facts corroborating Ludeña's case. According to Rodríguez, he had visited the house where Catalina was being held at Ludeña's behest. He asked her where she was born, and she replied Alcalá, but she could not remember her parish. She knew that it was the house of Rodrigo Caro and his wife Ysabel, on a wide street whose name she did not know. The witness knew Caro and the street in Alcalá de Guadaira where he lived, the Calle de la Mina, which was indeed very wide. The next day, Rodríguez continued his probing, and Catalina revealed that her father was a laborer from Gandil named Anton de Mairena. Her mother was Catalina Rodríguez. Bartolomé Rodríguez confided: "I knew the said Anton de Mairena; he was a short man with a dark complexion (*moreno*)." Moreover, the witness said that Catalina looked a lot like her father— stature (short), occupation (servant), demeanor (weak-minded), phenotype (dark), and likely with straight black hair. Was Catalina a *morena*, an Andalusian of lower-class background, or an *india*? Indeed, Catalina now admitted to Bartolomé Rodríguez that she had falsely testified to being an Indian "because they had terrorized me." Catalina's true identity now became the central problem facing the local representatives of Spanish justice in Havana. Their final decision had implications for the welfare of both Francisco de Ludeña and Catalina. Long incarceration in early-seventeenth-century prisons damaged both a person's health and finances.

After several weeks of inactivity in the case, Ludeña demanded action from the court, but this request only encouraged his opponents to take the offensive. On February 25, Francisco Báez appeared before the lieutenant general of Cuba, claiming that he had proved his case well enough "to secure victory." Catalina had confessed to being an Indian, and her admission was corroborated by many witnesses. He wanted the case settled. Whatever her true status, argued the alguacil on February 31, Francisco de Ludeña should be prosecuted for having transported her without a license. It seemed to Báez that Ludeña was conspiring to make it appear as though Catalina was a Spaniard in order to take her to Europe. He said that he had clearly and definitively demonstrated that Ludeña was breaking the law and thus should suffer the full penalties.

For his part, Ludeña responded on February 28, charging that the entire proceedings were tainted and that the witnesses supporting the accusers were untrustworthy and even dishonest. He did not mince words: "They are infamous men of evil conscience, and without fear of God." These allegations and the inquiry that followed delayed the decision on the original case until mid-March. Ludeña continued to press the attack, trying to discredit his accusers. He asked: "What of the witness Juan de Sequera? Had he not been forced to serve ten years as an oarsman in the galleys?" "What were his crimes," and why was witness Gerónimo de Valdes forced into galley service in Cartagena? And Juan Delgado, were not he and his father of the same name both infamous morisco rebels, exiled from Spain? And Padilla, the butcher in Cartagena, was he not publicly shamed in the city and finally exiled from the Indies? What was the background of witness Francisco de Castilla? Most important, however, what about the public executioner, Fernández Jaramillo? Was he not forced into galley service for deserting to the Moors in North Africa? Did he not commit murder in Cartagena? Were not his ears cut off as a sign of his criminality? Did he not wreak havoc in Havana before he was selected as public executioner, and even afterward? And who authorized such a criminal to serve the crown when he had repeatedly stolen, killed, and lied? How and why had such a den of criminals been assembled to give testimony against Francisco de Ludeña, a royal notary?

As much as his enemies in Havana in early 1606 may have wanted to ignore Ludeña, his charges could not easily be silenced. The notary was an educated man with substantial connections in both Spain and the Indies, even if he was not the most caring and benign of masters. Ludeña wanted the testimony of those witnesses against him to be stricken from the record, arguing that the word of such people could not be trusted. Indeed, in the next weeks he did provide even more convincing evidence that many of his accusers were petty criminals at best and traitors to the king or even murderers at worst—a veritable rogues' gallery.

Simón de Padilla, the butcher in Cartagena, had been found guilty of using false weights and had been put in the stocks. Juan Delgado was a branded morisco, son of another morisco, a butcher of Seville. Public executioner Fernández Jaramillo had a long criminal record. Most recently, María Rodríguez, the wife of a chief pilot of the galleys, reported that about a month earlier, while at home in bed, she had been awakened about midnight by a loud noise in the yard. She got up to investigate and discovered Fernández Jaramillo with another soldier who was shouting: "Well, you scoundrel and thief, in the house of an honorable lady! You have come and jumped over the walls to rob her." Fernández Jaramillo, in front of the soldier and the surprised María, "fell to his knees saying for the love of God, do not let anyone know, because I have entered as a person who has lost all reason, and I am drunk." According to the witness, this event occurred even after Fernández Jaramillo had been whipped and paraded through the streets of Havana because of his theft of some cheeses from Captain Alonso Ferrera.

Given these serious accusations, the judge decided to examine Juan Fernández Jaramillo a third time, on March 13, in the Morro fortress. He simply denied several of the accusations; others he ignored. Fernández Jaramillo did admit, however, that while stationed as a soldier in the North African frontier fortress of Melilla for a "piddling thing," he had been sentenced to the galleys as an oarsman for ten years without pay. Much of the service was in Cartagena de Indias. He further admitted that he had escaped, and Governor Acuña had then sentenced him to an additional five years in the galleys. At about that time his ears were cut off. His escape was just one of those spur-of-the-moment things, he lamented, and he did not deserve such a harsh disfigurement. For his alleged murder of a soldier in the plaza of Cartagena, Fernández Jaramillo admitted to a sentence of another two years in the galleys, again without pay. More recently, he conceded that for a certain case involving cheeses, the lieutenant general of Cuba had condemned him to two hundred lashes and an additional ten years of galley service. Nevertheless, Lieutenant Gendias and Antonio Fernández Farias persuaded him to take the office of public executioner in Havana, and for this they forgave him the ten additional years in the galleys. Fernández Jaramillo, of course, accepted the offer and "began to use and exercise the said occupation."

To press his case, Francisco de Ludeña continued to challenge the integrity of his accusers. On March 14, he related even more complete and damning information about his enemies. He called back for cross-examination Juan de Sequera, who was part of the company of Governor Acuña. Sequera testified that Fernández Jaramillo had served ten years in the galleys because "being a soldier on the Barbary Coast he had gone over the walls of the fortress and had wanted to join the enemy Moors." Furthermore, Sequera had seen him whipped publicly in the streets of Cartagena de Indias for having "absconded with some cheeses and bottles of oil from the storeroom of Captain Alonso Ferrera," leading to a sentence of ten additional years of galley service. Sequera, too, had been an important witness against Ludeña, but the notary's questions revealed that his reliability was suspect. Sequera admitted that he had been condemned in the city of Córdoba in Spain for taking part in an uprising. He received a term of eight years' galley service, which he completed in Cartagena under Governor Acuña.

Three days later, Ludeña presented his summation before Judge Suárez de Poago, concluding his defense by attacking those who had brought charges against him and pointing out the weaknesses and inconsistencies in their testimony. Ludeña charged that these hostile witnesses were "a band of lost and infamous people, and bad Christians"; they were "all of them exiled, and they had fled from Cartagena for crimes." Then, using what he believed to be flawless logic, he critiqued point by point the weaknesses in the testimony of his accusers. They did not provide the names of the girl's parents, her *encomendero*, or the parish in her indigenous village. If she really were an Indian, she should have been placed in the house of the general protector of the Indians, but she was not. It was clear to Ludeña that Catalina's testimony had been coerced and that her words should have been more closely scrutinized from the very beginning of the judicial process. He lamented that the investigating official did not take such precautions, particularly when it was public knowledge that she had complained of the "force that had been applied to make her say that she was an Indian." Furthermore, the proper protections legally available for minors had been denied Catalina in this case. In conclusion, Ludeña asked that all the charges against him be dropped. Instead, he argued that his accusers should themselves face punishment for "having wanted to make of a Spanish girl, a daughter of Spaniards, an Indian, subject to servitude." He demanded justice and a conclusion to the case.

The following day, March 18, Judge Suárez de Poago gave his decision: "I find that regarding the . . . merits of the [case] . . . Francisco de Ludeña defended himself well enough. . . . I must absolve and do absolve in this instance the said Francisco de Ludeña." Despite this verdict, the tribulations of Ludeña did not end. His enemies persevered and took judicial action that left him in legal limbo. On April 8, Francisco Báez filed an appeal, directed to the president and judges of the Royal Audiencia of Santo Domingo. Such an action provided Ludeña's enemies in Havana and Cartagena de Indias with the excuse to keep him jailed and his properties sequestered. If Ludeña left for Spain, charges against him still would remain open. Furthermore, many important papers would still be under the control of his enemies.

When Ludeña, his wife, family, and servants did return to Spain several months later, it was only after a lengthy delay. The annual fleet remained in Havana harbor while the ships were checked for seaworthiness and provisioned. Ludeña and his party finally departed in late September or early October, at the height of the hurricane season. The return route took the ships off the Florida coast and west of the Bahamas, where they took advantage of the strong currents of the Gulfstream. The fleet would pass not far from Bermuda, in the mid-Atlantic, and then sail toward Cape San Vicente in Portugal. From there it was only a day or two to the Andalusian ports of Spain. They finally landed at Sanlúcar de Barrameda, at the mouth of the Guadalquivir River, and on October 20, 1606, the Ludeña household was taken into custody. Alcalde Licentiate Martín Hernández Portocarrero, of His Majesty's Council, along with don Melchor Maldonado, treasurer of the Casa de la Contratación, reviewed the documents of the passengers on board the ships that entered the harbor. On the vessel of shipmaster Antonio de Obregón the officials found "Francisco de Ludeña with his wife, one son, and a female servant, and some slaves." Because the party could not "show a license for their voyage" and the royal inspectors discovered the problem in Havana with an "Indian woman," the officials took immediate action. Ludeña and his companions were "taken into custody to be turned over to the jail of the Casa de la Contratación in Seville."

Here, in the records of the Casa de la Contratación, the modern historian finally encounters documents that unravel part of the mystery surrounding the true identity of Catalina. Like all Spaniards leaving for the Indies, Ludeña and his party needed permits to depart, which officials filed in the registers of the Casa de la Contratación. In most cases, the process proceeded quickly, but sometimes complications arose that led to costly delays. A royal letter authorizing the trip, however, could speed up the process. On September 30, 1591, in the palace at San Lorenzo, Philip II signed a letter authorizing Francisco de Ludeña, vecino de Seville, to travel to Tierra Firme with his wife, children, a male servant, and two women for their service. The document specified that the children and servants were not to be married. On the outbound voyage in the early 1590s, shipmaster Juan Camacho recorded the presence aboard of one Francisco de Ludeña, his wife doña Leonor de Valdes, and Mateo, Gerónimo, and María, their children, along with Juan López de Aguila, Juana de Mendoza, and Catalina de Villacis, all servants and natives of Seville. They carried a copy of the license to depart for Tierra Firme. It was standard procedure to briefly describe each traveler in order to prevent others from falsely taking their places. The descriptions are not as accurate as paintings, but they are the only evidence available to the historian. At the time, Francisco de Ludeña was forty-two years old, "of good body, a black greying beard and black eyes." Doña Leonor was forty, with a "clear rosy complexion and a mole on the middle of her nose." Mateo, aged nineteen, "had signs of a beard and a small wound on the right cheek," while thirteen-year-old Gerónimo had a "sign of a wound on the left eyelid." María was twenty, "white, and with a clear rosy complexion, and two small scars on the side of the face and another on the right arm." Juan López de Aguila was thirty, of a good body, with a straw-colored beard and two wounds on both eyebrows. Juana de Mendoza was "white, with a small mole in the temple on the right side."

Most important for unraveling the case and determining the veracity of Ludeña and his accusers, however, is the description of the servant, Catalina de Villacis. But here someone has tampered with the document. There is a small tear in the page where the critical text about Catalina was entered, and paper glued to cover the hole. All that can be discerned are the words, "de edad - - - p - - - - na [pequeña?] de cu - - [cuna?]" (aged - - -

small in a crib), a scar above the right eyebrow and another on the right cheek. Why was the correct age of Catalina alone removed from the original page, unless someone wished to falsify the record? The fragmentary, altered text suggests that Catalina was still in a crib, therefore an infant. But this contradicts the testimony given by Ludeña while in Havana. Furthermore, officials in Seville seldom recorded full descriptions of infants, mentioning details such as scars in the licenses. They tended simply to mention small children as just that—small children—with no further identifying information, unlike young and older adults, where they provided a fuller physical description. A full description of an infant "servant" is even more suspicious. There is also the curious addendum dated December 23, 1595, signed by one Juan Caxal, for the ship *San Pedro* that confirms boarding by "Francisco de Ludeña and his wife and children, because his servants did not appear." This document, too, is torn at the most critical points, with paper glued on to cover the gaps. Who tampered with the records—Ludeña, or perhaps his enemies in Havana, who had access to his papers when his properties were sequestered? And who is *this* Catalina? Is she an Indian, or the orphan whom Ludeña claims to have taken into his household, or even someone else?

From jail in the port of Sanlúcar de Barrameda, Francisco de Ludeña wrote on October 21, 1606, complaining of his rapidly worsening plight; moreover, his wife was now seriously ill. He reminded authorities that he had returned to Spain on the *Santa María la Rosa* and that he remained unjustly incarcerated. He lamented the embargo of his property, especially of a black slave named Ysabel, pleading, "I have need of [the slave] for my personal service and for my wife, who has already received extreme unction and is at the point of death, and the said slave is ready to give birth." Ludeña requested that the slave and her clothing be released so she could serve her master and mistress, regardless of her advanced pregnancy. The treasurer and judge, don Melchor Maldonado, complied immediately and ordered the transfer of the party to a jail in Seville. Although the relevant documents are missing, the party apparently posted bond and was freed for fifteen days, with the stipulation that they appear at an agreed-upon time before the jailor of the Casa de la Contratación in Seville. Sometime between October 21 and November 16, doña Leonor died.

Nevertheless, the royal prosecutor (*fiscal*), Diego Lorenzo Navarro, pressed charges against Francisco de Ludeña on November 16 in Seville. That same day, Ludeña appeared and, in his name and that of his son Gerónimo, requested that the justices hear testimony in the case. He also asked that Catalina, who was under twenty-five and therefore legally a minor, be assigned a guardian, Francisco de Mesa, a *procurador* (solicitor) of the Royal Audiencia. Two days later, the court of the Casa de la Contratación complied with both petitions.

The officials took Ludeña's sworn "confession." He was now listed as fifty-seven years old, and he testified that he had been the king's notary in Seville several years before departing for the Indies. Court attorneys then asked if he had returned to Spain with his wife, children, and servants this year in the fleet commanded by General don Francisco del Corral "without orders or license . . . carrying as he did much merchandise, gold and silver, without registering it." Ludeña admitted that he did sail with his wife and one son as well as with one slave and a servant woman, proceeding from Cartagena de Indias, where they had resided for some time. The group first traveled on the ship of Juan Martínez de Murgia to Havana, but when this vessel began to take on water, they transferred to the ship of Antonio de Obregón. Ludeña "carried the license of the governor and royal officials and the Inquisition of the said city of Cartagena." In Havana, however, the lieutenant governor of Cuba had "taken all the baggage that I had, among which they took the said license." The justices then asked him if he had brought one "Catalina india who at present is in your service," despite knowing the laws prohibiting the transport of Indians to Spain from the Indies. He replied no, that he had dealt with these charges in Havana, where he had been imprisoned, "and I was freed because she is a Spanish woman, a native of these kingdoms, raised in Alcalá de la Guadaira." The same day the officials also took the sworn testimony of Gerónimo, whose evidence corroborated that of his father. Gerónimo, too, provided critical testimony that the license authorizing their return to Spain remained among the properties seized in Havana.

Officials of the Casa de la Contratación took the testimony "of a woman imprisoned in the jail of the Royal Audiencia" on November 18, 1606. The young woman "says that she is Catalina de Mairena and is seventeen years old, and is a servant of Francisco de Ludeña." She reported that she had returned from Tierra Firme and was a native of Alcalá de la Guadaira. When asked why she had confessed in Havana that she was an Indian from Cartagena, she replied: "I said it because the lieutenant of Cartagena advised me to say it." Catalina told the court officials that he had actually forced her to say that she was Indian. Asked if she had come without an official travel license, she replied that she had served Francisco de Ludeña from the time that he left Spain in the company of Judge Milla until their return. Moreover, she had traveled in the service of her master, with his license.

Two days later, solicitor Francisco de Mesa appeared before the president and justices of the casa to speak on behalf of his clients, Francisco, Gerónimo, and Catalina. He argued that there was no legal cause not to free them, and they certainly did not constitute a public danger. Furthermore, he declared that Diego Rodríguez Sierra, a wealthy Seville silk merchant, had agreed to post bond for the imprisoned Ludeña and his household. His efforts prevailed, and on that day, three officials of the court signed the release order.

For Ludeña, the whole affair had been a close call, fraught with risks. Shipping an Amerindian and illegal merchandise back to Spain was a serious crime, and his position had been made especially precarious by the confiscation of his papers in Havana. Did those papers include damaging reports on colonial officials in Cartagena and Havana, which motivated the American officials who brought charges against him? Certainly, his personal situation and the family's became even more unfortunate by the death of his wife. Nevertheless, he did secure his freedom, and documentation about his case in the court of the Casa de la Contratación ended.

Fortunately for anyone interested in unraveling the case, the paper trail in the Archivo General de Indias is extensive and fills many gaps in the story. Although someone (Ludeña or his enemies) tampered with his original license to travel to the Indies, other papers exist because both the originals and copies of supplementary documents regarding Ludeña's voyage to the New World were filed elsewhere in the Casa de la Contratación.[9] The critical piece for reaching the "truth" is the license authorizing Catalina de Villacis to travel to the Indies as a servant of Francisco de Ludeña. In these papers the original Catalina is described in detail, and she could not be the same seventeen-year-old who testified in Seville in 1606. According to the documentation, on December 19, 1591, Ludeña had appeared before the casa to request an authorization, which he signed in his own hand, for Catalina de Villacis to accompany the family as one of two female house servants. Two days earlier, Catalina had presented witnesses attesting to her background and "purity of blood," a requirement that was not easy to circumvent because the crown was exceptionally diligent in attempting to keep "undesirables" from the Indies. Pedro Suárez, a tailor, testified that he had known Catalina from as long as he could remember. She was a native of Seville, from the parish of San Pedro, unmarried (*soltera*), and her parents and grandparents were Old Christians, untainted by the blood of Muslims, Jews, or anyone recently converted to the Catholic faith.[10] The family had never been called before the Inquisition. Two other witnesses confirmed his statement, and the description of Catalina provided by all three witnesses was consistent—she was about thirty years old, small of body, with a scar above the right eyebrow and another on the right cheek. In the documentation used in Ludeña's defense in 1606, Catalina's age was removed along with the term "small of body" (*pequeña de cuerpo*). Someone had left just enough text so that it appeared to read, or could be read, as "pequeña de cuna," an infant girl in a crib.

Who, then, was the Catalina who accompanied Ludeña in 1605? Was she Catalina india, Catalina de Mairena, or Catalina de Villacis? Where was the real Catalina de Villacis, now about forty-five years old? Did she really go to the Indies, and was this Catalina india perhaps her daughter? Or were the charges against Ludeña in Havana really true? And what of the story of the servant girl, the orphan Catalina from Alcalá de la Guadaira, who had been taken in by Ludeña's family fifteen years or so ago? Was she brought by them to the Indies without an official license? She was, it seems, the person responsible for the events narrated in the record. Her charges, true or false, brought into action the legal representatives of the royal government in the Indies. What were her motives? How could she be so easily forced to testify under oath that she was an Indian when she was not? Had she been so mistreated by Francisco de Ludeña and his wife that she acted in revenge? Were there personal reasons why she might have hoped to remain in Cartagena de Indias rather than return to Spain? Was she sexually linked to Gavilán the barber, or to someone else? We do know that Ludeña was lying in his testimony. But how far did the lie extend?

The real identity of Catalina india remains a mystery. Certainly, her case demonstrates the caution that historians must use in their search for the "truth." Evidence is always suspect and must be examined from all angles. Court cases, with multiple testimonies from competing parties, often permit scholars to probe for answers, but multiple points of view are rare in colonial documentation. Too often, historians hear only one voice—that of a colonial bureaucrat, a clergyman, or a person in the strongest position of power and authority. But which of the witnesses was telling the "truth"? We know that witnesses lied, even under oath. If the evidence today is ambiguous about Catalina's identity, then what of her contemporaries who tried to label her "Indian"?

The varied descriptions provided by witnesses in the case permit a slightly better understanding of the nuances of colonial descriptors of caste and class. And in the early-seventeenth-century Spanish Caribbean, it was the "perception" that counted most often. What made Catalina an Indian or mestiza in the minds of the witnesses was color and physical attributes together with her menial occupation. Yet other witnesses testified that she looked like her father—small, dark, or moreno. If she were a Spaniard and simply resembled her father, her occupation as a servant would not have been uncommon for the daughter of a day laborer in Alcalá de la Guadaira. Unfortunately, authorities in the Indies obscured Catalina's true background and used her for their own ends. Officials in Cartagena de Indias and Havana, for whatever reasons, were clearly manipulating her identity to exert pressure on Francisco de Ludeña. He, in turn, manipulated her identity to protect himself and his family. Catalina's own shifting statements, back and forth from Indian to Spaniard, probably reflect not so much her confusion as her attempt at survival in a male-dominated world where she was merely a pawn in the hands of those in power. Her identity would change in keeping with the relative strength of those who controlled her life and her voice.

QUESTIONS FOR DISCUSSION

1. Do you think the problems of racial identity would have been easier or harder to resolve in the Caribbean, far removed from central regions of the Spanish Indies, such as central Mexico or the Andes?
2. How did Catalina's gender complicate the issues surrounding the resolution of her identity?
3. Why might the authorities in Havana have had a vested interest in prosecuting the case against Francisco de Ludeña?
4. Why did Catalina testify both to her Amerindian and her Spanish identity? Did the issue of her identity have the potential to change her life in either case?
5. How might the historian deal with conflicting evidence in a case such as this one? Does the evidence in this case lead you to think that Catalina was a Spaniard or an Amerindian?

NOTES

1. Claudio Esteva-Fabregat, *Mestizaje in Ibero-America* (Tucson: University of Arizona Press, 1995), sharply contrasts the different attitudes in Anglo versus Hispanic America. Catalina's story was uncovered during research for another project in Spain in 1998–1999 under support of a fellowship from the American Council of Learned Societies and Florida International University. The author thanks the students and faculty of Tulane University for their comments at a presentation in March 1999, and especially Alexandra Parma Cook for constructive criticism.

2. Unless otherwise noted, the quotes are taken directly from the case in Seville's Archivo General de Indias, Contratación 151B, ramo 6.

3. The protector general of the Indians was a position bestowed on someone, usually with legal experience, who was charged to assist in the defense of Amerindians. Bartolomé de las Casas was the first to be given the office in 1516, by Cardinal Jiménez de Cisneros. By the early seventeenth century there were many salaried Indian defense attorneys scattered throughout the Indies. See Lewis Hanke, *The Spanish Struggle for Justice in the Conquest of America* (Boston: Little, Brown, 1965).

4. Licentiate Melchior Suárez de Poago served as royal fiscal in the Audiencia of Panama from January 30, 1613, to February 19, 1619, when he was appointed fiscal of the Audiencia of Quito, where he served until retirement in 1647. Ernesto Schäfer, *El Consejo Supremo y Real de las Indias* (Seville: Escuela de Estudios Hispanoamericanos, 1947), 2:472, 516.

5. The governor of Cartagena de Indias, don Pedro de Acuña, was named to office on October 26, 1592. On December 24, 1599, he was appointed governor of the Philippines, where he later died. His successor in Cartagena, don Jerónimo de Zuazo Casasola, was named to office on March 9, 1600. Schäfer, *Consejo de las Indias*, 2:526, 534.

6. Sexual exploitation of the conquered, male and female, is stressed by Richard C. Trexler, *Sex and Conquest: Gendered Violence, Political Order, and the European Conquest of the Americas* (Ithaca: Cornell University Press, 1995).

7. Lies under oath are frequent, as described in a case of one Spaniard charged with bigamy and illegal shipment of bullion to Spain; see Alexandra Parma Cook and Noble David Cook, *"Good Faith and Truthful Ignorance": A Case of Transatlantic Bigamy* (Durham: Duke University Press, 1991). The historian must even take care in analyzing ecclesiastical records. As W. George Lovell succinctly points out, Dominicans and

Franciscans could view and portray a series of events in an entirely different light, acting out of interests for their own order. See W. George Lovell, "Mayans, Missionaries, Evidence, and Truths: The Polemics of Native Resettlement in Sixteenth-Century Guatemala," *Journal of Historical Geography* 16, no. 3 (1990): 277–94.

8. For the city, see María del Carmen Borrego Plá, *Cartagena de Indias en el siglo XVI* (Seville: Escuela de Estudios Hispanoamericanos, 1983).

9. Archivo General de Indias, Contratación 5234B, no. 1, ramo 19.

10. In Archivo General de Indias, Contratación 5234B, no. 1, ramo 18 we learn her parish in her testimony about Juan López del Aguila.

SUGGESTED READINGS

The unsavory side of port cities in the circum-Caribbean during the sixteenth century is portrayed in John Esquemeling, *The Buccaneers of America* (New York: Dorset Press, 1987). For the seamy side of life in Seville, see Ruth Pike's *Artisans and Traders: Sevillian Society in the Sixteenth Century* (Ithaca: Cornell University Press, 1972) and Mary Elizabeth Perry's two books, *Crime and Society in Early Modern Seville* (Hanover, NH: University Press of New England, 1980) and *Gender and Disorder in Early Modern Seville* (Princeton: Princeton University Press, 1990). For the case of Catalina de Erauso, "the nun-ensign" who shocked Seville society in this period, see Stephanie Merrim, "Catalina de Erauso: From Anomaly to Icon," in *Coded Encounters: Writing, Gender, and Ethnicity in Colonial Latin America*, edited by Francisco Javier Cevallos-Candau, Jeffrey A. Cole, Nina M. Scott, and Nicomedes Suárez-Araúz (Amherst: University of Massachusetts Press, 1994), 177–205.

For motives for emigration, see Ida Altman, *Emigrants and Society: Extremadura and Spanish America in the Sixteenth Century* (Berkeley: University of California Press, 1989). The trials of crossing the Atlantic are beautifully detailed by Carla Rahn Phillips, *Six Galleons for the King of Spain: Imperial Defense in the Early Seventeenth Century* (Baltimore: Johns Hopkins University Press, 1986). To examine socially defined sex roles, see Asunción Lavrin, ed., *Sexuality and Marriage in Colonial Latin America* (Lincoln: University of Nebraska Press, 1989); Steve J. Stern, *The Secret History of Gender: Women, Men, and Power in Late Colonial Mexico* (Chapel Hill: University of North Carolina Press, 1995); and Ann Twinam, *Public Lives, Private Secrets: Gender, Honor, Sexuality, and Illegitimacy in Colonial Spanish America* (Stanford: Stanford University Press, 1999).

Part II

The Mature Colonial Order, 1610–1740

During the seventeenth century, a more stable colonial social, political, and economic order developed in the Spanish Indies. By 1600, the Spaniards had subjugated the major Amerindian peoples, ended the squabbles among the initial conquistadors, and imposed an imperial bureaucracy to ensure their political dominance. Over time, however, the fiscally strapped Spanish crown began systematically selling appointments to most key colonial bureaucratic posts, which allowed *Creoles* (people of European descent born in the Indies) to gain unprecedented political clout, which they often used to advance local rather than imperial interests. During these years, the settlers also laid the foundations of a prosperous market economy tied to Europe. Silver mining remained a cornerstone of the colonial economy, but as production stabilized in Mexico and declined in South America, investment capital increasingly flowed to other prosperous economic sectors such as agriculture, grazing, manufacturing, and artisan production. With the economic diversification of the Indies, commercial exchanges expanded beyond the convoy system of transatlantic shipping, as trade links in legal and contraband merchandise evolved in the Caribbean and the Pacific, extending even to Spain's Asian possessions in the Philippine Islands.

For its part, the Roman Catholic Church had converted thousands of Amerindians, but persistent signs of enduring indigenous religious practices disturbed many in the Church hierarchy. In fact, some churchmen in the Andes initiated systematic efforts to "extirpate" indigenous religious practices. Nonetheless, widespread acceptance of Church rituals and popular devotions demonstrated the inroads made by Roman Catholicism throughout the Indies. In short, a hegemonic colonial political, social, and economic order slowly became entrenched during the long period from 1610 to 1740.

In Brazil, the seventeenth century saw not only the consolidation of royal institutions but also the instability and conflict occasioned by the Dutch invasion and occupation of Salvador da Bahia (1624–1625) and much of the captaincy of Pernambuco (1630–1654). The Portuguese crown dispatched royal governors to each of the major provinces, with a governor general in Salvador (called viceroy after 1720) who theoretically supervised the other provincial leaders. In reality, his powers outside of Bahia were strictly limited, as each governor controlled his own province and communicated directly with Lisbon. It was not until 1609, however, that Portugal established a high court in Salvador da Bahia, which heard criminal and civil cases and appeals from lower courts. A municipal council in the major cities also administered local affairs in their immediate jurisdictions. The entire bureaucracy, however, was much smaller than that in Spanish America.

The economy of Brazil remained mainly focused on sugar, produced on large plantations (*engenhos*), and, from the 1690s, on gold mining. The capital-intensive engenho consisted of large cane fields and a mill to process the cane and, for a fee, the crops of neighboring small-scale producers, into sugar. The demand for labor at the mills eventually exceeded the supply of Amerindian slaves, so plantation owners began importing Africans. It was the very success of the sugar economy in Brazil that attracted the Dutch invaders, who sought to control this profitable colonial industry. After expelling the Dutch, the crown provided a fleet of warships in 1649 to guard the annual convoys of merchant vessels involved in the sugar trade. The discovery of gold and diamonds in the 1690s in the interior provinces of Minas Gerais, Mato Grosso, and Goiás added a new dimension to the export economy, and the ensuing mining boom prompted a major movement of people from the coast. By the eighteenth century, Brazil, too, had begun to establish a more stable colonial social, political, and economic order.

The chapters in part II deal with the struggles of a diverse group of individuals who were attempting to cope with a hegemonic colonial order. Ursula de Jesús was an African slave living as a servant in the Convent of Santa Clara in Lima who later became a mystic, famous for having divinely inspired visions and conversations with souls in purgatory. Despite gaining her freedom and leading an exemplary life in the convent, Ursula could not escape the racism of her day. Indeed, she had even internalized some of these prejudicial attitudes, admonishing slaves who disobeyed their masters or had pretensions above their social station. Young Agustina Ruiz, a single mother living in Querétaro, Mexico, had visions, but they differed greatly from those of Ursula de Jesús. When she was interrogated before the Inquisition in 1621, Ruiz admitted to regular masturbation but also claimed to have been the lover of a number of saints, such as Saint Nicholas de Tolentina, Saint Diego, and even Jesus and the Virgin Mary. The inquisitors thought her claims preposterous; they also firmly believed that these visions of Ruiz could only be the work of Satan. Although Ruiz repented, admitted her guilt, and begged for mercy, the Holy Office sentenced her to three years of service and religious instruction in a Mexico City convent. While Ursula de Jesús and Agustina Ruiz accepted the basic values of the hegemonic colonial order, the Afro-Brazilian slave leader, Zumbi, resisted them by ruling Palmares, a coalition of communities of escaped slaves in the interior of Bahia that survived from the 1590s until its downfall in 1694. During the turbulent years of the Dutch occupation of Pernambuco, Palmares grew to between twenty thousand and thirty thousand inhabitants, an independent state based on a mixture of African and European customs. Zumbi, its most formidable military and political leader, defeated several Portuguese military expeditions until the final successful assault in 1694 and his capture and death the next year.

The journey of the Jeronymite friar Diego de Ocaña highlights the rise of the diverse forms of popular piety in the seventeenth century. In contrast to Ursula de Jesús, who lived in one of the proliferating urban religious houses in Lima during the period, Ocaña traveled through the countryside and to provincial capitals, such as Saña on the north coast of Peru, to spread the popular devotion of Our Lady of Guadalupe. To this end, he made small paintings of the Virgin of Guadalupe (which he claimed were divinely inspired), and when one of these images gained fame for its curative powers, it attracted the attention of a disreputable local parish priest who wanted it for his own private collection. The encounter between Ocaña and the priest gives us a glimpse into notions of divine intervention in human affairs, popular piety, and clerical fears about heterodoxy.

The resistance and agency of the indigenous peoples and those of African descent also formed a common theme during the seventeenth century. Felipe Guaman Poma de Ayala's failed attempt to gain control over lands claimed by both his family and a rival group of Andeans, the Chachapoyas, demonstrates how well indigenous elites understood and manipulated the Spanish legal system. His sense of injustice at the hands of the colonial legal system prompted Guaman Poma to write his now famous text, *El primer nueva corónica y buen gobierno*, which simultaneously presented the author's version of the history of the Andean region and his scathing denunciation of the corruption and bad governance of the colonial government and most of the Roman Catholic clergy. Another victim of Spanish justice was Ana de Vega, a *mulata* faith healer brought before the Holy Office of the Inquisition on charges of practicing witchcraft. When Ana de Vega healed a Spanish woman of a mysterious illness, the faith healer diagnosed the cause of the malady as witchcraft, blaming her patient's own daughter-in-law. After she recovered from her illness, the woman's son-in-law, Francisco Sambrano, denounced Ana de Vega to the Inquisition for curing without a license, fraud, and using witchcraft to divide his family. In the end, the court ruled against Ana de Vega, convicting her of being a witch. As so often happened, the inquisitors found the testimony of a Spaniard more compelling than the word of a poor, marginal, mulata faith healer, who appeared to possess unsettling and mysterious healing powers.

SIX

Ursula de Jesús

A Seventeenth-Century Afro-Peruvian Mystic

Nancy E. van Deusen

Seventeenth-century Lima was a rapidly growing cosmopolitan viceregal capital whose population rose from nearly twenty-five thousand in 1619 to perhaps as high as eighty thousand by 1680. This demographic growth ended abruptly, however, in 1687, when a devastating series of earthquakes struck, forcing people to flee the destruction, famine, and diseases that ensued. Lima was also the seat of the viceregal court, the most important royal audiencia in the realm, and the center of a prosperous colonial economy, at least until the tragedy of 1687. The crown made Lima the commercial entrepôt for the Andean region, and each year highland silver mines (particularly the famous "red mountain" at Potosí, in Bolivia) shipped bullion to the capital. Here it was exchanged for European wares (gathered from the trade fairs at Portobelo), illicit contraband merchandise, or colonial products from overland and seaborne trade routes. In addition, the city's urban population had become highly stratified: émigrés from Spain and Creoles occupied the highest social positions, followed by those of mixed racial ancestry (castas); then came the Amerindian residents of the city's indigenous sector (called the cercado), and the African freedman and slave populations. In short, for most of the century the viceregal capital was a vibrant, sophisticated urban center with a diverse citizenry.

A reflection of Lima's prosperity was the plethora of stately churches, monasteries, convents, and other religious buildings constructed during the seventeenth century. As the religious capital of the viceroyalty, Lima was the seat of an archbishopric as well as the Holy Office of the Inquisition and most of the principal monasteries or convents of the religious orders operating in South America.

Each of these ecclesiastical organizations had its own edifice, ranging in splendor from the imposing cathedral in the central plaza to more modest parish churches in the cercado. These buildings formed the center of a vital religious life that included veneration of the cross, cults of the saints, and ritual use of music, dances, and prayer. Such expressions of piety reflected the grandeur of the capital, but they also mirrored colonial ideals about social stratification. A person's role in a religious festival, seat in the cathedral at important services, and admission to certain religious orders or sodalities (cofradías) depended on social status. Even convent life was rigidly hierarchical, with nuns of the black veil occupying the highest rank, followed by nuns of the white veil, novices preparing to take their vows, donadas *(servants recognized for spiritual gifts or contributions to the community), and regular servants, who tended to worldly needs—washing, cooking, cleaning, and other household chores.*

One of the servants in the large and prestigious Convent of Santa Clara was a black slave, Ursula de Jesús. According to her later writings, Ursula began serving a wealthy nun of the black veil, but she chafed at her humble post, displaying signs of vanity and a rebellious spirit. After narrowly escaping death from falling into a deep well, however, Ursula changed her ways and led an exemplary and holy life. In fact, she became a well-known mystic who had divinely inspired visions and the ability to communicate with souls in purgatory. Over time, her reputation led one of the convent's nuns to purchase her freedom, and Ursula became a respected donada valued for her piety and visions. Despite her reputation, Ursula could not escape racial prejudices against Afro-Peruvians, even in the Convent of Santa Clara. She could never hope to attain the status of a nun or even gain a small measure of the recognition accorded to the Creole mystic Saint Rose of Lima. Nevertheless, her piety and links to the divine served as models to other women of color in Lima. Even today, in Lima's poor neighborhood of Barrios Altos, where the Convent of Santa Clara still stands, people continue to recount tales of her miraculous visions and her holiness.

One day, just as Ursula de Jesús, an Afro-Peruvian religious servant (donada), finished taking communion in the Convent of Santa Clara in Lima, the ghost of the deceased Licenciate Colonia appeared to her, asking her to plead with Jesus Christ to have mercy on his soul. Although he claimed that the intervention of the Virgin and Saint Rose of Lima had aided him, he continued to suffer terrible and interminable anguish in purgatory. He then explained that his flagrant mistreatment of his slave, Francisca, had determined in part his lengthy sentence. Shocked by this request, Ursula went into a meditative trance to communicate with Jesus Christ, who confided to her that this soul faced perpetual torture and damnation and that her supplications would be of no use.[1]

Such otherworldly requests for intercession directed to the holy women of convents by those in purgatory were not considered remarkable in colonial Latin America. What is indeed remarkable about this petition is that the spirit of a high-ranking colonial official contacted a former slave of African descent and that many of the elite nuns in her religious community had faith in the mystical abilities of the unassuming but powerful Afro-Peruvian servant in their midst. The question to be addressed here is how Ursula de Jesús, an enslaved woman of humble origins, gained both the experience and authority to claim such transcendent abilities as well as a reputation for sanctity that only a few achieved during that period.

Born in 1604 in Lima, Ursula inherited her status as a slave from her mother, and the two resided with their owner, Gerónima de los Ríos. Ursula spent her formative years in a large household filled with African, Spanish, and Peruvian people who shared and exchanged elements of their distinct cultural traditions. Both familial and occupational positions placed her owner in contact with a number of highly placed peninsular members of *limeño* (resident of Lima) and Andalusian societies. Like other elite Spanish women, Gerónima actively engaged in business negotiations (usually giving power to a male figure to represent her), especially the buying and selling of slaves. She had no children, but the household consisted of other family members, including her niece, Inés de Pulgar, and a few orphans as well as an abundance of Spanish, *mestiza*, and black girls working in her service as cooks, laundresses, maids, and gardeners.

Ursula's early childhood years replicate the circumstances facing many slaves who spent their lives working for others and whose family relations and destinies remained intricately linked to their patrons. Like many young girls living in a society where Catholic tenets often dictated cultural norms, Ursula developed a particular devotion to the Virgin of Carmen and prayed the rosary and fasted once per week. But she was unique in other respects. In 1612, Ursula went to live with a wealthy *beata* (pious laywoman) and mystic named Luisa de Melgarejo Sotomayor (1578–1651). During her years in doña Luisa's household, she met a number of men and women deeply committed to mystical practices. Although in 1617 she then entered the Convent of Santa Clara to serve Gerónima de los Ríos's niece, sixteen-year-old Inés, her unconventional spiritual education expedited her change in status from a slave serving her mistress into a freedwoman working in the service of God.

We have access, fortunately, to the inner musings and experiences of someone who easily could have slipped into oblivion because, at the request of her spiritual confessor, Ursula recorded her visions and mystical experiences. Her diary, kept between 1647 and her death in 1666 and later copied and altered by her confessor, accesses three important issues current during a period of spiritual efflorescence in seventeenth-century Lima. First, as a woman of color and a mystic, Ursula faced particular choices and contingencies that elite women living in convents did not. Second, although female visionaries claimed a degree of objectivity as conduits of divine knowledge, Ursula's recorded visions revealed the social tensions resulting from her experience of racism and the maintenance of social hierarchies characteristic of the convent and society at large. Undoubtedly, her singular experiences affected the choices she made.[2] Third, her visions enhance our knowledge of popular spirituality and notions of the beyond because Ursula specialized in communicating with departed souls caught in the fires of purgatory and desiring redemption.

According to the Jesuit chronicler Bernabé Cobo, by 1630 the "mystical body" of the "Christian Republic" of Lima had reached a level of piety comparable with that of the best European cities. Six "sumptuous" convents for females and fourteen male monasteries formed an integral part of the urban landscape, and Cobo estimated that in 1630, 3,600 individuals lived in monastic institutions, including more than 1,000 nuns, 1,000 servants, slaves, and laywomen in convents, compared with 1,126 priests and 500 donados, servants, and slaves in male monasteries.[3] In addition, mystical practices already condemned by Inquisition authorities in Spain reached their zenith. A number of Jesuit friars, many of whom served as the confessors of famous beatas, including Luisa de Melgarejo, explored the tenets of mysticism and influenced a generation of young male and female charges. Ursula's short stint in Melgarejo's home brought her in direct contact with a number of "living saints": individuals recognized by the community as worthy of sanctification, including doña Luisa herself. As mystics they claimed to receive divine knowledge through visions and "mental prayer"—direct, unmediated union with God—and served the Lima community as prophets and healers. The general populace, including influential authorities such as the wife of the viceroy, frequently solicited their spiritual advice on marriage, health, lost objects, and auspicious travel dates. Doña Luisa's celestial revelations circulated throughout Lima, and Saint Rose (1586–1617) was said to consult her confidante's writings.[4] Ursula also met a number of beatas who openly discussed theological matters. Unfortunately, many of these women were tried and, with the exception of Luisa de Melgarejo, convicted by the Holy Inquisition in 1625.

Although the Inquisition attempted to curtail what it considered to be heterodox forms of Catholic expression, young black women such as Ursula were fortunate to participate actively in the spiritual renaissance occurring in Lima, either through direct, intimate relations with Creole mystics or through their own efforts. For instance, many wanted to be Saint Rose's spiritual protégées, including Mariana, a native Andean servant who introduced the servant of God to a famous pious *cacica* (female ethnic leader), Catalina Huanca. Mariana diligently obeyed her mistress by placing lime on Rose's hands when she was told that they were pale and lovely, and later she confessed under duress that the saint wore a tunic of rough pigskin under her Dominican habit.[5] Unobtrusive, submissive devotional practices could also be found among exemplary casta men and women who generally served as donada/os in convents or as members of a Third Order of the Regular clergy. Frequently mentioned in the convent chronicles composed at the time, they were also recognized for their spiritual gifts and contributions among both the religious community and Lima's inhabitants. The Franciscan chronicler Diego de Córdova y Salinas, for instance, extolled the virtues of Estephanía de San Joseph (d. 1645), a *mulata* freedwoman and beata who charmed the elite with her vibrant personality; she preached daily sermons, tended to the sick and the poor, and collected alms for the nuns of Santa Clara. Her mestiza companion, Isabel de Cano, sewed mattresses for the sick and also spoke in public about spiritual matters. Word traveled throughout Lima that Francisco de la Concepción, a humble African donado, could appear in two places simultaneously and had the gift of prophecy. Hundreds of rich and poor limeños knew of the sensational curative abilities and charitable efforts of the Dominican mulatto Martín de Porras (1579–1639) long before his elaborate funeral procession took place. Not only did casta men and women situate themselves within the pantheon of Lima's popular "saints," but the cult of the Señor de los Milagros (an image of Christ) grew steadily during Ursula's lifetime and reached a fever pitch among people of African descent following the 1655 earthquake.

While aware of the various forms of popular religious expression in the "world," Ursula's main contacts after 1617 remained with holy women cloistered in the Convent of Santa Clara. Founded in 1605, it attracted scores of elite women who aspired to become nuns of the black veil. Those who could afford to pay only a modest dowry or who were not members of the aristocracy often became nuns of the white veil. Race and economic status were certainly key in perpetuating an assemblage of "durable inequality," and yet humility, strict observance of the rules, and spiritual gifts also served to elevate status within the convent.[6] A few of Ursula's contemporaries deserve specific mention. Catalina de Cristo worked as a baker in the convent; swore before the abbess that Saint Clare awakened her each morning by saying, "Let's go and knead the dough, Catalina"; and also reported seeing souls in purgatory during Requiem Masses.[7] In another example, Agustina de San Francisco had the reputation of supervising the slaves (including Ursula) and servants working in the convent with a firm but kind hand. Juana de Cristo gave spiritual counsel to the convent's servants and at night slept on a wooden plank in tribute to Christ's suffering on the cross. Another nun, Gerónima, signed her name "Slave of the Blessed Souls of Purgatory" and collected alms to pay for masses that might release them from their temporary prison. She kissed the feet of the dead (including blacks), and during Requiem Masses she imitated the corpse by covering herself with a shroud while the choir sang.

The original constitution of the order, written by its founder, Clare of Assisi (d. 1253), encouraged all able sisters to do manual labor and share in communal tasks.[8] She hoped that the nuns of the order would devote themselves to a life of poverty and independence in a self-sufficient environment. However, medieval convents supported a much smaller population. In the seventeenth century, Santa Clara in Lima required huge capital investments to support a population that grew by nearly 20 percent between 1630 and 1650 and consumed vast quantities of supplies. Each month the residents ate at least 140 chickens and large amounts of wheat flour and sugar; hundreds of pesos were spent on corn to feed the chickens raised in coops inside the cloister, on cords of wood for the ovens in the kitchen, and on the organ.[9] Male carpenters transported goods and repaired and built additions to the convent, but it depended chiefly upon female workers housed there.

In spite of Saint Clare's wishes, the convent maintained a large female servant population, in part because the majority of the nuns of the black and white veils disdained manual labor. During Ursula's lifetime, nearly 20 percent of the total convent population consisted of servants and slaves who served individual nuns and carried out communal tasks. For twenty-eight years, Ursula was one of hundreds of women whose exhausting daily work regime afforded no spare time to contemplate religious matters. Each day she attended to the needs of her *ama* (owner) in her cell: she prepared her food and washed her clothing and linen. Once those tasks were completed, Ursula worked with the other servants in the kitchen and infirmary until late each evening.

Although extremely hardworking, Ursula described herself during her years in bondage in the convent (1617–1645) as self-centered, temperamental, and vain. Like many slaves in Lima, she was known for her frippery and desire to wear stylish clothing. However, an event occurred in 1642 that transformed Ursula's life and permanently altered her reputation for vanity. Angry that she had lent a skirt to someone who returned it soiled, she washed it and then spread it out to dry on a plank covering the mouth of a deep well in the center of the convent. While she was arranging the skirt, the platform she stood upon collapsed, leaving Ursula suspended above the pit and trying to hold on, literally, for her life. Unable to help her, the nuns and other witnesses fervently prayed that she would not suffer a painful death. Ursula claimed that her own supplications to the Virgin of Carmen rescued her, and miraculously she recovered her balance and gained enough leverage to reach safety.

This fortuitous event led the now deeply humbled Ursula to sell her finery and dedicate her spare moments to prayer. From her brush with death she gained a sense of a greater purpose in life and beseeched God to instruct her in spiritual matters. The nuns began referring to her as a "servant of God," as Ursula now took pride in the exacting labor required of her and subjected herself to even more demeaning and burdensome tasks. In the infirmary she cared for the most contagious and repulsive patients and volunteered to wash infected clothing and rags wet with loathsome pus. Whenever she felt repugnance, she would place the rags in her mouth. Such mortification resonated with the sufferings and Passion of Christ and, above all, with his humanity.

Indeed, Ursula's sense of self-sacrifice, humility, and charity toward others conformed to notions of sanctity among holy women and men of the period. Her spiritual "résumé" replicated a common hagiographic model: a life of vanity and worldliness followed by a miracle and subsequent spiritual conversion. Like other holy women in Latin America and Catholic Europe, Ursula began to have visions and reported in her diary that she communicated frequently with Jesus Christ. Her "education" may seem odd to someone in the twenty-first century, but many female visionaries admitted to having intimate, emotional communication with God and other celestial beings. Still, in order to conform to contemporary notions of humility, they expressed astonishment that such a "worm," "ant," or lowly being as themselves would merit divine attention. Ursula echoed this sentiment. One day, while meditating, Ursula felt a tremendous desire to kiss the hand of Christ. She reported "experiencing" his presence and watched as he freed his nailed hand from the cross and placed it on her mouth. Deeply grateful for this divine favor, she asked, "My Lord, am I Saint Catherine [of Siena] or Saint Gertrude?" to which the Lord responded, "I am the one who benefited them and I am able to benefit you." Stunned by this reply, the humble Ursula wondered how she could possibly be compared to two famous saints who were noblewomen and who received "gifts" and personal visits from Christ.

In many ways, Ursula's path followed that of many other female visionaries, with one important exception: she was still a slave. After 1642, misunderstandings between Ursula and her owner developed because she neglected her daily work in order to attend to spiritual matters. By 1645, she felt despondent and desperate and requested permission to leave the convent to search for a new owner.[10] Concerned that the convent might lose a gifted holy woman and that Ursula's spiritual "career" would be cut short, doña Rafaela de Esquivel, a nun of the black veil, purchased Ursula's freedom—a considerable expense for that period. Ursula appreciated doña Rafaela's generosity but declined a subsequent invitation to become a donada for several reasons. Although the circumspect Ursula no longer wanted to leave the convent, neither did she want to continue a life of servitude, which the status of donada might prolong. Clauses in "letters of freedom" often specified that freed slaves should continue to "assist" their owner for a determined number of years. Like many freedwomen, she was proud to be her own mistress after forty-one years in bondage and wished to be "free" from draining communal tasks to devote herself entirely to God's service.

Ursula also resented the convent's donadas, whom she considered to be pompous. The religious servants would have considered her, as a slave, to be of a lower status and may have mistreated her. In retrospect, however, Ursula regretted her vanity and tenaciousness. After receiving a "sign" from heaven when several religious objects in the main chapel caught fire, and encouragement from a black novice about to take her vows as a donada, Ursula decided to follow the same course in 1646.

In fact, becoming a donada clearly presented Ursula with the best option to pursue her spiritual interests in a more dedicated and untethered fashion. Many donadas of Santa Clara held more prestigious posts than the servants and slaves of the convent. Some were *sacristanas*: they cleaned religious objects and washed the linen for the altar. Each morning they prepared the chapel for Mass by lighting candles and ensuring that the flowers, incense, and religious objects were readied for the priest. Others rang the bell to announce the liturgical hours; those with great strength carried the heavy cross during the religious processions held within the convent. The nuns welcomed donadas who showed a flair for fashioning candles for processions, festivals, and special masses. Finally, many convents boasted several donadas renowned for their remarkable expressions of piety, including a reputation for mortification and other acts of humility or mental prayer.[11]

Religious servants were a significant presence in Santa Clara; a 1633 report enumerated forty-seven professed donadas and sixteen novices, representing 26 percent of the total population of female religious.[12] Nearly all were native Andeans or castas; like Ursula, a few girls of African descent had received their freedom. Many were illegitimate or orphaned and had few family ties outside the convent. Most applicants were under the age of twenty and had spent years working in the service of a nun as a *criada* (servant). Cloistered since childhood, a donada was guaranteed economic and social security that the dangers and cruelties of the world could not provide. Moreover, a life in the service of the Holy Virgin seemed a natural recourse to many applicants. Still, most candidates were judged on their ability to carry out communal tasks and serve individual nuns. If they were fortunate, a nun would sponsor their vocation by promoting their candidacy to the religious community and by paying the required dowry of 500 pesos.

Once she decided to become a donada, Ursula spent the year 1647 preparing for her formal profession. She earned the reputation of being exceptionally pious because she lived with "singular advancement of her spirit, continuous mortification of her senses, and [served as a] rare model of penitence, and repeated fasts." Her evenings were spent lying prostrate before an image of Christ in the choir; she also wore a hair shirt and a crown of thorns hidden beneath her hair together with iron-studded straps around her waist and arms. On her back she carried a cross with barbs tightened with a bodice made of pigskin, with the bristles turned inward to intensify the effect. Each day she whipped herself before retiring and once again at four in the morning. Ursula professed on June 13, 1647, the day of the Holy Trinity, "with great devotion and humility." At that decisive moment, she expressed a fervent desire to comply strictly with her vows of poverty and chastity and obedience to the rules of the Order of Saint Clare.

From 1647 until her death in 1666, Ursula's spirituality—and particularly her ability to intercede on behalf of souls trapped in purgatory—continued to grow. The nuns of Santa Clara, her numerous confessors, and the Lima community considered her to be unusually gifted and blessed. For two decades, Ursula became intimately familiar with the world of dead souls, who began communicating with her in the belief that her prayers might alleviate their suffering in purgatory. In her diary, she recorded these phenomenal otherworldly "visits" from a variety of individuals: priests revealing their peccadilloes, nuns regretting their impudent conduct, or servants and children recounting the grave illnesses and excessive work that they had endured. Often she heard the voice of Jesus Christ and felt his presence or saw images of him, her guardian angel, or the Virgin Mary. Each offered assistance in alleviating the suffering of the pleading souls in purgatory who appeared frequently before her.

Most Catholics in early modern society believed in free will, which corresponded with the conviction that each person, after death, was judged before a holy tribunal and then sentenced to a specific length of time in purgatory in order to purge his or her sins. All souls knew that their stay in purgatory was temporary and salvation and access to heaven guaranteed. Depending upon the gravity and number of transgressions, "time" spent in this intermediary space between heaven and hell varied from several hours to several centuries. Only the most unsullied souls went directly to heaven; most resigned themselves to the fact that they would have to spend some time in purgatory. As one spirit explained to Ursula, "In order to go to Heaven, souls had to be purified with fire: to become like the purest crystal—without a single imperfection—before entering into Glory."

Once in purgatory, many awakened, as though their life had been a dream and they then witnessed their wasted hours and acts of folly. This realization formed an initial stage of their purgation along with the knowledge that their sins might have been expiated by prayer, contrition, and good works. Many reported being subjected to horrible torments, including extreme temperatures: from flames licking at their ethereal bodies to being plunged into icy waters. While in a deep trance, Ursula once had this vision of souls close to hell: "She saw an enormous and ferocious mouth of a formidable dragon, and inside, multitudes of souls covered in voracious flames. It was like when a pot boils and bubbles appear: some rising to the surface, others disappearing below. The descending souls plunged beneath with a terrible force and [she could see] them all completely water-logged and lodged in between horrible flames of burning tar and brimstone. But, once again, they would return to the surface, in strife and in constant motion."

The obsession with purgatory and sordid details of tales of horror and woe found in Ursula's diary reached a fever pitch in seventeenth-century Lima—to some degree because the dead formed an integral part of the lives of the living. Family members expressed concern for those in the beyond through prayers and requests for masses or by fasting and buying indulgences. They believed that these efforts could accomplish two goals: they might alleviate the suffering and diminish the length of time of their loved ones' stay in purgatory, and their charity might eventually assist their own case. In Lima, masses said for souls in purgatory were popular; in the cathedral alone, priests said three thousand masses each year for departed souls. Even the nuns of Santa Clara founded chaplaincies on behalf of the souls of purgatory, and Ursula herself established a confraternity in the name of the Virgin of Carmen, known for saving lost souls. [13]

Saving souls in purgatory was seen as a selfless and beneficial enterprise, both for the living and the dead. Intercession on behalf of troubled souls eased the concern of the living for their loved ones; served as a source of moral authority and as a disciplinary measure for those involved in similar wrongdoing; provided a direct, celestial education for the holy women working as intercessors; and offered visionaries such as Ursula the opportunity to gain a sense of power and authority which, under other circumstances, might evade them.

Communication with those from the beyond was believed to be real, but why would the souls of the dead wish to "speak" with Ursula? Many holy women throughout early modern Catholic Europe and Latin America experienced visions of departed souls, particularly of family members or people to whom they had been close. Several of the singular beatas circulating in Lima during Ursula's adolescence, including Luisa de Melgarejo, reported seeing the souls of Church dignitaries in purgatory; described the torments of souls; traveled to heaven, hell, and purgatory; or predicted whether the living would be condemned or saved. Most of these women, however, lived quiet, unremarkable cloistered lives. And of these, only a few accepted the difficult, lifelong task of releasing souls in purgatory. Those who did, like Ursula, believed that God had chosen them for that purpose.

Ursula's diary is unique because she communicated with souls from all walks of life. Among the deceased nuns who approached her, a number lamented that they had not paid enough attention during Mass: they whispered in the choir or spread malicious gossip. The spirit of one nun who had spent years in purgatory said, "Don't admire us, Ursula, twice I held the position of Prelate and now I am paying [dearly] for my faults." She expressed a commonly held belief that male and female religious had a greater moral responsibility than laypeople. If they sinned and disobeyed the convent's rules or the Ten Commandments, they suffered harsher punishment in the hereafter. Ursula asked the nun's spirit if many souls from Santa Clara were in purgatory, to which it replied, "Yes." It explained to Ursula that those Brides of Christ who spent their time in business negotiations instead of spiritual endeavors would pay a high price for their cupidity in the beyond. Ursula also inquired after the soul of her beloved doña Rafaela, the nun who had purchased her freedom, and a voice assured her that Rafaela had ascended into heaven.

Despite her status as a donada and freedwoman, Ursula's spiritual authority prevailed on certain occasions. Once, Christ explained to her his disappointment in the lax morals of his brides. He ordered that celestial "decrees" be posted in the choir enjoining the nuns to center their thoughts upon spiritual matters before, during, and after Communion. The nuns were required to deliberate on the ways they had been remiss. This was a tall order because it forced Ursula to criticize indirectly nuns who had been her superiors for decades. Fortunately, both her confessor and the abbess took the directive seriously, and no one in the community doubted its veracity. The abbess called a general meeting and read out the reforms dictated to Ursula from Christ. Clearly, the threat of purgatory served as a reminder that nuns and servants would be judged accordingly before the eyes of God. As Christ once explained to Ursula, even the ashes of the most powerful viceroy could easily dissipate in water. Perhaps Ursula's "reform" visions were also far more effective than any ecclesiastical visitation from the archbishop because they originated within a humble woman who understood the hierarchical structure of the convent and her place within it.

Concerns with racism and race relations were a constant in Ursula's life. Acutely aware of the centrality of patron-client relations as well as the necessary attributes of obsequiousness and humility for those in bondage, she never forgot her former position as a slave. This is evidenced by the fact that deceased younger and older slaves and servants frequently asked her to intercede on their behalf and to advise the living that they should behave honorably. One female slave appeared in her earthly form in the hope that Ursula would recognize her. She feared becoming one of the many lost, forgotten, and "orphaned" souls (*ánimas solas*) in purgatory without anyone to care about their well-being. Another slave explained that she had committed a mortal sin for having had a licentious love affair with a nun (causing a tremendous scandal), but that her prayers to Saint Clare and to Saint Francis had saved her from the flames of hell. She thought that her thirty years in purgatory were well deserved, but Ursula pleaded to God on her behalf—arguing that she had served the community well—in an effort to reduce her punishment. On another occasion, Ursula awakened with a horrible fright at 3:00 a.m. because she felt the presence of the soul of a dead slave who had worked as a cook and baker in the convent. She had erred by paying more attention to her own needs than to those of the "common good," and she advised Ursula to bring this matter to the attention of the abbess so that others would become aware of the consequences of their pernicious conduct.

Ursula's diary entries often recorded complaints about the demands of pampered nuns, the onerous kitchen work, and the trial of being spat upon and ridiculed. Frequently, when she asked Christ why she had to work excessively long hours, he reminded her of the excruciating suffering that he had endured during the Passion. On one occasion she wrote: "Saturday, I was exhausted from so much cooking and other things, desiring only to be in the mountains where there are no people. I turned to God and said, were it not for Him I would not persevere in this. He responded that although the Son of God was quite well off in His kingdom of glory He came to suffer travail for our sake." And about one difficult companion she wrote: "I am such a bad black woman. Sometimes I feel—I don't know what—toward my companion, with all her scolding I don't know how to get along with her. If I ask her, bad, if I don't ask her, worse. I can't find a way. Other times she will say, why don't you take your provisions, and I go and ask for alms for the infirm. Or, why don't I cure them? And other things of this nature that make me laugh. God only knows how I survive, and they tell me to suffer all that is offered me."

At times, Ursula found herself caught between her position as a visionary and her position as a freed black woman. She was not the only one to face this dilemma. The mulatto friar, Martín de Porras, dealt valiantly with the stark realities of racism and yet was known to admonish slaves who disobeyed their masters.[14] Ursula understood that slaves and servants often suffered the cruelties of abuse, physical exhaustion, and unjust recrimination but also comprehended the fact that they were property. On one occasion, the convent set off fireworks in honor of the June celebrations of Corpus Christi. In the tumult, a large ember landed on the head of a slave, causing a deep, mortal gash. Still, Ursula's concern rested not with the slave but with his master, a priest well known among the nuns. She felt troubled by the inconvenience that the loss of his slave would cause him. But when she begged Christ to have mercy on the poor, sick priest, a voice immediately chastised her:

> Ursula, it is not for the convenience of the owner that the servant should die. This [act] begins to open [the slave's] eyes to the world, and if he lives any longer he will lose [this knowledge] and it is better that he should die. When you are here sleeping in Heaven, the scales fall from the eyes, and each individual can see clearly that which is best for the salvation of the soul. This costs God a lot, and he is his Wise Majesty, the Universal Lord of the Heavens and the Earth, by whose hand pass so many things. The servants [in the world] all have a particular Providence.

Not all of Ursula's visions were laden with tales of anguish and suffering; she often witnessed the positive results of her efforts. After employing various means to ensure their safe passage from purgatory, many trans-figured souls—now radiant and dressed in flowing white garments— appeared to thank her before ascending to heaven. One servant whom she had "saved" described to Ursula how heaven differed, depending on one's "station" in life: "[In heaven] great harmony prevailed; everyone had their place according to their position; nuns belonged in one part, male religious in another, and laypersons and priests all occupied their places in order and harmony. Indians, blacks, and other people were punished in accordance with their standing and the obligations of their class."

In the realms of the beyond, everyone had a designated place that replicated the social hierarchies in the world, but those spaces also eradi-cated socially constructed differences. According to Ursula's visions, all souls were capable of ascending to heaven. For instance, the deceased María Bran, a slave of Santa Clara, appeared to Ursula dressed in an ecclesiastical garment tied with an ornately embroidered cord and wear-ing a crown of flowers similar to that of Saint Rose. María assured Ursula that blacks and donadas went to heaven, a concern that a white mystic would not have. The fact that a slave, dressed as a saint, would occupy a space in the lofty heights of purgatory and then enter "Glory" reveals Ursula's conception of purgatory as a place where social justice pre-vailed. From the point of view of a mystic who fought against racism and brutality her entire life, purgatory equalized differences, but it also func-tioned as a prism of the complex hopes and fears of a broad cross-section of Lima's colonial inhabitants.

Near the end of her life, Ursula became aware that she, too, would be granted a direct and safe passage to heaven because of her selfless efforts to help others. After suffering a mortal illness for over three weeks, Ursu-la died on February 23, 1666, and doña Leonor Basques, a well-respected nun of the convent, declared that the servant of God entered heaven in a state of ecstasy with her eyes raised toward the skies and her soul "nailed to the crucified Christ." She died a "good death" because she prepared her will, disposed of her worldly possessions, confessed her sins, and received extreme unction. The nuns of Santa Clara deeply mourned her passing, and a number of high ecclesiastical and secular authorities, in-cluding the wife of the viceroy, attended her funeral. Because of her lifelong devotion to Our Lady of Carmen, Ursula was buried beneath her chapel in the convent.

Ursula never gained the recognition that Saint Rose achieved in the seventeenth century. Nevertheless, she served as a model for women of color in Lima in small but significant ways. Five months after Ursula's death, the abbess petitioned for twenty-year-old Francisca de la Cruz to become a donada "following the example of the Mother, Ursula de Cristo." The nuns commissioned a casta artist to paint her portrait, and in 1686, one of her Franciscan confessors recopied and edited her diary. Today, religious histories mention her name only in passing. Until recently, people in the humble neighborhood where the Convent of Santa Clara is located were permitted to enter the vestibule to kneel before her image and pray for her intercession on their behalf.

QUESTIONS FOR DISCUSSION:

1. How did Ursula's condition as a slave affect her spiritual career?
2. Why was purgatory such a central feature in the lives of early modern colonial subjects?
3. What role did women play as intercessors between the living and the dead?
4. In what ways does Ursula's spiritual path replicate and depart from the lives of other holy women?
5. What does Ursula's life tell us about the different social tensions operating in colonial Latin American society?

NOTES

1. Most information on Ursula and the quotations cited in this chapter are derived from two manuscripts: the original diary, "Vida de la Hermana Ursula," Archivo del Monasterio de Santa Clara, Lima, Libro 5, 1928; and a biography based on the diary and written by a Franciscan confessor, "Vida de la Venerable Madre Ursula de Jesucristo," located in the Franciscan Archive of Lima, Registro 17, no. 45, n.d., 585r–603r.

2. Elizabeth Alvilda Petroff, "A Medieval Woman's Utopian Vision: The Rule of Saint Clare of Assisi," in idem, *Body and Soul: Essays on Medieval Women and Mysticism* (New York: Oxford University Press, 1994), 3–4.

3. Bernabé Cobo, "Historia de la fundación de la ciudad de Lima," in *Monografías históricas sobre la ciudad de Lima* (Lima: Imprenta Gil, 1935), 1:137, 233–34.

4. Juan Meléndez, *Tesoros verdaderos de las Yndias* (Rome: Nicolás Tinassio, 1681), 2:311.

5. Ramón Mujica Pinilla, "El ancla de Santa Rosa de Lima: Mística y política en torno a la Patrona de América," in *Santa Rosa de Lima y su tiempo*, ed. José Flores Araoz et al. (Lima: Banco de Crédito del Perú, 1995), 195.

6. Charles Tilly, *Durable Inequality* (Berkeley: University of California Press, 1998).

7. Diego de Córdoba y Salinas, *Crónica franciscana de las Provincias del Perú*, ed. Lino G. Canedo (Washington, DC: American Academy of Franciscans, 1962), 900.

8. Petroff, "A Medieval Woman's Utopian Vision," 66–79.

9. Archivo Arzobispal de Lima (henceforth AAL), Monasterio de Santa Clara, Leg. III, exp. 23, "Cuentas del monasterio . . . 1626 hasta 1629," 1r–2r.

10. Church authorities were responsible for the physical and spiritual well-being of slaves, and ecclesiastical law stated that a slave who suffered excessive brutality from his owner could petition a judge to be resold.

11. Francisco Echave y Assu, *La estrella de Lima convertida en sol sobre sus tres coronas* (Antwerp: Juan Baptista Verdussen, 1688), 228–33.

12. AAL, Monasterio de Santa Clara, Leg. IV, exp. 42, "Relación de religiosas y donadas del Monasterio de Santa Clara," 1633.

13. Archivo General de la Nación (Perú), Protocolos, Sebastían Muñoz, 1643–45 (February–March 1645), no. 1192, "Fundación de capellanía, doña Francisca de Aguilar, monja en Santa Clara." On masses in the cathedral, see Echave y Assu, *La estrella de Lima*, 72–75.

14. J. P. Tardieu, "Genio y semblanza del santo varón limeño de origen africano (Fray Martín de Porras)," *Hispania Sacra* 45 (1993): 572.

SUGGESTED READINGS

For a critical English-language edition of Ursula's complete diary, see *Ursula de Jesús, The Souls of Purgatory: The Spiritual Diary of an Afro-Peruvian Mystic* (Albuquerque, 2004). Amaya Fernández Fernández et al., *La mujer en la conquista y la evangelización en el Perú* (Lima, 1997), includes a brief biography of Ursula de Jesús, as does Alice Wood, "Religious Women of Color in Seventeenth-Century Lima: Estefanía de San Joseph and Ursula de JesuChristo," in *Beyond Bondage: Free Women of Color in the Americas*, edited by David Barry Gaspar and Darlene Clark Hine (Urbana, 2004), 286–316. Luis Martín's *Daughters of the Conquistadores* (Albuquerque, 1993) provides an insightful overview of convent life in the Viceroyalty of Peru. Kathryn Burns treats the economic and social realities of Cuzco's nuns in *Colonial Habits: Convents and the Spiritual Economy of Cuzco, Peru* (Durham, NC, 1999). Nancy E. van Deusen's *Between the Sacred and the Worldly: Recogimiento in Colonial Lima* (Stanford, 2001) and Fernando Iwasaki, "Mujeres al borde de la perfección," *Hispanic American Historical Review* 73, no. 4 (1993): 581–613, both examine forms of spiritual expression among women in seventeenth-century Lima. On donadas in colonial Lima, see Nancy E. van Deusen, "Donadas (Religious Servants) in Colonial Lima," in *Africans to Spanish America: New Directions*, edited by Sherwin Bryant and Ben Vinson III (Bloomington, 2012). The best monograph on slavery in colonial Lima is Frederick Bowser, *The African Slave in Colonial Peru, 1524–1650* (Stanford, 1974).

Both English- and Spanish-language excerpts of female spiritual writings in Peru, Mexico, and Spain are provided in Electa Arenal and Stacey Schlau, eds., *Untold Sisters: Hispanic Nuns in Their Own Works* (Albuquerque, 1989); and Asunción Lavrin gives a general overview of Latin American female spirituality in "Women and Religion in Spanish America," in *Women and Religion in America*, vol. 2, *The Colonial and Revolutionary Periods*, edited by Rosemary Radford Ruether and Rosemary Skinner Keller (New York, 1983), 42–78, which includes a translation of the life of the mulata terciary Estefanía de San Joseph. Finally, Jacques Le Goff's *The Birth of Purgatory* (Chicago, 1986) and Gil Fernández Martínez's *Muerte y sociedad* (Madrid, 1993) enable the reader to understand the medieval and early modern European attitudes toward death and the afterlife that influenced Ursula and other visionaries.

SEVEN

Agustina Ruiz

Sexuality and Religiosity in Colonial Mexico

Zeb Tortorici

By the early seventeenth century, Spaniards had consolidated their political, social, and economic power in the Viceroyalty of New Spain (see map 1). The viceregal capital at Mexico City was the political and economic hub of the vice-royalty, whose merchant guild (consulado) *controlled the thriving transatlantic trade with Spain. After 1561, all this Atlantic commerce went in legally sanctioned convoys* (flotas y galeones) *that left Seville for designated locations in the New World to exchange European wares for colonial products, particularly precious metals from the silver and gold mines of New Spain and Peru (see map 2). These commercial transactions took place in the viceroyalty's principal port of Veracruz, popularly known as the "throat"* (garganta) *of New Spain. San Luis Potosí, one the towns where Agustina Ruiz lived, formed part of a series of silver mining towns north of Mexico City, while her other home, Querétaro, supplied woolen textiles and foodstuffs to the mining zones. These northern towns were organized by the seventeenth century into a series of regional markets connected through Mexico City to the emerging economy of the Spanish Atlantic world.*

In consolidating its rule in New Spain, the Spanish crown, in partnership with the Church, sought to impose a rigid Catholic orthodoxy over its possessions in the Viceroyalties of New Spain and Peru. Catholic clergymen had accompanied the original conquistadors, and the Church launched a moral crusade to evangelize all of the twenty to twenty-five million indigenous inhabitants of New Spain, even sending missionaries to convert Amerindians in the transitional or frontier areas. The Spaniards viewed Catholicism as an essential ingredient in forming a stable, moral society. As a result, they viewed any breaches in

Catholic orthodoxy as a sign of social disorder, capable of threatening the moral foundations of colonial society. To police Catholic orthodoxy, the crown established an ecclesiastical court, the Holy Office of the Inquisition, with central offices in the viceregal capitals of Mexico City and Lima in 1569, where they began functioning after 1571. The Inquisition had no jurisdiction over the indigenous inhabitants of the New World, who were considered neophytes with the legal status of children, but everyone else was subject to its authority. Even foreigners from Protestant countries unlucky enough to be shipwrecked or captured in battle off Spanish colonial shores in the Caribbean or the Pacific were subject to prosecution as heretics by the Inquisition. Crimes such as bigamy, blasphemy, heresy, witchcraft, solicitation in the confessional, or any other forms of unorthodox religious views fell under the jurisdiction of the Holy Office of the Inquisition. In short, the policies of the Spanish crown sought to establish an Atlantic system that was closed to any pernicious outside influences, particularly any religious rituals or heretical beliefs capable of undermining the moral fabric of colonial society.

Twenty-year-old Agustina Ruiz was a young, poor, and uneducated single mother who found herself alone, without family support, in Querétaro, Mexico. On January 23, 1621, she unexpectedly ran afoul of the Inquisition by failing to complete her confession of sins to fray Manuel de Santo Tomás, a local commissary of the Holy Office. When brought before the inquisitorial court, she admitted to one of the lesser sins, masturbation, but she also spoke in graphic terms of having long-term sexual relations with a series of saints, such as Saint Nicholas of Tolentino, Saint Diego, and even Jesus and the Virgin Mary. To her judges, such events were impossible, and they viewed her visions as a foul desecration of the faith. The inquisitors ruled that the devil had tricked Ruiz, visiting her in the form of these holy figures. Agustina Ruiz ultimately admitted her guilt and begged the court for mercy, but the justices sentenced her to spend three years in a Mexico City convent, where she would serve the nuns and receive suitable religious instruction. Ruiz, however, did not see her visions as heretical. Rather, she viewed her sexual relations with these holy figures as proof of her own piety and of her devotion to her faith, as well as a demonstration of their love for her. Although she probably recognized that her visions contravened orthodoxy, she remained very proud to have been chosen as the sexual partner of these iconic figures of Roman Catholicism. In addition, her curious mingling of religious and sexual metaphors was not entirely unique in her day. A number of Roman Catholic mystics, including Saint Teresa of Ávila and Saint Rose of Lima, recalled an intense pleasure and pain experienced when having visions of the divine, which they expressed in terms that closely resembled the idioms of sexual intercourse. While the case of Agustina Ruiz clearly went well beyond the experiences of most early modern Roman Catholic mystics, her case and its resolution provide rare and unusual insights into the complex relationship between sexuality and the popular spiritual devotion of common folk in seventeenth-century New Spain.

On January 23, 1621, fray Manuel de Santo Tomás, a Spanish priest and commissary of the Holy Office of the Inquisition in Querétaro, Mexico, came forth to denounce twenty-year-old Agustina Ruiz for failing to complete a confession that she had begun with him a few weeks earlier on the eve of *Pascua de Reyes* (Feast of the Three Kings). He informed the Inquisition that Ruiz had begun to confess her sins to him in a Carmelite convent, asking for mercy and forgiveness for having, since the age of eleven, carnally sinned with herself nearly every day by committing the act of pollution (*polución*)—masturbation. Most unsettling to the priest, however, was not the act of voluntary "pollution" itself but rather the vivid, obscene, and sacrilegious descriptions that accompanied Ruiz's fantasies. According to the priest's denunciation, Ruiz confessed that she had spoken "dishonest words" with Saint Nicholas of Tolentino, Saint Diego, Jesus Christ, and the Virgin Mary, all of whom had "join[ed] themselves with her in different ways, with her underneath them, and from the side, and her on top of them, and also with her lying facedown while they conjoin themselves with her through both of her dishonest parts."[1] Given that the primary aim of the Holy Office of the Mexican Inquisition—established in 1569 by royal decree of Philip II of Spain and founded in 1571—was to extirpate heresy, it is no surprise that the Mexican Inquisition would take an interest in Ruiz, who was eventually sentenced to spend three years in a Mexico City convent.

SEXUAL TRANSGRESSIONS AND THE CHURCH

The case of Agustina Ruiz before the Inquisition provides a unique and richly detailed example of female sexuality and religiosity in colonial New Spain through the experiences of one young woman charged with a variety of heretical sins relating to her visions, her actions, and her body. A gap between orthodox types of sexual behavior described in Church treatises on moral theology and everyday transgressions often developed among ordinary citizens, who failed to practice fully the teachings of their religion or who simply interpreted religious doctrine in unorthodox ways.[2] Many of those whose actions and sexual behaviors fell short of Church teachings, however, frequently envisioned themselves as good Christians and steadfastly maintained that their actions did little or nothing to challenge Church dogma. The fact that these transgressors did not view their sexual practices as violating religious teachings opens up new ways to view sexuality and its complex relationship to religion and spiritual devotion.

One of the more unique aspects of the Ruiz case is its explicit (and exceedingly rare) reference to female autoeroticism, a topic that seldom appears in the documentary record, particularly among poorer laywomen such as Agustina Ruiz. Most theologians saw masturbation as a masculine sin, which, at least in theory, deeply concerned the Church. On the other hand, colonial confessional manuals and some Inquisition cases clearly demonstrate that masturbation was not always described solely as a male problem. More importantly, masturbation seldom concerned the Church on any practical or enforceable level. Even in Europe during the later Middle Ages, when theologians began to associate masturbation more closely with the "sins against nature" of sodomy and bestiality, masturbation was a lesser concern for churchmen, who viewed it as a relatively unimportant sin compared with these other, more "wicked" sexual transgressions.[3] Indeed, masturbation played only a minor role in the hierarchical drama of sexual sins. In fact, confessional manuals remain one of the few places even to mention the sin of masturbation.

The increased importance of these confessional manuals is linked directly to Counter-Reformation Catholicism after the Council of Trent (1545–1563), which sought to reemphasize the central role of the sacraments in the everyday lives of Catholics. After Trent, regular partaking of penance and the act of confessing the insinuations of the flesh—one's thoughts, desires, voluptuous imaginings, and movements of the body—were deemed an important part of salvation.

In colonial Latin America, bilingual confessional manuals were important tools for Spanish priests, who often utilized them as guides to confess native populations in indigenous languages. The 1634 *Confessionario mayor*, for example, was written in Spanish and Nahuatl by a secular mestizo priest, Bartolomé de Alva, and it remains one of many confessional books from early Mexico dealing with intimate matters that the Catholic Church wished to regulate. Such texts obviously may not be used as guides to what individual women and men actually did in private, but they clearly demonstrate the Church's concerns with the broad sweep of sexual conduct. Specific topics (tied to biblical prohibitions against killing and adultery in the fifth and sixth commandments) that Alva mentions in his *Confessionario mayor* include abortion, midwifery, witchcraft, incest, masturbation, sodomy, adultery, rape, bestiality, menstruation, and prostitution. Some of the concerns recorded by Bartolomé de Alva regarding women are reflected in the following questions, to be asked by priests in the confessional:

> Here is what the women will be asked. Were you menstruating sometime when your husband or some other man had sexual relations with you? Did you repeatedly feel your body, thinking of a man, and wanting him to sin with you? Did you do it to yourself with your hands, bringing to a conclusion your lust? When your husband was drunk: did he have sex with you as a woman, or sometimes did he do the disgusting sin [sodomy] to you? Did you restrain him? Were you responsible for dirty words with which you provoked and excited women? When you cohabited with some woman: did you show and reveal what was bad in front of those who had not yet seen the sin? Did you

ever pimp for someone? On account of you, did they know themselves through sin, you yourself provoking a woman for whom you had summoned someone? Did you know the failings of your mother or your father, your children and your relatives, your household dependents that they were cohabiting, and you did not restrain them? When they were drunk and intoxicated in your home, there, committing before you sins unworthy of doing: didn't you restrain them? Did you just look at them?[4]

In spite of the confessional guides, there are few historical records, apart from some solicitation cases and a number of self-denunciations, which reveal the actual conversations that took place between priests and their penitents in the confessional. Furthermore, while the confessional guides demonstrate a clear preoccupation with the supposedly dangerous and disorderly nature of female sexuality, neither criminal courts in colonial Mexico nor the Holy Office of the Inquisition—unless some potential heresy was involved—worried much about regulating female masturbation or same-sex sexual activities between women.

In the minds of contemporaries, some forms of "desire" need not be sexual in nature. Many pious men and women in colonial Mexico, including Agustina Ruiz, fervently sought spiritual salvation alongside their intense love for Jesus, the saints, and the Virgin Mary. They desired these holy figures, both men and women, on physical, sexual, emotional, and spiritual planes. For the women and men of colonial Mexico, desire—broadly defined by its everyday sexual, spiritual, corporal, and emotional materializations—was omnipresent. Desire manifested itself through hunger, thirst, lust, and carnality but also through the equally common forms of devotion, rapture, and religiosity. For women like Agustina Ruiz, desire in these spiritual arenas commonly functioned symbiotically and constantly influenced the decisions, acts, and beliefs of individuals who were often merely trying to live with conflicting desires, Church teachings, and daily pressures.

THE TRIAL OF AUGUSTINA RUIZ

When the priest made his formal charge against her in 1621, Agustina Ruiz was a twenty-year-old unmarried woman living with her seven-year-old son, Francisco, in the house of Alonso de Garibaldi and his wife, María Meneque. She had been born in the city of Puebla to a bricklayer named Alonso Bernal and his wife, Catalina de la Trinidad, who both died, leaving the young Agustina without any means of support. After the death of her parents, Ruiz lived with a neighbor in Puebla until she was "tricked" around the age of eleven or twelve into going to Mexico City by a certain Diego Sánchez Solano, the eventual father of her son, Francisco. According to her testimony before the Inquisition, after three years in Mexico City—still a virgin and an unmarried young woman (*doncella*)—Sánchez Solano convinced her that they should get married, after which they engaged in sexual relations, and she became pregnant. As was common in Mexico at that time, the two never did actually marry but lived together in the state of concubinage. It was only after the unexpected death of Sánchez Solano a few years later that Agustina Ruiz moved to San Luis de Potosí for three years before ending up in Querétaro.

In the course of her trial Ruiz related how, two months earlier, her "brother," Cristóbal Felipe (perhaps he was a lover, whom she later planned to marry, rather than a brother), had sent her and her son from San Luis Potosí to the home of Alonso de Garibaldi and his wife, María Meneque, in Querétaro with instructions to remain there until he came for them. While Agustina Ruiz was not placed in an official *recogimiento* (a house where women were confined and separated from the influence of the outside world), her involuntary placement in this house by a close male relative had a similar function—both to punish and to protect. Starting in the late sixteenth century, it became common to place divorced women, prostitutes, women involved in marital disputes, or those accused of bigamy, adultery, or concubinage in recogimientos. In colonial Mexico and Peru, as in Spain, the recogimiento served to protect female vulnerability and a supposed predisposition to sexual deviance and lasciviousness. In a similar way, by placing the young and unwed Agustina Ruiz in a private household, Cristóbal Felipe was "protecting" her (with or without her consent), like the many other women who were forced behind the walls of recogimientos. This placement likely served simultaneously to punish, protect, and separate Ruiz from the outside world and its sinful influences since she had already proved to be especially vulnerable to them in the past.

Her confessor denounced Agustin Ruiz to the Inquisition when she failed to finish her initial confession on the eve of Pascua de Reyes and receive absolution for her sins. Because it was already late in the day when Ruiz started her confession and her confessor deemed it necessary to ask her a number of other questions, he told her to return the next day to complete her confession. Ruiz did return, but she left the church before her confessor, fray Manuel de Santo Tomás, could see her. After many days passed without her return, the priest sent for her at the house of Garibaldi. As she entered the confessional, he said that he merely desired the best for her soul, and she replied that she felt somewhat faint because of fasting and would return that same day after she ate something at two o'clock. When she failed to return, the priest denounced her to the Inquisition, which quickly took up the case.

Like so many other men and women brought before the Holy Office, in her first testimony on February 6, 1621, Ruiz stated that she had no idea why she was being questioned by the Inquisition. She said that she knew nothing when she was asked whether she or anyone close to her had said, done, or committed anything that appeared to be against the Holy Catholic faith or evangelical law of the Church. Only when she was asked more specifically about the conversations between her and her confessor a few weeks earlier did she admit to having told him about touching herself and having had "bad thoughts and bad images" of Jesus, the Virgin, and the saints for years. In this first confession, she denied ever having told her confessor that she eroticized Jesus, the Virgin, or the saints, although this is something she later admitted, and she denied ever having masturbated in church, as her confessor alleged, but instead testified that she did so only at home in the comfort of her bed.

Then inquisitors questioned Ruiz in detail about her accounts of masturbation and the accompanying desecrating fantasies. They first asked Ruiz whether it was true that she had touched herself since the age of eleven. To this she replied that "since the age of eleven until six months ago she committed the sin with her hand by touching her dishonest parts, realizing that she was carnally communicating with the saints, Jesus, and the Virgin. These acts took place more or less three times a day for the last nine years." In response to other questions posed to her, Ruiz stated that no one saw her or heard her while in the act of pollution, nor had she told anyone aside from her confessor of her visions and actions. They also asked whether the "dishonest words" that she exchanged with Jesus, Mary, and the saints were those used to name the "dishonest parts" of men and women. While Ruiz admitted to all of these accusations, she asserted that she had stopped touching herself six months earlier, although she never mentioned why.

During Ruiz's first declaration, the inquisitors asked her some twenty-one questions about her actions and beliefs surrounding her autoerotic experiences. Many questions, however, remained about what Ruiz actually did and what she believed, in large part because of her vague answers describing her visions. Did Ruiz merely fantasize that Jesus, Mary, and the saints came to her to exchange lewd words, kisses, and embraces? Or did she believe that they had actually appeared to her and had tangible contact with her? At first, Ruiz did not question the reality of her visions. What is clear throughout Ruiz's first testimony, however, is the intense religiosity and devotion that she ascribed to her acts and visions. Ruiz framed her relationships with the saints, Jesus, and the Virgin in terms of divine sanction and gratitude toward her and confessed that "they showed that they were thankful to her with the words they spoke to her — dishonest and amorous words that corresponded to those used to describe the dishonest parts of men and women." Both amorous *and* dishonest in nature, the words spoken to Ruiz by her divine visitors signaled the intense love and devotion they felt for her and that she felt for them.

In her second declaration, taken shortly after the first, Ruiz began to succumb to the intense pressures and fears that she felt upon realizing that her case was not going to be taken lightly by the inquisitors. Ruiz strangely and suddenly—especially after going into so much detail with her confessor and in her first declaration to the Inquisition—retracted all previous testimony and alleged that she was suffering from a certain *mal de corazón,* or "illness of the heart." Given that the ubiquitous mal de corazón in the early modern Spanish world could refer to a variety of physical, spiritual, and emotional maladies—including vertigo, swooning, spasms, heart troubles, loss of consciousness, apoplexy, and melancholy—it is difficult to determine from what exactly Ruiz suffered. Ruiz unsuccessfully sought to convince the inquisitors that because of her malady, she did not remember anything from her first declaration. Inquisitors were skeptical of her professed mal de corazón, and shortly after this second testimony Ruiz, described as "small in body and skinny, with brown skin . . . [and] a small birthmark above her right eyebrow," was taken out of the home of Alonso de Garibaldi and María Meneque and placed in the care of Andrés de Montoro, the head of the textile factory, who put her in a presumably more trustworthy home. There, "in the good company of women," she would not be allowed to leave or to speak with any man unless given permission by the commissary of the Inquisition.

After her relocation, the Inquisitors extracted a third confession from Ruiz on April 1, 1621. This confession—repeatedly referred to by Ruiz as her "true confession"—not only confirmed much of her first confession but went into far greater detail than any previous testimony. In what is only a small segment of this confession, Ruiz asserted that the saints, Jesus Christ, and the Virgin appeared to her in the following manner:

> They came to her with their dishonest parts physically excited. Each of them explained how they wanted to see her both loved and desired, and for this reason they came down from heaven to earth. As they hugged and kissed her, their passions became inflamed, and they began to exchange dishonest words similar to those a man speaks to his wife in the act of carnal copulation. And with regard to the Virgin, who came to her in her bed to hug and kiss her, they would sit with their dishonest parts rubbing against each other. Of all the rest, it was Jesus who gave her the most in terms of dishonest words and acts. For Jesus told her that he had made her so beautiful and gracious, much to his liking, so that she would be his whore [*puta*] and so that he could enjoy himself with her.[5]

It was after this statement that inquisitors explained to her that "it is a Catholic truth that the saints in heaven, Jesus Christ, and the Virgin do not sin, cannot sin, and could not have come down from heaven to earth in order to do and say the things that she has confessed that they said and did. Instead, it was the devil." According to the logic of the inquisitors, it must have been the devil, who, taking the physical form of Jesus, Mary, and the saints, had tricked Ruiz into believing what she did. Immediately after hearing this explanation by the inquisitors, Ruiz admitted her guilt and formally acknowledged that all along the devil had tricked her: "Her soul was in a state of error and had offended God, the saints, and the Virgin with the moral turpitude and lewdness . . . and she asks Him [God] for forgiveness." Ruiz admitted to her crimes to mitigate her guilt in the affair, and then she pleaded for mercy from the inquisitors.

ASSESSING THE CASE OF AGUSTINA RUIZ

Throughout her testimony and before accepting the inquisitors' interpretations of her fantasies, Ruiz painted a picture of sincere and even singular devotion. An important part of this devotion was Ruiz's relationship with the Virgin Mary. Given her visions and imaginings of the Virgin—in which the two hugged, kissed, and rubbed their "dishonest parts"—this case also broaches the topic of (fantasized) same-sex physical and spiritual desire between women. Like so many young women accused of such forbidden sexual fantasies, Ruiz undoubtedly failed to understand the gravity of her offense. Because of her naïve belief in her visions, she became a target of the Inquisition.[6]

Another important component of Ruiz's expression of her devotion was its simultaneous sacralization and vulgarization. When speaking of her fantasized experiences with Jesus in her third confession, she stated that "before having carnal copulation, Jesus would have her and tell her, 'I put you in my soul.' To this she would reply, 'My eyes, your *carajo*, I put your *carajo* in me.' And Jesus asked, 'Where will you put it?' And she responded, 'In my *coño*, which is yours.'"[7] According to Ruiz, Jesus then told her that he was having sex with her because "you are my soul and my life and the one whom I love above all else." The use of the Spanish verb *meter*—to put or place one thing inside of another—is used in reference to Jesus's spiritually putting Ruiz in his soul as well as his physically placing his member inside of her. For Ruiz, the devotional metaphors of putting herself within the heart and soul of Jesus, and vice versa, transcend the spiritual plane to the physical and the sexual. The pious desire for spiritual salvation manifests itself through Ruiz's belief (expressed vernacularly) that it was she who, over anyone else, was the soul, the life, and the beloved of Jesus.

This description of heavenly love alongside intense physical and spiritual joy also raises the issues of bridal mysticism and spiritual union with Jesus so common among the early modern female mystics. The notion of the exchange of hearts between Jesus and the mystic, the metaphor of marriage with Christ the bridegroom, and the transformation of carnal desire into spiritual desire are central to the tradition of Christian mysti-

cism. Although it is unlikely that Agustina Ruiz was influenced by widely publicized accounts of female mystics such as Saint Catherine of Siena
(d. 1380), Saint Teresa of Ávila (d. 1582), or the only recently deceased
Peruvian mystic, Saint Rose of Lima (d. 1617), it appears that there are a
number of similarities and overlaps, given the highly erotic language
used by mystics to describe the ineffable nature of the ecstasy of their
mystical experiences. The important difference, however, was that
Ruiz—given her lack of a clerical education and likely scant exposure to
the rhetoric of the mystics—used vulgar street language to describe her
own unique mystical experiences.

Just as Ruiz used the language of penetration to describe the simultaneous physical and spiritual love of Jesus for her, Saint Teresa of Ávila
told of how a beautiful angel with his great golden spear "plunged [it]
into my heart several times so that it penetrated to my entrails. When he
pulled it out, I felt that he took them with it, and left me utterly consumed by the great love of God. The pain was so severe that it made me
utter several moans. The sweetness caused by this intense pain is so
extreme that one cannot possibly wish it to cease, nor is one's soul content with anything but God."[8] A purely sexual reading of the mystical
experience in this context or even a forced implication of the sexual or-
gans would be an "unjustified oversimplification," yet in many mystical
experiences it is through the idiom of sexual pleasure that the ineffable
nature and ecstasy of intense physical and spiritual union with Jesus is
most closely approximated.[9] For Ruiz, it was ultimately this desire for
spiritual salvation that merged with the desire for physical salvation and
that manifested itself through the acts of copulation with Jesus, who was
both spiritually and physically in love uniquely with her. Ruiz recognized and knew that some of her actions and visions contravened religious dogma, and still she continually described her interactions with Jesus, the Virgin, and the saints in ways that elucidate the erotic nature of
her piety and spirituality. Indeed, this impoverished, ordinary woman
demonstrated great pride at having been chosen for these remarkable
sexual experiences with Jesus, the Virgin, and the saints. The testimonies
offered by Ruiz show not only the conflicts between the sexual, the mystical, and the spiritual but also how often these spheres worked together
and reinforced one another.

Despite the fact that her confessor, who had denounced her initially,
came to regard her merely as "an attractive yet luxurious and vainglori-
ous girl," the Inquisition doggedly worked to uncover the heresy involved in her sins. On April 22, 1621, inquisitors sentenced Ruiz to imprisonment in the official jails of the Inquisition in Mexico City. While her
son, Francisco, remained in Querétaro, the inquisitors made Ruiz travel
to Mexico City, bringing only white clothing and, if she had the money,
one hundred pesos to cover the costs of transport and food while in
prison. It was here, in the prisons of the Inquisition, that she recounted

her final declaration, in which she candidly discussed how and when her visions began. Even her earliest eroticization of the saints began with an intense devotion to and desire for religious iconography. It is here that she provides an important key—the role of trauma—to better understanding her visions and mystical experiences. Her earliest visions, as she told the inquisitors, occurred shortly after the unexpected and violent death of her husband-to-be, Diego Sánchez Solano, in a fire while she was pregnant with her son. In search of solace, she went to visit a neighbor, who had a painting of Saint Nicholas of Tolentino mounted on a small altar. Ruiz said that the painting was so beautiful that she fell intensely in love with the saint. In her third confession she related that "with this image [in mind], she went to her house and that same night, lying in bed while she began to touch her shameful parts in order to pollute herself, she saw an image of Saint Nicholas that reminded her of the said [sexual] act, and, in effect, she consummated this act as if she were really sinning with him."

Ruiz then related how, for several days after this vision, she had similar visions of and experiences with Saint Diego, Jesus Christ, and the Virgin Mary. The very next morning, while she was still lying in bed, she again began to touch herself and think about the image of Saint Nicholas. She then saw him suddenly "enter through the door of the house, donning his priest's attire, which was full of resplendent stars." He came close to her bed, touched her face with his hand, and told her many "tender endearments and flatteries." He then got on the bed, lifted his clothes, placed himself on top of her, and had "carnal access" (*acceso carnal*) with her. She related how the following night Jesus appeared to her in a similar manner, telling her that he had "a great desire to see her and enjoy her," after which she had sex with him. On the third night after Sánchez Solano's death, she consummated the sexual act with Saint Diego and, on the fourth night, with the Virgin. Given that these visions began with her desire to find solace in that painting of Saint Nicholas, all of Ruiz's visions perhaps make the most sense if seen as a form of dissociation from her everyday reality and the traumas of her childhood and adolescence. The document can merely hint at the painful experiences of a young girl whose parents died when she was young, who had to move around between Puebla, Mexico City, San Luis Potosí, and Querétaro, who got pregnant at around age twelve (most probably through coercion of some sort, given that she said she had been "tricked" into going away with the father of her child, who eventually engaged in sexual relations with her under a promise to marry her), and who survived the death of her child's father while she was still pregnant with her son. Her eroticization of Jesus, the Virgin, and the saints was much more than a sexual manifestation of her spiritual piety. Ruiz's visions were likely a complex psychological defense by someone who had been severely emotionally and physically traumatized. Agustina Ruiz's radical reinterpretation of

Church discourse that Jesus loved her was a manifestation of her desire to be loved and perhaps an unconscious attempt to come to terms with an extreme sense of abandonment caused by the deaths of those close to her.

The final issue worth noting is the specter of priestly sexuality and the role that it may have played in the Ruiz case. The desires of priests and inquisitors assiduously interrogating, listening, and recording deserve some attention. Priestly sexuality—though negated by the Church through required vows of celibacy—has been recorded in a variety of solicitation cases in which priests sought sexual favors from their female and male penitents, but in this case it appears only as an obscured and invisible presence. [10] While priestly sexuality is successfully concealed in the background of Ruiz's overt sexuality, it may have influenced her reception and punishment. While some inquisitors expressed their un-abated surprise at the detailed descriptions of Ruiz's masturbatory fanta-sies and experiences, sexual titillation may have partly contributed to this surprise and even intensified it. Just as Ruiz was deeply affected by the painting of Saint Nicholas of Tolentino and based a large part of her sexual imagery on religious iconography and things that she encountered in her everyday life, the inquisitors interrogating her were likely influ-enced on both spiritual and corporal levels by her declarations. Yet the inquisitors expressed their "desire" for Agustina Ruiz (and her testimo-ny) in their determination to interrogate her, record her detailed utter-ances, punish her, and then "save" her. While we have nothing in the way of a historical record to prove how the priests and inquisitors per-sonally dealt with the testimonies of Ruiz, the inquisitorial gaze and the specter of priestly sexuality were never far removed.

CONCLUSION

As evidenced by this case, the divisions between obscenity, desecration, devotion, and the holiest of religious ecstasies—mediated in the historical record by colonial filters and notarial procedures—were thin or, at times, nonexistent. The same might be said for our present-day notions of colo-nial "order" and "disorder." As stated at the outset, Agustina Ruiz was eventually sentenced to be a recluse for three years in the Convent of the Conception of Nuns in Mexico City—a seemingly ironic punishment for someone whose crime was to sexualize the very religious iconography that would be ubiquitous and unavoidable in a convent. In addition, she was forced to see a medical doctor of the Holy Office of the Inquisition in order to determine whether or not she was pregnant (she was not) and was ordered to receive the sacrament of confirmation. The case presented here ultimately depicts a woman who largely saw herself as a devout Catholic and who never sought to contravene religious dogma overtly, despite the fact that inquisitors framed her visions as acts of symbolic desecration.

The account of one woman's thoughts, actions, and desires demonstrates how sexuality, erotic visions, and physical desire sometimes merged with religious devotion. More importantly, this singular case provides us with an extremely rare glimpse—through an extended discussion of female autoeroticism and accompanying religious fantasies—into the multiplicity of desire and the wide range of female erotic comportment in colonial Mexico. In an effort to deal with intense pain, loneliness, and mal de corazón, Agustina Ruiz partly ordered her life through her symbolic reinterpretation of religious discourse and found at least some form of solace and comfort that the Inquisition could only see as disorderly, defiling, and heretical—even while recording it in salacious detail. While historians may never know what happened to Agustina Ruiz throughout the rest of her life, it is likely that even after her inquisitorial imprisonment and the three years that she spent in a Mexico City convent away from her son—or perhaps because of it—Agustina Ruiz never looked at Jesus, the Virgin, and the saints in quite the same way that Christian theological discourse and the Holy Office of the Inquisition had intended.

QUESTIONS FOR DISCUSSION

1. Do you agree or disagree with the assertion that Agustina Ruiz's thoughts and actions represented a challenge to Spain's colonial project in early-seventeenth-century Mexico? Why or why not?
2. Did Ruiz's religious visions deviate from or originate within Catholic orthodoxy and iconography?
3. Might Agustina Ruiz have been treated the same by inquisitors were she a Spanish nun, an African or *mulata* slave, a Nahuatl-speaking indigenous woman, or a poor mestizo male rather than a young mestiza woman? To what extent can an individual's ethnicity, social standing, and place in the community influence his or her treatment by criminal and ecclesiastical authorities?
4. If the visions and thoughts of Agustina Ruiz represented a challenge to (or a perversion of) Catholic religious doctrine, why was she not punished more harshly? What were the ultimate goals of the Holy Office of the Inquisition in Mexico? How does our understanding of religious orthodoxy change if we acknowledge that erotic mysticism was an important component of both popular and official religious devotion?

NOTES

1. Bancroft Library MSS 96/95 5:4, fol. 2. All excerpts are taken from this Inquisition case. For more on this case and others like it, see Zeb Tortorici, "Contra Natura: Sin, Crime, and 'Unnatural' Sexuality in Colonial Mexico, 1530–1821" (PhD diss., University of California, Los Angeles, 2010).

2. Any close reading of this case, however, should be placed within a proper historiographical framework. Historian Asunción Lavrin, in an influential essay, examines the gap between the proper types of sexual behavior described in treatises of moral theology like confessional manuals and the everyday transgressive behaviors of the population at large. Regarding the vast number of criminal and Inquisition cases that deal with sexuality, Lavrin asserts the following: "These cases were either self-confessions or denunciations of breaches of the ecclesiastical norms, and they represent the reality of daily life for those who failed to practice fully the teachings of the church." See Lavrin, "Sexuality in Colonial Mexico," in *Sexuality and Marriage in Colonial Latin America*, ed. Asunción Lavrin (Lincoln: University of Nebraska Press, 1989), 51.

3. Thomas Laqueur, *Solitary Sex: A Cultural History of Masturbation* (New York: Zone Books, 2003), 136.

4. Bartolomé de Alva, *A Guide to Confession Large and Small in the Mexican Language, 1634*, ed. Barry D. Sell, John Frederick Schwaller, and Lu Ann Homza (Norman: University of Oklahoma Press, 1999), 105–9.

5. BANC MSS 96/95 5:4, fol. 12.

6. In colonial Latin American archival sources, references to same-sex sexuality between women are, at best, exceedingly rare, making this case even more significant. Historian Ligia Bellini, in the only full-length study of same-sex sexuality between women in colonial Latin America, asserts that the young women prosecuted for *sodomia foeminarum* (sexual relations between women, including the insertion of "objects") in colonial Brazil were clearly not cognizant of the gravity of their crimes, often interpreting their own actions as sexual games or experimentation. Bellini rightly concludes that what all these women have in common is that "they put into practice what they desired in certain moments." Ligia Bellini, *A coisa obscura: Mulher, sodomia, e Inquisição no Brasil colonial* (São Paulo: Brasiliense, 1987), 31.

7. The Spanish-language vernacular terms *carajo* and *coño* refer, respectively, to the genitals of the man and of the woman.

8. Teresa of Ávila, *The Life of Saint Teresa of Ávila by Herself*, trans. J. M. Cohen (New York: Penguin, 1957), 210.

9. Georges Bataille, *Erotism: Death and Sensuality*, trans. Mary Dalwood (San Francisco: City Light Books, 1986), 224.

10. For more on the crime of solicitation in the early modern Iberian world, see Stephen Haliczer, *Sexuality in the Confessional: A Sacrament Profaned* (New York: Oxford University Press, 1997).

SUGGESTED READINGS

Given that there are few works specifically about the intersection of female sexuality and spirituality in colonial Latin America, the suggested readings offered here are meant to guide students to the larger historiography on sexuality and the "sins against nature" (sodomy, bestiality, and masturbation) in the Spanish and Portuguese colonies in the Americas. There are a few important works, however, that have focused on the intersections of female sexuality and spirituality in colonial Mexico specifically. Jacqueline Holler, in "'More Sins Than the Queen of England': Marina de San Miguel before the Mexican Inquisition," in *Women in the Inquisition: Spain and the New World*, edited by Mary E. Giles (Baltimore: Johns Hopkins University Press, 1999), has examined the 1598 Inquisition trial of a Mexico City holy woman, Marina de San Miguel, who confessed having erotic religious visions and sexual relations with priests and another holy woman and was convicted of *alumbradismo* (claiming to have been personally and spiritually illuminated by the Holy Spirit). Nora E. Jaffary, in *False Mystics: Deviant Orthodoxy in Colonial Mexico* (Lincoln: University of Nebraska Press, 2004), discusses a number of fascinating cases of popular mysticism. Asunción Lavrin, in her momentous *Brides of Christ: Conventual Life in Colonial Mexico* (Stanford: Stanford University Press, 2008), dedicates one chapter to questions of gender, sexuality, and the crime of solicitation in the convent. Last, although its focus is largely Spain, Sherry Velasco's *Lesbians in Early Modern Spain* (Nashville: Vanderbilt University Press, 2011) is an important contribution to the field and provides necessary Iberian background to the context of colonial Latin America. Scholarly interest in colonial "homosexuality" began essentially with Serge Gruzinski's 1986 "Las cenizas del deseo," translated into English as "The Ashes of Desire: Homosexuality in Mid-Seventeenth-Century New Spain," in *Infamous Desire: Male Homosexuality in Colonial Latin America*, edited by Pete Sigal (Chicago: University of Chicago Press, 2003). Since Gruzinski's publication, Brazilian scholarship, led by Luiz Mott, has paved the way for historians researching similar topics. Some of Mott's work, translated into English, can be found in Harold Johnson and Francis A. Dutra, eds., *Pelo Vaso Traseiro: Sodomy and Sodomites in Luso-Brazilian History* (Tucson: Fenestra Books, 2007). Federico Garza Carvajal's *Butterflies Will Burn: Prosecuting Sodomites in Early Modern Spain and Mexico* (Austin: University of Texas Press, 2003) uses law codes, theological discourse, and criminal cases to explore the discourses of masculinity that played into the burning of sodomites in Spain and Mexico. Finally, the contributors to *Sexual Encounters/Sexual Collisions: Alternative Sexualities in Colonial Mesoamerica*, a special issue of *Ethnohistory* 45, no. 1 (Durham: Duke University Press, 2007), have examined historical and ritualized instances of sodomy, solicitation in the confessional, hermaphroditism, and cross-dressing among indigenous peoples. A more extensive historiographical discussion of works dealing with the "sins against nature" can be found in Zeb Tortorici, "Against Nature: Sodomy and Homosexuality in Colonial Latin America," *History Compass* 10, no. 2 (2011): 161–78.

EIGHT

Zumbi of Palmares

Challenging the Portuguese Colonial Order

Mary Karasch

Sugar exports fueled the economy of Portuguese Brazil in the seventeenth centu-ry, and as profits from European sales increased, sugar planters imported more slave labor, especially from Angola. These enslaved Africans proved to be a more efficient, productive labor force than the Amerindians. Large sugar plantations dotted the landscape in the Northeast, sometimes employing hundreds of slaves who planted the crop, cut the cane, and processed it into sugar loaves and aguardiente *(white rum) for sale in coastal urban centers, such as Salvador in Bahia and Recife in Pernambuco. Few of these complex operations were entirely self-sufficient in basic supplies (manioc, corn, beans, livestock, etc.), which they bought from farms and ranches in the interior. Finished goods and many artisan products came from the nearest urban marketplace. In short, the economic life of much of coastal Brazil revolved around sugar production, supported first by indigenous and later by a mixture of Amerindian and African slave labor.*

Slaves in Brazil resisted bondage in numerous ways: work slowdowns, sabo-taging of machinery or tools, violence, and flight. By the seventeenth century, settlements of fugitive slaves called quilombos *or* mocambos *emerged in the frontier zones. Most of these mocambos in the Northeast region were small encampments, but one settlement, called Palmares, developed into an indepen-dent confederation of eleven towns that spanned the rugged frontier zones in the states of Alagoas and Pernambuco. At its peak, Palmares was an autonomous state, based on African political and religious customs, with between twenty thousand and thirty thousand inhabitants. Probably founded in the 1590s after a slave revolt, the eleven mocambos of Palmares survived for one hundred years* supported by agriculture, fishing, hunting and gathering, trading, and raiding nearby Luso-Brazilian settlements and plantations. The Portuguese and the Dutch mounted many expeditions to conquer Palmares, but each suffered defeat by its determined defenders. The final, successful assault on Palmares took place in 1694, when a Luso-Brazilian force of thousands of men encircled the main mocambo of Macaco, battered down its walls with artillery, and then captured and looted the town. The smaller, weaker mocambos also fell to the attackers, who took the few surviving captives to sell as slaves in Rio de Janeiro. For the Portuguese, Palmares represented not only a military danger but also a beacon to all slaves intent on resisting colonial authority. Such a threat to the social and political order was unacceptable and had to be destroyed, regardless of the cost.

The most famous "great chief" or king of the Palmares confederation was Zumbi, who forcibly overthrew his predecessor, Ganga Zumba, for failing to mount an effective resistance against the Portuguese. Although Zumbi was born in Palmares, he was captured by a military expedition and raised in Porto Calvo by a Catholic priest, Antônio Melo, who baptized the boy and taught him both Latin and Portuguese. At fifteen, however, he ran away and returned to Palmares, where he ultimately usurped the position of great chief from Ganga Zumba in 1677. Given the scarcity of women in Palmares, many females had multiple husbands, but leaders such as Zumbi could have one or more wives of their own. Indeed, popular traditions record that Zumbi's wife was Dona Maria, a white woman captured from her father's sugar plantation by a raiding party from the federation. Nevertheless, upon becoming the king of Palmares, Zumbi became a formidable political and military leader convinced that peace with the Portuguese promised only betrayal and enslavement. As a result, he fought off each Portuguese and Brazilian military expedition sent against Palmares until the final, successful conquest of Macaco in 1694. Zumbi escaped the carnage following the capture of Macaco only to fall into an ambush in November 1695; his body was mutilated, and his severed head was displayed in Recife. Although Palmares and its most famous leader had perished and the Portuguese colonial notion of order had prevailed, Zumbi's memory continued to inspire all those who sought freedom in Brazil.

Mythic hero, or traitorous enemy? Zumbi of Palmares is a man of legend celebrated in the movie *Quilombo* and honored by Afro-Brazilians every year in November. He was born in 1655 and died resisting capture in 1695. His life and the drama of Palmares, which have been told and retold in Brazil for centuries, have inspired generations of slaves and their descendants. It is one of the defining moments in colonial Brazilian history that reveals both the order—that is, the colonial system and its profound inequities—and the disorder (in the view of the Portuguese) of the slaves who escaped their world of *engenhos* (sugar plantations) and *senzalas* (slave barracks). In contrast, however, I would argue that the order was in Palmares and the disorder was on the coast, as fugitive slaves re-created in the forested hillsides of Palmares their own autonomous society, free of slavery and of Portuguese colonialism. This chapter will, first, define quilombos; second, describe Palmares before the revolt that brought Zumbi to power; and third, assess the role of Zumbi in the final years of Palmares before its destruction by the great army of the 1690s. It will conclude with the elevation of Zumbi to a national hero who inspires those who struggle against or endure the legacies of slavery in modern Brazil. In myth and popular belief, Zumbi has not died but lives on to continue the struggle of his people.

Wherever slavery existed in colonial Brazil, settlements of fugitive slaves were sure to be nearby. They came to be called quilombos from the Jaga term (*ki-lombo*) for a fortified camp in Angola, and their inhabitants *quilombolas*. An alternate term, mocambo, derives from *mukambu* in Quimbundo, another Angolan language. In the case of Palmares, as in much of the Northeast region, the more common usage was mocambo. They were often no more than small encampments where a group of slaves could hide out from their masters and overseers. Others grew to considerable size under the leadership of kings or queens. Those that existed on the fringes of plantations or mining camps sometimes served as temporary respites where slaves could escape from work for a brief period before being returned to the rigors of life as a slave.

Palmares, however, was different. It evolved into an autonomous community in the interior of the states of Alagoas and Pernambuco and posed a military threat, especially under Zumbi, to Portuguese colonial society on the coast. Its very success challenged the colonial order on the coast in a way that no other mocambo had ever done, and its destruction, so the Portuguese hoped, would deter all other such attempts in the interior of Brazil. But they were wrong. Slaves did not give up the struggle for freedom and formed quilombos as long as slavery lasted, or they learned from the brutal destruction of Palmares to remain hidden and preserve their autonomy in secret until discovered by the outside world a century after the abolition of slavery in 1888. They could escape destruction because they either settled in remote regions of Brazil, such as Kalunga in Central-West Brazil, or the quilombos of the Amazon region and Mato Grosso, or they remained small and did not pose a military threat.

In contrast, Palmares was both remote from the coast yet close enough for expeditions to reach it. The mocambo took its name from a region where palm trees were plentiful—that is, *palmeiras* (palm groves) in Portuguese. A seventeenth-century description suggests why fugitives took refuge there. It was "a naturally rugged site, mountainous and forested," where the light could not penetrate and lush vegetation impeded one's steps and obscured the trunks of trees.[1] The tangled forests were penetrated by numerous rivers, which provided secure sources of water, even in the dry season. In addition to the hostile vegetation, Palmares included a series of tall mountains with sharp escarpments. One of them was shaped like a stomach (*barriga*); hence it was named the Serra da Barriga, from which the inhabitants were able to view the region all around for a great distance and flee to the interior upon the approach of a hostile expedition. In the Serra da Barriga of what is now the modern state of Alagoas, formerly a part of the captaincy of Pernambuco in the colonial period, was constructed the principal mocambo of Palmares, known as Macaco.

The chroniclers do not document when the first fugitive slaves fled to the Serra da Barriga. Décio Freitas, one of the historians of Palmares, argues that the first to establish themselves in a mocambo were a group of fugitives from a sugar plantation in the south of the captaincy of Pernambuco at the end of the sixteenth century. They had risen in revolt and killed their masters and overseers. If Freitas is correct, then Palmares began in a slave revolt of the late sixteenth century. When they chose to flee to the interior, these runaways were invading unknown lands, reputedly controlled by hostile Indian nations. What they found, however, in the Serra da Barriga was a terrain so difficult that even the Indians avoided it. According to tradition, about forty fugitives made it to the mountains and there built the first thatched-roof huts.[2] Their daring brought them freedom, and this generation died as free men who never again had to work on a sugar plantation.

The ancestors who began Palmares forged a new society in the mountain fortress. Reconstructing its "golden age" before the 1670s, when internal dissension combined with destructive expeditions led to disaster, is somewhat difficult because historians are dependent on outsider accounts and/or popular traditions. At the beginning of the seventeenth century, aggrieved planters began to complain about the blacks of the Serra da Barriga who were raiding their plantations for women. Not only did they capture black women but also white women and their daughters, *mulatas* (women of mixed African and European ancestry), and Indian women. Some women, however, may have fled voluntarily to escape abusive spouses and masters or, in the case of at least one prostitute, life on the streets of Recife. Since their numbers were small in the early seventeenth century, the men of Palmares also recruited other men to join them, including Portuguese soldiers who were fleeing forced recruitment. Whether plantation slaves were stolen, as in the Luso-Brazilian traditions, or voluntarily opted for freedom is unclear from the sources. There is no doubt, however, that recruiting through either capture or persuasion was a marked feature of the early period in the history of Palmares. In 1597 a Jesuit priest complained that the "first enemies are the blacks of Guiné [Africa] in revolt, who are in some mountains, from where they come to make assaults and give some work."[3]

As they recruited their new members, the black, mulatto, Indian, and white inhabitants of Palmares created an economy based on subsistence agriculture, trade, and raiding. The first Palmarinos may have lived by hunting, fishing, and gathering palm products and cultivating the small plots of land they planted with corn and manioc, but as the settlement evolved, so, too, did the diversity of economic activities needed to sustain thousands of people. The basic communal principle that challenged Portuguese mercantile and capitalist ideals on the coast was that all property belonged to the mocambo, with the exception of one's own personal property. As a spy reported, "Everything was [belonged to] of all and nothing was of no one." In other words, as Freitas concludes, "the palmarino blacks had created a communitarian economy of self-subsistence."[4]

Families received the land on the condition that they give any surplus to the community. To obtain access to land, one had to belong to the community of the mocambo; later one had to be a part of a particular polyandrous family. A new recruit had to submit to a long period of trial, including raiding and capturing a replacement for himself, after which he would be incorporated into a family and given access to land. Men were the labor force; women were the ones who organized and supervised the work as "chiefs of the family." Each woman might have as many as four or five husbands who labored for her and their household, which was obviously an inversion of patriarchal Luso-Brazilian society on the coast.

The basis of the economy was agriculture. Two weeks before planting began, the families cleared the fields using the techniques of slash-and-burn agriculture, although the burnings must have announced their presence to neighbors and expedition leaders. Working together, they tilled the fields, planted the seeds, and harvested the crops. Because the soil was so fertile, they could plant two crops of corn each year. Their workday comprised six hours from dawn to noon as opposed to the twelve- to eighteen-hour days on coastal plantations. At the end of the harvest, they feasted and danced for a week. Their labor was not devoted to Europe's consumers of sugar but to their families. They harvested food crops—that is, corn, beans, manioc, sugarcane, and sweet potatoes. Any surplus was deposited in a warehouse located in the center of the town for the benefit of the mocambo—its chiefs and warriors, its children, the old, and the sick. They also set aside a surplus for emergencies, especially drought and external attacks. Additional foodstuffs were traded to nearby planters for manufactured items that they could not make themselves.

They also exploited tree crops, especially bananas. They planted orchards of fruit-bearing trees such as mangoes, which must have provided them with vitamin-rich fruits and fruit drinks. They also harvested the rich resources of the palm trees. They ate the palm fruit with manioc flour or made it into an oil to be used in lamps or as butter. They even ate the large worms that lived on the trees. With palm leaves they covered their houses and wove mats and baskets. For their clothing they wove cloth from tree bark and used the husk of the palm fruit to make pipes. They undoubtedly enjoyed palm wine as they smoked their pipes.

For animal protein, they hunted and fished and raised chickens and pigs but did not raise cattle, which suggests that pastures were unavailable or that they easily acquired beef by raiding or trading for cattle with nearby ranchers. The chroniclers certainly complained about the blacks of Palmares killing cattle. The quality of their diet was reflected in their fine physical shape. When the captives from Palmares were paraded through the towns, the malnourished poor marveled at their health and strength.

Sometime after settling in the mountains, Palmarinos solved one of the most difficult challenges that faced quilombolas—that is, obtaining iron and weapons. Initially, they raided nearby plantations for iron weapons and tools, but they soon found a source of iron ore, which they mined. Since many Africans had worked iron before their enslavement in Brazil, they undoubtedly applied their knowledge to iron mining and smithing. In the Serra da Barriga, they placed the forge next to their religious "temple" and council house, which suggests an African religious attitude toward the significance of iron. Although they were unable to make firearms, they could meet most of their needs for tools and weapon points. They also acquired firearms and gunpowder in tribute from the whites whom they permitted to live on their lands. Their ceramics included Amerindian pots and jars and delftware imported from Holland.[5] They also used hammocks and carved objects of wood.

What they could not make, they then had to acquire by trade or raid. The Palmarinos traded their surplus foodstuffs not only for guns and salt but also for manufactured goods. Since sugar planters tended to focus on monoculture and did not plant enough food for their slaves, the Palmarinos ran a thriving trade in corn and manioc with nearby planters who protected them, since they were dependent on Palmares for food for their slaves. Portuguese complaints about the white protectors and tributaries of Palmares help to document the ways in which it was linked to the local economy. Its residents did not live in isolation or avoid contact and relations with whites.

In this way, the people of Palmares lived by agriculture, fishing, hunting and gathering, trade, and raiding for an entire century. They were able to exploit the same environment without exhausting their food sources while at the same time increasing their population size. Furthermore, they were able to produce a sufficient surplus to maintain a political and military elite and militia forces that defended their towns from attack. They even had settlers who lived on their lands and paid them tribute. Zumbi was supported from this surplus, and he and his people may have suffered from hunger only in time of war, drought, or crop failures.

The culture and society of Palmares are more difficult to describe. According to Governor Francisco de Brito Freire, they spoke their own new language, which at times appeared to be from Guiné or Angola, or Portuguese, or Tupi, a coastal Indian language. Whites could not understand their language and had to speak to them through interpreters.[6] How those interpreters had learned the Palmarino language is uncertain, but Zumbi could also speak Portuguese and knew Latin. He would not have needed an interpreter to communicate directly with the Portuguese.

Just as their language was a mixture—apparently a Creole language—cultural traits appear to have been drawn from both the Africans and Amerindians. The majority were black men who were increasingly removed from their African traditions as the generations passed, although new runaway Africans tended to reinforce some cultural traditions. Amerindian captive women brought their languages and cultures and undoubtedly transmitted them to their children and grandchildren. The central position of women in Palmares must have tended to reinforce the Amerindian influence. The fabrication of ceramics in Amerindian forms and designs is suggestive of the strength of their culture.

Since women were rare, especially at first, and highly valued, the Palmarinos evolved codes of conduct around polyandrous marriages to avoid constant fighting over women. The polyandrous family was the basic social unit of Palmares, and family relationships were established through the maternal line. The best surviving description of the polyandrous households of Palmares derives from a document of 1677, which gives a summary of a spy's report. He had lived among the Palmarinos for six months.

> Each black who arrives at the mocambo [who has] fled from his masters is soon heard by the council of justice, which has to know his intentions because they are greatly distrusting, nor are they trusting solely due to the fact of being [a] black who presents himself; that as soon as they certify the good intentions of the black who comes, they give him [a] wife which he possesses along with other blacks, two, three, four, and five blacks, since [there] being few women they adopt this style to avoid conflicts; that all the husbands of the same wife live with her [in] the same mocambo, all in peace and harmony, in imitation of a family, . . . that all these husbands are obedient to [the] woman who orders all in life as in work; that to each of these families the chiefs [*maiorais*], in council, give a piece of land to cultivate, and that the woman and her husbands do; . . . that in war they impress all in the moments of greatest need, without exception of the women who on those occasions appear more like *feras* [wild animals] than persons of their [own] sex.[7]

On the coast of Brazil, this lifestyle stood in marked contrast to the patriarchal planter-dominated society in which powerful white men lorded it over large households of women, including a wife, mistresses, and numerous slave concubines. Zumbi's mother may have ordered her household of men and children before losing her newborn to raiders from the coast, or she may have been one of the wives in a chiefly household, since the chiefs were permitted to have more than one woman. Ganga Zumba, Zumbi's predecessor, had three: a mulata and two black women. The children born in the quilombo of polyandrous or polygynous marriages never knew slavery. Zumbi, however, was the exception because he had been born free in Palmares but was then raised in the household of a Catholic priest after he had been stolen away.

The religion practiced in Palmares is uncertain, but it is unlikely to have been that of the *orixás* found in Candomblé, a contemporary Afro-Brazilian religion. Due to the slave trade from Congo-Angola to Brazil after 1580, the majority of Palmarinos were probably Central Africans. According to tradition, the first fugitives to settle Palmares were Ango-lans.[8] There was also a minority of slaves imported in that period from what are now the modern countries of Ghana and Benin. Ganga Zumba was an Ardra from the slave coast, and he may have followed practices more similar to Dahomeian Vodun. Zumbi had been raised Catholic by a priest, as had other Palmarinos who kept statues of Jesus Christ, Our Lady of the [Immaculate] Conception, and St. Brás in the "church" in the largest mocambo of Palmares in 1645. There are references to priests and to non-Christian religious specialists at Palmares, and even the name Ganga Zumba suggests *nganga*, a common term for a religious specialist in Central Africa. Did Zumbi continue to practice some, if not all, of his Catholic beliefs, or did he abandon them for the new religion he found in Palmares, which may have been a mixture of Central African, Christian, and Amerindian religious traditions? There is one glimpse in the docu-ments of a young Zumbi continuing to maintain a relationship with the priest who had raised him in his household, risking capture on three separate occasions to bring him gifts. Were Zumbi's furtive visits those of an adopted son to a beloved father or of a Christian to a respected priest? Or was there a forbidden sexual relationship between the priest and the young Zumbi? Because of his capture at an early age and his intensive education in Portuguese, Latin, and Church teachings, apparently Zum-bi's religious formation was Luso-Brazilian in contrast to the more African and Amerindian quilombolas. On the other hand, he clearly chose a Central African name with religious and chiefly connotations after he was free to do so.[9]

Those who followed the more African religious traditions in Palmares were undoubtedly concerned with protection and security. Shrines with statues, amulets, and charms may have been common. Religious special-ists would have been needed to protect the Palmarinos from spiritual harm, but they did not rely solely on spiritual safeguards. They fortified their towns with walls of wood or stone and, in time of war, with tall palisades and hidden traps with sharp-pointed poles that impaled men and horses. Before the Dutch invasion, the Palmarinos had a great council that met in the council house and elected a chief or a maioral who had many powers but not the absolute ones of a hereditary king or dictator. The most crucial decisions were resolved in a popular assembly. Thus, the early image of the leader of Palmares is of a nonhereditary and elected chief who had to consult an assembly. His subjects were few—

perhaps no more than one thousand in the Serra da Barriga in the 1630s. All this changed, however, with the Dutch invasion, which transformed the colonial Northeast and enabled thousands of slaves to flee to Palmares. Zumbi was born a year after the expulsion of the Dutch in 1654, and he entered a more complex society—that is, a confederation of town-sized mocambos led by the great chief, Ganga Zumba, in the 1670s. Under his leadership, Palmares had grown to enormous size. Macaco had eight thousand inhabitants, while Amaro may have had five thousand. Some twenty thousand to thirty thousand men, women, and children may have lived in the eleven mocambos of Palmares.[10]

The personal history of Zumbi of Palmares begins shortly after the expulsion of the Dutch from Pernambuco in 1654. A year later, the governor of Pernambuco sent an expedition against Palmares. Confident in having defeated a powerful European enemy, the Portuguese governor commissioned Brás da Rocha Cardoso to lead an expedition of six hundred men to eliminate their "internal enemy" who had grown in strength and numbers during the Dutch wars. Although the expedition of 1655 failed to destroy Palmares, the troops took prisoners, including a newborn who was only a few days old. The little boy was given as a present to a Portuguese parish priest, Antônio Melo, who served in the district of Porto Calvo until he returned to Portugal in 1682. The priest baptized the child Francisco and later taught him to read. By the age of ten, the boy knew both Latin and Portuguese. Until age fifteen, Francisco lived in a clerical household as the priest's servant and assisted him in his religious duties, such as saying Mass. Many priests in the colonial period maintained large households that included slave women, and some may have cared for Francisco and imparted their values and religious beliefs. At the same time, the priest undoubtedly taught him Catholicism. The young Francisco may have absorbed both Afro-Brazilian and Portuguese beliefs and expressed them as an altar boy. The traditions do not make it clear whether the priest treated him kindly, as an adopted son, or badly, as a captive.

Suddenly and inexplicably, the teenager fled the life that he had known and took refuge in Palmares in 1670 at the age of fifteen. The reasons are uncertain. Had he continued to maintain contact with the people of Palmares and with his mother's family during the long years of exile as a priest's servant? Or had a particular act of cruelty or racial discrimination led him to flee the slave society of the coast? A more sinister motive is hinted at in a denunciation registered with the Inquisition. The charge against Padre Melo was sodomy. Did the young Francisco flee to escape unwanted homosexual abuse?[11] The latter theory seems unlikely because Zumbi later returned at the risk of his own life to give presents to Padre Melo, which suggests that he was fond of his adopted father. Because Padre Melo maintained a relationship with Zumbi until his return to Portugal, his enemies may have falsely denounced him to the Inquisition to ruin his reputation. Nevertheless, by 1685, Zumbi had a wife and children. According to popular traditions from Alagoas, his wife was Dona Maria, a white woman who was the daughter of a sugar planter of Porto Calvo and who had been captured by the Palmarinos. When the theatrical dance of Quilombo is performed in Alagoas, she appears as Zumbi's queen, who at the end of the performance is handed over to an influential white man after the destruction of Palmares. Oral traditions suggest that within Palmares she had become a person of stature, who was no longer held against her will. When whites raided quilombos elsewhere in Brazil and discovered captive white women, they returned them to their families. Instead, Zumbi's wife (and his children?) were treated like fugitive slaves. Otherwise the usual sources do not refer to her except in one letter in which the Portuguese offered freedom to Zumbi, his wife, and children if he would make peace.[12]

Except for the brief visits to the priest who raised him, Francisco's future lay with Palmares. Perhaps because of his knowledge of the outside world as well as his literacy skills, he rose rapidly within the mocambo of Osenga, located near Porto Calvo. Two years after his return to Palmares, he was elected maioral. Reflecting his reintegration into Palmarino society, he changed his name to Zumbi and his mocambo was renamed Zumbi. At eighteen years of age in 1673, he led a force that defeated an expedition led by Antônio Jácome Bezerra and achieved the rank of *cabo de guerra*. Two to three years later, in 1676, he courageously resisted the attack of the expedition of 280 men led by Major Manuel Lopes, who invaded and burned one of the mocambos that then had two thousand houses. The Palmarinos suffered heavy losses, and Zumbi was wounded in the leg. After this battle, one chronicler described him as "crippled."[13] In spite of that setback, it took him only four years more to become the general commander of the Palmarino militia forces as general of arms (*mestre de campo*). Zumbi thus led the militia forces when they confronted the expedition of Fernão Carrilho, which killed so many Palmarinos in 1677.

The former altar boy had quickly earned the trust and respect of the Palmarinos for his leadership abilities, but where had they come from? Padre Melo testified to his intelligence in a letter he wrote about Zumbi, but who had trained him to lead men into battle? The sources are silent. His political skills, however, were honed when he challenged Ganga Zumba, the chief of the mocambo of Macaco and great chief of the confederation of mocambos. Although the Portuguese called him *rei* (king), Ganga Zumba had to consult a council composed of the chiefs and cabos de guerra of each mocambo. Zumbi, in the role of chief of his mocambo, must have participated in the deliberations of the council. As a cabo de guerra, he was also subject to the commander general of the militia. Since Ganga Zumba's powers were not absolute nor based on hereditary rights, he ruled at the wishes of the council of chiefs. In order to survive, the Palmarinos required a strong political and military leader able to mobilize the people in defense of Palmares. If he failed or showed weakness, the very existence of Palmares would be threatened.

That threat came in the powerful expedition of Fernão Carrilho, who attacked Palmares in 1677, killing many, wounding Ganga Zumba, capturing Field Commander Ganga Muiça, and taking numerous captives back to slavery on the coast. His people blamed Ganga Zumba for this disaster, accusing him of being drunk when he commanded one of the military forces. In all of the mocambos except for Macaco, popular assemblies called for Ganga Zumba's removal. When the great council in Macaco took up the question, Zumbi assumed a leadership role and spoke for the opposition. He denounced Ganga Zumba for "military ineptitude" and corruption and used his oratorical skills to wage a "legal" battle to remove him. In spite of his efforts, however, he lost. Ganga Zumba remained as great chief of Palmares to the distress of those who feared the consequences of his inept leadership.

The opposition (possibly led by Zumbi) soon began to conspire to remove him by force. Learning of the plot against him, Ganga Zumba struck first by deciding to make peace with the governor of Pernambuco. He sent to Recife a delegation that included two of his sons to ask for "peace and friendship." In the words of an anonymous chronicler,

> The appearance of those barbarians caused amazement, because they came naked, and with their natural parts alone covered. Some wore their beards in braids, others wore false beards and mustaches, and others were shaved, and nothing more. All were husky and powerful, armed with bows and arrows, and carrying only one firearm. One of the king's sons rode a horse because he still bore an open bullet wound that he had received during the fighting. [14]

The peace accords negotiated in 1678 included the provisions that those who made peace would receive lands at Cucaú and be able to trade openly with their neighbors, and that all blacks born in Palmares were free vassals of the king of Portugal. But the price for peace and the right to occupy Cucaú was Ganga Zumba's agreement "to return all the runaways who had come from our populated places." [15] Since native-born Palmarinos had ties of friendship and family with the former slaves who had joined them, they feared that their family members and friends would be forced back into slavery on the coast. The peace accords thus cost Ganga Zumba majority support. Only three hundred to four hundred persons agreed to follow him to Cucaú, where he established a separate community under Portuguese "protection."

With Ganga Zumba no longer resident in Macaco, Zumbi seized the initiative. Using the militia forces of his mocambo, he moved against the mocambos that had remained loyal to Ganga Zumba. Some he took by force of arms, others by the power of persuasion. After consolidating his power over the other mocambos, he unified all adult men into a great army that then conquered Macaco, an easy victory because Ganga Zumba and his followers had retreated to Cucaú. With Ganga Zumba isolated and defeated, the great council then elected Zumbi as the head of the confederation of mocambos. What Zumbi had achieved was a palace coup in which he had seized upon popular discontent to organize militia forces that had unseated an unpopular ruler. His daring victory was then legitimized by the great council.

As Zumbi consolidated his power in Macaco and prepared for future wars, Ganga Zumba's people faced incursions on their land by white planters seeking their fugitive slaves. Supporters of Zumbi in Cucaú also plotted to seize weapons and foodstuffs to take to the defense of Palmares; but when they were discovered, they struck first, poisoning Ganga Zumba and killing his principal advisers. The Portuguese then took advantage of the conflict to repress Zumbi's supporters in Cucaú and executed four of the principal conspirators and enslaved two hundred others. Ganga Zumba's attempt to live at peace in Cucaú in the midst of a slave society had divided the people of Palmares and ended tragically with his death in 1680.

Perhaps Zumbi and the Palmarinos concluded that to make peace was to be betrayed and enslaved. Why they henceforth fought the Portuguese and the planters so tenaciously may have been due to the terrible lessons learned at Cucaú: the Portuguese were not to be trusted, and to live in peace with them would only lead to enslavement. To preserve their freedom, they had to resist and fight for their people and their own way of life. What is clear from the documentation is that a newly unified and revived Palmares under the leadership of Zumbi took the offensive. Troops of forty to fifty men attacked plantations and towns, carrying off slaves, foodstuffs, and weapons. One wonders if they particularly raided plantations where their former comrades had been reenslaved. Not even the great sugar mill owners were safe from attack as they traveled from the coast to their plantations. For a period of thirteen years (1680–1693), Luso-Brazilian expeditions were ineffectual in stopping Palmarino attacks. Troops raised by forced recruitment in Bahia and Pernambuco were unable (or unwilling?) to defeat the Palmarinos. Thus, Zumbi and his people lived in freedom because they were able to defeat militarily all the small expeditions sent against them.[16] In 1685 the king of Portugal tried to make peace with Zumbi and offered to pardon him if he would move to an *estancia* (ranch) with his wife, children, and captains, where they would receive royal protection from enslavement. Was Zumbi tempted to abandon his people? We can only judge from his behavior, because he continued to fight and did not make peace.[17]

That same year of 1685, Zumbi was helped by a great epidemic of yellow fever that struck coastal Brazil for the first time. The severity of its impact on Europeans meant that the colonial forces were unable to organize large expeditions. The year 1690, however, marked a shift in government policy from the support of small, poorly trained, and badly organized forces to the recruitment and provisioning of an enormous expedition designed to conquer Palmares and enslave its people. To attract men, the government promised the lands of Palmares to the victors.

First, the government ordered convoys of foodstuffs sent to Porto Calvo, the town where Zumbi had been raised. From there, they constructed a road to move oxcarts of supplies to the Serra da Barriga. A month later, three thousand unruly recruits arrived, including prisoners from the jails of Recife, whites, Indians, *mamelucos* (*mestizos*), and even blacks organized in "Henriques" (regiments). By the time that they had gathered all of the men together, they had raised an army of nine thousand, the largest ever put together in the colonial period. Included in this great army were the men from São Paulo (Paulistas), who were led by Domingos Jorge Velho. Thus, Zumbi and the Palmarinos were to face an army larger than the Dutch had sent to capture Pernambuco.[18] Unfortunately, the documents do not reveal the size of Zumbi's army.

The final assault on Palmares began with an attack of one thousand men led by Domingos Jorge Velho, but Zumbi and his men easily repulsed them. The governor of Pernambuco then sent Bernardo Vieira de Melo to reinforce them. Once again, Zumbi and his troops defeated them. Palmares was then protected by hidden shafts that killed men who fell into them as well as by a great palisade that encircled the defenders of Macaco. On January 5, 1694, as Zumbi went to inspect the fortifications of Macaco, he saw the approaching artillery of the huge expedition. According to tradition, he questioned the sentry who had failed to warn the people of the army's approach: "And you let the whites encircle us? Tomorrow we will be invaded, and dead, and our wives, and children [will be] captives." He then ordered the negligent sentry executed and convened his war council.[19]

Meanwhile, the great army was attempting to surround Macaco and cut off all routes of escape. While the army closed in, the people of Macaco slipped out in the early morning at about 2:00 a.m. All but the rear guard led by Zumbi had left the town when a sentry spied the fleeing Palmarinos and opened fire. Zumbi and about five hundred men then fought desperately at the edge of a steep precipice in the black of night. In the confusion, many tumbled over the side while the fortunate ones escaped to the forest, but so many had been wounded that their flowing blood "served as [a] guide to our troops." The survivors were then hunted down by the troops of Vieira de Melo, who reported killing two hundred men, saving the lives of only the women.[20]

At dawn the artillery batteries broke the walls of Macaco and the troops sacked the town, killing any of the defenders who remained. According to Frei Loreto de Couto, the troops advanced on Macaco "cutting and killing all they met" until there was no place to put all the bodies.

Only 510 captives survived to be taken and divided as slaves among the victors in Porto Calvo. Macaco itself was looted and burned. After Macaco's destruction, the victorious army fell on the weaker mocambos and continued to kill the men and capture the women and children. Few of them lived, however, because the mothers killed their children so that they would not be enslaved and afterward starved themselves to death. Eighty of the survivors were sold as slaves to Rio de Janeiro.[21]

The victorious troops returned to the coast with their captives and left the Paulista Domingos Jorge Velho to "clean up." Rather than pursue the fugitives from Palmares, he seems to have furthered his own interests by "acquiring" cattle from nearby ranches and contrabanding captive blacks for sale in Bahia. Meanwhile, Zumbi could not be found. Somehow he had escaped the slaughter at Macaco with perhaps two hundred of his people. At this time, he remained hidden in an effort to regroup his small band of men.

Once the governor learned that Zumbi had escaped, he put a price on his head. However, Zumbi continued to raid for arms and ammunition. He was seen at the town of Penedo and recognized by the scars from his wounds. Nonetheless, he and his men remained in the area of Penedo. One of his principal lieutenants was a mulatto named Antônio Soares of Recife, who was captured on one of the raids. A Paulista and his men tortured Soares to reveal Zumbi's hiding place. Although Soares initially refused to inform on Zumbi, he yielded after receiving the promise of his life and his freedom and led the Paulistas to the forests, possibly in the Serra Dois Irmãos. At dawn, Soares left the forest and called out, "Zumbi! Zumbi! Zumbi!" When Zumbi appeared, Soares walked up to him like Judas going up to Christ. Rather than kiss him, however, he plunged a dagger into his stomach.[22]

Although severely wounded, Zumbi fought valiantly, as did his companions who came to his aid. Only one of them survived. Zumbi died in the fighting on November 20, 1695. The Paulista and his men delivered his "small and thin body" to the officials of the city council of Porto Calvo. An examination revealed fifteen gunshot wounds and innumerable blows from other weapons; after his death he had been castrated and mutilated. The last degradation by his enemies occurred in a public ceremony in Porto Calvo, in which his head was cut off and taken to Recife, where the governor had it displayed on a pole in a public place. His objective was to destroy the belief that Zumbi was immortal. The mulatto Soares received his reward of a pardon, ratified by the Overseas Council in 1696, and lived to an advanced age in Recife.[23]

Zumbi's betrayal and death, however, did not eliminate his influence or appeal to the slaves of Brazil and their descendants. Some of his followers who escaped the destruction of Palmares continued to live freely in quilombos, and the memory of Zumbi and Palmares led slaves to flee to quilombos as long as the institution existed in Brazil. Unlike Palmares, however, many remained hidden and unconquered, and their descendants lived in freedom until discovered in the twentieth century. They now claim rights to lands given to them by the Constitution of 1988.

In the cities of contemporary Brazil, Afro-Brazilians celebrate Zumbi's life and honor his memory each year on November 20. He has become the epic hero of Afro-Brazilians who celebrate his courage, leadership qualities, and heroic resistance. On the other hand, many in Brazil ignore him. One senses a reluctance to make him a national hero because he and the Palmarinos offered a direct challenge to Luso-Brazilian life and culture as well as to the colonial order. A society in which women organized the households, the people worked on a communal basis, and elected black leaders governed a multiracial society that included tributary whites was the opposite of the colonial society on the coast. Zumbi was a powerful black leader who had defeated numerous Luso-Brazilian expeditions, and Luso-Brazilian authorities who had imposed a patriarchal, racially stratified, and inequitable colonial order on the coast could not tolerate such a man. Perhaps the former altar boy fought so valiantly for his people because he knew both worlds—the world of slavery and racial discrimination in which he had been raised, and the world of freedom and autonomy to which he escaped at the age of fifteen.

QUESTIONS FOR DISCUSSION

1. How and why did Palmares survive for about a century?
2. In what ways was Palmares different from most quilombos?
3. Why is Zumbi the symbol of freedom to Afro-Brazilians?
4. Why did Zumbi seize power and refuse to make peace with the Portuguese?

NOTES

1. Décio Freitas, *Zumbi dos Palmares* (Luanda: Ministério da Cultura, 1996), 7. My thanks to Flávio dos Santos Gomes for this reference.
2. Ibid., 7–8.
3. Ivan Alves Filho, *Memorial dos Palmares* (Rio de Janeiro: Xenon Editora, 1988), 5.
4. Freitas, *Zumbi*, 10.
5. The evidence for Amerindian and European pottery in Palmares is from the archaeological investigations reported by Pedro Paulo de Abreu Funari, "A arqueologia de Palmares," in *Liberdade por um fio: História dos quilombos no Brasil*, ed. João José Reis and Flávio dos Santos Gomes (São Paulo: Companhia das Letras, 1996), 26–51. This chapter also includes maps and the only known picture of Palmares from 1647 (p. 33).
6. Freitas, *Zumbi*, 12.
7. Ibid., 11–12.
8. For Angolans as fugitives, see Ernesto Ennes, *As Guerras nos Palmares* (São Paulo: Companhia Editora Nacional, 1938), 24.
9. Freitas, *Zumbi*, 21.

10. Ibid., 15–16. Freitas believes that the total population of the mocambos did not exceed twenty thousand.

11. My thanks to Matthias Röhrig Assunção in a letter of October 13, 1999, for calling my attention to the *Veja* article of May 24, 1995, on the theory that Zumbi was a homosexual. The historian Luiz Mott located the denunciation of Padre Melo to the Inquisition; but Freitas, while considering the hypothesis "plausible," has not found any allusion to a sexual relationship in the correspondence of Padre Melo.

12. On Zumbi's wife, see "Quilombo" [of Alagoas] in *Dicionário do Folclore Brasileiro*, ed. Luis da Camara Cascudo, 5th ed. (Belo Horizonte: Editora Itatiaia, 1984). A brief and incomplete version in English is "'White Man Won't Come Here': A Twentieth-Century Folk Memory of Palmares," in *Children of God's Fire: A Documentary History of Black Slavery in Brazil*, ed. Robert E. Conrad (University Park: Pennsylvania State University Press, 1994), 377–79. The document that refers to the peace offer to Zumbi, his wife, and his children is reprinted in Décio Freitas, *Palmares: A Guerra dos Escravos*, 3rd ed. (Rio de Janeiro: Edições Graal, 1981), 144.

13. Edison Carneiro, *O Quilombo dos Palmares*, 4th ed. (São Paulo: Editora Nacional, 1988; Brasiliana, vol. 302), 40.

14. "The Great Seventeenth-Century *Quilombo* of Palmares: A Chronicle of War and Peace," in Conrad, *Children of God's Fire*, 375.

15. An English summary of the peace treaty and its provisions is in ibid.

16. Carneiro, *Quilombo dos Palmares*, 43–44. He lists at least thirteen expeditions between 1672 and 1694 that Zumbi would have fought against.

17. For the peace offer of the king of Portugal in 1685, see Freitas, *Palmares*, 143–44.

18. Freitas, *Zumbi*, 24.

19. Zumbi's words are recorded in document 54, "Requerimento . . . de todos os officiaes e Soldados do terço de Infantaria São Paulista de que hê M.e de Campo Domingos George [sic] Velho," in Ennes, *Guerras nos Palmares*, 323.

20. Freitas, *Zumbi*, 25.

21. Ibid.; Carneiro, *Quilombo dos Palmeres*, 163.

22. Freitas, *Zumbi*, 26–27.

23. Ibid., 27.

SUGGESTED READINGS

Four brief biographies of Zumbi are Décio Freitas, *Zumbi dos Palmares* (Luanda: Ministério da Cultura, 1996), which is the best; Severino Vicente da Silva, *Zumbi dos Palmares* (São Paulo: Edições Paulinas, 1990); Joel Rufino dos Santos, *Zumbi* (São Paulo: Ed. Moderna, 1985); and Leda Maria de Albuquerque, *Zumbi dos Palmares*, 2nd ed. (São Paulo: IBRASA; Brasília: Instituto Nacional do Livro, 1978).

General histories of Palmares, some with published documents, include Jayme de Altavilla, *O Quilombo dos Palmares* (São Paulo: Comp. Melhoramentos, 1931); Ivan Alves Filho, *Memorial dos Palmares* (Rio de Janeiro: Xenon Editora, 1988); Edison Carneiro, *O Quilombo dos Palmares*, 4th ed. (São Paulo: Editora Nacional, 1988; Brasiliana, v. 302); Ernesto Ennes, *As Guerras nos Palmares* (São Paulo: Companhia Editora Nacional, 1938); Décio Freitas, *Palmares: A Guerra dos Escravos*, 3rd ed. (Rio de Janeiro: Edições Graal, 1981); and Mário Martins de Freitas, *Reino Negro de Palmares*, 2nd ed. (Rio de Janeiro: Biblioteca do Exército, 1988). Additional printed documents on Palmares are in Robert Edgar Conrad, ed., *Children of God's Fire: A Documentary History of Black Slavery in Brazil* (University Park: Pennsylvania State University Press, 1994) and Leonardo Dantas Silva, ed., *Alguns Documentos para a História da Escravidão* (Recife: Editora Massangana, 1988).

On quilombos in Brazil, see João José Reis and Flávio dos Santos Gomes, eds., *Liberdade por um fio: História dos quilombos no Brasil* (São Paulo: Companhia das Letras, 1996); Richard Price, ed., *Maroon Societies* (Garden City, NY: Anchor Books, 1973); and Stuart B. Schwartz, "Mocambos, Quilombos e Palmares: A Resistência Escrava no Brasil Colonial," *Estudos Eonômicos* 17 (1987): 61–88.

Author's note: As of 2011, Silvia Hunold Lara is completing research on Palmares in Recife, Pernambuco, and Portugal. Her future book will significantly update more recent historiography on Palmares and include new documentation that she has discovered since this chapter was originally published in 2002.

NINE

Diego de Ocaña

Holy Wanderer

Kenneth Mills

Spreading Christianity was central to the Spanish colonial enterprise in the New World, and Roman Catholic clergy founded convents and churches as they sought both to convert the Amerindian population and to police the faith among all Christians. Evangelizing took place not only in major cities such as Lima or Mexico City but also in smaller provincial centers such as Saña, on the north coast of Peru. In the sixteenth century, the rural economy of northern Peru had revolved around the city of Trujillo, yielding bountiful harvests of wheat, corn, beans, rye, grapes, olives, and fruits. Trujillo remained home to the region's most prominent European families, and it was also the seat of local government, a bishopric, and the location of several important religious houses. By contrast, Saña (founded in 1563) remained a smaller place, nestled among the forbidding sand dunes of the coastal desert, with only a parish church and three convents. Nevertheless, in the seventeenth century Saña experienced greater economic prosperity with the introduction of sugarcane cultivation, which later would become the foundation of the local economy and make it the preeminent city in the region. When the Hieronymite friar Diego de Ocaña visited the area in 1599, however, Saña was still a small provincial city with an ethnically diverse population in need of spiritual guidance and supervision.

The familiar festivals, saints' days, and devotional objects associated with Catholic devotion provided stability and structure to Spanish society in Iberia and the New World, but the crown and clerical authorities believed that they could also pose serious dangers if the laity did not adhere to orthodoxy. The Inquisition policed the actions of all but the native Andean population, but by

151

1610 in the Archbishopric of Lima, clerical and lay officials would initiate visita-
tions to the Amerindian parishes to root out or "extirpate" not only lingering
pre-Christian religious practices but also what were viewed as errant forms of
Christianity. Apart from such direct efforts to maintain the faith, churchmen
also monitored the veneration of holy images such as Our Lady of Guadalupe
from Spain or New World devotions such as the Virgin of Copacabana, the
original image of which was enshrined in 1583 on the eastern shores of Lake
Titicaca in what is today Bolivia. These powerful expressions of faith could win
new peoples to Catholicism in the New World, but officials of the Church hierarchy also wanted to ensure that the laity adhered to pure Catholic principles. In
the seventeenth-century Spanish Empire, the lines dividing Church and state
remained blurred. For the crown, preserving Roman Catholic orthodoxy formed
a bulwark against social disorder and political chaos, particularly in the remote
provinces of the Indies.

The mission of the Hieronymite friar Diego de Ocaña was designed to advance the spread of an important popular devotion, the "miraculous" sculpted
image of the Virgin of Guadalupe from the kingdom of Extremadura in what is
today western Spain. Ocaña and his companion, Father Martín de Posada, were
sent from Extremadura to the Viceroyalty of Peru as agents (demandadores) to
inspect existing centers of devotion to the Virgin to correct errant practices and
to gather alms for the home sanctuary and monastery. It was within the purview
of a demandador to judge an existing image and its community in error and
thus unauthorized and in need of replacement. Before arriving in Saña on the
arid north coast of Peru, however, the elderly Posada died, leaving Ocaña to
carry on their mission alone. Once in Saña, the now hungry and bedraggled friar
found a thriving cult of the Guadalupan Virgin in a nearby valley under the
supervision of the Augustinian order, leaving him little hope of controlling devotions to the Extremaduran Virgin at this shrine or seeking alms. Feeling himself
divinely inspired, however, Ocaña went on to paint images of the Virgin of
Guadalupe to enshrine elsewhere, which he hoped would become an authoritative
new series of Marian shrines in Peru all providing alms and answering to the
Hieronymites at the home shrine in Extremadura. One of his portraits gained
fame for its curative powers in Saña and attracted the attention of a covetous and
unsavory parish priest who invited the impoverished and near-starving Ocaña to
his house. An elaborate negotiation ensued, with the friar torn between his mission of religious control and propriety and his need for food and the means to
continue his journey. In the end, Ocaña accepted the wily priest's offer of silver
for the portrait, not as payment, he insisted, but as a donation that would allow
him to continue his mission throughout the Spanish Indies. Like many devoted
religious, Ocaña saw himself as an instrument of divine power, and his retelling
of this curious affair displays both self-justification of his faith and his employment of "playful" picaresque motifs from the popular literature of the day as a
means of allaying his concerns. The author of this chapter contends that study-
ing this episode in Ocaña's journey reveals what the Hieronymite most feared
and, indeed, a special concern he shared with not a few of his missionizing

contemporaries in the era following the Council of Trent — a fear of being ineffec-
tual and forgotten or, even worse, of becoming an inadvertent spark of Christian
heterodoxy and error.

Diego de Ocaña was a Castilian and a friar of the Order of Saint Jerome. As an agent of his home monastery at the sanctuary of a miraculous image of the Virgin Mary, Our Lady of Guadalupe, in the Villuercas mountains of Extremadura in western Spain, he traveled to and through much of Spanish South America between 1599 and 1605, gathering alms, propagating devotion, and recording what he found. Most of what can be learned about Ocaña begins with what he himself wrote, drew, and rendered in watercolor and ink sketches in a cross-genre account of this journey created en route.[1]

Ocaña wrote and sketched principally for his Hieronymite superiors and brethren in Guadalupe, but he also heeded a succession of royal commands for all kinds of information about the Indies "from any person, lay or religious," who traveled there.[2] Thus, significant sections of his manuscript amount to highly purposeful reporting with these religious and imperial interests in mind; Ocaña attempts to bring narrative order both to the series of devotional centers he founded and to his various experiences. That said, his manuscript also has a powerful personal dimension. He was not composing an "autobiography" in the modern sense or even engaged in "life writing" in the manner of the explorations of self pursued by his saintly contemporaries and their disciples. His kinds of self-revelation emerged more indirectly.

After introducing Diego de Ocaña and his role as a representative of the holy image of Our Lady of Guadalupe, my principal way of capturing something of his life and significance in a short chapter is to explore this indirectness as well as to illuminate a small event at the edge of larger things, centering on one of Ocaña's many apparent departures not only from the focus of his journey but also from the main trunk of his narrative. On the surface, the incident seems a detour and appears to document a simple change of fortune along the way — the kind that Ocaña and his readers expected from their traveling heroes, fictive and otherwise. Yet the entertaining respite from apparently more serious matters that this friar's excursion into the world might seem to offer is not really a respite at all. The episode is one of a number in the manuscript that, while light in tone and told with an amusing flair, is also heavy with unease and revealing of Ocaña's larger predicament. It represents one in a succession of narrative episodes in which Diego de Ocaña seems to steal away — and consequently to steal his readers away — from his central mission and into his creative mind; yet I contend that the story's uncertainty is registered for a reason, which requires close consideration alongside Ocaña's most deliberate narrative forays. While his telling of a single incident cannot encapsulate him, it reveals "more" than he, and other churchmen, could express in any other way. Students of evangelization, missionary activity, and religious change in various social and ethnic communities in colonial Latin America run the risk of depending too fully on an established assembly of examples and texts to fire their understanding. Diego de Ocaña's revealing episode offers a fresh angle on the uneven transplantation and multiform communication of Catholic Christianity in colonial settings, suggesting that much of what was generated by early modern religious enterprise lay beyond a missionary's control.

DIEGO DE OCAÑA AND THE MISSION TO PERU

Diego de Ocaña was born around the year 1570 in Ocaña, near Toledo. All that is known of his early youth is that he made his way to the shrine of Our Lady of Guadalupe in Extremadura. This home of the carved image of the Virgin Mary had attracted pilgrims and prayers since at least the early fourteenth century. There, the boy entered the monastery of the Hieronymites, the Virgin's guardians since 1389. He made his full profession of vows in the Order of Saint Jerome on June 8, 1588, on that day choosing the promise of a spiritually full but sequestered life of prayer, obedience, and manuscript illumination in the convent's bustling scriptorium.[3] His days in Guadalupe were, in fact, numbered, lasting a little more than a decade. On January 3, 1599, as a late replacement for another friar, Diego de Ocaña and an older Hieronymite companion, Martín de Posada, were bound for the New World.[4]

Among the royal privileges and entitlements conferred by a series of medieval and early modern Castilian monarchs on the Hieronymite guardians of Guadalupe was the right to send out representatives to inspect and spread devotion and to gather alms that would maintain a cult befitting the Mother of God and assist in the care of the thousands of pilgrims who flocked to the sanctuary each year. Ocaña and Posada were two such agents, called demandadores, or questors, from the house at Guadalupe who, in the age of King Philip II, extended their field of operation beyond the Spanish and Portuguese heartlands and into what the Hieronymite chronicler and future prior of the monastery of Guadalupe, Gabriel de Talavera, in 1597 called—in apparent reference to any number of newly contacted peoples—"the most remote regions of the Indians."[5] Ocaña and Posada crossed the Atlantic and passed through the Caribbean and over the isthmus of Darién before sailing down the north coast of South America as far as the port of Paita, where the older man, already gravely ill, died in a rented room on September 11, 1599. Ocaña carried on alone, traveling through much of Spanish South America until late 1605, at which point he went to New Spain, where he died in Mexico City in 1608.[6]

Gabriel de Talavera viewed matters, including demandadores, from the lofty perspective of the home sanctuary. He placed his monastery's holy wanderers within a universal network of alms collection and divine favors that linked not only diverse and expanding terrestrial settings of Catholic Christendom but also heaven and earth, God's designs being realized through Hieronymite actions. Yet the extra-European paths of these representatives from Guadalupe were not nearly so well trodden as Talavera dreamed. If the Virgin of Guadalupe had become known and venerated in certain American parts, the Hieronymites—who had been, at best, sporadically involved in New World expansion and who remained without their own monastery there—most often were not. False alms gatherers in all manner of habits abounded, and even legitimate ones such as our two demandadores from Guadalupe could expect cautious, if not cool, receptions as they arrived in cities and towns. They had to be carefully introduced and authorized by official papers carried both from their Hieronymite superiors and from the crown.

From such papers as well as from the reporting of their activities such as the detailed account made by Ocaña within the larger surviving relation of his journey, it is clear that urban centers were these representatives' principal targets and that their brief was extensive.[7] Guadalupan demandadores expected a contribution from the coffers of any municipality that could afford it. Ocaña also mentions begging alms door to door, often assisted by the legitimating and cajoling presence of some respected local notable. Yet a demandador promoted devotion and collected alms, augmented, if possible, by the founding of religious associations (*cofradías*) among the laity. The recruited groups of pious men and women were themselves to be governed by hand-picked local stewards (*mayordomos*) among whose chief tasks were the maintenance of the flow of alms and bequests and the choice of secure successors to their office. People and piety were organized around sacred images of Our Lady, which the Guadalupan agents either inspected and approved or, as in Ocaña's case, might even make and then put directly into a cofradía's care. Ocaña wrote of how the Virgin Mary herself guided his hand as he created seven painted renderings of the original sculpted image of Our Lady of Guadalupe, at least five of which he saw enshrined in South American churches (in Lima, Potosí, Chuquisaca [La Plata, today Sucre], Cuzco, and Ica).

Ocaña also orchestrated an array of devotional activities, a kind of audiovisual assault on a city or town's different social communities that included programs of preaching, special masses, elaborate local festivals and processions, and even theatrical performances to promote the Virgin of Guadalupe, attract people to join a lay religious association, and inspire local residents to give alms and veneration. Ocaña himself delivered sermons, but in diverse and populous places such as the great mining center of Potosí (in what is today Bolivia) he also recruited others, including local preachers gifted in native Andean languages as well as in Spanish.[8] The sermons as well as the hymns and a play composed by Ocaña himself were peppered with miracle stories exemplifying the history and power of Our Lady of Guadalupe.

The ultimate goal in each setting was a new sacred foundation, a fresh beginning for a local cult of the Virgin. Yet some of these beginnings were only achieved at the expense of existing Guadalupan images whose cults, in Ocaña's estimation, had grown untethered from obedience to the shrine of the original image in Extremadura. Demandadores in the late sixteenth century were scrutinizing and correcting local devotion even as they were exciting it. In this sense, these agent-inspectors reflected their centers, in Ocaña's case, the increasingly jealous attitude of the home monastery of Guadalupe, and also the caution of the larger Catholic Church in matters surrounding the veneration of images and relics (and also the related authorization of miracles and human sanctity) in the years following the promotion of the decrees of the Council of Trent (1545–1563). The Holy Council of Trent had charged its bishops across Catholic Christendom to ensure "the legitimate use of images" and to be wary of any person who holds "impious opinions," who promotes dangerous errors or improper attention to any likeness of Christ or the saints, or who proposes to set them up and keep them outside of churches, where the "due honour and reverence [that] is owed them" could be given. It was thus within Ocaña's principal task to bring and maintain devotional order in a particular Marian corner within the Christianizing Indies. He was to visit and inspect existing Guadalupan cults in the New World, with an eye to reforming or otherwise counteracting any wayward devotion and replacing any unauthorized images that he might find. And he was also to ensure—beyond the amounts needed by local devotees for basic maintenance and the purchase of wax and other necessities—that an appropriate bulk of any alms gathered in the name of Our Lady of Guadalupe was flowing back to the home shrine in Extremadura. In short, it mattered greatly how, where, and with whom his images came to rest.

Ocaña's efforts to spread and maintain correct devotion to the original image and cult of Our Lady of Guadalupe in promising places in the Indies were capped off by his own narratives describing what he had done and experienced as a demandador. These narratives were a crowning part of his orchestrations. In them, he both fantasized about and attempted to fasten down the cultic beginnings he wanted to achieve. He thought, too, of his readers. As the first champion and participant-teller of these new sacred foundations of Our Lady of Guadalupe, Ocaña sought to influence the consequences of his actions and how they might be remembered.

It is easy to be carried along by Ocaña's needful purpose and systematized narrative effort toward new and secure devotional foundations, to concentrate on his dream of control and permanence. Indeed, being carried along in this way is an important part of the central task of trying to understand Ocaña's priorities and ways of seeing. But it is only a first part. The reader's engagement with what Ocaña trumpeted should not obscure what he could not help but whisper, and all else that he included. Indeed, as I shall attempt to exemplify through a presentation of one episode among a number of its kind, the Hieronymite also tells of traveling, and faring, much less certainly. He finds himself, more often than expected, at a considerable distance from his determined choreographies of alms collection and propagation, experiencing an America which — far from receiving his Extremaduran Mary with open arms and bending to his will — threatens his mission's primary purpose by thwarting his aims of establishing or correcting centralized control over Guadalupan devotions in Spanish America.

The fact that Diego de Ocaña does not look away or suppress all record of his risk taking in such instances compels attention. Rather than closing down his narrative task at such moments, Ocaña writes *through* them. In fact, he writes in a detailed and entertaining fashion about a number of apparent misadventures — and, as we shall see in the example below, he even stirs a dose of humor and a dollop of adventure into his telling of what happened when things grew perilous and went awkward and awry. As Judith Butler and others have explored in other contexts, in the broadest human terms, Ocaña's responsibility "to give account" to his intended readers is so highly developed that, far from muffling his remembered moments of anguish and uncertainty, he embraces them.[9] He does so because they are golden opportunities to demonstrate his humility before all that "America" — and ultimately God himself — has put in his path; they are chances to account for himself as a human who, in keeping with his early modern Catholic Christian thought, does not hold the reins of destiny. And he does so because his contemporary readers were deeply conditioned to receive, indeed to expect, the very protagonist and adventure he was giving them. His own and his readers' familiarity with apostolic journeys and the lives of Christ and the saints as much as with romances of chivalry, picaresque novels, and missionary reports and contemporary chronicles from the Indies east and west, led them to expect narratives that served up people whose meanderings and missteps, accidents, foibles, resourcefulness, and feats of perseverance beneath God's gaze were every bit as integral to their meaning as were their grand quests and stated aims. Diego de Ocaña's own "willingness to become undone," in Butler's expression, is shared on the page — and it is to this precise act of narrative imagining and sharing of how he was "undone" in his relationship with others and before apparent obstacles that I am drawing attention when I say that he is "writing *through*" such episodes.[10] It is to just such a moment and to Ocaña's unveiling of himself as just such a compelling human purveyor of a Catholic Christian religion to others in challenging circumstances that we now turn.

THE INCIDENT IN SAÑA

Diego de Ocaña arrived in Saña (just south and east of what is today the city of Chiclayo) in the northern coastal region of Peru in late September 1599, having buried his companion and fellow Hieronymite, Martín de Posada, in the port of Paita only a few days earlier. Saña was at this time an abundant provincial town in a well-watered valley of this arid region. Pueblos of Indians remained, even after the devastation wrought on native numbers by waves of disease in the coastal zone. The pueblos surrounded a substantial and growing Spanish settlement that included a parish church and the convents of three religious orders.

In another valley only four leagues (about twelve miles) away was a shrine dedicated to an image of Our Lady of Guadalupe, an already famous sculpted likeness that had been in the care of Augustinian friars near Pacasmayo since 1563. Ocaña was drawn there, and he marveled at the Augustinians' fine house, at their school and their extensive properties, and especially at the wealthy and thriving cult of Our Lady, which commanded alms and veneration up and down the coast of Peru. The image had its stirring foundational legend and was now famous for miracles, with pilgrims arriving even from the viceregal capital of Lima to the south.[11] It may have been sought by a Spanish devotee and carved by an approved sculptor as a faithful likeness of the original, but from Ocaña's perspective, devotion to Our Lady of Guadalupe on the north coast had gone wrong. From promising beginnings, the cult had strayed and transformed into an example of thriving disobedience. Neither in the northern coastal region nor (as Ocaña would discover) in populous Lima was any thought given to the original image of Our Lady of Guadalupe, and not a peso of alms raised in her name was being sent to the Spanish home sanctuary. The image's Augustinian guardians had quietly declared a kind of religious independence and had no intention of operating their satellite shrine differently. Alms, rents, and other incomes gathered in the name of the Virgin of Guadalupe would stay in this American place.

Ocaña later presented his short sojourn in Saña as the point at which he began to formulate not only a clearheaded response to the rival image of Our Lady of Guadalupe but also his larger strategy for founding devotional centers elsewhere. He had seen the established prosperity and devotion at the Augustinians' shrine, and he judged it locally insurmountable. "I could do nothing in this town," Ocaña later wrote, referring to Saña, "beyond empowering two people [to oversee collection and dispatch] in case someone sought to make a donation to Our Lady of Guadalupe of the kingdoms of Spain through their will or by some other means." Appreciating the Augustinians' foundation and shrine (and thinking it unassailable) "was one of the things . . . which moved me to build chapels in Lima and in other places," he explained.[12] And these plans for a rival image in populous Lima (in 1600, a city of some twenty thousand) were only the beginning. For it was then that this demandador would truly get to work. Within such chapels, Ocaña planned to position portrait copies, images of Our Lady of Guadalupe which, with the Virgin's help, he himself would paint and see approved by ecclesiastical authorities. Around these new images he would recruit lay religious associations and organize festivals and liturgical devotion, intensive programs of preaching and, of course, systems of alms collection that he meant to be protected in perpetuity. These would be the sacred beginnings that he could then champion as a first chronicler.

Ocaña's understanding of himself as a messenger, a conveyor of authority, is a recurring theme in his story. By virtue of the fact that he came from the sanctuary of the original miraculous image, he saw himself as many others would have seen him: as an instrument of God and his mother Mary. More particularly, he perceived himself as one whose lack of formal artistic training beyond some manuscript illumination in the scriptorium at Guadalupe would be overcome, like any other obstacle — from a tempest at sea to a worn-out mule. He wrote of how the Virgin herself guided his brushstrokes. Ocaña described himself further as the carrier of a simple and legitimate spiritual authority — "a friar from her [Mary of Guadalupe's] own house" who could paint faithful copies, "so very like the one in Spain." The fresh and direct connection to the original image and shrine is what is important. He counted on devotees in the New World to appreciate the authenticity of his channel to the heavens and also on their capacity to share at least some of his understanding of how the celestial court functioned.

Two principal messages on this score were exemplified in his own sermons, just as they would have echoed through those delivered by preachers whom he recruited to his cause. The first concerned the proven power of the Virgin Mary in her advocation of Our Lady of Guadalupe as a prime intercessor before God. And the second asserted Ocaña's capacity to deliver the goods, in contrast to what he had only to imply were the lesser and even dubious claims to such authority ventured by the conveyors, guardians, and devotees of certain other images. His criticism of the Augustinian foundation at Pacasmayo could remain implicit. Ocaña's understanding of Mary of Guadalupe as a permanent and singular advocate for all kinds of people partook of a highly developed Marian theology in shrines such as the one in Extremadura. Moreover, his attachments to orthodox power and devotional propriety reflected not only his home monastery's increasing sensitivity toward the proliferation of image copies but also broader caution which, in the face of deep criticisms from Protestant as well as internal Catholic reforms, he shared with other contemporary churchmen when it came to the veneration of images and relics and the investigation of purported miracles.

As justified as Ocaña may have felt as a creator and dispenser of holy images in New World settings, however, there were concerns and dangers that he did not mask. Like many other missionaries who found themselves in evangelization settings far from the comfort of confirming centers, he was taking important matters into his own hands. Later in his manuscript, as he was taking stock of the various images he had gone on to paint and enshrine in Peru, his recognition of this fact of his initiative prompted a revealing defensiveness. "I know full well," Ocaña explained to his readers, both Hieronymite and otherwise,

> that there are and will be those in Spain who argue that it is not wise to make these images [as I have done]. But, for these reasons, they will begin to see their importance. For now, and each year hence, from wherever there is a house and image of Our Lady of Guadalupe, many alms will leave the Indies which [otherwise] would have stayed. And now the *majordomos* [of the lay religious associations he founds]—who are like demandadores, and whom I leave [in office]—are masters of all, and [themselves] remain subordinate to the Justices and the royal and ecclesiastical courts which will annually take account of the alms they have collected.[13]

What Ocaña does not include in this passage—especially a discussion of the arguments of the nameless critics who he suspects will question the wisdom of his actions—seems more significant than his overt defense of the devotional centers he has founded and the reassertion of his dream of permanence and perpetual alms. Rather than gliding over his sense of the dangers that the painted image copies might bring to the mission of asserted or replenished control of local devotions to Our Lady of Guadalupe de Extremadura, his insecurity is registered. And within his self-defense and line of reasoning is the glimpse of self-awareness, which perfectly invites us toward a closer examination of Ocaña's adventures in Saña.

THE TEMPTATION OF DIEGO DE OCAÑA?

In the days before his arrival in Saña, the reality of severe want, of life alone on the road, and of the possibility of his own insignificance began to press on Ocaña. Traveling overland through the coastal desert, even with a native Andean guide who knew the area, there was the danger of becoming disoriented, of losing the trail, and of draining the last drop of water from their gourds. Somewhere in the sands stretching between the city of Piura and the "Indian town" of Olmos, Ocaña recalled musing further. Like the path he and his guide were traveling, he seemed dangerously close to disappearing. "As soon as the horses pass," he observed, "the wind fills their footprints [with sand], and there is no trace." In Ocaña's case, the prospect of himself and the Virgin of Guadalupe being forgotten almost as soon as they passed arose from more than a contemplated erasure of his way through the sand. Impermanence had a name. Fray Diego del Losar ("de Losal" in Ocaña's rendering), also from the shrine in Extremadura, had been a Hieronymite predecessor who traveled throughout Peru for some twelve years promoting the advocation of Our Lady of Guadalupe. Del Losar was little remembered by people whom Ocaña met, and he became for Ocaña a powerful reminder of all that might not come of his own efforts. There was barely more memory of Diego del Losar than if he had not been there at all, Ocaña recorded, and what had happened with del Losar could happen with him: "As soon as his back was turned, all would come to an end, be abandoned and forgotten."[14]

When Ocaña reached Saña, only a few days later, the place turned out to be a site in which his resolve would be challenged and adjustments would be necessary. In short, his lofty initial plans for countering the Augustinians' shrine and avoiding the apparent failures of del Losar by painting and enshrining an image in Saña as the first among many within a veritable empire of images of Our Lady that might endure in Lima and other carefully chosen places beyond would have to be reconsidered. Ocaña had spent his last real on the rented horses and the Indian guide who had accompanied him into town. He was starving, without the means to continue, casting about for options and forced to act. In his manuscript, Ocaña worked to make sense of some further adventures in Saña. "Finding myself in need," he explained, "I began to sell some of the things I carried, my appealing images in particular. I had a very striking image I made in Panama, and I brought it out for some people to see. They took it to a person who was ill and, before everyone's eyes, he [soon] appeared well; and I said that if they paid me, I would leave it there."

News of the apparently miraculous recovery of this person—and doubtless of the visiting friar's offer, too—spread, and Ocaña was soon fielding requests. But humans (neither Ocaña nor the individual townspeople) were not acting alone. According to the Hieronymite, the people "begged and pleaded" with him to leave the image behind. He claimed to have been surprised neither by the miraculous cure nor by the local burst of requests for the image. Interest in the image was, for him, evidence of a devotion awakened by God, a celestial reward after the Virgin of Guadalupe had heard her friar's call and interceded on his behalf. "I had earlier prayed to Our Lady," Ocaña explained, "[asking] that they [the townspeople] would take a liking to her portrait."

For the praying friar turned chronicler of the incident, God's miraculous cure had drawn fervent interest in his image at just the right moment, very much as his readers—familiar with the *topoi* of the holy wanderer, abandoned to fate, enduring all manner of suffering and trusting in God—would have expected. One of the people who came forward to see the Hieronymite's image begs attention. He was "a rich and inquisitive priest." Indeed, Ocaña presents this cleric as a crude and single-minded collector of curious sacred objects, not the stable and influential sort of person whom Ocaña characteristically sought out to assist his local missions, let alone to take an image of the Virgin into his care for the future. The priest, for his part, seems to have regarded Ocaña as a fellow down on his luck from whom something remarkable and powerful might be gotten. He also appears to have assumed that Ocaña was a little like him, one who might both appreciate and serve his collecting passion. The priest invited the Hieronymite back to his home to show off the many *curiosidades* that he had collected in his oratory. Ocaña claims to have accepted the invitation not out of politeness or any particular desire to see the fruits of this man's obsession, but because he was famished. As it turned out, he saw in this rich priest someone likely to be able to produce even more than a decent meal. As the Hieronymite's stomach rumbled, the story continued—a story that, as I have hinted, contains more meaning than might first meet the eye. A seemingly amusing comedy in the manner of the day is also an elaborate dance between religious propriety and caution on the one hand, and worldly temptation and even the prospect of heterodox danger on the other. What Ocaña leaves out in his reporting of the various steps in this dance seems as illuminating as what he chooses to relate.

His reservations about the acquisitive priest notwithstanding, Ocaña arrived with his locally renowned image of Our Lady of Guadalupe hidden, literally, up his sleeve. After showing Ocaña around his oratory crowded with oddities and sacred marvels, the priest came straight to the point: he was hoping to make his next acquisition. And what he proposed was simple enough: if Ocaña would only leave his painted image of the Virgin of Guadalupe with him, the priest would be all too happy to help the needy friar on his way.

Here, Ocaña's self-conscious need to account for his actions is notable. He first stresses to the priest the care he has taken to follow his order's restrictions about personal property and the receipt of money by any friar who finds himself on the road. It was imperative that he not break the rule, or even seem to do so, for either kind of departure offended God and set a scandalous example to laypeople.[15] He writes of his polite and public response to the priest's unseemly directness as having been an expression of how pleased he would be to leave his image amid so fine a collection for no recompense at all. Yet behind the spoken effort not to oblige the priest to pay him, he confessed a more private thought. "Relieving my need," he admitted, "mattered more to me than all his indiscretion." Ocaña had been praying again, and he owned up to how eager he had been for matters to proceed precisely as the priest was suggesting:

"I was at my wit's end and at such a point that, like another Esau, I would have sold my birthright for a bowl of lentils."[16]

As Ocaña's relation of the episode continued, it grew simultaneously more tense and entertaining. Like the knight errant and *pícaro* so popular among readers of his time, Ocaña's carefully remembered self struggled gamely to keep up appearances, with little to fall back on apart from his wit. It was as if the famished yet painstaking friar and the crude and worldly priest had been preparing for the roles all their lives. The cleric ventured some details, saying that if Ocaña would just part with the miraculous image, he would give him a bar of silver to support his mission and travels. Yet even in Ocaña's desperation, this assurance was not enough. The Hieronymite's asides confirm that he felt obliged by his vows to play a more innocent figure than he could possibly have been at this stage. "But, sir," he claims to have ventured, "what is the value of a bar of silver?" The priest's quick answer was a further inducement and just the right touch to allow Ocaña to advance a step further. While most *barras* of silver were worth about 250 pesos, the priest explained, he would give Ocaña one that would easily fetch 300. With this offer, according to the Hieronymite, the priest began pleading that he accept the arrangement. Ocaña wrote that the comforting prospect of three hundred pesos' worth of silver coming as a kind of gift from a pleading man made him swallow hard at his good fortune: here he was refusing to take payment, and the offer in exchange was more than he had dreamed of! After going quiet for some time, the Hieronymite wrote that he burst out laughing at this further evidence of God and Mary answering his prayers and causing the priest to implore him to accept the silver in this way.

Ocaña snapped back to attention when he realized that the priest was taking his reaction the wrong way. Fearing that the traveling friar was a clever campaigner laughing off the three hundred pesos as a paltry sum, or perhaps imagining that some monkish reluctance to receive payment still lingered, the priest began begging the Hieronymite to reconsider. According to our author, the priest cried that he would give Ocaña anything he desired, just as long as he left the portrait copy in his oratory. This heightened level of beseeching was, of course, even better. It provided further reassurance, if any were required, both for Ocaña and for his Hieronymite readers in Guadalupe that vows were kept and propriety observed. The friar was acting as any wandering religious would act in dire circumstances, thinking only of how to proceed with his mission. Ocaña writes that he calmed the priest by assuring him that the painting of the Virgin of Guadalupe would be his and by saying once more to the man that if he had not been in need, he would have parted with it to so discerning a devotee for nothing.

Even with his prospects so suddenly improved and the necessity of some funds for making his way met, Ocaña's vow of poverty and commitment to a mission in which every real raised in alms to support his home sanctuary's pilgrims was carefully accounted for meant that he needed to register grave concerns and insist on his purpose. The sight of the large bar of silver made Ocaña distinctly uncomfortable. He could not relax with the temptation, like the lump of a misdeed, right there in front of him and everyone else. Ocaña even asked whether the priest was able to pay him its worth in reales to help it disappear. When the priest, having gotten what he wanted, finally invited his guest to share the supper for which the friar had been longing, Ocaña felt so nervous in the presence of his prize that he declined the meal for which his stomach longed. He wrote that he considered it better to leave quickly, before his host began to gaze tenderly on the silver and think better of the exchange.

Ocaña's story raced to its conclusion: it was time to entertain with a somewhat inglorious getaway. The Hieronymite instructed his servant to hide the silver in his cloak and carry it directly to the inn, where he would meet up with another servant who was waiting, bored and disconsolate at their impoverished predicament, and watching their belongings. Ocaña describes the scene that the travelers later must have reflected on together. When the man who had been waiting saw the first servant enter, sweating under a load, and then throw a silver bar to the ground, he began to cheer up. "All three of us," Ocaña wrote, "delighted to find ourselves, at last, with money, called for the innkeeper to bring us something to eat." Yet the Hieronymite still could not quite relax. He remembered that "I asked them [the innkeeper and his family or helpers] to close the door, and I instructed that if anyone came looking for me or asking after me they should say that I was nowhere to be found (*que no estava en el mundo*)."

Ocaña tried to capture how he felt, explaining that he meant precisely what he wrote; rendered more literally, he was wishing not to be found in the world and also feeling not *of* or *in* it: "It is true that, just then, I was not there," he added.[17] I interpret his statement and repeated insistence as Diego de Ocaña's underscoring of the predicament in which he found himself in Saña and as an accounting for himself and his interactions there. For here was one who, very early in his American journey, had found his purpose as a mobile agent of control and correction of sacred Marian images threatened if not thwarted. He was ultimately a fleeting presence in a very local place. And the fate of the image he had left with the collecting priest—much less any devotion that might surround it— would remain quite beyond his control. The Hieronymite's predicament is heightened because what happened in Saña begged the question of his mission and of images and local Christianities around them in general. His quitting of the field of action, his shutting himself and his fellows away, and his expressed desire not to be found in the world for that moment suggest that Ocaña realized what he was sharing and accounting for: the limits of his own capacity to know and control the religious devotion he and others like him were charged with setting in motion.

Behind a tavern door with his two servants, still feeling a little deprived of his senses and strength but taking some solace in having solved the puzzle of how he would obtain mounts and continue down the coast to Lima, Ocaña recalled trying to shut himself off from deeper uncertainties about what he had done in Saña. He was finally about to eat his fill. Yet just seeing and touching the bar of silver was somehow not enough to persuade him that either it, or his adventure, was real. "It seemed to me that it was a dream, and that I did not have it [the silver] for certain." It was not the last time that Diego de Ocaña would describe what he saw before him and what was happening to him in America as a dream.

CONCLUSION

For a demandador charged with the foundation and inspection of holy images in secure settings—places in which devotion would be regular and monitored, and from which a steady supply of alms would flow—Diego de Ocaña was paying what may at first seem to us a surprising amount of attention not to the fate of an image he had created but to a newly acquired hunk of silver. The principal questions at which I have hinted above may be put more explicitly in conclusion. What about the portrait copy of Our Lady that he left behind in the oratory of a priest of questionable piety? Where precisely would the image be placed, and what would be the arrangements for its care and protection as well as for the alms that might be gathered in the name of Our Lady of Guadalupe? Was the painting now a curiosity within a larger private collection and around which a local bore could spin marvelous stories? Or would reports of the local miracle spread, leading others to visit and venerate the image in a shrine that would grow, perhaps far from the unsavory priest's grasp? These are the possible futures about which Ocaña was nothing short of obsessed in other urban centers in Peru, but he was not in a position to face them in Saña.[18]

It can be tempting to view the episode in Saña as atypical and largely unimportant. Arguably, events there unfolded so differently from how they developed in one of Ocaña's orchestrated acts of foundation or correction in Lima, Potosí, Chuquisaca, Cuzco, or Ica that the two kinds of action are unrelated. In Saña, once Ocaña had abandoned any idea of founding a devotional center to rival the Augustinians at Pacasmayo, it might be tempting to suggest that he was simply using anything at his disposal to relieve a bitter want and to proceed to the larger centers in which he would truly go to work, more carefully performing his demandador's functions of spreading correct devotion and of gathering and guiding alms. But, then, why did Ocaña write of his experience in Saña in the way that he did, opening himself up, justifying and entertaining in equal measure, and—most crucially—not concealing difficult matters that he might well have reported differently or not at all? What happens if we do not look away—if we do not cleave his adventure in Saña from the company of his larger narration of a purposeful journey as if it were only light entertainment, the desperate measure of a traveler in need, or the act of a friar with an eye on bigger prizes?[19] What happens if we take the episode seriously as a revealing invitation toward Ocaña's manner of seeing and accounting for what he was doing?

Two matters seem most pertinent. First, Ocaña was a friar who had joined a religious order and pledged his life to obedience and service to God and a miraculous image of his mother; he prayed often and, as I have emphasized above, he expected divine involvement in worldly affairs. The Hieronymite had carefully recorded reasons for believing himself one of God's favored servants. Aboard a ship, descending the face of a cliff, crossing a swift river, considering his own survival within a building collapsed by an earth tremor, menaced by people he does not know or understand, and in seemingly countless other predicaments in the Indies, Ocaña reminds the reader of his manuscript of how he understood his own fate to be in God's hands. His expectation of heavenly help and comfort meant that for Ocaña there was a special opportunity, not something to fear or avoid, in elaborating a narrative about experiences such as the one he had in Saña. Our Lady of Guadalupe and God were looking out for him, placing certain people in his path, moving human hearts. Ocaña literally could not have seen himself or explained things in any other way.

Second, narrating such an episode was an opportunity for playfulness—albeit an early modern Castilian friar's kind of playfulness—that was not appropriate at points in the manuscript in which he was reporting his official foundational and reformative efforts to his superiors. It was a reader's and a writer's playfulness, an awareness of his reader, which may well, in the end, have been part of what fueled a censorious superior's decision not to shepherd Ocaña's posthumous manuscript to publication. To fuel these more personal and revealing portions of his account, Ocaña could draw on his familiarity with contemporary genres of literature that featured the adventures and changes of fortune of a various band of God's human instruments with whom the friar, as a traveler in a strange land, could easily identify. As I hinted above, the incident that became a "detour" or "trial" or "challenge" in the life of an exemplar or protagonist was a crucial and comfortably repetitive feature in most tales of apostolic suffering, in hagiographic narratives, and in all manners of edifying stories, including those from contemporary chroniclers of the Indies. And such elements were just as integral to the plots of the popular romances of chivalry (one of which Ocaña explicitly cites at another point in his manuscript), to their more pious offshoots, the so-called *libros de cabellerías-a lo divino*, and to picaresque literature. There is not space to exemplify these influences sufficiently here. But suffice it to say that, together, these merging literary forms of the early modern Spanish world provided highly developed, elastic, and entertaining patterns into which a lively writer such as Ocaña could tip the details of his own experiences. Such events and close scrapes as happened to Ocaña in Saña positively invited such a tipping. Rather than simply distorting his record of an actual happening, these patterns enabled Ocaña's telling and his extraction of meaning from it while, in the process, coating real events in a contemporary and (he hoped) receivable humor, thus considerably enhancing his narrative's appeal for contemporary readers.

Indeed, the future remained a region of hope. Dreams of permanence were not fully punctured—in part, because, for Ocaña, uncomfortable reality seemed to intrude as expected, almost on cue. Diego de Ocaña, the divinely inspired creator of painted images of the Virgin of Guadalupe and the orchestrator of new sacred foundations meant to overcome all barriers in the Andes, does not so much go absent as step aside for a necessary moment. Diego de Ocaña, the wanderer and writer, arrives to reflect on the various tests of his devotion and effect of his prayers. Saña and other places in America became proving grounds for his trust in the Marian protector and in her influence before God. Such experiences left him shaky but undeterred. As he came to compose his account of them, he sought both to reveal and to console himself, to find a little protection in the telling even as he portrayed the experience in words. The act of writing allowed him to cast his mind back to Saña, to try and sort out what had occurred there; I have contended that his attempting to write *through* this and other such events brought the prospect of expressing humility and of achieving some greater understanding of himself and his actions. As we have seen, Ocaña's humility comes with both a knowing grimace and a quiet grin. Giving a written account of an episode such as that in Saña allowed him to acknowledge and take a few crucial steps away from his haunting sense of impermanence, to do so away from his memory of that place surrounded by shifting sand. The events in Saña were fleeting, and the acquisitive priest is an extreme example and not representative of everyone. Yet in terms of Ocaña's dawning realization of the imperfect and transitory nature of what he, like other Christian missionaries, might achieve, much less control in the Indies, Saña foretells a great range of other places where, over the next half-dozen years, the Hieronymite would also leave an image of Our Lady among people, having done his best to secure the foundation but ultimately hoping for the best.

Little wonder he would express that for a moment at least he did not wish "to be found there" in that realm of futility or worse. If not with his paintbrushes, then with his pen, ink, and paper Ocaña would creep back from a frequently jarring world toward the more certain walls of the cloister in Guadalupe for which he longed. Yet his simultaneous determination to come out from behind those walls, to tramp around in the world rather than only escape and transcend it, and his enthusiasm for attempting to account for a great range of what he did and experienced there means that Diego de Ocaña will never quite disappear.

QUESTIONS FOR DISCUSSION:

1. What are the principal limitations and advantages caused by the fact that much of what we can learn about Diego de Ocaña and his journey derives from his own account?
2. Restating a question posed within this chapter: why did Ocaña write of his experience in Saña in the way that he did, justifying and entertaining in equal measure but not concealing matters he might well have reported differently or not at all?
3. What factors most inspired and informed Diego de Ocaña's understanding of himself and his actions?
4. What does Ocaña mean when—away from the priest's oratory and the whole experience in Saña—he writes that he was "nowhere to be found," not in the "world"?
5. What does the consideration of Diego de Ocaña's relation of his thoughts and behavior in Saña in September 1599 contribute to our understanding of evangelization and its aftermaths in colonial settings?

NOTES

1. Biblioteca de la Universidad de Oviedo, Spain, M-204, is untitled, but it has been called the "Relación del viaje de Fray Diego de Ocaña por el Nuevo Mundo (1599–1605)." See the new and serviceable scholarly edition, Diego de Ocaña, *Viaje por el Nuevo Mundo: De Guadalupe a Potosí, 1599–1605*, ed. Blanca López de Mariscal, Abraham Madroñal Durán, and Alejandra Soria (Navarra: Universidad de Navarra; Madrid: Iberoamericana; Frankfurt: Vervuert; México: D. F. Bonilla Artigas Editores; Monterrey: Instituto Tecnológico de Estudios Superiores de Monterrey, 2010) and Kenneth Mills, "Diego de Ocaña (ca. 1570–1608)," in *Guide to Documentary Sources for Andean Studies, 1530–1900*, ed. Joanne Pillsbury (Norman: University of Oklahoma Press, 2008), 3:457–64.

2. *Real cédula* of Philip II to the chancellería of the Nuevo Reino de Granada and other officials in the Indies, San Lorenzo, August 16, 1572; Marcos Jiménez de la Espada, ed., *Relaciones geográficas de Indias*, Biblioteca de Autores Españoles, vol. 183 (Madrid: Ediciones Atlas, 1965), *Perú*, vol. 1, 50.

3. Archivo del Real Monasterio de Guadalupe, Leg. 39. Ocaña must have been at least eighteen years old by this date in 1588, the minimum age for entrants according to the Hieronymites' constitutions, "because at a younger age they cannot understand the rule they take." Biblioteca Nacional de España, Madrid, Ms. 1099, "Compilación de las constituciones extravagantes de la Orden de S. Gerónimo desde su principio hasta el año de 1513," Título 7, fol. 7v.

4. On his late inclusion as one of two monks permitted and commissioned by an ailing King Philip II, see Archivo General de Indias, Indiferente General, Leg. 2869, Tomo 5, fols. 165v, 168r–169v, 207r; and Carlos G. Villacampa, *La Virgen de la Hispanidad o Santa María de Guadalupe en América* (Seville: Editorial de San Antonio, 1942),

Appendices, docs. 4–10: 325–31. Martín de Posada and Diego de Ocaña set sail from Sanlúcar on February 2, 1599.

5. *Historia de Nuestra Señora de Guadalupe* (Toledo: Thomas de Guzman, 1597), Observaciones, Treatise 4, fol. 454r.

6. Archivo del Real Monasterio de Guadalupe, Códice 61 (Necrología de monjes, 1600–1747), fol. 7r.

7. Accounts were composed by other Hieronymites who traveled across the seas on behalf of the monastery of the Virgin of Guadalupe, but the pressures of space do not allow their treatment here. Suffice it to say that none of the surviving records is as extensive or articulate as Ocaña's "Relación."

8. Ocaña's reporting of his sojourn of some fourteen months in the great mining center of Potosí, while not entirely typical, was the culmination of these first tellings. See Kenneth Mills, "Diego de Ocaña's Hagiography of New and Renewed Devotion in Colonial Peru," in *Colonial Saints: Discovering the Holy in the Americas, 1500–1800,* ed. Allan Greer and Jodi Bilinkoff (New York and London: Routledge), 2003; and idem, "Diego de Ocaña e la organizzazione del miracoloso a Potosí," in *Il santo patrono e la città. San Benedetto il Moro: Culti, devozioni, strategie di età moderna,* ed. Giovanna Fiume (Venice: Marsilio Editori, 2000), 372–90.

9. Judith P. Butler, *Giving an Account of Oneself* (New York: Fordham University Press, 2005).

10. Ibid., 136.

11. Rubén Vargas Ugarte, *Historia del culto de María en Hispanoamérica y de sus imágenes y santuarios más celebrados* (Lima: Imprenta "la Providencia," 1931), 454–56. Ocaña writes of the shrine on the north coast (in 1599) at "Relación," fol. 213v. On the Guadalupe of the north coast from a later and supremely Augustinian point of view, see Antonio de la Calancha, *Corónica moralizada,* ed. Ignacio Prado Pastor (Lima: Imprenta de la Universidad Nacional Mayor de San Marcos, [1638] 1974–1981), esp. vol. 4, 1225–1385. See also the celebratory Francisco de San Joseph, *Historia universal de la primitiva y milagrosa imagen de Nuestra Señora de Guadalupe* (Madrid: Antonio Marín, 1743), chs. 24 and 25, 168–84.

12. Ocaña, "Relación," fol. 30r. Unless otherwise noted, from this point forward all quotations of Diego de Ocaña are from "Relación," fols. 29r–32v.

13. Ocaña, "Relación," fols. 214v–215r.

14. Diego del Losar was a native of Puente del Arzobispo, near Toledo, who professed his vows in the monastery at Guadalupe in 1563. Sebastián García, *Guadalupe de Extremadura en América* (Guadalupe and Madrid: Comunidad Franciscana de Guadalupe and Gráficas Don Bosco, 1990), 109.

15. Biblioteca Nacional de España, Madrid, Ms. 1099, "Compilacion de las constituciones," Título 8: de lo concerniente lla honestidad de nra. religión, fol. 8v.

16. In the Bible, Esau, son of Isaac, notoriously sold his own birthright to his brother Jacob; his is an "edgy" example for Ocaña, for he also lived for the moment and held nothing sacred. See Genesis 25:29–34.

17. Sebastián de Covarrubias's third sense of *mundo* (world) in 1611 catches an essential portion of what Ocaña meant here. Covarrubias (translated by the author) writes: "Sometimes 'world' means the instability [or fragility] of things, their changeability." *Tesoro de la lengua castell ana o española,* ed. Felipe C. R. Maldonado, rev. Manuel Camarero (Madrid: Editorial Castalia, 1995), 768.

18. See Mills, "Diego de Ocaña's Hagiography."

19. In the introduction to their edition of Ocaña's manuscript, López de Mariscal, Madroñal Durán, and Alejandra Soria draw no attention to the episode or others like it. In his earlier edition of Ocaña's "Relación," Arturo Álvarez, for his part, offers an awkward apology for the incident, reassuring the Hieronymite's new generations of readers that "the hardships he [Ocaña] suffered in the course of his odyssey excuse the freedom [the lack of preoccupation, *desenfado*] with which he relates to us such human anecdotes as this one from Saña." Arturo Álvarez, *Diego de Ocaña, Un viaje fascinante por la América Hispana del siglo XVI* (Madrid: Studium, 1969), 48, n. 31.

SUGGESTED READINGS

Diego de Ocaña's untitled manuscript resides in the library of the University of Oviedo, Spain, catalogued as M-204, and called the "Relación del viaje de Fray Diego de Ocaña por el Nuevo Mundo (1599–1605)." Evidence within the manuscript suggests that Ocaña drafted and illustrated the work between 1599 and 1607. As noted, the "Relación" can now be studied widely in the edition by López de Mariscal, Madroñal Durán, and Alejandra Sorio (2010), which replaces the problematic modern edition by Arturo Álvarez, *Diego de Ocaña, Un viaje fascinante por la América Hispana del siglo XVI* (Madrid: Studium, 1969), which was reprinted in paperback, with additional editorial omissions and changes in the interests of brevity, as *A través de la América del Sur* (Madrid: Historia 16, 1987).

Sustained discussions of Ocaña have been few, but readers might begin with Kenneth Mills, "Diego de Ocaña (ca. 1570–1608)," in *Guide to Documentary Sources for Andean Studies, 1530–1900*, edited by Joanne Pillsbury, 3:457–64 (Norman: University of Oklahoma Press, 2008). For background, consult especially Francisco de San Joseph, *Historia universal de la primitiva y milagrosa imagen de Nuestra Señora de Guadalupe* (Madrid: Antonio Marín, 1743); Germán Rubio, *Historia de nstra. Sra. de Guadalupe; o sea: Apuntes históricos sobre el origen, desarollo y vicisitudes del santuario y santa casa de Guadalupe* (Barcelona: Industrias Gráficas Thomás, 1926–1927); and Carlos G. Villacampa, *La Virgen de la Hispanidad o Santa María de Guadalupe en América* (Seville: Editorial de San Antonio, 1942). Also notable is Rubén Vargas Ugarte's pioneering work that discusses Extremadura's Our Lady of Guadalupe and Ocaña within a helpfully larger Marian theater in Spanish America: *Historia del culto de María en Hispanoamérica y de sus imágenes y santuarios más celebrados* (Lima: Imprenta "La Providencia," 1931). More recent, still surveying, but usefully juxtaposing Ocaña's work with an account produced by a Hieronymite successor in the Andes is Javier Campos y Fernández de Sevilla, "Dos crónicas guadalupenses de indias," in *Guadalupe y Extremadura, toda en la evangelización de América*, edited by Sebastián García, 47–54 (Madrid: Talleres Gráficas Don Bosco, 1993). Exploring Ocaña as a special kind of early modern travel writer is Elena Altuna's insightful "'En esta tierra sin memoria': El viaje de Fray Diego de Ocaña (1599–1605)," *Revista de Crítica Literaria Latinoamericana* 22, no. 43–44 (1996): 123–37. For more on Ocaña as a Hieronymite *demandador* and for a more fulsome bibliography in general, see Kenneth Mills, "Diego de Ocaña e la organizzazione del miracoloso a Potosí," in *Il santo patrono e la città. San Benedetto il Moro: Culti, devozioni, strategie di età moderna*, edited by Giovanna Fiume, 372–90 (Venice: Marsilio Editori, 2000); idem, "La 'memoria viva' de Diego de Ocaña en Potosí," *Anuario del Archivo y Biblioteca Nacionales de Bolivia* (1999): 197–241; and idem, "Diego de Ocaña's Hagiography of New and Renewed Devotion in Colonial Peru," in *Colonial Saints: Hagiography and the*

Cult of the Saints in the Americas, 1500–1800, edited by Allan Greer and Jodi Bilinkoff (forthcoming). A perilously decontextualized study of Ocaña's manuscript illustrations is pursued in Beatriz Carolina Peña, *Imágenes contra el olvido: El Perú colonial en las ilustractiones de Fray Diego de Ocaña* (Lima: Pontificia Universidad Católica del Peru, 2011).

An understanding of Ocaña's time in the Monastery of Guadalupe in Extremadura is best gained from the contemporary Gabriel de Talavera, *Historia de Nuestra Señora de Guadalupe* (Toledo: Thomas de Guzman, 1597). But readers seeking sound context and information in English on the Extremaduran image and sanctuary of Guadalupe as well as on the development of Spanish Hieronymites at Guadalupe and elsewhere are directed to Gretchen Starr-LeBeau, *In the Shadow of the Virgin: Religious Identity, Inquisition, and Political Authority in Guadalupe, Spain* (Princeton: Princeton University Press, 2008); Albert A. Sicroff, "The Hieronymite Monastery of Guadalupe in 14th and 15th Century Spain," in *Collected Studies in Honour of Américo Castro's Eightieth Year,* edited by M. P. Hornik, 397–422 (Oxford: Lincombe Lodge Research Library, Richard Kronstein Foundation for the Promotion of Jewish and Cognate Studies); and J. R. L. Highfield, "The Jeronimites in Spain, Their Patrons and Success, 1373–1516," *Journal of Ecclesiastical History* 34, no. 4 (1983): 513–33. On the monastery and shrine as a miraculous pilgrimage site, see especially Françoise Crémoux, *Pèlerinages et miracles à Guadalupe au XVIe siècle* (Madrid: Casa de Velázquez, 2001); and also the ranging compilation by Sebastián García and Felipe Trenado, eds., *Guadalupe: Historia, devoción, arte* (Seville: Editorial Católica Española, 1978).

TEN

Felipe Guaman Poma de Ayala

Native Writer and Litigant in Early Colonial Peru

Rolena Adorno

Before the European invasion in 1532, the Andean peoples had no formal system of alphabetic writing. In Tawantinsuyu the quipu, *a system of knotted cords, communicated meaning through the color, texture, size, form, and arrangement of the cords. Quipus did not attempt to reproduce phonetic sounds as in European script. Instead, they imparted numerical information and some basic narrative ideas much as today's road signs do (such as the red, octagonal "stop") without using alphabetic symbols. Trained specialists, known as* quipucamayocs, *interpreted the quipus by examining and manipulating the knotted cords. They could then pass on this information to interested parties, much like literate European scribes.*

Although Andeans continued using quipus early in the colonial period, by the late sixteenth century Spanish officials became suspicious and even hostile to evidence drawn from them. Since any such information was decipherable only by an Andean, it could not be verified independently by a European. Spaniards feared investing the power of recordkeeping solely to native quipucamayocs and judged the knotted cords much inferior to European alphabetic writing. Clerical authorities also feared that the mysterious quipus might represent a link to Andean religious beliefs. This attitude led Spanish friars, entrusted with converting the Andeans to Roman Catholicism, to learn the principal indigenous languages and translate them into alphabetic script. As a result, by the early seventeenth century, quipus gave way to alphabetic writing in Castilian and, to a lesser extent, in the principal indigenous languages, Quechua and Aymara.

The efforts of European missionaries to translate Andean languages into alphabetic script and to teach Andeans Castilian Spanish (the most common language in Spain) ultimately encouraged an impressive but brief Andean literary awakening. The production of literary texts written in Castilian and in indigenous tongues culminated in 1615 with the completion of Felipe Guaman Poma de Ayala's masterpiece, El primer nueva corónica y buen gobierno. *This massive manuscript (nearly 1,200 pages, of which 399 are full-page illustrations) was written mostly in Castilian with occasional passages in the author's native Quechua, and it provided a history of the Andes before and after the founding of Tawantinsuyu, the Quechua name of the Inca empire. It also focused on the abuses perpetrated by the Spaniards on the conquered population since 1532 and made sweeping proposals for colonial reform. Guaman Poma's intended audience for his work was King Philip III of Spain.*

By the time that Guaman Poma finished his opus, the Andean author Juan de Santa Cruz Pachacuti Yamqui Salcamaygua already had written his Relación de antigüedades de este reyno del Pirú *(1613), and the mestizo author El Inca Garcilaso la Vega also had produced the first part of his famous history, the* Comentarios reales de los Incas *(1609), the second part of which would appear posthumously under the title* Historia general del Perú *(1617). Meanwhile, the Spanish priest Francisco de Avila had compiled a collection of oral accounts of Andean religious traditions, written entirely in Quechua and known today as* Ritos y tradiciones de Huarochirí *(circa 1610). Despite the production of texts about the Andean past by indigenous and mestizo authors in the early seventeenth century, this literary renaissance ended abruptly, and future Andean authors would write only in Castilian. Moreover, none of the later works attained the majesty, scope, and originality of these earlier ones, particularly the* Nueva corónica y buen gobierno *of Guaman Poma.*

During his lifetime, Felipe Guaman Poma de Ayala went from collaborating closely with the colonial regime to denouncing its abuses. One important clue to this change in attitude may be found in documents relating to disputes over lands in the valley of Chupas (in Huamanga) between the kinsmen of Guaman Poma and an ethnic group, the Chachapoyas, originally from northern Peru, who also had settled in the region. In the series of litigations between the parties, the Chachapoyas and the Guaman/Tingo family accused each other of being recent interlopers. The legal dispute dragged on until 1600, when the Chachapoyas gained the upper hand by claiming that Felipe Guaman Poma (the leading figure in the litigation for the Guaman/Tingo clan) was not a member of the Andean elite but, on the contrary, a humble Andean named Lázaro. By discrediting Guaman Poma, the Chachapoyas won their case and secured the lands. For his part, Guaman Poma was sentenced to two hundred lashes and a two-year exile from the city of Huamanga and its six-league radius. It was a bitter blow that no doubt led Guaman Poma to rethink his position regarding the colonial regime that he had so loyally served in the past. The vehicle for his protest was Nueva corónica y buen gobierno.

The life story of the Andean Felipe Guaman Poma de Ayala draws together two great changes that occurred in Peru in the early Spanish colonial period: legislation affecting the civil status of members of the native populations under colonial rule and the introduction of alphabetic literacy and European book culture. Guaman Poma's inherited Andean ethnic status was downgraded as a result of actions begun during the administration of the viceroy Francisco de Toledo, and his life experience included the acquisition of literacy in the Spanish language and, ultimately, his writing of his remarkable book. In its own day, that manuscript book was not published. Recognized today as one of the notable cultural achievements of Spanish colonial Peru, the *Nueva corónica y buen gobierno*, available for reading on the website of the Royal Library of Denmark, is inscribed in the UNESCO Memory of the World Register (see figure 10.1).

Guaman Poma's story illustrates the challenges that arose in the early colonial period for members of the first generation of ethnic Andeans born in Peru after the Spanish Conquest. The record of that experience, contained in his book as well as in his legal petitions and a brief letter he wrote to the Spanish monarch, spans a twenty-year period (1594–1615). His writings reveal how indigenous Americans made a place for themselves in the mixed, colonial and indigenous, society to which Spanish colonialism introduced them. They reveal the transformations of outlook that defined his personal experience as well as those of many other native-born, Spanish-speaking Andeans who occupied the "space in between," the "contact zone" between native Andean and colonial Spanish societies.

Guaman Poma earned his livelihood in ways that were typical of Andeans who were fluent in Spanish and who could therefore negotiate between Andeans and non-Andeans, including Europeans, Creoles (individuals born in America of European parentage), and enslaved black Africans. His example shows how social roles and identities could evolve in the course of a single individual's lifetime when it coincided with the establishment and consolidation of the Spanish colonial regime. His story is also that of a seemingly ordinary individual who achieved an extraordinary feat in writing his startling chronicle of Andean history (*Nueva corónica*, that is, "new chronicle") followed by his bold, comprehensive treatise on colonial reform (*buen gobierno*, or "good government").

The significance of Guaman Poma's manuscript book for our understanding of Inca civilization and the early colonial period in the Andes is considerable. It provides a source of basic information about Andean institutions available nowhere else, and its documentary value has been demonstrated by its extensive use in fundamental studies of Andean economic organization, pre-Columbian Andean civilizations, Inca law, and even the Andean system of weights and measures. As a text that makes use of the Quechua language within a half century of its initial transcription into alphabetic writing, it offers insight into the early colo-

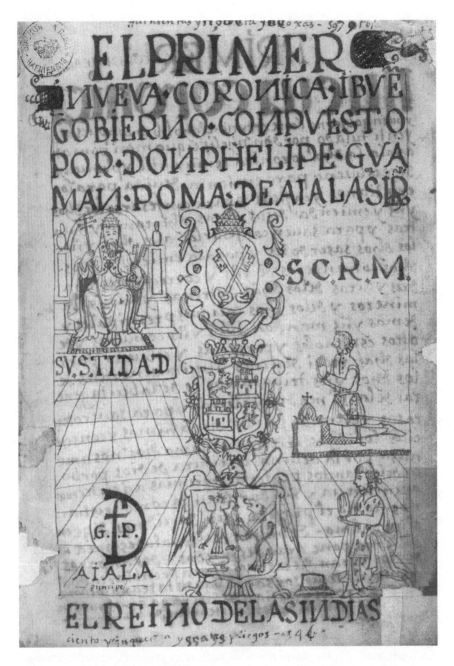

Figure 10.1. Frontispiece of Guaman Poma's *Nueva corónica y buen gobierno*.
Source: Courtesy of the Royal Library of Denmark, Copenhagen.

nial uses of the language, by Quechua and Spanish speakers alike. Guaman Poma's work has been an invaluable source for the study of the symbolic organization of the Andean world. The *Nueva corónica y buen gobierno* is of interest to us today because of the light it sheds on members of Andean-born, Quechua-speaking generations that, for their own survival, long served the offices of Spanish colonial administration—only to reach a final state of disillusionment with the colonial promise to order post-Conquest society according to Christian principles and to make justice available to all.

Guaman Poma's *Nueva corónica y buen gobierno* provides a record of that disillusionment. To make a case against the Spanish domination of Andean society, he argues that there had been no "just cause" to conquer Peru and that, in fact, there had been no military conquest because Andeans accepted Spanish rule peacefully. To demonstrate his arguments, he rewrites the history of the conquest in this "new chronicle," claiming that the Incas did not resist the Spanish invasion but were instead subdued by the miraculous visions of saints, such as Saint James (Santiago Mayor), pictured in figure 10.2. It was clear to Guaman Poma, however, that Spanish colonizers were in the Andes to stay. So he adds to his account of pre-Columbian Andean and Spanish Conquest history a long treatise on "good government," that is, on how to make Spanish colonial governance responsive to Andean needs and to prevent the ruin of Andean society. A visual summary of his account of the Andean peoples' colonial masters pictures them as predatory beasts about to devour a pious Andean begging for mercy (see figure 10.3). Yet to understand the relationship between his itinerant life and the writing of his book, we need to understand his ancestral background and how its prerogatives were modified (for the worse) in colonial times.

Guaman Poma was descended from *mitmaqkuna*. In Inca times, these were members of ethnic communities sent out with special privileges by the Inca to settle areas the Incas had recently conquered, to provide military garrisons along the vulnerable eastern borders of the kingdom, or to populate potentially productive but uncultivated lands. While mitmaqkuna obeyed local administrative rule in their new place of residence, they maintained the dress and symbols of their ethnic homeland. Their duties were to teach the superior ways of Inca culture, primarily the solar religion and the imperial language (Quechua), and to facilitate the local communities' assimilation into the Inca empire. Guaman Poma's *mitmaq* ancestors originated in Huánuco and were sent to settle in Huamanga, probably in the fifteenth century (see figure 10.4). After the arrival of the Europeans in 1532, the status and prestige of mitmaqkuna not surprisingly suffered a decline because the concept took on new meanings: the ambassadorial settlers who in earlier times represented the Inca's power and prestige and carried out his imperial mission were now viewed as

Figure 10.2.   Guaman Poma's drawing of Saint James (Santiago Mayor, the patron saint of Spain) illustrates his argument that the Incas did not resist the Spaniards' invasion of Peru. Guaman Poma, *Nueva corónica*, 406. *Source:* Courtesy of the Royal Library of Denmark, Copenhagen.

Figure 10.3. Guaman Poma's allegorical drawing of the Andeans' colonial masters as predatory beasts. Guaman Poma, *Nueva corónica*, 708. *Source:* Courtesy of the Royal Library of Denmark, Copenhagen.

ordinary newcomers, outsiders—here the relevant Spanish term is *forasteros*—to the communities they inhabited.

This was a precarious situation for families or clans like those of Guaman Poma because the Spanish colonial regime invented new distinctions to differentiate among migrant groups. (Not adept in Quechua, the Spanish colonizers typically called them *mitimaes*). In the 1570s, the Spanish viceroy Francisco de Toledo (1569–1581) fixed permanent residences for the mitmaqkuna, cutting them off from their homelands by assigning them to the places where they were residing at the time. This separated them and their descendants from the local *ayllu*, the basic kin unit of native Andean society, which held title to collective lands, organized cooperative labor teams, and carried out other collective functions.

The Spanish colonial administration at first divided the indigenous peoples into two clearly defined categories: (1) *originarios*—this Spanish-language term referred to native-born members of traditional, organized Andean settlements, and (2) *forasteros*—this Spanish-language term referred to migrants, outsiders. In relation to it, the Quechua-language term, *yanakuna*, which morphed in Spanish into *yanacona*, referred to Andeans who were detached from their ayllu affiliations and lived in the service of Spanish colonists, most often in cities. Anyone branded as a yanacona had been effectively stripped of his or her ethnic origin and identity, and people who had been long-ago migrants were regarded as forasteros, regardless of the length of their residence in their present communities and in spite of the degree of their assimilation to the region they inhabited. A little later, in the seventeenth century, colonial officials attempted to make further distinctions between those they called *forasteros revisitados*, those "who live in their respective *ayllus* because their ancestors were born here and were integrated into these communities," and "*forasteros advenedizos*, newcomers and other recent arrivals who at present are found within the *ayllus* but leave at will."[1] The result was a hodgepodge in which local ethnic identities were disrupted and an Andean's ethnic identity all too frequently became a question of improvisation to keep up with the pigeonhole to which he or she was assigned by colonial authorities. The "forastero advenedizo" designation would impinge on Guaman Poma.

Guaman Poma's account of his experience offers a glimpse into what the mitmaq heritage meant in colonial times. When he set out to defend his interests in lands he claimed in the area of Huamanga, he identified himself in legal petitions as both a member of the local native elite and as an appointee of the Spanish colonial government. Later, in the *Nueva corónica y buen gobierno*, Guaman Poma called himself an "administrator, Indians' advocate, deputy of the administrator of the colonial district." In the course of writing his chronicle he boldly elevated his title from local ethnic lord (*cacique principal*) to prince: "*capac ques prencipe*" (*qhapaq* means "prince"). (These "edits" are visible on Guaman Poma's manu-

Figure 10.4.   Map of Peru. Henrik Maribo, designer. Reproduced from Rolena Adorno, *Guaman Poma and His Illustrated Chronicle*, 10. *Source:* Courtesy of Museum Tusculanum Press, Copenhagen.

script, digitized on the Royal Library's website.) Guaman Poma obviously felt the need to enhance his traditional inherited rank as well as to lay claim to higher status within the colonial hierarchy. Such claims would have been a typical way for those of mitmaq heritage to insert themselves into the colonial mainstream.

By his own account, Guaman Poma was born "after the time of the Incas," and he declared himself to be eighty years of age when he finished writing his book.[2] Although his calculations are unlikely to be precise, he was probably born sometime between the mid-1530s and the mid-1550s, and from the dates he mentions in his chronicle we know that his death occurred after the year 1615. While Guaman Poma claimed Huánuco as his ancestral home, Huamanga (today's Ayacucho), the city in the Andes of south central Peru, was the site of his recollections of events from the period of his youth as well as the focal point of his decade-long litigation to support claims to hereditary properties. The province of Lucanas, located in the southern Andean region of present-day Peru, about one hundred miles to the south-southeast of Ayacucho (Huamanga), was another major site of his activities (see figure 10.5). He traveled through Lucanas as a church inspector's assistant in the late 1560s, worked there as a low-ranking colonial Indian administrator in the late 1590s, and settled there after 1600.

As a native Andean "assimilated" to Spanish language and religion, Guaman Poma would have been known as an *indio ladino*, that is, as someone who was presumably proficient in Castilian, Christian in belief, and Hispanicized in custom. "Indio ladino" was a colonial term applied by Europeans, never one of self-identification by Andeans. Denoting ostensible assimilation to Hispanic language and religion, the term "ladino" also connoted negative values of craftiness, cunning, and untrustworthiness. Because of the effective erasure of elite status that its use commonly implied, the term "indio ladino" was never used by Guaman Poma to refer to himself (although he used it to refer to others). He surely felt the sting of its negative connotations when he mentioned that he and others were scorned as *ladinejos* or *santicos ladinejos*, that is, as great and impertinent talkers, overzealous converts, or busybodies.

FROM HUAMANGA TO LUCANAS, LIMA, AND CUZCO: SERVING CHURCH AND STATE

Guaman Poma's activities first come into view for the period of the 1560s through the early 1580s. He writes of having served the ecclesiastical inspector (*visitador*) Cristóbal de Albornoz in identifying practitioners of traditional Andean religion in the first campaigns to "extirpate idolatry" in early colonial Peru (see figure 10.6). Although he does not picture himself here, Guaman Poma shows Albornoz supervising the punish-

Figure 10.5. Map of the Departments of Ayacucho and Apurimac, noting areas of Guaman Poma's activity. Henrik Maribo, designer. Reproduced from Rolena Adorno, *Guaman Poma and His Illustrated Chronicle*, 11. *Source:* Courtesy of Museum Tusculanum Press, Copenhagen.

ment of an Andean man, weeping, as carried out by another Andean member of the priest's inspection team. (We may surmise that the man's tears are occasioned not only by the humiliation of public punishment but by torture that precipitated his forced confession.) It is likely that Guaman Poma's own, earlier recruitment to the church inspection team had occurred in Huamanga and that its mission was Albornoz's 1568–1570 campaign to the provinces of Soras, Lucanas Laramati, and Lucanas Andamarca (see figure 10.5). (In his chronicle Guaman Poma mentions the names of inspection team personnel who participated in this specific tour, and he cites the names of Andeans punished by it, as recorded in Albornoz's own reports.)

Albornoz's extirpation-of-idolatry campaigns probably provided Guaman Poma with his earliest significant exposure to the policies and practices of the missionary church in native Andean communities. He expresses approval of Albornoz's work and points out that the priest punished the practitioners of Taki Unquy, a radical nativist movement that preached the triumph of Andean gods over the Christian god, advocated rejection of all that was European, and coincided with the threat of armed rebellion against the Spaniards from the neo-Inca stronghold at Vilcabamba. (Albornoz has been broadly credited for the suppression of the Taki Unquy movement.) Guaman Poma's reference to the practitioners of Taki Unquy as "false shamans" (*hechiceros falsos*) suggests that he viewed its leaders as hypocritically exploiting for their own personal or political gain the traditional rituals that in Inca times had been mounted for the expulsion of illness and to which their current native followers continued to adhere.

Guaman Poma also reveals his familiarity with the provincial Church councils held in Lima to establish and refine policies for evangelizing the Andean peoples. His enthusiastic support of its decrees on a broad range of topics suggests that he viewed rigorous and thorough evangelization as a pressing need in Andean society. Guaman Poma's militant defense of the need for surveillance of the Andean communities to stamp out prohibited traditional religious practices, as well as his detailed exposition of such practices, suggest that his religious perspective was orthodox and inflexible, neither syncretic nor ambiguous.

This stance reflects the early outlook that he must have developed when he accompanied Albornoz on his inspection tours, but it also reveals his later need, as an Andean author writing to the Spanish king, to insist unequivocally on his strict adherence to the Roman Catholic Christian faith. At the same time, Guaman Poma sternly criticizes the Spanish missionary clergy who failed in their pastoral duties or subverted it by corrupt actions. Thus pro-Christian and anticlerical, Guaman Poma expresses, in representing himself as a self-appointed adviser to the king, his views about the need for missionary guidance and reform.

In addition to his knowledge of Church council edicts, Guaman Poma's mention of some of the men who participated in the important Third Church Council, convened in Lima in 1582–1583, suggests that his skills as an interpreter may have been employed there. Yet his references to one of the council's principal theologians, the Jesuit José de Acosta, as well as to Luis Jerónimo de Oré, a Franciscan priest from Huamanga, and the secular priest and author Miguel Cabello Balboa evoke them not as persons whom he had met or worked for but rather as authors of the books they had written (and therefore he had read). In general, the priests who populate Guaman Poma's chronicle are overwhelmingly those who

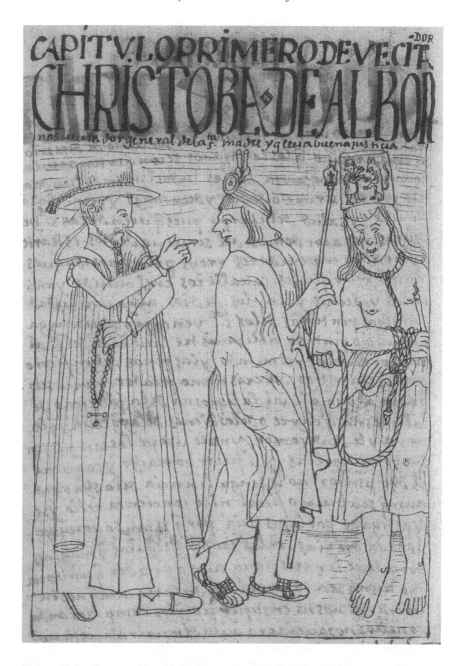

Figure 10.6.   Guaman Poma's early employer, Cristóbal de Albornoz, a Spanish priest, punishes an Andean practitioner for engaging in traditional ("idolatrous") religious practices. Guaman Poma, *Nueva corónica*, 689. *Source:* Courtesy of the Royal Library of Denmark, Copenhagen.

served in local Andean parishes in the provinces of Lucanas Andamarca, Soras, and Aymaraes in the southern Peruvian Andes (see figure 10.5).

Guaman Poma vividly recounts events that seem like firsthand recollections from the Viceroy Toledo's administration of the 1570s, which occurred decades before he began writing his book. The Toledo regime was important to Guaman Poma because he personally endured some of the economic and social consequences wrought by the viceroy's policies and their later enforcement, particularly with regard to the shifting colonial status of the mitmaqkuna. Guaman Poma summarizes the legislation promulgated by Toledo, and he recounts Toledo's inspection tour of the viceroyalty. This was carried out, according to Guaman Poma, after the resettlement program of native communities was undertaken. (These were the *reducciones*, whereby native communities were forcibly moved out of their traditional dispersed homelands and relocated to larger Spanish-style towns, where taxes (tribute) could be levied on them and their labor in the cyclical state corvée labor service (*mita*) could be assigned and supervised more efficiently.

Guaman Poma describes Toledo's late 1570 journey from Lima to Cuzco, starting his account with Toledo's visit to Huamanga and reporting events of the subsequent journey to Cuzco as if he had been a firsthand observer and participant. Narrating Toledo's reception in the city of Huamanga, he describes a highly theatrical and symbolic act which the viceroy carried out at the Inca site of Vilcashuaman, from whose stone step pyramid the Inca had presided over his court. Toledo, Guaman Poma writes, ascended the steps to the Inca's low throne (*usnu*) and was "received like the Inca himself by all the principal lords"; he then commanded the oldest and most highly ranked Andean lord in attendance to ascend to the top of the pyramid and be honored with him.[3]

The symbolism of that event, however, could not match the symbolic and real implications of another: Toledo's execution in 1572 of the last surviving Inca prince, Túpac Amaru. As if again he had been an eyewitness, Guaman Poma re-creates the powerful scene in which the fifteen-year-old Inca prince is beheaded (he was actually garroted) while noble Andean men and women witnessing the event wail inconsolably in protest and grief. Eyewitness or not, Guaman Poma would have heard many times the account of Túpac Amaru's capture, his humiliating entry into Cuzco, and his unjust execution.

In general, Guaman Poma's assertions reflect the attitudes and actions of the Andean provincial elite from the mid-sixteenth century onward. On the whole, the native elite responded eagerly to the chance to seek offices and privileges in the colonial system. From the 1550s onward, native lords had served as subordinates to Spanish administrators (Guaman Poma's documented experience is an example), and they continued to compete for positions in the colonial bureaucracy even after the reorganization of native society under Toledo. In the 1570s the viceroy revamped the ethnic power structure, institutionalizing state control over the succession of *kurakas* (Andean lords) and converting them into agents of the state for overseeing the directed activities of the local community. Toledo had dismissed Inca rule as illegitimate and tyrannical, and he attempted to fuse the fragmented, local hereditary non-Inca leadership with low-ranking colonial governmental functions.

Overall, Toledo's legacy in Peru at the end of the sixteenth century is crucial to interpreting Guaman Poma's position and claims. Like many other Andeans in his situation, Guaman Poma participated in the official transactions of the civil administration, yet his colonial affiliations were no match for those of the ethnic group against which he and his kin competed for disputed lands. Guaman Poma's case illuminates the situation of Indians designated as forasteros, discussed earlier, and illustrates the principle that "land-tenure cases were among the most hotly contested within the colonial judicial system. The rising value of land and the shrinking assets of indigenous communities provoked bitter disputes. Migration complicated the debates over land inheritance and titles in ways which were reflected in the courts throughout the seventeenth century."[4]

IN LIMA AND HUAMANGA: LITIGATION AND LEGAL DEFEAT

During the six-year period from 1594 to 1600, Guaman Poma served as an interpreter and witness in proceedings in Huamanga that confirmed land titles and implemented the policies resulting from Viceroy Toledo's reducciones. Guaman Poma knew well that in the world of colonial affairs, the written word was the essential means by which to document abuses and demand the redress of grievances. In the *Buen gobierno* he repeatedly insists that, like him, other Andean elites must become literate in Spanish to be able to carry out their traditional duties and to participate fully in the Spanish legal system. He makes this point in a drawing of an Andean commoner enumerating his grievances on the fingers of one hand while an Andean lord, dressed in European garb and sitting at a desk, drafts in Spanish the complaint that later will be submitted to the colonial authorities (see figure 10.7).

At the same time, during the period 1594–1600, Guaman Poma was busy in legal pursuits of his own, defending in the courts his and his kin's claims to lands in the valley of Chupas, just a few leagues from the colonial city of Huamanga. In the map he drew to accompany his petitions and substantiate his claims, the city of Huamanga occupies the center (see figure 10.8). Guaman Poma's adversaries in the legal disputes that culminated in his expulsion from Huamanga in 1600, the Chachapoyas, were an ethnic and possibly a linguistic group originating in the eastern highlands and western Amazonian slopes of today's northern

Figure 10.7. An Andean commoner, hoping to have his claims adjudicated by the Spanish colonial legal system, dictates his complaints to an Andean lord. Guaman Poma, *Nueva corónica*, 784. *Source:* Courtesy of the Royal Library of Denmark, Copenhagen.

Peru. The Inca had assigned them to the Quito area, where they were living at the time of the Spanish invasion. The Chacha groups were "small homogeneous enclaves forming a far-flung net of small mitmaq operations" located "at the outskirts of former aboriginal sites which had been converted into Inca centers," possibly with "responsibility for controlling the interaction of aborigines with the privileged population of the new citadels."[5]

The Chachapoyas had not been conquered until the reign of the Inca Huayna Capac (1493–1527), but when the Spanish took over Peru the Chachapoyas quickly assimilated themselves into the royal forces as "modern soldiers," continuing the role they had played in late Inca times. This occurred when in mid-1538 the powerful Chachapoyas allied themselves with Spanish royal troops to defeat the rebellion of Diego de Almagro the Younger in one of the most important battles between the Spanish crown and rebellious conquistadors in the 1540s. After the royal victory, the Spanish governor settled the Chachapoyas nearby at Santa Lucía de Chiara in the valley of Chupas (the site of Guaman Poma's claim; see figure 10.5) and exempted them in perpetuity from tribute payment in recognition of their loyalty and military prowess. They were identified as being in service to the "justice officials of this city [Huamanga] and the royal crown."[6]

The struggle over the lands of Chiara—and Guaman Poma's clan's troubles—began in 1586, when in Lima the viceroy, Fernando de Torres y Portugal, granted the lands located some two leagues from the city of Huamanga to the Chachapoyas under the leadership of their lord, don Baltazar Solsol. Reasons given were their status as mitmaqkuna as well as their ongoing service to the crown in law enforcement in Huamanga. Their receipt of this land grant was thus presumably based on need and merit. The lands are described in the decree as being vacant, that is, unencumbered by any current legal claims to ownership, "for more than fifty years, since they had been the lands of the Inca."[7]

Just two months after the lands of Chiara were surveyed in February 1587 and the Chachapoyas established themselves there, a member of the Tingo-Guaman families claimed and received title to the same lands from the same corregidor's deputy. The next recorded legal action occurred a full seven years later, in September 1594, when the rights of the Chachapoyas were confirmed. Again, just a few months afterward, the Guaman-Tingo families' claim to Chiara of April 1587 was also upheld. Notwithstanding the protests of the Chachapoyas, local colonial authorities honored the renewed Tingo-Guaman claims. During the following three years, both parties filed petitions and counterpetitions, each side accusing the other of being recent immigrants, "forasteros advenedizos," to contradict their claims as longtime residents and landholders. It looked as if Guaman Poma and the Guaman-Tingo families would prevail: On September 5, 1597, the Royal Audiencia (the highest civil and criminal

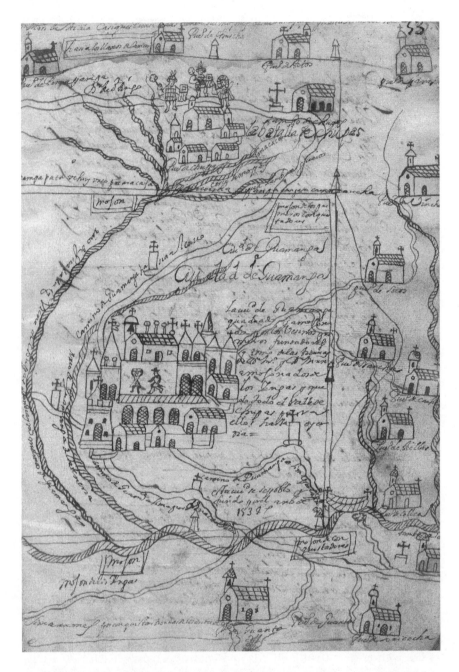

Figure 10.8.   Map of the Huamanga area drawn by Guaman Poma in pursuit of his land claims. *Source:* Courtesy of Dr. Alfredo Prado Prado, Presidente, Centro de Investigación y Promoción Amazónica, Lima, Peru.

court in the viceroyalty) ruled in their favor, and Guaman Poma carried the documents confirming the land titles from Lima back to Huamanga.

Regrettably for Guaman Poma, however, the legal advocate representing him and his clansmen referred in the court documents to one of Guaman Poma's relatives as a "yanacona," which harked back to the stigmatizing designations that turned native Andeans into immigrants in their own land in Toledo's time. The reference to—in effect, an accusation of—the status of one of Guaman Poma's family members as someone detached from the ethnic community cast a shadow over all of them as recent immigrants and potential outsiders to the Huamanga area. If not native to the area, the argument went, then Guaman Poma and his people were recent immigrants without land rights and, if making false claims to local lands, could be branded as impostors. That is exactly what happened: the tide of events now turned dramatically against Guaman Poma.

On March 23, 1600, in Huamanga and before the corregidor's deputy and justice official Pedro de Rivera, the Chachapoya leaders Domingo Jauli and Juan Sota accused Guaman Poma of falsely presenting himself as a cacique who called himself don Felipe; they claimed that he was instead a humble Indian named Lázaro. They charged that this "don Felipe/Lázaro" had secured a royal order to have the Chachapoyas' lands surveyed under false pretenses and that he had then failed to appear on the designated date at the Chiara site where the survey was to have been carried out. The municipal notary accompanying the survey team corroborated the Chachapoyas' claim.

As a result, Guaman Poma's doom was sealed. On December 18, 1600, the Chachapoyas' rights to Chiara were confirmed, and a criminal sentence was imposed on Guaman Poma. As condemned in the verdict, he was labeled an impostor of evil intentions, a "common Indian who, through deceit and trickery, called himself a cacique and was neither a cacique nor a person of rank, but yet he subordinated Indians so that they respected him as such."[8] He was sentenced to two hundred lashes to be administered publicly and condemned to two years of exile from the city of Huamanga. If he violated the conditions of the sentence, his exile would be doubled to four years. The costs of the suit, furthermore, were to be borne by him. On December 19 the sentence was proclaimed publicly in Huamanga.

Why had Domingo Jauli singled out Guaman Poma for criminal charges? Guaman Poma was clearly the most persistent of Jauli's adversaries as well as the most successful. Twice, Guaman Poma had traveled to Lima to appear before the Royal Audiencia, and on both occasions (September 10, 1597, and March 6, 1599) his land titles were confirmed. Under such circumstances, Jauli evidently could triumph over Guaman Poma only by convincing the authorities that Guaman Poma was an impostor—a fraudulent representative of the clan whose land claims had been unjustly upheld by the highest court in the viceroyalty. Getting Guaman Poma out of the way was tantamount to nullifying the claims he made on his own and his kinsmen's behalf.

Were the assigned corporal punishments and banishment unusual? Were they carried out? According to the *Siete partidas*, the fundamental legal code in sixteenth-century Castile that was carried over to Indies legislation, committing false actions and misrepresenting the truth of matters constituted some of "the greatest evils man can commit," and banishment or death was considered appropriate punishment. Although it is not known whether the corporal punishment was administered to Guaman Poma, his banishment surely was effected. Losing these legal battles and later acknowledging them only by allusion in the *Nueva corónica y buen gobierno*, Guaman Poma nevertheless let slip the observation, in discussing the pretensions and criminal activities of "common Indians," that he first became aware of such social disintegration—Andean society being turned "upside down"—when he began his travels, that is, "in the year that we left, of 16[0]0 and afterward."[9]

IN LUCANAS AFTER 1600: WRITING TO EXPOSE INJUSTICE

We know what happened to Guaman Poma after 1600, thanks to his letter of February 14, 1615, to King Philip III, announcing the completion of his *Nueva corónica y buen gobierno*.[10] Guaman Poma's experience during those post-1600 years was probably limited to the Lucanas region because the twenty-odd settlements and the majority of local colonial officials he names in his chronicle pertain to the province of Lucanas. He describes local events that span the years from 1608 to 1615, and he discusses noteworthy occurrences of the years 1611, 1612, and 1613. (He cites an inspection of the local priests and parishes in Lucanas as part of a general tour carried out in 1611, and he remarks that he had been imprisoned at the time for seeking to defend local Andean citizens whom he represented as an appointee of the colonial administration.)

It was during this period in Lucanas that Guaman Poma's artistic apprenticeship was carried out. That is, he worked for the Mercedarian friar Martín de Murúa, whose two manuscript chronicles of Inca history include more than a hundred drawings made by Guaman Poma. Murúa was working as a parish priest in the province of Aymaraes, located in the present-day department of Apurimac. (These settlements are highlighted in figure 10.5.) Guaman Poma's detailed account of Murúa's conflicts with the local native community, his discussion of local Andean governance in Yanaca (the native settlement where Murúa lived), and his mention of a score of traditional customs that were practiced there but prohibited by the Church point to his considerable acquaintance with that community. From recent investigations, we know that Guaman

Poma could not have worked with Murúa before 1596 and that his period of collaboration necessarily extended beyond 1600, which is when their artistic relationship developed.

Guaman Poma probably turned to the writing of *Nueva corónica y buen gobierno* at this time, inspired or enabled, in part, by his work with Murúa. Guaman Poma wrote his long prose text mostly in his semiliterate Spanish with occasional sections (unreadable to the king) in Quechua. His heavy reliance on pictures, particularly regarding the colonial abuse of the native population, reveals that he considered his drawings to be the most direct and effective way of communicating his ideas to the king and persuading him to take remedial action. Guaman Poma entreated the king to publish his book, insisting that it should be used to fulfill the pressing needs of instructing Spanish colonial officials in the proper conduct of their offices and ensuring the just treatment of the Andeans.

Guaman Poma had thus met his goal of giving Philip III an account of ancient Andean history from the beginning of time through the reign of the Incas and informing the monarch about the crisis in Andean society that was a result of Spanish colonization. Guaman Poma called his account of Andean history "new" not only because he denied the military conquest of Peru by the Spanish but also because his version of pre-Columbian history would be utterly without precedent to readers of the Spanish-authored histories of Peru then in print. That is, he presented an elaborate and complex cosmology weaving the dynasties of the Andean past into a Christian model of universal history and making the Incas not the first and only great Andean dynasty but the last one, succeeding the earlier royal dynasty of the Yarovilcas of Allauca Huánuco, from which he claimed descent.

With respect to the topic of good government, Guaman Poma attempted to show the king that colonial exploitation, wanton violence, and European diseases were bringing an end to Andean civilization: the traditional Andean social and administrative hierarchies were being dismantled, and the native Andeans were being exploited in the mines and in the countryside and went fleeing to the cities, where they engaged in the dissipated lifestyles of rogues and prostitutes. Meanwhile, the mixed-race *mestizo* population was increasing at an alarming rate due to miscegenation. As a result of all these phenomena, the ethnic Andean population was in sharp decline. The picture he painted, in short, was one of impending doom.

Having fashioned himself as a trustworthy adviser to the king, Guaman Poma depicts this role in a hypothetical interview, visualized as a face-to-face meeting with Philip III for which Guaman Poma's presentation of his chronicle, held here in his hand (see figure 10.9), is the written surrogate. As if his chronicle were an account of his merits and services (*relación de méritos y servicios*), which was the standard Spanish means for seeking the monarch's favor, Guaman Poma presents as his merits (his ancestors' aristocracy and deeds) his descent from the ancient Yarovilca dynasty that preceded the Incas and his grandfather's and father's service to the Incas as well as to the Spanish crown. As his services (his own service to the crown), Guaman Poma cites the sacrifice of his personal life and livelihood to survey colonial society, outline its abuses, propose its remedies, and submit his findings to the king. When he finished his beautifully illustrated book, Guaman Poma wrote a letter to the king, dated it February 14, 1615, at Lucanas, and traveled over the Andes to Lima to deposit his manuscript book for dispatch to Spain and the royal court in Madrid.

THE *NUEVA CORÓNICA Y BUEN GOBIERNO*: IN MADRID AND COPENHAGEN

Did Philip III personally receive and read Guaman Poma's book? Probably not, although the manuscript surely arrived at the Spanish royal court, where the manuscript book was acquired in the 1650s or 1660s by a Danish diplomat and collector of Spanish books who came upon it while ambassador to the court in Madrid. As a result, Guaman Poma's autograph manuscript arrived at the Danish royal court, and it has been part of the Danish royal collection of books and manuscripts, now located at the Royal Library of Denmark in Copenhagen, since the 1660s. The intrinsic interest of the nearly four hundred drawings no doubt ensured the work's survival, and its powerful anticlerical, anti-Spanish critique, attributing to the Spaniards in Peru endless cruelty and greed, all in pictures, must have served well the interests of the ideological war waged by the Protestant countries of northern Europe against the Roman Catholic countries of the south, especially Spain.

Did Guaman Poma believe, to the end, that writing his exposé to the Spanish king would serve the cause of justice and right the wrongs perpetrated against the Andean peoples? His near-final words in the book suggest that he was losing faith in that prospect: "There is no god and there is no king. They are in Rome and Castile."[11] We can read this to mean that Guaman Poma perceived a void: the powerful European authorities imposed in Peru to create a new social order and to bring Christian justice to the Andes were absent; they neither protected nor ensured the well-being of the Andean peoples materially, socially, or spiritually. Guaman Poma here reveals that he has given up hope for remediation, for himself, for the native populations, and for Peru itself. In fact, Guaman Poma's early occupation as a church inspector's assistant and in other low-ranking administrative offices, his failed legal disputes in claiming ancestral lands, and the final project of writing his book—pursued as his only avenue of social intervention when all others were closed to him—bespeak the precariousness of native Andean life under colonial

Figure 10.9. With the *Nueva corónica y buen gobierno* in hand, Guaman Poma imagines an interview with King Philip III. Guaman Poma, *Nueva corónica*, 975. *Source:* Courtesy of the Royal Library of Denmark, Copenhagen.

rule. Even more than the itinerancy of such a life, Guaman Poma's personal testimony reveals the ambiguities and internal contradictions of the colonial experience.

QUESTIONS FOR DISCUSSION

1. What do you think the greatest challenges would have been to the "cultural identity" of someone in colonial society, such as Guaman Poma, identified as an indio ladino? What might those challenges have been for a Creole (someone born in America of European descent and parentage) or a recently emigrated Spaniard?
2. Why do you think Guaman Poma would have put materials in his book (Quechua language texts, for example) that would be unintelligible to his designated reader, king Philip III of Spain?
3. What benefits and dangers do you think individuals from traditionally oral cultures, such as Guaman Poma, would have seen in the institution of alphabetic writing and the distribution of texts and documents made possible by printing?
4. How dependent do you think the missionary church would have been on native assistants for evangelization and the "extirpation of idolatries"?
5. What might be the major political, economic, and social consequences of a native community's forced migration and resettlement? What might be the effects on the individual as well as the community?

NOTES

1. Ann Wightman, *Indigenous Migration and Social Change: The Forasteros of Cuzco, 1570–1720* (Durham, NC, 1990), 54.
2. Felipe Guaman Poma de Ayala, *El primer nueva corónica y buen gobierno*, ed. John V. Murra and Rolena Adorno, Quechua trans. Jorge L. Urioste (Mexico City, 1980), 1104. Entire manuscript available online at the website of the Royal Library of Denmark, http://www.kb.dk/permalink/2006/poma/info/en/frontpage.htm.
3. Guaman Poma, *Nueva corónica*, 447.
4. Wightman, *Indigenous Migration*, 135.
5. Frank Salomon, *Native Lords of Quito in the Age of the Incas: The Political Economy of North Andean Chiefdoms* (Cambridge, 1986), 160.
6. Juan A. Zorrilla, "La posesión de Chiara por los indios chachapoyas," *Wari* 1 (1977): 49–64, at 59.
7. Ibid., 51, 57.
8. Ibid., 63.
9. Guaman Poma, *Nueva corónica*, 886, 918.
10. This letter is digitized and translated into English in Rolena Adorno, *Guaman Poma and His Illustrated Chronicle from Colonial Peru/Guaman Poma y su crónica ilustrada del Perú colonial* (Copenhagen, 2001), 79–86, and is available online at the website of the Royal Library of Denmark, http://www.kb.dk/permalink/2006/poma/info/en/front page.htm.

11. Guaman Poma, *Nueva corónica*, 1136.

SUGGESTED READINGS

For Guaman Poma's own writings, see the Royal Library of Denmark's online digital edition of the original *Nueva corónica y buen gobierno* manuscript (http://www.kb.dk/permalink/2006/poma/info/en/frontpage.htm), both for its 399 drawings and the transcription of its Spanish prose text, originally published in Felipe Guaman Poma de Ayala, *El primer nueva corónica y buen gobierno*, edited by John V. Murra and Rolena Adorno, Quechua translations by Jorge L. Urioste (Mexico City, 1980; reprint, 1992). For Guaman Poma's letter to Philip III announcing the completion of his work, see its Spanish transcription and English translation in Rolena Adorno, *Guaman Poma and His Illustrated Chronicle from Colonial Peru/ Guaman Poma y su crónica ilustrada del Perú colonial* (Copenhagen, 2001). Frank Salomon discusses the writings of Guaman Poma and his peers from the perspective of Andean categories of historical and cosmological thought interpreted under colonial circumstances in "Chronicles of the Impossible: Notes on Three Indigenous Peruvian Historians," in *From Oral to Written Expression: Native Andean Chronicles of the Early Colonial Period*, edited by Rolena Adorno (Syracuse, 1982) and "Testimonies: The Making and Reading of Native South American Historical Sources," in *Cambridge History of the Native Peoples of the Americas: Part 3: South America*, edited by Frank Salomon and Stuart B. Schwartz (1999). Rolena Adorno examines the visual and verbal compositional features of the chronicle and the meanings given by Guaman Poma to his work in *Guaman Poma: Writing and Resistance in Colonial Peru* (Austin, 2000). In *The Polemics of Possession in Spanish American Narrative* (New Haven, 2007), Adorno examines Guaman Poma's work in light of colonial reformist writings, specifically those of Bartolomé de las Casas.

The Americas Society's multiauthored *Guaman Poma de Ayala: The Colonial Art of an Andean Author* (New York, 1992) provides insights into Guaman Poma's art at the intersection of Andean and European traditions. The interdisciplinary volume *Transatlantic Encounters: Europeans and Andeans in the Sixteenth Century*, edited by Kenneth J. Andrien and Rolena Adorno (Los Angeles, 1991), discusses the political, economic, social, and symbolic forces shaping colonial Andean society and highlights Guaman Poma as a central source and subject. On the important topic of colonial migration and its impact on Andean society, see Ann Wightman, *Indigenous Migration and Social Change: The Forasteros of Cuzco, 1570–1720* (Durham, NC, 1990). For the forastero in literature, see the novel *Deep Rivers* by José María Arguedas, translated by Frances Horning Barraclough (Austin, 1978). For the complexities of religion and ritual in the post-Conquest Andean world, see Sabine MacCormack, *Religion in the*

Andes: Vision and Imagination in Early Colonial Peru (Princeton, 1991) and Kenneth Mills, *Idolatry and Its Enemies: Colonial Andean Religion and Extirpation, 1640–1750* (Princeton, 1997). Steve J. Stern's *Peru's Indian Peoples and the Challenge of Spanish Conquest: Huamanga to 1640* (Madison, 1982) and Karen Spalding's *Huarochirí: An Andean Society under Colonial Rule* (Stanford, 1984) examine the process of change in Andean society from pre-Columbian to midcolonial times, the former focusing on Guaman Poma's home territory and the latter on the province about which he had much to say at the end of his work. For an illuminating study of the vital yet conflictive role that indigenous adjuncts like Guaman Poma played in the Andean Christian church, John Charles's *Allies at Odds: The Andean Church and Its Indigenous Agents, 1583–1671* (Albuquerque, 2010) is indispensable.

ELEVEN

Ana de Vega

Seventeenth-Century Afro-Mexican Healer

Joan Bristol

After the turbulent Conquest era had passed, Spain's empire in the Indies underwent a long period of political expansion and socioeconomic transition. By the early seventeenth century, the crown imposed an extensive imperial bureaucracy to govern the empire, supported by the moral authority of the Roman Catholic Church. Its clergymen had evangelized millions of Amerindians, and they attempted to impose rigid orthodoxy over all Europeans, Amerindians, and Africans living in the empire. The principal institution policing the purity of the faith was the Holy Office of the Inquisition, centered in Mexico City and Lima. Despite the Church's apparent successes, clergymen found troubling and persistent signs that Amerindians and Africans continued clinging to pre-Christian religious beliefs, and all too many European settlers had lapsed into deviant religious practices. The Inquisition did not have jurisdiction over Amerindians, who were regarded as neophytes in the faith and not subject to its discipline, but the Holy Office vigorously prosecuted any Jewish converts (known as conversos) who clandestinely practiced their old faith, along with Old Christians guilty of sins such as bigamy, blasphemy, heresy, and one of the most serious forms of religious error, witchcraft. The Inquisition sought to ensure that the Spanish Atlantic remained essentially a Roman Catholic world.

For many Christians, religious deviancy remained a potent sign of Satan's presence in their world. To seventeenth-century Spaniards, the devil was not an abstract force but a very real, tangible presence in their world, and his mission was to undermine the good in society and replace it with evil. Satan tempted lesser men and women in the real world every day, leading to corruption and sin.

The forces of evil could also enter the world as demons or even take possession of individuals or physical objects in the natural world. The role of the Holy Office of the Inquisition was to stamp out any deviant religious beliefs and practices in the New World in order to combat the corrupting influence of the devil and his minions. Some acts of religious error were relatively minor affairs, but others, such as heresy and witchcraft, were extremely dangerous and had to be rooted out and extirpated. This was particularly important in the New World, where the millions of new Amerindian and African converts were so easily swayed by the devil's clever forms of deception and delusion. Even Old Christians could run afoul of the Holy Office and suffer the consequences of their corrupt behavior. In this way, the Inquisition served as the moral bulwark protecting fundamental moral values, and its judges had a responsibility to prosecute any deviant religious views that threatened the well-being of the broader society. Such attitudes were not present merely in the Spanish Atlantic, however; in the Salem, Massachusetts (in England's North American colonies) witch trials of 1692, twenty-eight people were executed or condemned by Puritan authorities.

In 1647 the Holy Office of the Inquisition in Mexico City took up the case of a free mulata *living in Puebla, Ana de Vega, who stood accused of witchcraft. Her problems began when a licensed physician proved unable to cure María Sambrano of a mysterious illness. The woman's desperate husband took her to Ana de Vega, a well-known healer, who diagnosed the cause of the illness as witchcraft, perpetrated by the woman's own daughter-in-law, Ana de Morales. María began to recover under Ana de Vega's treatment, and when her son, Francisco Sambrano, heard of his wife's alleged witchcraft, he became enraged and threatened to kill his wife. When Francisco had calmed down, his wife convinced him that she was innocent of witchcraft and instead blamed Ana de Vega for stoking her husband's anger against her. Although a social and racial inferior to the Sambranos, Ana de Vega's healing power gave her sufficient influence within the family to turn Francisco against his wife temporarily, but soon he denounced Ana de Vega to the Inquisition for curing without a license, committing fraud, and using witchcraft to divide his family. The Inquisition immediately began compiling its case against Ana de Vega, who fit the popular profile of a witch—she was single, of Afro-Mexican descent, lower class, and a faith healer. Church authorities often found such marginal social figures suspicious and thought that their dubious healing powers derived from some evil pact contracted with the devil or his minions. In the end, Ana de Vega defended herself by pleading that she was weak, ignorant, and stupid, with no real healing powers, but to no avail. The Inquisition ruled in favor of Francisco Sambrano and convicted Ana de Vega. This case indicates a great deal about the role of the Inquisition in policing public morals and also about popular notions of healing and social hierarchy that led the Sambranos and the Holy Office to turn against the suspicious mulata faith healer from Puebla.*

In 1647 a Spanish man named Juan Garcia Sambrano brought his wife, María Sambrano, from their home in Guexocingo to the city of Puebla, approximately twelve and a half miles away, "to cure her of a grave sickness."[1] The physician who treated her, Doctor Bartolomé Parejo, soon reached the limits of his expertise and stopped treating her "for not finding the quality (*calidad*) of the said sickness." He advised Juan and María to consult "a female healer of female indispositions (*achaques*) to cure her."[2] At that point Ana de Vega, a free mulatta who lived in Puebla, was called in. According to María, Ana de Vega diagnosed her illness as the result of witchcraft. The healer said that someone had sprinkled powders on María's body and that these were "so harmful that if she had drunk them she would not live [even] four days."[3] Ana treated the sick woman for a few days in Puebla and continued the treatment when María returned to Guexocingo, administering potions, ointments, and "other medicines," including several enemas.[4] In one of María's evacuations Ana found "a white thing like a little stick (*como palito*)" that she identified as a dead worm and claimed was a sure sign of witchcraft.[5] The healer revealed to María that a woman named Ana de Morales had bewitched her. This alleged culprit was María's daughter-in-law, the wife of her son Francisco Sambrano.

WITCHCRAFT IN COLONIAL MEXICO

Francisco Sambrano had not been present when Ana de Vega had treated his mother, and he was understandably alarmed when he heard news of Ana de Vega's diagnosis. He visited Ana de Vega in Puebla, hoping to find out more about his wife's supposed involvement in his mother's illness, and the healer repeated her allegation. Although Ana de Vega refused to reveal how she knew that Ana de Morales was to blame, Francisco believed the healer. He reported that he began "exclaiming against [his wife], [his wife's] daring, and the bad conscience in her conduct."[6] According to Francisco, Ana de Vega took advantage of his great fury to persuade him to buy powders and other objects from her that he could use to kill his wife. Francisco also planned to use the powders to kill Ana de Morales's parents, who he suspected had helped their daughter with the spell. His rage was not just a passing emotion. After he left Ana de Vega, Francisco proceeded to get rid of his property, according to him, even selling his herd of cattle for a lower price than it was worth. He claimed that he did this in order "to freely execute his intent, to commit the said murders."[7] He purchased a horse and hid some of his possessions in a ravine outside the city, presumably so that he could flee there after committing the murders. Reflecting on his actions later, however, Francisco concluded that he was "tricked by his suspicions, conceived against . . . his wife and her parents and by the credit that he gave to the . . . mulatto healer."[8]

Although Ana de Vega's words were enough to convince Francisco of his wife's guilt, he also received what seemed to be material evidence in support of her accusation. When Ana de Vega instructed Francisco to secretly look through Ana de Morales's belongings, he found a knot of hair in his wife's desk. Twisted in it was an object that he described as being "like intestine (*tripita*), dry with some stitches of *pita* [aloe fibers] sewn in it."[9] Ana de Vega lit the object on fire, and Francisco described how it writhed as it burned and how the healer shouted, "look at the said spell, how it is certain."[10] When Francisco found a packet of opium poppies (*adormideras*) and another packet that contained two objects "that seemed to be dried flesh" among his wife's possessions, Ana de Vega assured him that these, too, were part of the spell.[11] Hearing this, Francisco stormed off to confront his wife, "blind with anger and bile (*colera*) and indignation" because all that "the said mulata healer had affirmed" seemed to be even more certain.[12]

When Francisco finally confronted his wife, however, he heard a different explanation of the items he had found. Ana de Morales readily acknowledged that she owned these items. Yet she denied any wrongdoing. Instead, "with great tears and oaths, and exclamations that she made to heaven," Ana de Morales claimed that the whole story was a lie and that Ana de Vega had tricked Francisco into turning against her.[13] Francisco experienced a rapid change of heart after speaking with his wife. Persuaded of Ana de Morales's innocence and believing her allegations that Ana de Vega had manipulated him, Francisco went to the local commissioner of the Inquisition and accused Ana de Vega of curing without a license, committing fraud, and using witchcraft.[14] Ana de Vega was first imprisoned in the public prison in Guexocingo and was later placed in the secret prison of the Inquisition in Mexico City, where she spent six months as her trial for witchcraft unfolded.

HEALERS IN COLONIAL MEXICAN SOCIETY

The story of Ana de Vega illuminates the role of Afro-Mexican healers in colonial society and their relationships with other colonial residents. This story comes to us from an Inquisition case in which witnesses gave their descriptions of what they saw and experienced. The Inquisition investigated cases in which Catholics were accused of heresy—contradicting or acting against church doctrine—and the Mexican Inquisition was mainly concerned with offenses such as blasphemy, bigamy, and witchcraft, the crime of which Ana de Vega was accused. Inquisition files include denunciations of alleged criminals, witness testimonies, formal accusations, confessions or other declarations by the accused, inventories of the possessions of the accused, and the sentences for those convicted of crimes. Inquisition cases are especially useful for learning about people who did not produce firsthand written records, in this case including Afro-Mexicans. The different witness testimonies together provide a broad perspective on events and allow an understanding about witnesses' values, ideas, and even how they identified themselves in relation to others. Yet Inquisition documents must be analyzed carefully. Because of its nature as an institution meant to police and control the residents of New Spain, individuals appearing before this body, whether as accusers or as accused, must have chosen their words carefully for maximum effect. They may have wanted to convince Inquisitors of the guilt of those they accused, or (in the case of testimonies by the accused) they may have been advertising their innocence and trying to avoid harsh punishments such as whippings, public humiliation, separation from their property, and exile. Thus, thinking about Ana de Vega requires paying attention to the reasons that she, Francisco Sambrano, and other witnesses appeared before the Inquisition. It is also important to consider the motivations of these witnesses to tell the Inquisitors about particular events in particular ways. Even though Ana de Vega's Inquisition file is a highly mediated text, it reveals a great deal about Ana de Vega's work as a healer, the way that others valued that work, and the ideological framework in which residents of New Spain lived.

On the surface, Ana de Vega's experience with her clients seems to reflect Spanish ideals of social hierarchy. Because Spaniards believed that Native Americans and people of African descent were meant to serve them, it makes perfect sense that a mulatto healer was called to minister to a Spanish woman by tending to her bodily needs. Ana de Vega gave María an enema, applied ointments to her body, and examined her excretions. In other words, María's family literally regarded Ana de Vega as the appropriate person to call in situations that required getting one's hands dirty. On closer examination, however, it seems clear that Ana de Vega was not always in an inferior position in her relationship with María and her family. María, her husband, Juan, and her son, Francisco, deferred to Ana de Vega. They respected her diagnoses and followed her instructions closely, and they continued to do so even after Ana accused a member of their own family of witchcraft. Why did they place such great trust in a mulatto woman, supposedly inferior to them because of her ethnic background and class position? What prompted them to later change their minds and accuse her of witchcraft? What does this case explain about the opportunities, and the limits on these opportunities, that Afro-Mexicans had in New Spain?

Spaniards like María Sambrano and her family consulted healers for several reasons. One important motivation for consulting a healer was the lack of licensed medical personnel. Spanish men were the only people allowed to become physicians, and between 1607 and 1738, only 438 men earned medical degrees in Mexico. These men could not satisfy the medical needs of even the minority Spanish population of New Spain, much less the majority non-Spanish population.[15] Physicians and other licensed medical professionals (including empirics, who handled tasks such as pulling teeth, mending bones, treating hernias, and midwifery) had to be certified by the *Protomedicato Real*, established in Spain in the fifteenth century and in New Spain in the sixteenth century.[16] To be licensed, the Protomedicato required medical personnel to have *limpieza de sangre* (purity of blood), indicating lineage that was free from non-Christian background. The concept was originally developed in Spain to discourage mixing with Jews and Muslims; in the Americas it generally referred to people whose lineages were not mixed with African or Amerindian background. Although this rule was not always strictly enforced, particularly in the case of midwives, generally non-Spanish healers were not licensed to practice medicine, and many people in New Spain could not find doctors to consult. Even when doctors were accessible, many families could not afford the fees that physicians charged and used healers as their first recourse.

The Sambrano family was not forced to consult Ana de Vega because of a lack of access to licensed doctors or lack of money, however, since they did consult a physician initially. In this case, the Spanish physician's failure to cure María played a role in her family's decision to consult Ana de Vega. This decision is not surprising given the state of colonial medicine. Theoretically, there was a sharp distinction between the scientific or academic medicine used by physicians and the remedies used by healers. In practice, however, most men and women saw both trained physicians and healers as viable, and sometimes equally effective, options when they were ill or otherwise afflicted. The scientific medicine that physicians practiced was based on humoral theory, developed by the ancient Greek physicians Hippocrates and Galen, which held that illness could result from an imbalance in the four basic humors and could be cured with drugs or foods that had the opposite qualities of the humors. For instance, chickpea broth was a treatment for epilepsy, which physicians diagnosed as being caused by too much black bile, one of the humors. Black bile had cold and dry properties that the broth, categorized as hot and wet, would balance out.[17] Other techniques for restoring the humors included cupping (creating suction on the patient's skin), purging, inducing vomiting, and bleeding.[18] These techniques did not reliably heal sick people and in many cases probably made them sicker. Thus, the Sambrano family's decision to move on to Ana de Vega after consulting a licensed physician was a common one.

Ideas about ethnicity may also have helped create a demand for Afro-Mexican and other non-Spanish healers. Spaniards defined Africans, Amerindians, and their descendants as unrefined, irrational, and close to nature. The idea that non-Spaniards were more in tune with the natural world may have led many to believe that natives, Africans, and their mixed descendants had special abilities to cure.[19] This would have been particularly appealing when Spanish medicine failed. Thus, many structural factors combined to make healers essential to colonial society and its residents.

In addition to these more structural issues, María and her family may have trusted Ana de Vega because she presented herself in an authoritative way as an expert healer. According to María, Ana de Vega diagnosed her immediately and without any hesitation after her examination. The healer's speed and certainty must have reassured María and her husband and given them hope. Their experience with the healer was certainly different from the experience with Dr. Parejo, who had not even been able to diagnose María's illness, much less treat her. Furthermore, when María asked Ana de Vega how she knew that Ana de Morales had bewitched her, María claimed that the healer provided her with descriptions of successful cures she had worked. In effect, Ana de Vega presented her experience as a credential in the absence of the kind of official qualifications that licensed physicians could supply. According to María, Ana even claimed that she had cured another of Dr. Parejo's patients when he and some "*comadres*" (in this case, probably female healers or midwives) had incorrectly diagnosed a sick woman as pregnant. Instead, Ana had contended that the woman was bewitched. This diagnosis was confirmed when, after taking Ana de Vega's remedy, the sick woman discharged three demons with horns.[20] Offering a final reason for María to trust her, Ana de Vega claimed that Ana de Morales had sent a black woman to Puebla to buy the witchcraft that she used against María from indigenous sellers. According to the healer, she had paid them fourteen pesos.[21] Such accounts of successful treatments, as well as Ana de Vega's detailed information about Ana de Morales, must have increased María's confidence in the healer and her diagnosis.

The material results that Ana de Vega produced must also have contributed to the family's decision to trust her. First, Juan and Francisco both reported that María felt better after Ana had administered the enemas.[22] Second, Francisco claimed, his belief that his mother had been bewitched was bolstered by Ana de Vega's assertion that the worm found in María's evacuations was proof of witchcraft.[23] Even Ana de Morales agreed that this evidence had given Ana de Vega's accusation against her an air of truth, although she disagreed with her conclusions.[24] Finally, finding the suspicious objects in his wife's belongings sealed Francisco's belief in her guilt. Granted, some of Francisco's misgivings about his wife predated Ana de Vega's involvement with the family. He reported that several years earlier, Ana de Morales's parents had poisoned him in order to stop him from taking their daughter away and that he had been sick for three years after this incident.[25] This certainly made it easier for him to believe in his wife's guilt. According to Francisco, however, it was the evidence that Ana de Vega led him to, and her interpretations of this evidence, that confirmed his suspicions of Ana de

Morales. He trusted the healer because she produced what seemed to him unimpeachable proof of his wife's betrayal.

The Sambrano family gained hope from Ana de Vega's treatments, and perhaps María's improved health was due to Ana de Vega's cures as well. Ana de Vega also gained benefits from her work. Her most tangible reward was money. Curing was an occupation, and healers practiced their art for profit. Yet Ana de Vega also received other, less tangible benefits from being a healer. The trust that she gained from her clients translated into respect, as María and her family accepted her diagnoses, used her potions and ointments, and consulted her even after María returned to Guexocingo from Puebla. This trust translated into authority over others' actions as well, since Francisco decided to kill his wife and her family based on his belief in the healer's abilities. Such respect and authority may have made curing a desirable profession for non-Spaniards. This authority was short-lived, however, and ultimately it was Ana de Vega, rather than Ana de Morales, who was punished for witchcraft. How did Ana de Vega go from being respected as a healer to being convicted as a witch and a fraud?

ANA DE VEGA, WITCHCRAFT, AND THE INQUISITION

One reason for her change in status from "healer" to "witch" had to do with the way the two activities became blurred in the minds of colonial people. Although the crown and Church defined "witchcraft" and "healing" as distinct activities, most men and women probably saw them as points on a continuum of methods capable of regulating the body and its place in the world. The ability to identify witchcraft was complicated by the lack of a single definition, since the terms *hechicería* and *brujería* were used to explain a diverse group of activities, including demonic involvement, divination, and cases in which individuals used powders and herbs to control others. A fourteenth-century Inquisitors' manual used in Mexico claimed that the use of "philters" (magical potions) and certain divination techniques could be heretical if the user had an explicit connection with the devil. According to the manual, however, there were different degrees of diabolic involvement, and they were not all equally heretical.[26] In the end, decisions about unacceptable activities rested with individual Inquisitors who interpreted cases and issued edicts, and these definitions were not always consistent.[27] Ideas about the difference between healing and witchcraft were also influenced by individual situations. Patients like María Sambrano and their families were probably more concerned with recovering their health than they were with the crown's and the Inquisition's definitions of acceptable curing techniques. Often they were ready to overlook suspicious curing techniques, at least for a time, if they experienced relief from their symptoms or were given hope of improvement.

Another answer to the question of how the Sambrano family lost their trust in Ana de Vega and began thinking of her as a witch rather than a healer lies in the relationships among the parties involved in the case. The authority that Ana de Vega earned from curing María was based on fragile foundations, and the Sambrano family's trust in the healer crumbled quickly when it was tested. María testified that she had misgivings about Ana de Vega's diagnoses from the healer's first visit, claiming that she was often "raising objections" in her exchanges with the healer, asking questions about how she arrived at her diagnoses. In fact, it was María's questions that led Ana de Vega to boast about other cures that she had performed. These were then used as evidence in the case against her. María also claimed that she had been worried that Ana de Vega was putting María's son, Francisco, in danger by stirring up his anger against his wife. María said that she and her husband had begged the healer to replace the lethal powders that she had sold Francisco with useless ones.[28] Since María's doubts did not stop her from continuing the treatments, it may well be that she emphasized her suspicions in retrospect to make herself seem less complicit in the affair. Nonetheless, even by taking María's testimony with a grain of salt, it seems that the seeds of suspicion against Ana de Vega were sown early in her relationship with the Sambrano family.

The fragility of Ana de Vega's authority was made manifest when Francisco believed his wife's protestations of innocence over Ana de Vega's accusations. Ana de Morales claimed that she had legitimate reasons for possessing the objects that Francisco had found in her desk. She explained that the piece of "intestine (*tripita*)" that had been burned was the umbilical cord of their son, which had been cut and saved by María Sambrano herself. The two pieces of dried flesh were relics of a Carmelite friar who was venerated as a saint in Querétaro. The poppies had been purchased as a cure for illness.[29] These objects were the kinds of materials that could be used for witchcraft, yet Francisco believed his wife's explanations that they were beneficial. Ana de Vega's authority was not strong enough to withstand Ana de Morales's denial.

The loss of the Sambrano family's trust put Ana de Vega in a far more vulnerable position than she had been in before she met them. When Ana de Vega lost her influence over María Sambrano's family, she was put under the scrutiny of the Inquisition, an institution that did not recognize the authority she had accrued through healing. The crimes of which Ana de Vega was accused fell into two categories. First, witnesses claimed that she was a liar and a trickster who pretended to cure but in fact did not have the proper skills. In his denunciation, Francisco explained that Ana de Vega did not have the "science, or knowledge, of a healer and doctor (here he used the female term, *médica*)."[30] He claimed that "with-

out having the letter of examination of the Protomedicato of this kingdom nor the license of the Justicia Real to be able to [practice medicine],
with approval of the doctors, of the said city of [Puebla de] Los Angeles,"
she "goes curing, and tricking, the sick, taking their money unjustly."[31]

The second set of accusations against Ana de Vega followed from the
first. According to Francisco, she was not merely ignorant. Instead, he
claimed that she was a witch who was in league with the devil. He
offered several pieces of evidence. First, Francisco explained that his desire to kill his wife and her family "could not have been a natural thing"
and that Ana de Vega had controlled him and stopped him from exercising his free will.[32] Francisco's indigenous servant, Pablo, provided another piece of evidence. As Pablo later recounted in his own testimony,
when he had accompanied Ana de Vega back to Puebla from Guexocingo, they had seen two natives walking toward them. The healer predicted
that one of them would take off his hat and turn his face away from them.
When this happened, Ana de Vega explained to Pablo that the man was a
witch and that she had cured someone whom he had bewitched. That
was why he took off his hat to her.[33] According to Francisco and other
witnesses who repeated the story, however, this prognostication itself
was evidence of witchcraft. Francisco and others also offered Ana de
Vega's reputation as evidence, claiming that she was well known in Puebla as Anica the sorcerer (*bruja*). This reputation was well founded, according to Francisco, since Ana de Vega lived like a witch. Not only had
she sold him lethal powders to use on his wife and in-laws, her house
was full of suspicious materials. He claimed that bunches of hair hung
from the rafters and that jars of remedies were everywhere.[34] Finally,
according to Francisco, Ana de Vega's appearance provided the final
evidence that she was a witch. He testified that "the said mulata, has such
bad appearance and countenance in her face, and reversed eyes, and
blond hairs, that her ugliness [indicates that she is a] witch, as this de-
nouncer presumes and understands, by the things that he saw in her
house."[35] Perhaps the "blond hairs" appalled Francisco because a blond
mulatta challenged ideas about how non-Spaniards were supposed to
look—the possibility that non-Spaniards could have European-like physical characteristics upset the racial hierarchy of New Spain, in which
members of different racial groups were supposed to be easily identified
and kept in their places. Francisco's assertion that he knew Ana de Vega
was a witch because of how she looked certainly drew on a larger ideology that held that moral difference could be read on the body through
racial and other physical signs. Essentially, Francisco was arguing that if
Ana de Vega looked like a witch, she must be one. Francisco was familiar
with commonly accepted definitions of witchcraft, and he cast his testimony in these terms in order to bolster his case.

Ana de Vega understood popular ideas about witchcraft as well, as
we see in her attempts to explain her activities in a way that might be

acceptable to inquisitors. In her first response to the accusations against her, Ana de Vega claimed that many were lies. She denied that she had said that María was bewitched, and she said that Francisco had looked through his wife's things on his own initiative, not on her recommendation. She did agree that she had cured those who were bewitched and explained in detail how she made and used her remedies, probably hoping to establish herself as an expert healer. She claimed that she did not use witchcraft herself, however. According to her, she "had not cured with things of the demon but rather with things of God."[36]

Eventually, however, given the amount of evidence against her and the fact the inquisitors were proceeding with the case, Ana de Vega realized that she would make her predicament worse if she continued to claim innocence. She capitulated, confessing that she had diagnosed María's illness as witchcraft, tricked Francisco into believing in his wife's guilt, and sold Francisco the powders and objects that he planned to use to kill his wife and her parents. This confession may have been strategic, since it saved her from torture.[37] Ana de Vega used the language and concepts of the Inquisition strategically as well, to defend herself. She tried to excuse her actions by portraying herself as weak and ignorant, in contrast to the cunning and evil person that the other witnesses had described. She then reversed Francisco's accusation that she was in league with the devil by claiming that she herself had been tricked by the devil into accusing Ana de Morales.[38] In her final testimony, Ana de Vega claimed that she was, in fact, not a skilled healer at all. Instead, she said, she treated her clients "by guess . . . asking the Indian herbalists what is good for this or that sickness," and she "does not know the devil nor has any pact with him but rather with God and the Holy Virgin."[39] Finally, Ana de Vega claimed that the only "stupidity (*torpeza*)" that had inspired her was a desire for money and "to have enough to sustain herself."[40] Her tactics were unsuccessful, however, and in the end Francisco's version of events prevailed.

Inquisition cases are rich sources of information because they contain multiple perspectives on events. This richness of perspectives also makes it very difficult to piece together a single story from Inquisition testimonies, since each party had his or her own motivations for presenting the story in particular ways. It is impossible to know whether to believe Ana de Vega's story or Francisco's. In the end, the inquisitors believed both Francisco's accusation and Ana de Vega's final confession, and they found her a "heretic, witch, apostate of our holy Catholic faith; excommunicated witch, invoker of the demons, with vehement suspicions, [of a] pact with them, liar, perjurer, thief by way of healer, instigator, and concealer of accessories in her evil."[41] On March 30, 1648, she was punished in a public auto-da-fé. She received two hundred lashes and was exiled from her home in Puebla.

CONCLUSION

Neither Ana de Vega nor her case was particularly unusual in seventeenth-century Mexico. Several hundred Afro-Mexicans were brought to the Inquisition and accused of witchcraft during the sixteenth and seventeenth centuries. Of these, only twenty-six were, like Ana de Vega, convicted of the crime.[42] Yet the number of accusations shows us that Afro-Mexicans were involved in practices, many associated with healing, that others might have found suspect. This case also demonstrates the meaning of curing for Afro-Mexicans themselves and about the benefits they hoped to receive. The most immediately obvious benefit that Ana de Vega and other Afro-Mexican healers received was monetary. Although they could not hope to become wealthy, successful healers might support themselves. Less tangibly but just as importantly, they might also gain honor in the form of status and reputation. Healers were important members of their communities who were valued and relied on in times of trouble. While Afro-Mexicans were denied many opportunities and had few protections because of their social position, work as healers gave them opportunities to gain profit and even power. Yet the case against Ana de Vega also reveals that Africans and their descendants occupied profoundly vulnerable and unstable positions in New Spain's society, even within the context of the non-Spanish population.

Finally, the case of Ana de Vega reveals how power and authority were constructed under Spanish colonialism. The way that Ana de Vega and others like her used curing techniques illustrates the sometimes fluid and contingent nature of power and authority in New Spain. Official hierarchies seemed to recede into the background when Spaniards entrusted their bodies to black and mulatto healers. These hierarchies were quickly reasserted, however, when Spaniards felt threatened by these healers and their unofficial forms of authority. In many ways, Ana de Vega and others like her stood at the nexus of order and disorder in colonial Spanish America. Her clients hoped she would bring order, in the form of health, into their lives. Yet they also feared the potential for disorder that might come from placing their bodies in the hands of an Afro-Mexican woman. When their fears became too great, they turned to the authority of the Church and state, as embodied in the Inquisition, to reassert their status and social standing.

QUESTIONS FOR DISCUSSION

1. Do you think Ana de Vega was guilty of witchcraft? Why or why not?
2. What were the goals of the different people involved in this case when they testified at the Inquisition? Focus on one of the people

involved and find examples of ways that he or she chose specific words or included specific information to influence inquisitors' opinions.

3. What did Ana de Vega gain from her work as a healer? What did she lose? What did members of the Sambrano family gain and lose from their relationships with Ana de Vega?

4. Would Ana de Vega have come in contact with any of the other people whose biographies appear in this book? Under what circumstances might she have met these people, and what kinds of relationships might they have formed?

5. Does this seem like an event that could have happened only in the past? What are the similarities and differences between the world described in this case and the time and place that you live in?

NOTES

Parts of this chapter were previously published in "From Curing to Witchcraft: Afro-Mexicans and the Mediation of Authority," published in the *Journal of Colonialism and Colonial History* 7, no. 1 (2006): 1–37. Reprinted with permission by The Johns Hopkins University Press. Copyright © 2006 Joan Cameron Bristol and The Johns Hopkins University Press. Parts of this chapter were also previously published in *Christians, Blasphemers, and Witches*, published by the University of New Mexico Press. I thank the University of New Mexico Press for permission to republish these sections.

1. Archivo General de la Nación (hereafter AGN), Inquisición 429.4 1647, 220.
2. Ibid.
3. Ibid.
4. Ibid., 212.
5. Ibid., 229v.
6. Ibid., 212v.
7. Ibid., 213.
8. Ibid.
9. Ibid., 213v.
10. Ibid.
11. Ibid., 214.
12. Ibid.
13. Ibid.
14. Ibid., 214v–215.
15. John Tate Lanning, *The Royal Protomedicato: The Regulation of the Medical Professions in the Spanish Empire*, ed. John Jay TePaske (Durham: Duke University Press, 1985), 139. For population figures, see Gonzalo Aguirre Beltrán, *La población Negra de México* (1946; Mexico: Ediciones Fuente Cultural, 1989), 219.
16. Guenter B. Risse, "Medicine in New Spain," in *Medicine in the New World: New Spain, New France, and New England*, ed. Ronald L. Numbers (Knoxville: University of Tennessee Press, 1987), 13–15; Lanning, *The Royal Protomedicato*, 17, 175–83.
17. George M. Foster, "Relationships between Spanish and Spanish-American Folk Medicine," *Journal of American Folklore* 66, no. 261 (1953): 203.
18. J. Richard Andrews and Ross Hassig, introduction to *Treatise on the Heathen Superstitions That Today Live among the Indians Native to This New Spain* (Norman: University of Oklahoma, 1984), 31–32. María del Carmen Anzures y Bolaños, "Johannes Steinhoffer, médico y misionero jesuita en el noreste de Nueva España en el siglo XVIII," in Juan de Esteyneffer, *Florilegio medicinal*, ed. María del Carmen Anzures y

Bolaños (1712; reprint, Mexico: Academia Nacional de Medicina, 1978), 43–45; Foster, "Relationships," 202–3.

19. Healing powers and witchcraft are often associated with unknown or foreign elements and, although blacks and mulattos, even natives of Africa, were quickly acculturated into Spanish society and lived among other colonial residents, they were constructed as marginal in the Spanish system. Julio Caro Baroja claims that people tend to associate mystical powers with those they consider inferior because they come to be seen as more "natural," and Solange Alberro uses Caro Baroja's idea to explain why Spaniards went to indigenous healers. Julio Caro Baroja, *Vidas mágicas e Inquisición* (Madrid: Taurus, 1967), 1:49; Solange Alberro, *Inquisición y sociedad en México 1571–1700* (México: Fondo de Cultura Económica, 1988), 300. Cases in which Spaniards paid or forced natives and Afro-Mexicans to take peyote in order to find lost things or find missing people (including runaway slaves) suggest that they may have thought that these people had special attributes. They may also not have wanted to take the peyote themselves. For examples, see AGN, Inquisición 339.89 1620; AGN, Inquisición 356 (sin expediente); AGN, Inquisición 356.160 1626; AGN, Inquisición 366.27 1629; AGN, Inquisición 486.76 1621.

20. AGN, Inquisición 429.4 1647, 229v–230.

21. Ana de Vega's claim reflects Laura Lewis's assertion that blacks and mulattos were usually intermediaries between Native Americans and Spaniards in matters pertaining to witchcraft. Ana de Vega also claimed that she herself had obtained many of the materials that she used in curing from "indios herbolarios," although it is possible that she said this in order to shift the blame for her supposed "witchcraft" onto others. Lewis, *Hall of Mirrors: Power, Witchcraft, and Caste in Colonial Mexico* (Durham, NC: Duke University Press, 2003), 153–58.

22. AGN, Inquisición 429.4 1647, 220.

23. Ibid., 213v.

24. Ibid., 224.

25. Ibid., 212v.

26. Nicolau Eimeric and Francisco Peña, *El manual de los Inquisidores*, trans. Francisco Martin (Barcelona: Muchnik Editores, 1983), 83–84.

27. Luis Sala-Molins, introduction to *El Manual de los Inquisidores*, trans. Francisco Martin (Barcelona: Muchnik Editores, 1983), 14.

28. AGN, Inquisición 429.4 1647, 229v.

29. Ibid., 224–24v.

30. Ibid., 214v.

31. Ibid. The Protomedicato Real, which replaced the Protomedicato General, had been established in New Spain just the year before, in 1646. It was intended to reform the institution. Francisco may have emphasized Ana de Vega's unlicensed status hoping that inquisitors would take the charge of practicing without a license more seriously in light of the recent changes in the Protomedicato.

32. Ibid., 215.

33. Ibid., 218v.

34. Ibid., 213.

35. Ibid., 215. Ugliness was presented as a suspicious characteristic in other cases as well. See the testimonies about Leonor de Vargas, suspected of witchcraft, who was described as "fat and ugly-faced (*fea de rostro*)" (AGN, Inquisición 296.3, 18).

36. AGN, Inquisición 429.4 1647, 250v.

37. Ibid., 268v.

38. Ibid., 267v.

39. Ibid., 268v.

40. Ibid., 271v, 280.

41. Ibid., 278.

42. *Abecedario de los Relaxados Recosiliados y Penitenciados en la Nueva España*, Huntington Library Manuscript Collection 35096.

SUGGESTED READINGS

For information on the Mexican Inquisition, see Solange Alberro, *Inquisición y Sociedad en México 1571–1700* (México: Fondo de Cultura Económica, 1988). Noemí Quezada has written about healers and the court in "The Inquisition's Repression of *Curanderos*" in *Cultural Encounters: The Impact of the Inquisition in Spain and the New World*, edited by Mary Elizabeth Perry and Anne J. Cruz (Berkeley: University of California Press, 1991).

For ideas about witchcraft, see Laura Lewis, *Hall of Mirrors: Power, Witchcraft, and Caste in Colonial Mexico* (Durham, NC: Duke University Press, 2003) and Martha Few, *Women Who Live Evil Lives: Gender, Religion, and the Politics of Power in Colonial Guatemala* (Austin: University of Texas Press, 2002).

Information about colonial Mexican medicine can be found in John Tate Lanning, *The Royal Protomedicato: The Regulation of the Medical Professions in the Spanish Empire*, edited by John Jay TePaske (Durham, NC: Duke University Press, 1985) and Guenter B. Risse, "Medicine in New Spain," in *Medicine in the New World: New Spain, New France, and New England*, edited by Ronald L. Numbers (Knoxville: University of Tennessee Press, 1987).

A good source for general information on Afro-Mexicans is *Black Mexico*, edited by Ben Vinson III and Matthew Restall (Albuquerque: University of New Mexico Press, 2009). This volume gives a sample of articles by authors who have done larger studies on Afro-Mexican history.

Part III

Reform, Resistance, and Rebellion, 1740–1825

When the last Habsburg king of Spain, Charles II, died childless in 1700, it took fifteen years of bloody conflict to ensure the succession of Philip V, the French Bourbon claimant to the throne. As the new king surveyed his devastated patrimony, the pressing need for commercial and fiscal reforms became obvious. The transatlantic trade with the Indies had reached its nadir, and contrabandists plied the Caribbean and Pacific with impunity. Policymakers in Madrid desperately searched for ways to reinvigorate commercial ties with the colonies and increase revenues for the empty royal coffers. At first, their effort to revive Spain and its empire involved attempts to curb smuggling, curtail the power of the Church, modernize state finances, establish firmer political control within the empire, end the sale of bureaucratic appointments, and fill the depleted royal treasury. The loss of Havana in 1762 to the British during the Seven Years' War produced even more sweeping reform measures.

During the reign of Charles III (1759–1788), the crown began dispatching royal inspectors (*visitadores*) to various parts of the Indies to gain information and begin the process of making administrative, fiscal, commercial, and military reforms. By 1750 it had ended the sale of appointments to all high-ranking colonial offices and began replacing Creoles with younger, well-trained, peninsular-born bureaucrats. Officials in Madrid also created two new viceroyalties in regions of South America famous for being centers of contraband trade: New Granada in 1739, and the Río de la Plata in 1776 (see map 3). In many areas of the empire the crown also sent out a series of intendants (responsible for administration, fiscal affairs, justice, and defense) who linked provincial magistrates with audiencias of the major cities. The government also shored up local defenses, enlarged the fleet, and built up the regular army and local militias. To pay for these costly reforms, colonial authorities raised taxes and created royal monopolies for the sale and distribution of key goods such as tobacco. Finally, the crown ended the transatlantic fleet convoys in 1740 and allowed individual licensed merchant vessels from Spain to trade with South America while keeping the fleet system for New Spain. Although this remedy increased colonial commerce, the Madrid government went further and allowed free trade with the empire between 1778 and 1789. It was a time of sweeping imperial changes.

Under the leadership of its chief minister, Sebastião José de Carvalho e Melo, Marquis of Pombol, Portugal also initiated reforms designed to tap the resources of its chief colony in Brazil. Like his counterparts in Bourbon Spain, Pombol sought to increase tax yields, secure colonial defenses, and expand commercial ties between colony and metropolis. A particular concern was Portugal's reliance on Great Britain for manufactured goods needed in both the homeland and Brazil as well as the large quantities of British contraband goods entering the colony. Pombol promoted Portuguese industries to curtail dependency on the British and to supply Brazilian markets. Moreover, to regain control over the colonial trade, the chief minister abandoned the fleet system in 1765 and chartered three monopoly companies (which allowed only limited foreign participation) to trade with Brazil. He also revamped the colonial administration in Portugal and Brazil by establishing a new royal treasury in 1761 to centralize accounting, collect taxes more efficiently, and control expenditures. While these innovations had some impact on renovating the colonial ties with Brazil, Pombol's fall from power in 1777 limited their long-term effectiveness. Finally, lower gold production by 1750 and the slow decline of the sugar economy in Brazil also curtailed the success of the reform effort.

While the Bourbon reforms in Spanish America and Pombol's innovations in Brazil resulted in increased revenues and enhanced colonial commerce, they also produced a number of specific grievances in the Indies. In some areas, this unrest exploded into violent upheavals (such as the Rebellion of the Barrios in Quito in 1765, the Comunero Revolt in New Granada in 1781, the Túpac Amaru and Túpac Katari revolts in the Andes in 1781–1783, and the Inconfidencia Mineira in Minas Gerais in 1788). Nevertheless, Spain's and Portugal's rule continued unchallenged in most of the regions of their empires until Napoléon's army invaded the Iberian Peninsula in 1807 to attack Portugal, a close ally of Great Britain, the French emperor's most bitter foe.

The Portuguese king, dom João VI, along with the entire court (nearly twelve thousand people), fled in a British fleet to Brazil, where he ruled from 1808 to 1820. The king made profound changes in the colonial relationship, such as initiating free trade for Brazil, removing restrictions on manufactures, and granting British subjects extraterritorial rights. These changes culminated in his decision to raise Brazil to the status of a kingdom coequal with Portugal in 1810. When João VI reluctantly returned to Portugal in 1820, he left his son and heir, Pedro, in Brazil to rule as regent. After the Lisbon government reduced Brazil to colonial status and recalled Prince Pedro, Pedro declared Brazil's independence, winning it

Map 3. The Viceroyalties of Peru, New Granada, and the Río de la Plata and the Viceroyalty of Brazil in the late eighteenth century.

with minimal bloodshed in 1822. The prince became the country's first emperor, Pedro I.

After his invasion of Spain, Napoléon forced its king, Charles IV, to abdicate on May 6, 1808, and his heir, Ferdinand, to renounce his rights to the succession. Napoleon then placed his elder brother, Joseph, on the throne, which led to a popular uprising against the French usurper. This tumult in Spain prompted a serious constitutional crisis in both Spain and the Indies, where many believed that without a legitimate monarch, power reverted to the people. As a result, Creole elites felt emboldened to establish provisional *juntas* in many major cities of the empire, usually to rule until a legitimate monarch was restored. Local Spanish authorities crushed many of these juntas, and others fell later to the Spanish armies sent by Ferdinand VII when he returned to the throne in 1814. Nevertheless, bloody wars for independence ensued that ultimately led to the independence of Mexico and Central America in 1822 and of South America by 1825.

As part of their reforms, the Spanish government allowed citizens born out of wedlock to purchase an edict of legitimation (*cédula de gracias al sacar*) that erased the "defect" of their birth. These edicts also allowed people to buy the honorific title of "don" and permitted those of mixed racial ancestry to purchase "whiteness." A wealthy mulatto merchant from Panama, Pedro de Ayarza, sought to purchase a cédula to raise his own social status and that of his three sons. Although the crown granted "whiteness" to one son, officials in Madrid denied it to Ayarza and the two younger ones, which demonstrates the difficulties involved in negotiating race and status in the uncertain world of the Spanish Indies. Problems of gender also plagued citizens in eighteenth-century Spanish America, such as a female merchant from Quito, Victorina Loza. Quito's economy had experienced a long decline as textile imports from Europe eroded the market for locally produced woolen textiles, leading to an outmigration of males seeking better economic prospects elsewhere. Resourceful women such as Loza took advantage of the opportunities provided by the relative shortage of men in the city to become merchants, a male-dominated job in most of the Indies. Nevertheless, Loza needed a husband to travel the difficult overland trade routes. After her first spouse died, she married a younger man, Francisco Xavier Sánchez de la Flor. Although this union proved to be an unhappy one, the tough and practical Victorina Loza remained a successful merchant, even in the uncertain and declining economy of Quito.

The great reforms of the eighteenth century had little impact on the life and loves of Captain José Antonio da Silva, who lived in the rural parish of Santana in the province of São Paulo, Brazil. Although da Silva married a woman who was his social equal, he also carried on sexual affairs with women beneath his station and fathered several illegitimate children. Despite contravening Church prohibitions against concubinage, da Silva's philandering did little to disrupt the prevailing social hierarchies of his day. Moreover, his slave mistresses actually reaped some tangible benefits from their relationship—wealth, higher status, and freedom for their children. In this way, Brazilian elites managed to perpetuate rigid hierarchies but also inadvertently allowed some social mobility. The lives of many ordinary people were swept up in the larger events of their day. A rumored slave revolt in 1795 in Buenos Aires, for example, allegedly led by the city's small French community, prompted local authorities to prosecute Juan Barbarín, a merchant apparently guilty only of believing in the principles of liberty and equality within the colonial social order. Barbarín was little more than an innocent pawn punished by colonial government officials who panicked at the prospect of revolution.

The controversial life story of Agustin Agualongo illustrates that not all poor people, slaves, and Amerindians flocked to the rebel banner during the independence struggles in the early nineteenth century. Although a humble painter, Agualongo became a major commander of forces loyal to Spain in the southern Colombian state of Pasto. Agualongo and his followers fought the insurgent armies of Simón Bolívar and his generals until his capture and execution in 1824, indicating the strength of loyalist sentiment in the region. Agualongo and his followers fought to gain a more inclusive nation that would protect their political rights and their traditional lands. Finally, a slave woman, Angela Batallas, used the prevailing political rhetoric of the independence era to demand her rights: she challenged the Great Liberator, Simón Bolívar, to grant her the freedom that was guaranteed in the public pronouncements of the Creole governments of the time. The turbulent years of reform, resistance, and independence allowed some of these colonial subjects, such as Angela Batallas, some additional opportunities for negotiating a more favorable place for themselves within society.

TWELVE

Pedro de Ayarza

The Purchase of Whiteness

Ann Twinam

Although historians have written a great deal about the military, fiscal, administrative, and commercial reforms in the Spanish Empire, they have paid less attention to the Bourbon social agenda. The crown issued a series of landmark pieces of legislation dealing with questions of birth and race in the Indies, beginning in 1778 with the Royal Pragmatic on Marriages. This edict attempted to bolster the colonial social hierarchy by giving parents more direct control over their children's marriage choices. Whereas the Church had generally taken a strong stand in favor of spousal choice, even in cases of unequal marriages, the pragmatic effectively allowed parents to appeal to royal officials, who could prevent the union if either the potential bride or groom had a "defect" of race or birth. In contradiction to the pragmatic sanction that impeded mobility, in 1795 the monarchy published a price list of favors called the gracias al sacar *that encouraged those with "defects" to move upward. Colonists who were illegitimate might purchase an official edict of legitimation (*cédula de gracias al sacar*) that erased the stain of their birth; people of mixed racial ancestry might purchase "whiteness" or even buy the honorific title of "don."*

These seemingly divergent policies concerning social and racial mobility stemmed from the piecemeal and occasionally haphazard nature of the Bourbon reform effort. They also embodied the long-standing Spanish tradition of allowing the king to alter rank, status, or heritage even when it involved an individual's birth or race. Such negotiations of race, class, and ethnicity were delicate matters that had to be scrutinized and adjudicated carefully by the Cámara of the Indies, a subgroup of the Council of the Indies, on a case-by-case basis.

A crucial principle guiding members of the cámara was the fundamental tension between status in the private world of individuals (family, kin, and intimate friends) and the public sphere (everyone else). Issues of race and illegitimacy were not necessarily immutably fixed at birth; a child might be known to be illegitimate or racially mixed by the private world of family, kin, and friends, but in the wider society this fact might remain secret. As a result, individuals could "pass" as legitimate or even as white and maintain their "honor" (public reputation) and social status despite any private "defects" in their birth or racial status. Passing also occurred when individuals who were illegitimate or racially mixed were able—given their family connections, wealth, education, and public service—to persuade outsiders to accord them the status of legitimates or whites in spite of their private reality. In this sense, questions of honor and status were negotiated and sometimes even contested, challenged, lost, or regained over time. Since honor was situated in the public sphere, a petitioner had to provide substantial evidence in a request for a cédula that he or she was seen by the community as a person of character. By granting an edict of legitimation or whiteness, the cámara was validating honor already acknowledged by the wider colonial society. Through its legislation such as the Pragmatic on Marriages and the cédula that legitimated and whitened, the crown sought to mediate and promote social order.

*The case history of Pedro de Ayarza gives a compelling example of the tensions that emerged over questions of race, honor, and status in the late eighteenth century. Ayarza was a well-respected Panamanian merchant with connections throughout the region, but he was also a dark-skinned man (*pardo*) of dubious ancestry. Nevertheless, prominent officials felt free to stay at his home; he was a captain in the local pardo militia regiment, and his wealth and commercial connections were unquestioned. In those ways he had informally "passed" in that he was often accepted and treated as if he were white.*

Ayarza was also a caring father. When his eldest son, Josef Ponciano, was denied a degree at the university in Bogotá because he was a pardo, the merchant began a legal process lasting from 1795 to 1807 to purchase official whiteness and the honorific title of "don" for himself and his three sons. Arguing that his many services to the crown, social standing in Panama, considerable wealth, and the virtues of his children (who were well educated) outweighed his defect, Ayarza spent a weighty sum on lawyers' fees to obtain whiteness through a cédula de gracias al sacar. Many officials in the Indies supported his request, while others feared the consequences of allowing the sons of a pardo merchant to obtain university degrees and, in the case of Josef Ponciano, to practice law. In the end, the members of the cámara declared Josef Ponciano "white" and a "don," but they failed to approve a change in status for Pedro de Ayarza and his other two sons, Antonio Nicanor and Pedro Crisólogo. This odd compromise left the family divided, with one member white and the others pardo, and demonstrates the difficult process of negotiating ethnicity, legitimacy, and honor in the closing decades of Spanish colonial rule.

Panamanian Pedro de Ayarza was a solicitous father, willing to sacrifice much for the welfare of his three beloved sons, Josef Ponciano, Pedro Crisólogo, and Antonio Nicanor. As they grew up he "observed . . . [their] great inclination toward a literary career," and so he decided to provide them with the best education possible.[1] He sent them away from their Portobelo home to attend a boarding school in Cartagena. When his eldest, Josef Ponciano, reached the age of twenty-one, he traveled with his twelve- and nine-year-old brothers to Santa Fe de Bogotá. He attended the university while they studied at the *colegio* of San Bartolomé. It was only in 1794, when Josef Ponciano was ready to graduate, that the family's troubles as well as this story began. Even though he had attended classes for three years, the university registrar and then the viceroy refused to let him graduate. The reason: the Ayarzas were pardos, and the Laws of the Indies and a royal cédula of 1765 specifically denied permission for racially mixed persons to receive university degrees.

And so father Pedro de Ayarza began a quest, from 1795 to 1807, to purchase whiteness for himself and for his sons. What Pedro could not know as he began this twelve-year campaign was that it would ultimately end with his family divided. His eldest son would eventually be deemed white and a don, while Pedro Crisólogo and Antonio Nicanor would remain pardos, as would Pedro himself. To understand how this outcome occurred is to probe critical years in the development of late-eighteenth-century Bourbon policies toward race, and particularly toward racial whitening. Tracing the principal players in the Ayarza quest for whiteness—Pedro and his sons, their friends and acquaintances in Panama and Bogotá, New Granadan viceroys and officials, and the Council and Cámara of the Indies as well as the minister of justice and King Charles IV—reveals intriguing variants on how pardo-ness was conceptualized together with the limits and extent to which it might be negotiated as the colonial era drew to a close.

The first question that naturally arises is: Why would a pardo from Panama ever believe that he could successfully plead with a Spanish monarch to make him white? Pedro had several excellent reasons to forward such a request. First, a historic Hispanic mentality had always validated the monarch's power to alter an individual's rank or heritage. Second, at the same time that Pedro petitioned, the crown issued a 1795 *arancel*, or price list of favors that might be purchased through a process known as gracias al sacar. One provision made it possible for pardos to buy whiteness while another set a price for the purchase of the honorific title of "don." Third, there were precedents of others who had been whitened. Understanding this background provides some framework for Pedro's initial optimism.

From the beginning of the Spanish state, monarchs had been able to alter rank and heritage, including race. As one Spanish historian succinctly characterized it, "The king counts more than blood" (*Mas pesa el rey que la sangre*).[2] Underlying the royal ability to transform status was a mentality that accepted a distinction between a person's private reality and any publicly constructed reputation. Since the monarch was superior to positive law, he could literally change an individual's public and legal persona. Throughout the centuries Spanish kings had declared persons who were *conversos* (of Jewish origin) to be Old Christians, transformed nonnobles into nobles, changed those born illegitimate into legitimates, and converted the nonwhite into white.[3] Echoes of the medieval origin of this bargain resounded when Pedro begged the king as "universal father" to demonstrate "clemency" toward "those vassals who demonstrate proper conduct in service to God and the monarchy."

By the end of the eighteenth century, the king was active only at the end of the process. Petitioners purchasing a gracias al sacar followed a well-defined routine.[4] They had to provide documentation concerning their birth, evidence of their service to the king, and letters of reference and recommendations from distinguished citizens. These were forwarded, sometimes with additional comments, by royal officials in the Americas—in the case of Pedro it was the viceroy of New Granada. The packet arrived at the Council of the Indies, which then sent it to the Cámara of the Indies, an elite subgroup composed of council officials who handled issues of patronage, or gracias. Within the cámara, attorneys (*fiscales*) first summarized the submitted documentation. They usually recommended approval or denial and then submitted a report to the cámara, which met and discussed the application. If the cámara's verdict was favorable, it was forwarded to the minister of the Indies and the monarch, who usually—but not always—gave final approval for the issuance of the official decree (cédula). In Pedro's case, he went a step further: he engaged an *apoderado*, a legal representative in Spain, to keep him informed of developments and to facilitate the movement of his case through bureaucratic channels.

Although the cámara had issued gracias al sacar for centuries, it was only in 1795 that a royal decree publicized, detailed, and expanded those privileges as well as set prices to be charged in the Americas.[5] In the case of whitening, the arancel fixed a price for *quinterones* (those of one-fifth mixed race) of 800 reales while, somewhat inexplicably, the presumably darker-skinned pardos paid a lesser 500 reales "for the dispensation of [that] quality." Another new provision charged 1,000 reales for purchase of the title of "don," an honorific that carried with it the assumption that the bearer was white, legitimate, and a person of honor. In a backhanded way, "don" proved to be another avenue for those who were legitimate but racially mixed to advance socially because those who received it were automatically considered white and persons of honor.

Certain provisions of the 1795 decree—for example, the granting of legitimations—were part of a Hispanic tradition of published and purchasable gracias reaching back to the fifteenth-century beginnings of the

Spanish state. These included the 244 eighteenth-century American legitimations explored in *Public Lives, Private Secrets*.[6] Others, such as whitening or the award of the title of "don," had only rarely been granted and had never been codified in a price list before 1795. This gap is notable because cámara officials appeared to have been surprised by some of the provisions in the 1795 legislation; they had apparently not been involved in either its compilation or composition.

On one level this may not be surprising, for in bureaucracies it is not uncommon for some officials to write legislation and others to enforce it. In this case, since the gracias al sacar was a moneymaking measure, bureaucrats in the treasury (Contaduría General) listed and priced the gracias to be sold. The result was that officials in the Cámara of the Indies had to deal with the social and racial consequences of a 1795 decree that either contradicted or altered their current policy. In the case of legitimations, the decree facilitated purchase by the offspring of adulterers or of priests even though the cámara had an established policy of denying such requests.[7] In the case of whitening or purchase of the title of "don," *camaristas* had to figure out how to award privileges that had rarely been granted and never before been institutionalized in a royal decree. Since Pedro's case started in 1795, when officials began to figure out their response, and extended to 1807, when some decisions were finally crystallized, it provides unique insight into the ways that imperial bureaucrats at a number of levels reacted to provisions concerning whitening and bestowal of the status of "don."[8]

It is notable that even though cámara officials had seldom officially erased an individual's defect of pardo-ness prior to 1795, they had implicitly done so on a few occasions, one of which bore directly on the Ayarzas' case. This was a ruling issued in 1765 after don Cristóbal Polo, a mulatto, had graduated from the university in Bogotá and had tried to practice law in Cartagena. When local lawyers protested, royal officials reviewed the case and decided that Polo's father's service in defense of that city and his own legal abilities were sufficient cause to admit him to the bar. Their decision additionally reveals how, with university graduation and admission as a lawyer, don Pablo informally leaped over discriminatory and social barriers. Even though no official cédula of whitening or title of don was ever issued, Polo's education and profession meant that he was thereafter considered to be white and was commonly to be addressed as "don."

Even though royal officials had decided in favor of this Cartagena lawyer, they had also issued a 1765 decree that his case should "not serve as an example" for other petitions. Officials ordered that henceforth the university in Bogotá should prohibit those ineligible by statute—presumably including illegitimates and the racially mixed—to enroll. That prohibition had later been violated when the eldest Ayarza son attended classes. Ironically, father Pedro de Ayarza tried to flip the 1765 decree because he cited it not as a prohibition for granting a university degree but as a precedent that such exceptions had already been made. Additionally, he admitted that the publication of the 1795 arancel for gracias al sacar had "inspired [him] to ask for this favor." And so it was within this context of Janus-faced precedents and ambiguous legislation that Pedro de Ayarza began to document his own accomplishments and those of his sons.

FIRST PETITION, 1795–1797

When asking for gracias, it was mandatory to demonstrate service to the king and the state. Pedro de Ayarza's first application, in 1795, provided a list of relevant activities. For twenty years he had served as a captain in the pardo militia, he had personally subsidized his militia company, he had never collected any of the salary due him, and he had managed the finances of the local parish church as well as the Franciscan monastery. A man of means and one of Portobelo's most prominent merchants, he was married, and all three sons were legitimate. Yet a knowledgeable observer might have noted what he had not done—although his wealth more than qualified him, he had never held local public office, almost certainly given that he was a pardo.

Documentation of Pedro's service brought another group into the gracias al sacar process—friends and notables to testify in his favor. From Pedro's perspective, it was essential to round up the most prominent witnesses to support his argument. Some of these no doubt testified because his patronage was valuable, others likely were personal friends, and some were advocates for his sons. Such recommendations were largely formulaic: a notary would take a prepared witness list and go from one person to the next, asking a series of questions crafted to elicit the sought-after answers. There are two aspects, however, inherent in this common type of colonial documentation that have often been underestimated. First, many witnesses did not follow the formula and give the pat or obvious answer—instead, their own authentic voices and comments sometimes emerged. Second, witnesses customarily used such testimony to send coded or implicit messages that went beyond the obvious affirmation of the facts. Cámara officials proved particularly alert to such transmissions. In Pedro's case, witnesses not only confirmed his service and wealth but also demonstrated the degree to which the Ayarzas were accepted by the white elite and thus the extent to which a gracias al sacar might not disturb the social and racial status quo.

Some of the highest officials in Panama and Colombia rallied to support Pedro's petition. In Portobelo, don Lorenzo Corbacho de Espinosa y Albares, the royal treasurer, noted that Pedro was a respected merchant—not an inconsiderable achievement for someone who was a pardo. Long-distance merchants had to lend and borrow money for extended periods, which meant that they had to be men of confidence and trust. These qualities were attributed to white merchants who were men of honor and thus denied to the racially mixed who lacked status. The treasurer confirmed, however, that Pedro was trusted by the commercial elites because "the merchants of Panama, Cartagena and other ports . . . consign to him with the greatest confidence." Cartagena merchant don Tomás Andrés Torres agreed. He observed the "lack of subjects . . . in Portobelo" of "equal circumstance" and noted that Pedro handled "all the business of that province . . . his intervention not only is useful to commerce and its individuals but necessary."

On a more personal note, the Portobelo treasurer, don Lorenzo, testified that Pedro received the "general applause . . . of all the persons of distinction of this city." His comments served to reassure royal officials that Pedro already informally enjoyed some of the privileges of whites, so his upward mobility would not disturb local notables. The royal official who oversaw Portobelo's mail service also validated Pedro's social acceptance. He noted that "the governors and all the other subjects of the first order without the least objection had visited and frequently visit [Pedro's] house." Another indication of this near-elite status was that when distinguished persons such as the archbishop of Nicaragua and the army brigadier passed through Portobelo, they lodged with the merchant.

Pedro de Ayarza's fine reputation extended beyond his home in Panama to the viceregal capital in Bogotá. Particularly telling here was how he was able to enlist Bogotano elites to support the whitening of his son, Josef Ponciano. Early in the case, the potential for whitening this eldest son became a particular focus of cámara officials. They seem to have been most impressed by the enthusiastic support accorded this university student not only by his professors but also by some of the most important people in the viceregal capital. A lawyer of the audiencia of New Granada, for example, recalled that he had known Josef Ponciano since his school days in Cartagena, where he had earned the "highest esteem because of his manners" and where he had been treated with "respect by the highest subjects." The lawyer added that his cousin, who happened to be the governor of Panama, had given him "fervent recommendations" concerning Pedro's eldest son.

Witnesses sent coded messages not only concerning the Ayarzas' social acceptability but also concerning their race. One of the few negative voices was that of the director of studies at San Bartolomé, who had been the first to deny Josef Ponciano's graduation. He made it clear that the Ayarzas did not have fair skin or straightish hair; they did not look white. When the official referred to Josef Ponciano's attempt to graduate, he mentioned the prohibitions of the 1765 cédula and added that it "seems to exclude . . . mulattos, which quality is notorious in this pretendent." This remark is notable because in other gracias al sacar cases, when petitioners were whiter looking, this factor worked to their advantage. Appearance did not apparently improve the chances of the Ayarzas.

Rather, when witnesses commented on the Ayarzas' race, it was to weigh it as an unfavorable "quality" that could be dismissed, given that it was counterbalanced by positive virtues that merited peer treatment. When audiencia justice don Francisco Xavier de Ezterripa praised Josef Ponciano's "good conduct," for example, he stated in reference to appearance that "in spite of this quality he has made himself deserving of the general esteem, and he is distinguished in civil treatment with those who are considered persons of the superior class." Don Josef Rey, a Bogotá lawyer who had known the university student for three years, praised his "irreprehensible conduct" that clearly demonstrated those "zealous principles of education that since childhood have inspired him." He concluded that Josef Ponciano was "deserving (in spite of this characteristic) of the greatest attentions that could be given in this place." Such enthusiasm was seconded by don Pedro Groot, the royal treasurer in Bogotá, who observed that Josef Ponciano had "enjoyed in this city the esteem of the most prominent and notable subjects who, aware of his good talents, do not disdain from consulting with him and favoring him, washing away whatever fault . . . of his birth." He added that the manner of the eldest Ayarza son more than made up for any "defect that could be noted" and that he was treated with "distinction and appreciation." One of his former teachers even awarded him the title of "don" prematurely in referring to Josef Ponciano in his testimony.

While the elites of Portobelo and Bogotá had considerable praise for Pedro and for his elder son, they were less specific about the virtues of the two younger boys, then thirteen and sixteen. Yet one of their professors at San Bartolomé had noted that all three brothers had won the "esteem of the most prominent persons" because of their "proper conduct," "modesty," "good education," and "courteous and Christian behavior." And so with these and a number of similar recommendations, Pedro's petition was forwarded through the viceroy in Bogotá to the peninsula for a decision by the Cámara of the Indies.

How did Spanish officials respond to this barrage of information? It is telling that when the document first arrived in July 1795, the cámara fiscal wrote a note in the margin that the price list for gracias al sacar charged 1,000 reales for "don" and 500 for dispensation of pardo. He did this even though Pedro had not asked to be whitened but rather to purchase the title of "don." Officials seemed aware that this was one of the first post-1795 gracias al sacar cases and so it might set some precedent for whitening in the Americas. The reviewing attorney was not sympathetic to Pedro Ayarza's petition. He applauded what he considered to be the "just opposition" of university officials and the viceroy who had prohibited Josef Ponciano's university graduation. He recommended that the cámara deny Ayarza's petition given that it ran against the "spirit of the law . . . and the cédula of 1765."

Such a negative recommendation did not augur well for full cámara review of the application, for camaristas usually agreed with the fiscal. This time, however, their first response was cautious. They acted as they often had in petitions for legitimation when the issue was unclear. They did what administrators usually do, that is, they delayed and asked for additional information. In this instance, they sent a request to the viceroy in Bogotá for more facts from the university concerning the Ayarza brothers.

When Viceroy José de Ezpeleta responded in May 1796, he forwarded a packet of even more laudatory letters of recommendation. Josef Ponciano's professors at San Bartolomé sent an unambiguous message: they hoped that his "good conduct and virtue would have its reward" given the "commendable personal characteristics of this individual." Such comments seem to have impressed the lawyer at the audiencia level in Bogotá because he recommended that the viceroy write a covering letter fully supporting Ayarza's petition. It is likely that Pedro never knew that this was one of the first, but not the last, times that various bureaucrats at different levels would support his petition, even though this favorable solution would never be carried out fully.

This time the stumbling block proved to be the viceroy in Bogotá. He agreed in his forwarding letter with the numerous witnesses who had testified to the "honor and excellent conduct" of Pedro Ayarza and of his older son. He also admitted that university officials as well as his own audiencia attorney had no problem in whitening Josef Ponciano. The viceroy was not as enthusiastic about the two younger Ayarzas, and he suggested that given their ages, it was too early to know how they would turn out.

Viceroy Ezpeleta then expanded the case beyond the personal situation of the Ayarzas, considering potential consequences on imperial policy. Specifically using the metaphor of the gatekeeper, he noted the "inconveniences" that might result from "opening the door for all others of the same quality that are in the same situation." These, if they also were of "good conduct," might apply for the "same dispensation." He also questioned the effect of the whitening cédula: if Josef Ponciano was dispensed from being a pardo, he apparently could "aspire to the offices and occupations" of whites; if he could not do so, "the gracias would be unfruitful." Since the viceroy was an accomplished bureaucrat, he only raised these issues and came down on neither side. He concluded that he had provided the requested information and left the making of higher policy decisions to his superiors.

When this letter reached Spain, the cámara's reviewing attorney noted the favorable recommendations as well as the cautions raised by the viceroy. He came decisively down on the side of the latter and recommended

yet again that the cámara deny the Panamanian's petition. Such a repeated denial was particularly ominous. Yet, in a surprising move, the
cámara still seemed unwilling to dismiss the case, perhaps again because
it was one of the first, and this was an issue they needed to resolve. And
so they resorted to an uncommon tactic, one employed only when they
were confused about what to do. They asked the secretaries of the viceroyalties of New Spain and Peru to comb their respective archives and
look for precedents where whitening had been granted. The secretaries
discovered two examples. One was from the Philippines, where in 1780
Dr. don Francisco Borla de los Santos, a racial mixture of Sangley and
Indian, had successfully applied to graduate from the university in Mani-
la even though he was a *mestizo asiático.*

Although the other example did not involve graduation from a university, it struck closer to the core issues at the heart of the Ayarza case. It
concerned a 1783 petition in which Bernardo Ramírez, the fountain keep-
er of Guatemala City, had asked to be treated as white given his many
documented services to the crown. In his case, royal officials had wa-
vered between the "fatal consequences" that might result when the
"Spaniards and Americans of distinction" heard of his mobility and their
desire to reward a subject who had shown "zeal, care, and love" that was
worthy of "remuneration and recompense." They decided against whitening but suggested that he be awarded a medal or militia post.

Both the Guatemalan as well as the Ayarza cases highlighted the contesting functions of the cámara as it represented the Spanish monarchy
and state. On one hand, as agents of the king the cámara dispensed a
gracias with almost medieval characteristics given the monarchical function to enhance the public status of deserving vassals who had served the
king and the state. On the other hand was the more contemporary, almost sociological concern of camaristas that local elites would be alienat-
ed if the state promoted social and racial mobility for those at the margin.
It is no accident that after the revolts of the 1780s (Túpac Amaru, the
Comuneros), cámara officials proved particularly solicitous of local feelings. The large majority (70 percent) of these Indies officials had served in
the Americas and were keenly aware of rising social and racial tensions.[9]

In one sense the Ayarza case proved to be a benchmark precisely
because Pedro and his sons were the perfect example of a new cohort that
was seeking upward mobility into late-eighteenth-century elite circles.
The Ayarzas met two elite standards: they were legitimate, and they were
rich. Only one aspect, the fact that they were pardos, legitimized the
official and informal discrimination leveled against them. Added to this
was the not inconsiderable variable in their favor that a flood of recommendations from elites in Panama and Colombia suggested that the
cámara's decision to whiten in this case might be a popular rather than an
unpopular choice. Faced with these conflicts, the cámara refused to make
the Ayarzas "dons" or to whiten Pedro and his two youngest sons. How-

ever, they ruled that for Josef Ponciano "the quality of pardo" should be "extinguished," and they agreed that he could graduate from the university. The ministry of justice and the king approved the ruling in January 1797, and the royal decree was published on February 15.

It is intriguing to note that in the archival *legajo* (bundle) that contains this documentation, there was a rough draft of a cédula that not only whitened Josef Ponciano but also his two younger brothers. An attached note then commented that the privilege was only for the eldest. It is unknown whether this was a mix-up in communication or whether the cámara had seriously considered whitening all the brothers. Pedro may again have come closer than he would ever know to attaining his goal. By 1797 he was not yet a "don," and the graduation of his remaining sons from the university remained in limbo. Josef Ponciano, however, was both a university graduate and white.

SECOND PETITION, 1799–1803

Back in Bogotá, the road was not entirely smooth for don Josef Ponciano, who, having graduated from the university, began an apprenticeship to practice as a lawyer. By 1800 a debate erupted between the two most senior lawyers in the viceregal capital as to whether the Panamanian should be admitted to the bar. One argued that many attended the university, received degrees, and yet never became lawyers; thus, don Josef Ponciano's graduation did not inevitably mean that he should be permitted to practice. The other lawyer disagreed. The fiscal of the audiencia asked the cámara to rule on what turned out to be a most substantive issue, the one raised originally by the viceroy: What did whitenings really do?

Meanwhile, in Panama, Pedro was again collecting letters of recommendation, planning for the graduation of his two younger sons, and nurturing his own hopes to become a "don." His second application, in 1802, detailed his additional services to the king, including his more than twenty-eight years as captain of the pardo militia. Twice he had subsidized Portobelo troops when supplies had failed to arrive and there was no money in the royal treasury since English pirates had held up the subsidy from Lima. He was yet to collect any salary from the state.

Pedro also argued that his younger sons, Pedro Crisólogo and Antonio Nicanor, were worthy, noting that he had "all the satisfaction that a father [might have] in the[ir] accomplishments." His sons, he rhapsodized, "have known how to honor the white hairs of their father" and were "worthy of [his] paternal love." He reminded officials of their "legitimacy," "good conduct, application, and literary progress," and asked that they receive "equal grace" to graduate from the university and that he and they might enjoy the "distinction of don." Pedro then tried a

father-to-father approach with the monarch: "I leave to the high consideration of Your Majesty what would be the feelings of a father reproached
by his two younger sons" given that "he had asked for the royal grace of
Your Majesty for the eldest." He exclaimed: "What would be the heart of
a father in not wanting to see his two youngest equally rewarded, for
[following the] example of the eldest, they have filled the desires of their
father in the attainment of such honorable inclinations."

And so Pedro's dream entered the bureaucratic chain yet again. It
rested first in the hands of the fiscal and viceroy in Bogotá, who forwarded it without comment to the fiscal and Cámara of the Indies. This
time, the reviewing lawyer's recommendations to the cámara divided the
Ayarza case into three parts: the two younger sons, Pedro, and the
Bogotá problems of Josef Ponciano.

Although the fiscal approvingly noted the "conduct" and "progress"
of students Pedro Crisólogo and Antonio Nicanor, he did not recommend that they receive university degrees. Instead, he concluded that
they were of an "age [where] they could begin another career and the
knowledge they had accumulated could serve them in whatever employment." He then expanded this decision to include all pardos, arguing that
they should not become lawyers given that occupations in agriculture
and commerce were "more similar to their condition and were of the
greater private and public usefulness." The question does arise, since
fiscales were invariably lawyers, if at least part of his reluctance concerning the Ayarzas was to prevent pardos from entering his own legal profession.

The fiscal's negativity also encompassed Pedro de Ayarza, for the
reviewing official was not impressed by his additional service to the
state. Even if he deserved some accolade, the cámara lawyer concluded
that he should be "rewarded in [some] other way." The official was especially disapproving of Pedro's desire to purchase the title of "don," complaining that such requests "confused the castes with the whites." The
Ayarzas were not total losers, however, for when it came to enforcing the
royal cédula that granted whiteness to Josef Ponciano, the fiscal agreed
that it should carry the full force of law. He recommended that the
cámara order that Josef Ponciano be permitted to practice as a lawyer and
that he should be called "don."

Just as in the first application, camaristas proved more sympathetic to
the Ayarzas than the fiscal did. They agreed that Josef Ponciano could be
a lawyer and a "don." The cámara, however, now seemed to be as much
concerned about Ayarza family unity as about pardo mobility. Camaristas worried about the "discord that might result from brothers finding
themselves in such different states of quality." And so, in July 1803, they
overruled the fiscal and decided to whiten Pedro's two younger sons. Yet
again, the Ayarzas may have never known how close they came to their
desired goal. In a rare reversal the next month, the ministry of justice and

the king overruled the cámara and refused to approve the whitenings, although they agreed that Josef Ponciano could be a lawyer and a "don." So the stage was set for Ayarza's third petition.

THIRD PETITION, 1804–1806

This time Pedro did not delay long—after all, by now his two youngest sons, Pedro Crisólogo and Antonio Nicanor, were twenty-two and twenty-five years old. In his 1804 repetition he asked the king to "receive with benignity the desires of these youths" to pursue a career even if "it would not be as glorious as Augustus, Demosthenes, and a thousand others equally disgraced by their [humble] birth, but useful to the public good." When in February 1805 Bogotá viceroy Antonio Amar forwarded the application, he noted "the same circumstances as the previous ones."

It was more than a year later, in August 1806, before the cámara fiscal reviewed the application one more time. He reminded camaristas that it had been denied in 1803 and added that it had been placed in the Contaduría General "with the others." This was an important development: apparently, the king and minister of the Indies had now ordered the cámara to table any applications concerning whitening. As the fiscal explained, the state needed to decide "as a general point if it was suitable or not to dispense such gracias and distinctions to the pardos and what in the first case ought to be conceded." Such a "resolution" needed the development of "necessary rules" so as to place pardo applications in a "common system." The fiscal also reminded the cámara of the opposition that had arisen at the University of Caracas when Lorenso María Bejarano had been whitened.

It seems unlikely that the camaristas needed any prodding to remember the Venezuelan reaction to the Bejarano case as well as to the 1795 gracias al sacar, given the howls of protest that had erupted from local elites. Venezuelan notables had overwhelmed officials with predictions of the dire consequences that would result if local pardos could purchase whiteness.[10] Feelings had run so high that the governor of Maracaibo had threatened an *Obedezco pero no cumplo* (I obey, but I do not comply), the rarely issued temporary veto of an imperial action deemed too dangerous to implement. In this case, he refused to publish the whitening provisions of the 1795 decree.[11]

Even given the order for administrative tabling and the Venezuelan situation, the cámara decided to give the Ayarzas another chance. They had been sensitized by the 1803 reversal of their decision to whiten the younger sons, however, and camaristas tended to retreat to conservatism when they had been overturned. So this time, they relinquished any decision making. Instead, they simply passed the documents up the administrative chain, noting that it would be "convenient to make all known to

His Majesty . . . so that he might decide what would be his royal will."
The response of the monarch proved to be equally enigmatic, for in December 1806 the cámara received a two-word reply: "Como parece," or
"As it seems." Since the 1803 denial was presumably to stand, the cámara
tabled the Ayarza petition with the others.

FOURTH PETITION, 1807

Six months later, the final Ayarza petition—a letter written by Pedro's
Spanish apoderado, don Manuel Antonio de Echevarria—arrived at the
Cámara of the Indies. He queried whether the opaque monarchical decision was valid since "the resolution was not clear on what point" the
decision had been based. He no longer sought to make Pedro a "don" but
pleaded for the future of the two younger Ayarzas. Noting that Pedro
Crisólogo and Antonio Nicanor had finished their university studies, he
pointed out that it would be a "sad thing to see all their work lost." He
again brought up the issue of family unity, reminding the cámara of the
"dissension" and "deformity" that would result from brothers in "such
different states of quality." He reminded the king that he had used his
"supreme authority" in granting such a gracias to don Josef Ponciano,
and he begged for "equal grace" for his brothers.

This petition arrived at the cámara in July 1807. By now the camaristas
had been rebuffed twice by their superiors, and they did not hesitate.
They ordered the case to be "united with the other cédulas," and so it sat
in limbo. Yet, as Napoléon marshaled his troops for the Spanish invasion
that would come the next year, events not only in Spain but also in the
Americas may well have opened up dramatic new options for the Ayarzas.

CONCLUSION

The case of the Ayarzas reveals how far one man willing to expend unlimited amounts of money and demonstrating enormous determination
might travel to overcome popular and official racial barriers at the end of
the colonial era. There were many times when Pedro came close. His
quest highlights both confusions as well as contradictions of disparate
players on varying levels. In his case, local elites rallied to support whitening, especially for the clearly gifted Josef Ponciano, yet the furor raised
by local elites elsewhere eventually spilled over to contaminate the Ayarza case and doom a favorable outcome. Back in Spain, camaristas also
had to confront their traditional roles as dispensers of gracias to worthy
petitioners altering status with their informed understanding of such al-
terations in the Americas. Their problems were only magnified by the
indecision of the highest policymakers, at the level of the monarchy and

the ministry of justice. What is clear in this confusion is that petitioners such as the Ayarzas, their friends and colleagues, the cámara, and the king and his highest officers were looking at issues of quality and of race with new eyes, even as the forces of revolution and independence mobilized to change the paradigm forever.

EPILOGUE

How did those transformations brought by independence change the lives of the Ayarza brothers? Did the family remain divided now that Josef Ponciano was white and a lawyer while his brothers Pedro Crisólogo and Antonio Nicanor remained pardos and unable to graduate from the university? Only recently, with the power of Google, has it become possible to find tantalizing digital traces concerning the later history of these brothers.[12] Josef Ponciano eventually left his law practice in Bogotá and settled as a merchant and lawyer in Lima; in 1833 he served on the Peruvian Supreme Court. Even though Pedro Crisólogo was not transformed into a white, he still used his university education to his advantage, for he became a priest, an occupation usually forbidden to pardos. Eventually he attained the prestigious post of vicar of his hometown of Portobelo, Panama. Antonio Nicanor served as an officer during the independence wars and became a "hero" recommended for promotion to Bolívar. In 1841 he was the representative of the city of Portobelo in Panama's first attempt to secede from Colombia. It appears that near the end of his life, Josef Ponciano returned home to Panama and reunited with his brothers. At least an 1839 notice that a judicial tribunal was now established on the isthmus listed a Dr. Josef Ponciano Ayarza as one of its first judges. Three years later, a Bogotá newspaper noted that the spot needed to be filled, given the death of the holder. While Josef Ponciano certainly benefited from his whitening to obtain the highest judicial posts, the education of his brothers combined with their changed world also permitted them significant opportunities for success.

QUESTIONS FOR DISCUSSION

1. Identify the varying groups involved in the Ayarza case. Explain their different attitudes toward the petition. Why were their views similar or different? Which groups were more influential in effecting the eventual outcome?
2. Discuss those ways that the personal situation of the Ayarzas reflected broader political, social, and racial trends characteristic of late colonial Spanish America.

3. If you could visit Colombian, Panamian, and Spanish archives and find out more about the Ayarzas and the ultimate disposition of their case, what information would you like to know? Why?

4. What does the personal history of the Ayarzas reveal about late colonial Spanish American views concerning public and private spheres, race, and social mobility?

5. What does the Ayarza case reveal about the underlying differences between the ways those in the Hispanic and the Anglo world viewed race and racial mobility? In what way was the racial discrimination leveled against the Ayarzas like that of the Anglo world; in what ways was it different?

NOTES

1. The primary sources for this chapter are the years of Ayarza petitions located in the Archivo General de Indias, Panama 292, no. 2, 1803. Unless otherwise noted, quotations derive from this source and will not be further noted. Parts of the case have been reprinted in Rodulfo Cortés Santos, *El regimen de "las gracias al sacar" en Venezuela durante el periodo hispánico* (Caracas, 1978), 2 vols.; and James F. King, "The Case of José Ponciano de Ayarza: A Document on *Gracias al sacar*," *Hispanic American Historical Review* (August 1944): 440–51.

2. José Antonio Maravall, *Poder, honor y élites en el siglo XVII* (Madrid: Siglo XXI, 1989), quotes Vélez de Guevara, 84.

3. Ann Twinam, *Public Lives, Private Secrets: Gender, Honor, Sexuality, and Illegitimacy in Colonial Spanish America* (Stanford, 1999), 50–51.

4. Ibid., 50–55.

5. Archivo Histórico Nacional, Madrid, Consejos Libros 1498, n. 4, 1795, contains the original. The 1801 version that increased costs is reprinted in Richard Konetzke, *Colección de documentos para la historia de la formación social de hispanoamérica, 1493–1810*, 5 vols. (Madrid: Consejo Superior de Investigaciones Científicas, 1958–1962), 3:2, n. 354, 1801.

6. Twinam, *Public Lives, Private Secrets*.

7. Ibid., 251–61, 275–88, 291–98.

8. In contrast to the more than two hundred gracias al sacar legitimations traced in Twinam, *Public Lives, Private Secrets*, only thirty-four pardos applied for grants of partial or full whiteness. In his monumental documentation of colonial social history, Richard Konetzke reprinted several cases: in 1687 a *moreno* had been appointed governor of a Panamanian province in spite of his race; several Cuban pardos in the 1760s had been permitted to study and practice medicine. Konetzke, *Colección de documentos*, 2:2n546, 1687; 3:1n177, 1760; 3:1n189, 1763.

9. Twinam, *Public Lives, Private Secrets*, 13–16, 54, 335–36.

10. Rodulfo Cortés reprints thirty-five key documents in volume 2 of *El regimen*.

11. Ibid., 67.

12. *Colección Documental de la Independencia del Perú* (Comissión Nacional del Sesquicentenario de la Independencia del Perú, 1972), 404; on Josef Ponciano's role as a merchant, see Peru, Supremo Tribunal de Responsabilidad Judicial, and José Antonio García y García, *Anales del Supremo tribunal de responsabilidad judicial* (Impr. Del Teatro, 1880), 63; for his service on the Peruvian Supreme Court, see Ricaurte Soler, *El Pensamiento político en Panamá en los siglos XIX y XX* (Universidad de Panamá, 1988), 28; on Pedro Crisólogo as vicar, see Francisco de Paula Santander et al., *Cartas de Santander-Bolívar: 1820–1822* (Fundación para la Comemoración del Bicentenario del Natalicio y el Sesquicentenario de la Muerte del General Santander, 1988), 295; on Antonio Nican-

or's promotion, see *United States Congressional Serial Set,* 1904, 322; on his role as a representative, see Juan Antonio Susto, "Esfemerides de mayo," *Loteria* 84 (May 1948): 4; on Josef Ponciano taking up the judicial post in Panama, see Diego Uribe Vargas, Beatriz C. Gutiérrez Montes, and Mario Iván Álvarez Milán, *El meridian 82: Frontera maritime entre Colombia y Nicaragua* (U. Jorge Tadeo Lozano, 1999), 285.

SUGGESTED READINGS

A brief commentary in English as well as some Spanish-language documents on the Ayarza case have been translated into English by James F. King, "The Case of José Ponciano de Ayarza: A Document on *Gracias al sacar,*" *Hispanic American Historical Review* (August 1944): 440–51. However, this article and document contain only a small part of the case. For an analysis of aspects of the whitening cases, see Ann Twinam's "Purchasing Whiteness: Conversation on the Essence of Pardo-ness and Mulatto-ness at the End of Empire," in *Imperial Subjects: Race and Identity in Colonial Spanish America,* edited by Andrew B. Fisher and Matthew D. O'Hara (Durham: Duke University Press, 2009), 141–66, and "The Etiology of Racial Passing: Constructions of Informal and Official 'Whiteness' in Colonial Spanish America," in *New World Orders: Violence, Sanction, and Authority in the Early Modern Americas,* edited by John Smolenski and Thomas J. Humphrey (Philadelphia: University of Pennsylvania Press, 2005), 249–72. Also see Ann Twinam, *Public Lives, Private Secrets: Gender, Honor, Sexuality, and Illegitimacy in Colonial Spanish America* (Stanford: Stanford University Press, 1999). Those who read Spanish can find further cases of whitening requests in Richard Konetzke, *Colección de documentos para la historia de la formación social de hispanoamérica, 1493–1810* (Madrid: Consejo Superior de Investigaciones Científicas, 1958–1962), 5 vols., although he usually prints selections rather than full cases. Santos Rodulfo Cortés, *El regimen de "las gracias al sacar" en Venezuela durante el periodo hispánico* (Caracas: Italgráfica, 1978), 2 vols., contains a volume of documents on the Venezuelan reaction to whitening.

THIRTEEN

Victorina Loza

Quiteña Merchant in the Second Half of the Eighteenth Century

Christiana Borchart de Moreno

Textile mills producing woolen cloth in the north-central highlands of the Audiencia of Quito served as the foundation of the regional economy. By the eighteenth century, however, a series of epidemics and natural disasters and the introduction of large quantities of higher-quality European goods combined to erode the prosperity of cloth manufacturers. Mill owners still sold their cheaper woolens to markets in New Granada to the north, but they lost ground in the more lucrative southern markets (especially Lima) to European imports and locally produced Peruvian woolens. The declining demand for Quiteño cloth (especially higher-quality paños) *also prompted a slow agrarian decline in the north-central highlands. Spanish rural enterprises had organized abundant land and labor resources to grow food, graze livestock, and produce woolen cloth for export. As the profitability of the mills declined, merchants throughout the audiencia began to organize the production of woolen and especially cotton cloth, usually through the "putting out" system. In this system, merchants gave advances of raw wool or cotton to local producers, often Andeans, who spun thread and wove cloth in their homes and villages for the merchant suppliers. This form of cottage industry was most common in the southern highlands, near the city of Cuenca, but it also was found in scattered towns and villages throughout the highlands. Apart from financing cloth production, merchants also traded in a host of local artisan goods such as rosaries, religious paintings, and sculpture. In short, the decline of the large mills resulted in not only hardship but also a changing commercial and economic landscape.*

239

By the second half of the eighteenth century, Quito began to evolve from a manufacturing and commercial center to more of an administrative and service-oriented city. The Bourbon reforms led to a plethora of new government agencies and new bureaucratic jobs for the upper-class peninsular and Creole populations. Most of the city's middle and lower classes, however, made more modest livings from small-scale enterprises that hardly compensated for the profits generated by the woolen textile industry in its heyday during the seventeenth century. Moreover, as the crown imposed higher taxes and administrative controls from the 1760s onward, even marginal economic activities suffered. When the government attempted to regulate the production and sale of aguardiente (cane liquor) and assume direct control over the sales tax in 1765, for example, it threatened to destroy these modest urban commercial and agrarian enterprises. As a result, riots known as the "Rebellion of the Barrios" erupted in the city. A popular government took control of Quito for over one year until royal troops finally entered the city and restored the audiencia to power. In the end, the overall economic decline of the district had serious repercussions in the city, whose population first stagnated and then began to decline by the end of the eighteenth century.

One of the merchants plying her trade in this uncertain economic climate was doña María Victorina Loza. One of four siblings from a middle-class Quiteño household, doña Victorina married an older man, Fernando Lucas de la Peña, a Popayán merchant who owned a shop in Quito. The couple operated the business together, with doña Victorina running the shop while her husband traveled frequently across the rugged Andean cordillera to sell his wares and procure merchandise for sale in Quito. When her husband died, doña Victorina married a much younger man, Francisco Xavier Sánchez de la Flor, probably to help collect debts and also to travel throughout the countryside, an activity unsuitable for a "respectable" woman. Doña Victorina was a tough, determined businesswoman, however, one of a growing group of female entrepreneurs in Quito. While her business flourished, however, her personal life did not; by 1790 her young husband had begun a sexual liaison with a woman in Quito. Doña Victorina tried to have Francisco manage her rural properties, but when he refused to leave the city and his mistress, she initiated legal action against him for squandering her assets. Throughout her life, doña Victorina remained a wily, determined, and willful merchant who operated successfully in the difficult economy of eighteenth-century Quito.

The first adventure in life was survival, which was no easy task for anyone born around 1740 in the northern Andes. This was especially true if a person lived in the straw hut of an Andean working on a hacienda or in an *obraje* (mill) or was even an independent cotton weaver in one of the numerous highland villages. It was even true, however, if someone resided in the comfortable house of a well-established Creole or *mestizo* (mixed Spanish and Amerindian) family in Quito, the capital of an audiencia district. Although there are no statistics, wills written in Quito in the second half of the eighteenth century show that parents frequently outlived one or more of their children.

Along with her four siblings, doña María Victorina, the daughter of Quito *vecinos* (citizens) don Manuel Loza and his wife, doña Tomasa Vásquez Albán, was confronted with the usual health risks of her time: frequent epidemics of smallpox, chicken pox, and measles. Moreover, Quito and the central and northern highlands of Ecuador suffered from frequent natural disasters, such as the severe earthquakes in Quito (1755), Latacunga (1757), and especially Riobamba (1797). This last quake caused the complete destruction of the town as well as extensive damage in regions as far north as Quito and its surrounding valleys. Volcanic eruptions such as that of Cotopaxi in 1740–1755 and 1768 and nearby Tungurahua in 1773 normally caused fewer deaths, since the surrounding areas were sparsely populated. But the expulsion of ashes and the resulting landslides often destroyed large agricultural and cattle-grazing areas. In 1785–1786 a period of heavy rains—described in terms similar to the El Niño phenomenon of recent decades—resulted in heavy losses of both Indian workers and flocks of sheep in the central highlands and forced the closing for several months of one of the biggest textile mills in the province. The consequences were felt in villages and towns as food shortages and damage to the already depressed textile industry affected large sectors of a society that still depended on the production and trade of woolen cloth.

In addition to these recurring epidemics and natural disasters, the Audiencia of Quito also suffered from several bloody and destructive riots and rebellions touched off by the Bourbon monarchy's attempts to reform the colonial administration and raise more revenue. The impoverished population perceived every change as a new threat to their already diminished economic prospects, and they reacted violently. Most indigenous rebellions took place in the principal textile-producing centers and must have resulted in declines in production and interruptions of commerce along the royal road that linked highland textile mills and rural producers of cotton cloth to markets in Lima, Popayán, and Barbacoas. The Quito rebellion of 1765 was one of the largest urban insurrections in the eighteenth-century Spanish Empire. Efforts to establish a royal aguardiente distillery and to assume direct control over the sales tax (*alcabala*) administration triggered the bloody uprising.

There is no document, diary, or letter to show the impact of this seemingly endless list of problems and disasters on Victorina Loza's life. But, as a citizen of Quito and an active part of its merchant community, she must have felt their impact even though they did not reduce her to "critical poverty," a modern expression that applies to many members, especially women, of Quito's popular classes. Not much is known of the Loza-Vásquez Albán family. Nevertheless, the parents of the household financed two daughters' admission to the Santa Catalina convent and provided dowries for the marriages of Victorina and her sister Antonia, indicating that they were a rather well-to-do family. None of the documents related to the family gives any hint about their ethnic status. Information about ethnicity is seldom found in official documentation from the era, not even in the census data of the second half of the eighteenth century, which usually distinguishes only four rather dissimilar ethnic categories: whites, Amerindians, free (probably black and mulattos), and slaves. The 1784 census lists 17,976 "whites" from a total in the Quito population of nearly 24,000, including peninsular and Creole Spaniards and mestizos. These mestizos must have formed the largest segment of this "white" category in the census since European immigration to the audiencia district was insignificant. Yet within this white and mestizo segment, the social and economic differences were enormous.

As in other parts of the Spanish Empire, modern scholars have tended to focus their attention on the extremes of the urban society: the titled and untitled nobility on one hand and the urban underclass or *plebe* on the other. This focus gives the erroneous impression that there was nothing in between these two extremes. According to a city council document produced in 1789, however, in Quito only about five hundred persons of both sexes could claim to be members of the titled and untitled nobility, a group that included peninsular and Creole Spaniards. This group represented under 3 percent of the urban population and included crown officials and large estate holders, descending from the original *encomenderos* and obraje owners, who also engaged in long-distance trade. Between this upper segment of the so-called white population and the large but not so clearly defined group at its bottom of artisans, peddlers, and unemployed, there was a small middle class. Most were merchants, who even in this critical half century were able to accumulate capital and afford a comfortable living, but without any prospect of entering the highest ranks of society.

The Loza-Vásquez Albán family probably belonged to this middling group of merchants engaged in trade with Popayán and its gold-mining district in the northern part of the audiencia district. To define a distinct Quito merchant class is difficult, at least in the second half of the eighteenth century, when nearly everybody from the upper class (audiencia justices, priests, and estate owners) to lowly indigenous weavers engaged in some sort of trade. Quito never had a merchant guild that in other parts of the empire at least made clear the distinction between wholesale and retail merchants. Nevertheless, documents from the period demonstrate the existence of numerous *pulperías*, *tiendas*, and *almacenes*. Pulperías provided for everyday needs by offering basic foodstuffs and other local and regional products; tiendas and almacenes offered a wide range of higher-quality products, especially locally produced and imported textiles. Tiendas tended to serve the general public, whereas the almacenes operated largely as wholesale businesses.

A second difficulty in defining the merchant class involved the fluctuating numbers of people, especially men, engaged in trade. There were a number of reasons for this fluid merchant population. First, Quito was a rather isolated marketplace, far away from the main ports of Cartagena and Callao and also distant from the areas where the locally produced textiles were sold. Second, the audiencia suffered from a severe lack of specie; most of the gold production in its most northern territories went directly to Popayán and Santa Fé. This difficult situation required mobility and the use of several commercial strategies for a merchant to remain in business.

The large Cartagena and Lima merchant houses, frequently owned by peninsular Spaniards, controlled the supply of European commodities. These enterprises could be contacted by mail or through local agents, who generally lived in the port of Guayaquil, not the audiencia's highland capital. Nevertheless, most of Quito's merchants established personal contacts with these main centers of commerce. They traveled themselves, for example, to Lima, selling their locally produced woolen textiles (higher-quality *paños* and more roughly woven *bayetas*) along the way, in the viceregal capital itself, and sometimes even farther to the south. They returned with European luxury products and metal wares, Peruvian wine, and occasionally some Chinese silk. Completing this trade circuit commonly took about two years if all went well. Another possibility was to send a hired agent to buy and sell on commission or to establish a joint venture, preferably with a family member. In these cases, one of the partners established himself for a number of years in Popayán, Lima, or Cartagena. Merchants from other parts of the Spanish Empire also set up shop temporarily or permanently in Quito. Only a few came from Spain, Cartagena, and Lima. Between Quito and Popayán or Pasto, however, there was a constant coming and going of people who established ongoing commercial and family connections in the capital city.

How did women enter this rather complicated pattern of trade? For a long time scholars thought that women engaged only in small-scale commercial and productive activities, such as bread baking and street marketing. In mid-seventeenth-century Quito, for example, a conflict over unfair competition took place between male owners and administrators of pulperías on the one hand and the so-called *gateras* or Indian women selling in the streets on the other. The only two female owners of a pulpería recorded in the city's records of that time clearly had no active part in the day-to-day running of the businesses. By the second half of the eighteenth century this pattern had changed dramatically; city records indicate that women not only owned and ran pulperías and different kinds of artisan shops, but they were also registered as a "vecina and merchant of this city." More than one woman also owned and operated a tienda, engaging in the long-distance trade with Lima and Popayán.

Victorina Loza, who never called herself a merchant in any notarial documents from the period, fell within this emerging group of female merchants. Her commercial training may have begun at home, where she must have learned to read and write. Her first marriage was to don Fernando Lucas de la Peña, a Popayán merchant who had settled in Quito. Her parents provided the dowry—probably some cash, clothing, household silver and linen, merchandise, and perhaps a slave, which was handed over to her husband to help him in carrying the "burdens of marriage." Although the precise amount of this dowry remains unknown, it was the only capital that doña Victorina ever received from her parents. In later years her brother, don Fulgencio, whose wife was also known as a merchant in Quito, cheated Victorina and her sister Antonia of their paternal inheritance. Husbands had the right to manage but not to spend their wives' capital, which had to be returned in case of divorce or widowhood. On the other hand, even if they had not received any capital, by law husbands owed their wives support, which consisted (using the common eighteenth-century formula) of "food and an annual change of clothes" befitting her social position. In exchange the husband could expect love, obedience, and a serene life.

After marriage the couple lived quietly in Quito, although don Fernando assuredly must have spent a lot of time traveling in order to stock the almacen run by his wife in his absence. They had no children of their own but adopted a foundling left on their doorstep, whom they named Fernando de la Peña. The love that doña Victorina always expressed for this son indicates that he was probably one of the many illegitimate children (registered as foundlings) in the city. Their biological parents were sometimes one of their adoptive parents, their brother or sister, or some other relative. Since Victorina's second marriage also remained childless, it is likely that the child, Fernando, was the offspring of a close relative.

After 1767 doña Victorina appears in court records suing several dilatory debtors. The commercial and legal affairs of the couple fell completely into her hands because her husband was listed as an "invalid with a well-known ailment." Don Fernando may have been older than his wife. The lawsuits portray doña Victorina as a competent and persistent businesswoman who did not give up, even if her debtors had left Quito. One such case, for example, involved a priest who owed her money for some *efectos de Castilla* (Spanish goods) purchased before he went as a missionary to the remote province of Maynas in the Amazon region. Nevertheless, doña Victorina persisted; some sixteen years after the lawsuit began, the executor of the priest's estate finally paid the debt. Another debtor, a shop owner himself, left his tienda to a sister and supposedly fled to Lima in 1769. In 1770 the dogged doña Victorina had his shop closed to prevent him from selling any items that might have come from her almacen. Because of information she provided, the debtor was finally located in Otavalo and brought to justice in Quito. Officially she had him imprisoned, but he apparently spent only a few daytime hours in a front room, leaving the jail for his meals and overnight. Soon other creditors joined in the legal action, and the recalcitrant former shop owner had to repay the debts within five years. Doña Victorina, however, insisted on having the man post bond, signed before a notary. He probably paid his debts because fifteen years later the man served as one of her lawyers.

Don Fernando Lucas de la Peña apparently died somewhere between the end of November 1769 and October 1771 because in October of the next year (1772) doña Victorina married for a second time. Her new husband was don Francisco Xavier Sánchez de la Flor, a Popayán merchant like don Fernando and perhaps even his former junior partner or employee. Why would a well-established widow, accustomed to managing her own business affairs, marry a penniless younger man? His motives are more understandable. A merchant without capital of his own could find employment only as a shopkeeper or as a traveling agent, with an income of about one hundred pesos per year and a place at his employer's dinner table (or two pesos, one for the man and another for the mule, for every eight days on the road). As the husband of doña Victorina, Sánchez de la Flor could manage a considerable fortune. When he signed a receipt for the dowry in February 1776, it was worth a total of 47,850 pesos and consisted of silver coin, a house in central Quito, merchandise in the almacen, jewels, household silver, clothes, and four slaves. The sum seems high for the day and probably included debts owed to doña Victorina that she considered collectible.

A principal motive for doña Victorina's decision to marry a second time was probably her need for a man to help in collecting the debts. Another may have been to have her young husband travel across the rugged Andean landscape to continue the trading patterns set by doña Victorina and her first husband (see figure 13.1). Don Fernando had not only left a house and an almacen but also some business contacts, especially with the Mosquera family, important estate holders and merchants in Popayán and its district. But contacts alone were not enough to maintain successful long-distance trade links. Quito was the point of departure for textile shipments that went north to Barbacoas and to Popayán and its environs, sometimes extending even to Santa Fé de Bogotá. The normal shipment of cloth to these northern provinces consisted of woolen bayetas and cottons, called *lienzos* or sometimes *tocuyos* (especially when they had been produced in the southern highlands near the city of Cuenca). The bundles of cloth were wrapped in coarse frieze, which was usually sold in the mining districts. Since few merchants owned textile mills, they had to purchase the cloth from manufacturers (called *obrajeros*) at the lowest possible price. Business with these obrajeros usually could be transacted in Quito, where many of the mill owners lived or at least kept part-time residences. Buying cheap bayetas, however, often involved traveling directly to the centers of production. Acquiring cottons produced by independent weavers required traveling to several Amerindian villages in the central and south sierra, even though weavers from the nearby village of Alangasí came to Quito themselves to offer their fabrics.

Going around the countryside on business was not an option for a respectable woman, and respectability was very important to doña Victorina. Women of the middle and upper classes could be seen traveling to their haciendas, escorted by servants or male relatives, or accompanying their husbands when they took up a new post within the colonial administration. But even in pulperías, business activities split along gendered lines, with the wives running the shop and their husbands on the road selling goods and getting fresh supplies. Only Amerindian women traveled "on business," such as transporting woolen fabrics from the village of Guano, near Riobamba, to the capital. As a result, the need to find a man to move around freely, maintaining business contacts and finding the best goods and prices, probably accounted for doña Victorina's decision to enter into such an unequal marriage. Moreover, having a husband gave a woman greater "respectability," which, in a general way, made matters easier in business and in the courts. Unfortunately, prospective husbands were scarce in Quito, as more and more young men were leaving the city in search of a better future in more prosperous regions. In less than twenty years the ratio in Quito went from 75.8 men per 100 women in 1781 to 53.3 in 1797. This imbalance between the numbers of men and women was evident in the increasing percentage of female shop owners, which grew from 29.7 percent in 1770 to 40.5 percent in 1802.

If don Francisco had cherished any dreams of gaining complete control over his wife's fortune, he must have been disappointed. Their union was apparently a marriage of convenience, and a lawyer even testified that doña Victorina and don Francisco had never shared a bed, although this assertion was never proved. Nevertheless, it was not uncommon in late-eighteenth-century Quito for a wealthy widow to take a poorer husband, offering economic security to the man who entered into the marriage as a sort of junior partner. In later years, for example, one woman who could not run her fringe-making shop because of guild regulations offered "decent meals and clothing every year" to a penniless fringe master, whom she later married. As the legal documentation indicates, doña Victorina never gave up complete control of her fortune, even though she respected the formality of having don Fernando appear as the head and legal representative of the business.

She even had don Fernando sign a power of attorney in July 1773 so that she could control their "joint" legal affairs. Initially she acted on her own only when her husband was traveling, but when he was in Quito, she asked his permission formally to pursue legal contracts and lawsuits. Don Fernando was obviously absent, for example, in 1778–1779 when she contacted obraje owners about buying bayetas and went to the alcabala office to sign documents that accompanied her shipments of these textiles

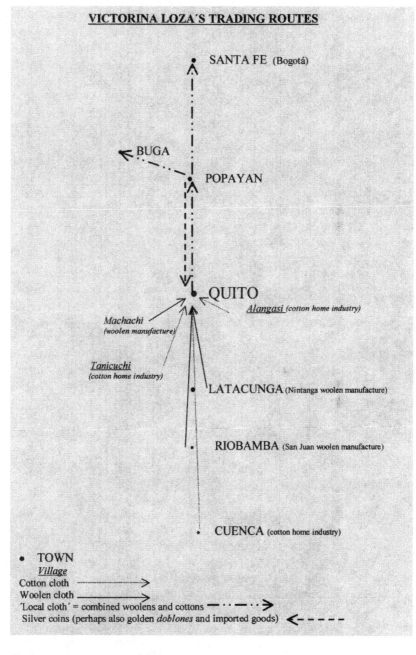

Figure 13.1. Victorina Loza's trading routes.

to Popayán. He was also absent in 1780 when she bought a small hacienda in the southwestern outskirts of Quito. In 1788, however, her husband signed all the trade permits, and that year he appeared as a leading textile merchant in the Popayán trade.

On the other hand, no records exist of any independent business dealings of don Fernando. In 1776 he received Spanish goods from his brother-in-law don Fulgencio, but only to put them in his wife's almacen. In 1783 he sold a slave from Popayán who had escaped to Ambato, south of Quito, and who had married there under false pretenses. In this transaction, however, he was only the representative of the owner, don José María Mosquera, his wife's most important business partner. In another slave sale he acted for don Miguel Alvares del Corro (from Riobamba), the representative of a Cádiz merchant. In 1785 he delivered to don Justo Castro (from Guayaquil) 1,019 pesos from doña Victorina, asking that Castro invest the money in "showy goods" for sale in Lima. This last deal seems to have been the couple's only attempt at establishing a new, southern business route. Doña Victorina's total lack of business contacts in the viceregal capital forced her to rely on a stranger who seemed to know what highland products were "showy" enough to attract attention in Lima. Moreover, the contract included buying European goods in Lima, which Castro would sell on his return trip. Doña Victorina was to receive her money and an 8 percent commission (the usual "one-way" commission was 4 percent at that time). Only four and one-half months later, don Francisco, representing his wife's interest once again, initiated a lawsuit against Castro, who had not even started his long journey to the south. Rumors about his dishonesty must have come to his creditors' attention because Castro had gone to jail twice before and was released only because of an infected leg wound. Nonetheless, he profited from the disagreements among his creditors and apparently never repaid these debts.

Although colonial lawsuits over business transactions rarely include correspondence between the litigants, in one of doña Victorina's trials, conducted by her husband, a few of her letters have survived. They offer intriguing insights into the discussions between obraje owners and merchants as well as into doña Victorina's way of doing business. Her opponent in the case was don Vicente Isidro Villavicencio y Guerrero, eldest son of Countess del Real Agrado and administrator of her obraje of San Juan, near Riobamba. The mill was a rather destitute establishment with thirty-two native workers and another nineteen in a nearby workshop for spinning. In November 1778 doña Victorina wrote a letter to don Vicente proposing a business deal. She needed about six thousand *varas* (one vara equals about thirty-three inches) of baize and offered to exchange European goods from her shop for the cloth. In the following March a meeting between them took place in doña Victorina's house.

At this meeting a bitter disagreement started. Don Vicente needed cash urgently, probably to repay debts or to cover some of the costs of assuming his new duties as magistrate of Trujillo. Nonetheless, his strained financial situation did not stop him from taking two pairs of English silk stockings at sixteen pesos as an advance on their proposed business deal. He also wanted an additional 300 pesos in cash for himself and another 300 pesos in goods, payable to don Mariano Donoso. The six thousand varas of baize were to be delivered the following September. Although doña Victorina had no ready cash, she offered to try and get at least half of the money within the following few days. Only a week after the supposed contract, don Vicente pressed again for the "promised" 150 pesos, and he also complained that the goods delivered to don Mariano did not amount to the promised 300 pesos. He urged her to complete the deal, terming her attitude as mere "child's play."

Doña Victorina responded that she had promised only an "attempt" to secure the money, not to deliver it. Moreover, she had never signed any contract agreeing to such terms. After all, she could not promise to pay cash (at a rate of two reales per vara) for baize that she would receive a full six months later. In addition, don Mariano, whose family owned estates in the nearby Machachi valley, had already made her a better offer: he could deliver the needed bayetas immediately. Moreover, doña Victorina still had contacts with the Nintanga obraje owned by the Mercedarian order, which could also provide the merchandise. As to the price of the merchandise delivered to Donoso, she stated:

> Your Grace tells me that I have given merchandise from my shop to don Mariano Donoso [worth] 193 pesos in expensive textiles, but because of the esteem I have for the foresaid gentleman and the friendship I profess for my lady doña Rosa his wife I gave him of the most florid and at the current prices at which I am selling at this moment for silver in cash, and if all this is contemptible he will not have to go through the trouble of taking another vara of cloth . . . and I am writing the same to don Mariano Donoso so that he will not come in for more expensive textiles.

She even told don Vicente that the textiles could be returned because in her almacen "they will not rot nor will I experience any damage."

In the second half of the eighteenth century the time had long passed when wealthy obraje owners sold their woolens directly in Lima or exchanged them for European goods to be sold for high profits in the Audiencia of Quito. Don Vicente, the future Count del Real Agrado, was not the only one who had to look for commercial intermediaries. Merchants routinely offered to exchange European goods for locally produced woolens because the supply of cash was extremely limited in the audiencia district.

Don Vicente not only failed to get the cash that he so desperately needed, but he also lost his lawsuit with doña Victorina. In November 1782 the president of the audiencia signed an order to have don Vicente arrested. As in similar cases, the debtor fled from Quito to avoid arrest, so in March 1783 the order was extended to Latacunga, Ambato, and Riobamba. Since the documentation about the lawsuit ended with this order, the fugitive probably agreed to send some baize from his obraje to pay for the goods that don Mariano had received from doña Victorina as part of the agreement.

Most merchants in the Spanish Indies tried to invest part of their money in landed estates. This goal was true not only for wealthy upper-class merchants who traded directly with Spain but also for the more modest ones engaged in interregional trade. Doña Victorina was no exception. She bought her first estate in 1776, in Luluncoto, an agricultural area in the suburban parish of San Sebastián, located in the rural southeastern periphery of Quito. In 1780 she obtained another small hacienda, called Lloa Chiquito, on the lower slopes of Mount Pichincha, at the outskirts of the southwestern parish of San Roque. Two years later she purchased a small holding in Collacoto, close to her first investment. These properties were situated in areas of small, landed estates devoted to agriculture and cattle grazing that supplied their owners and the urban marketplace with fresh food. Together with the plain of Añaquito, north of Quito, both areas attracted investments from merchants, but the properties also changed owners frequently. Most of the buyers and sellers belonged to the merchant community.

For doña Victorina the acquisition of land represented more than just gaining access to fresh foodstuffs for her household or for sale in local markets. Her main concern was the future of her adopted son, don Fernando, who had entered the priesthood. To give him a secure, regular income (one of the conditions for being ordained) she set up a "patrimonial foundation" in 1782 to provide him with 200 pesos per year from the income generated by these rural properties. Doña Victorina also sought even better investments for her son. In August 1785, for example, she sold her Luluncoto and Collacoto properties to a fellow merchant for 6,100 pesos: 4,880 pesos in cash, or perhaps merchandise from his shop, with the rest paid out in the form of an annuity yielding a 3 percent annual return. She later sold the Lloa Chiquito estate to another Quito merchant and invested the proceeds in a hacienda, El Tintal, near the village of Perucho, northwest of Quito, paying 8,400 pesos.

Although El Tintal saddled doña Victorina with a mortgage of 5,900 pesos, the estate was located in a subtropical sugarcane-producing area. During this period the sale of sugar and aguardiente still yielded considerable profits to landowners in the region, which probably justified the investment. The estate also became a refuge for doña Victorina, with a room and an oratory of her own, a formal garden with fruit trees, flower and medicinal herb beds, and a stable for her favorite riding mules. Haciendas in the Perucho region were small compared to the larger properties of Quito's nobility and the Jesuit order (until its expulsion in 1767), which were located in the principal sugarcane-producing regions in the Chota and Mira valleys and around the villages of Urcuquí and Salinas. Instead, Quito's middle-class merchants invested in the small- and medium-sized estates near Perucho to gain status and perhaps a higher rank in colonial society.

In November 1780 the merchant don Gregorio Betancourt had sold El Tintal for 8,400 pesos to don Carlos Araujo. The payment should have been completed within two months, but Araujo, who only a few years later would become one of the most important owners of sugarcane and cattle haciendas in the northern highlands, canceled the contract with the argument that he lacked sufficient cash to meet the terms of the deal. It seems likely, however, that it was not the lack of cash but the lack of a sufficient labor force that caused Araujo to withdraw. In 1780 don Gregorio affirmed that he had a great deal of sugarcane ready for grinding (worth between 4,000 and 6,000 pesos), but several witnesses stated that the area suffered from a permanent lack of native workers, which necessitated large capital outlays to attract farmhands from other regions. The estates obviously were not large enough to justify the acquisition of slave laborers.

Doña Victorina was aware of this labor problem, and so she started to "buy" the labor force needed to work on her own properties. The usual procedure was to purchase the debts of a native worker from another estate owner, offering either cash or merchandise. By this means she acquired thirteen workers over the years, one of them a mestizo. Most of the former employers were owners of small estates, perhaps in the same district. The biggest deal involved the Marquis de Villaorellana and his hacienda of Granobles in the Cayambe valley. A representative of doña Victorina's in the area somehow convinced seven laborers to leave Granobles and work on El Tintal. The marquis, whose family had been in serious economic difficulties for years, complained to local authorities and asked for 263 pesos in compensation. In the end, he had to settle for only one hundred pesos. The most interesting contract was signed with don Tiburcio Cabezas, the most important (or principal) cacique of Otavalo, who was paid thirty pesos in May 1799 in exchange for "the labor of his Indians" on the Tintal estate. Relying on indigenous authorities as intermediaries to secure workers was a procedure called *concertaje colectivo*, a form of labor contract in the Ecuadorian highlands, which has not yet been studied.

While her business operations ran smoothly, doña Victorina's private life suffered numerous setbacks after 1790. In early 1792, she signed a contract with her husband, leasing him El Tintal and the nearby potato-growing property of Ambuela and promising not to interfere in their management. Although claiming that she had leased the property because of her inability to run the haciendas herself, doña Victorina's real motive was different. She had been informed of her husband's infidelity with a woman in the parish of San Roque. Putting her husband in charge of properties outside of Quito was clearly an attempt to separate him from his lover. The strategy failed, however, since don Francisco had no intention of remaining on the remote haciendas, not only because of his lover but also because he wanted to speculate in mining operations. In the late eighteenth century, the audiencia experienced what one historian has called a "genuine mining psychosis." Local entrepreneurs such as don Francisco attempted to reverse the region's long economic depression by finding new deposits of precious metals, but most lacked both the capital and the technical expertise.

In November 1792, instead of taking direct legal action, doña Victorina wrote a secret letter to the president of the audiencia that denounced her husband's infidelity. She probably took this more discreet and secretive procedure to avoid a scandal. Nevertheless, she eventually pressed a legal suit against don Francisco for spending 29,000 pesos of her dowry. Hoping to reconcile with her husband, however, doña Victorina suspended her suit for two months, but in January 1793 she presented her claims before the court once again. In the meantime, her husband had begun legal proceedings before the bishop to annul their marriage on the grounds of a "legal impediment." To counter this action, doña Victorina included the statements about her husband's infidelity from several witnesses sworn to secrecy. The weight of the evidence against him was sufficient to have the court sentence don Francisco to jail for some time.

Apparently, imprisonment did not sober don Francisco or make him behave more cautiously. On March 5 at 11:00 p.m., one of the alcaldes accompanied by a few infantry soldiers, several ministers of the law, and a clerk knocked at the door of his lover's house and

> heard quick steps from the inside until, with some delay, they opened the door. Having entered, His Grace recognized the second room which serves as a bedroom; he found on a desk before the bed a skirt and shawl from Castile and in it lying asleep, naked to his underwear, don Francisco Xavier Sánchez de la Flor to whom the judge said, "I have come after you, get up and dress yourself quickly.". . . Meanwhile they looked for the accomplice who was not found in the same room but in the first one near the main door, buried in the bed under her mother's feet.

Don Francisco gave a common excuse to justify his presence in the house and in the bed of Magdalena Suárez. He claimed to have come to the house on "honorable business" but was surprised by a heavy rainstorm. Having been ill only recently, he feared for his health and stayed where he was. Despite offering this lame excuse, don Francisco went to jail, where he convinced the authorities that his lover, Magdalena, would present herself on the following day. When she did not appear, officials seized her mother and pressed both prisoners to disclose Magdalena's hiding place. Finally both were released, but don Francisco only after posting bail.

After these events, no possibility for any reconciliation between don Francisco and doña Victorina remained. Husband and wife became frequent litigants. Doña Victorina tried to recover both of her haciendas (El Tintal and Ambuela) and also sued to regain two slaves taken away by her husband, who had entered her property together with his lawyer to remove the slaves and some of his wife's belongings. Moreover, in 1796 don Francisco tried to sell two smaller properties, which, according to his own statement, were worthless without Ambuela. He assured the buyer that he would reclaim Ambuela from his wife, a procedure that he anticipated taking no more than six months. However, he lost all the suits and asked to be declared *pobre de solemnidad* (deserving poor), probably because he could not pay his debts. In 1803 his wife, certainly to avoid scandal and any additional demands by her husband, wrote her last will in the form of a "closed testament" to be opened only after her death.

In her last will doña Victorina mentioned her unhappy marriage only briefly, stating that she was "living alone for just reasons." Her beloved adopted son had died before doña Victorina, but her testament displays no bitterness or disappointment. Instead, it is an expression of her affection for the people who had accompanied her over the years and who were named in her bequests: her two slaves and two household servants, all females; her young lady of company, her cousin and clerk, and her surviving sister in the Santa Catalina convent; but most of all the two granddaughters of her sister, Antonia, and her two goddaughters, Nicolasita (the daughter of don Miguel Loza) and Regina Corral (the child of one of her lawyers). Her nephew, don Miguel Loza, inherited her estates.

The inventory of her possessions lists only ten pesos in cash. Instead of money, there was a formidable collection of jewels, worth more than 5,000 pesos. Some of them were simple strings of pearls, which may have served as savings in case of unforeseen setbacks. The most valuable piece was a Spanish diamond necklace worth 721 pesos, and perhaps the most unusual was a rosary made of alligator teeth set in gold. Some of the jewels were given to the Santa Catalina convent, while others went to pay for masses for the repose of her soul. The rest went to her goddaughters and her female relatives.

At the end of her life, doña Victorina's belongings totaled 38,054 pesos, which did not include the 29,000 pesos that she had been trying to claim, unsuccessfully, from her husband. In spite of all her troubles and the loss of part of her dowry, she had fared slightly better than her brother, don Fulgencio, who had left a total of 37,500 pesos to his three children. Doña Victorina died on November 25, 1805. A statement of twenty-five years earlier, very similar to some verses from the Old Testament dedicated to the "capable wife" (Proverbs 31:10–31), best sums up her life: "a person of much sense in her conduct, prudent in her undertakings and economical in her trades to secure her advancement without ever retracting from her negotiations . . . she behaves with more prudence than the most skillful merchant to which she adds virtuous behavior . . . fearful of God."

QUESTIONS FOR DISCUSSION

1. Why do you think doña Victorina was able to enjoy such a high level of independence in her business activities? How did the special conditions present in eighteenth-century Quito allow women to play such an active role in the economy?
2. Why did colonial bureaucrats take such an active role in matters of public morality, such as concubinage and adultery, when these had traditionally been the concern of Church authorities?
3. Explain what you think doña Victorina meant by saying that she lived alone "for just reasons?"
4. To what extent does doña Victorina seem to be accommodating herself to the prevailing social order, and how does she seem to resist it?

SOURCES

All the sources are from the Archivo Nacional, Quito (AN/Q). The basic information on doña Victorina and her family comes from a document that includes her last will, the inventories of her house and estates, and copies of the concubinage trial: Sin título (don Francisco Xavier Sánchez de la Flor sobre la testamentaria de su mujer doña María Victorina Loza), AN/Q, 3a Notaría, Juicios, 1805-XI-28.

Business Contacts

AN/Q, 3a Notaría, Juicios, 1767-X-19; 1769-IX-23; 1785-V-20.
AN/Q, Pesos, 1782-VI-28.

Don Francisco Sánchez de la Flor

AN/Q, 1a Notaría. Phelipe Santiago Navarrete, 1775–1776 (vol. 408), f.283r–284r; Thomas Pazmiño, 1781–1782 (vol. 419), f.361r–362r.
AN/Q, 3a Notaría. Juan Matheo Navarrete, 1772–1773 (vol. 63), f.219r–219v; Juan Rodríguez, 1795–1796 (vol. 73), f.172v–177v.

Landed Estates

AN/Q, 1a Notaría. Thomas Pazmiño, 1779–1780 (vol. 416), f.454v–458v; Thomas Pazmiño, 1781–1782 (vol. 419), f.306v–309r and f.358v–361r; Thomas Pazmiño, 1785–1786 (vol. 425), f.384v–386r and f.401v–404r.
AN/Q, 3a Notaría. Juan Narciso Osorio, 1779–1780 (vol. 66), f.129r–132r.
AN/Q, Tierras, 1784-VII-7.
AN/Q, Tierras, 1793-V-4.

Slaves

AN/Q, Esclavos, 1793-V-4 and 1793-X-18.

SUGGESTED READINGS

For general information on the socioeconomic situation of the audiencia district, see Kenneth J. Andrien, *The Kingdom of Quito, 1690–1830: The State and Regional Development* (Cambridge, 1995); for details on the Bourbon reforms in the area, see Christiana Borchart de Moreno and Segundo E. Moreno Yánez, "Las reformas borbónicas en la Audiencia de Quito," *Anuario Colombiano de Historia Social y de la Cultura* 22 (1995): 35–57. An analysis of epidemic diseases may be found in Suzanne A. Alchon, *Native Society and Disease in Colonial Ecuador* (Cambridge, 1991), whereas rebellions have been studied by Segundo E. Moreno Yánez, *Sublevaciones indígenas en la Audiencia de Quito desde comienzos del siglo XVIII has finales de la colonia* (Quito, 1985). Regarding the popular reaction to Bourbon tax innovations, see Kenneth J. Andrien, "Economic Crisis, Taxes, and the Quito Insurrection of 1765," *Past and Present* 129 (November 1990): 104–31, and Anthony McFarlane, "The Rebellion of the Barrios: Urban Insurrection in Bourbon Quito," *Hispanic American Historical Review* 49 (May 1989): 282–330. Both articles together with Martin Minchom, *The People of Quito, 1690–1810: Change and Unrest in the Underclass* (Boulder, 1994), offer insight into the eighteenth-century urban popular classes. Christian Büschges has studied Quito's upper classes in "Nobleza y estructura estamental entre concepto y realidad social. El caso de la ciudad de Quito y su región," *Jahrbuch fur Geschichte von Staat, Wirtschaft und Gesellschaft Latinamerikas* 33 (1996): 166–86.

Quito's interregional trade has been studied by John C. Super, "Partnership and Profit in Early Andean Trade: The Experiences of the Quito Merchants, 1580–1610," *Journal of Latin American Studies* 2 (1979): 266–81, and by Christiana Borchart de Moreno, "Circulación y producción en Quito. De la Colonial a la República," *Siglo XIX. Revista de Historia* 14 (July–December 1993): 73–97.

FOURTEEN

José Antonio da Silva

Marriage and Concubinage in Colonial Brazil

Muriel S. Nazzari

By the late eighteenth century, Brazil exceeded two million inhabitants, and the centers of population had shifted from the coastal sugar zones of the northeast to the southeastern captaincies. The discovery of substantial gold deposits by the 1680s in the interior prompted a major demographic shift to the frontier captaincies or regions of Minas Gerais, Mato Grosso, and Goiás as people of all racial and class backgrounds rushed to seek their fortunes in the gold fields. New transportation networks and commercial routes developed to serve these growing settlements, but by the 1750s gold production began to decline slowly. Nevertheless, the demographic center of the colony had shifted decisively. Bolstered by the importation of large numbers of slave laborers, sugar production expanded rapidly in the southeastern captaincies by the 1790s. This expansion also spawned the cultivation of foodstuffs, grazing of livestock, and production of other exportable commodities such as tobacco, cotton, rice, and, later, coffee. The transfer in 1763 of the viceregal capital from Salvador in Bahia to Rio de Janeiro reflected the socioeconomic changes that were transforming Brazil by the eighteenth and early nineteenth centuries.

At the periphery of these changes was São Paulo, long Brazil's gateway to the interior. In the seventeenth century, this city served as the staging ground for the expeditions of bandeirantes *who roamed the interior provinces from the Amazon to Spanish Paraguay in search of indigenous slaves for coastal plantations. These* bandeirantes *were some of the first to discover the gold deposits later in the century. Once the gold rush began, São Paulo prospered, supplying foodstuffs and serving as a conduit for commerce to and from the coast. In 1711 it was given the official rank of city, and by 1803, São Paulo had a population of nearly twenty-five thousand. As the city's economic role expanded, the local society evolved into an urban center with well-established social hierarchies.*

Captain José Antonio da Silva was a prominent citizen in the rural parish of Santana, in the province of São Paulo, and his life and loves mirror the social realities of the city and its hinterland. The social mores of the day required José Antonio to marry someone of the same social rank as defined by ancestry, honor, and race. In keeping with this custom, he married a suitable woman, doña Clara Maria Ribeira, but the couple had no children. His marriage and Church prohibitions against concubinage, however, did not stop him from engaging in a series of illicit relationships with women beneath his social station and siring several illegitimate children. By confining his sexual liaisons to women considered his "inferiors" in class, race, and wealth, however, José Antonio's dalliances did nothing to subvert the prevailing social hierarchies. In fact, they actually reinforced the patriarchal societal order. Ironically, several of the women in the rakish captain's life actually reaped some tangible benefits from their relationships with him. His wife, doña Clara Maria, ended her days a wealthy woman, even marrying a much younger man. Two of his mistresses, Gertrudes Pires and Ignacia Franca, also married well and even improved their social status—census takers changed their racial categorizations from bastarda *(meaning* mestiza) *or* parda *(meaning dark-skinned) to white. Two of his slave mistresses also managed to secure freedom for the children that they bore José Antonio. Despite every effort by Brazilian elites to impose rigid social hierarchies, as the life of José Antonio da Silva demonstrates, disorder often prevailed over colonial notions of order.*

In the realm of sexual relations, order was difficult to maintain in colonial Brazilian society. The Church prescribed marriage as the only acceptable context for a sexual relationship, envisioning a society in which most adults were married, except for religious. Although such an ideal had never truly existed in Europe, it was especially hard to achieve in the Americas, in part because of the difficulty in enforcing Church rules in a colonial society. Both the Church and the civil society believed that marriage should be between equals in age, fortune, and social status. *Qualidade* in Portuguese (or *calidad* in Spanish) was a complex term that included issues of ancestry and honor and, in the Americas, also came to embrace race.

Since most of the Portuguese settlers who went to Brazil in the early years were male, they found few European women to marry who were equals in "quality." As a result, they frequently formed liaisons with women of other races and lower social status that were condemned by the Church and seen as disorderly. But the resulting disorder in sexual relations in the Spanish and Portuguese colonies ironically helped to maintain a different sort of order in the highly hierarchical racial system that was evolving. Brazil was no exception to this process. Both scholars of the early colony and ordinary Brazilians of the twenty-first century well know that stable nuclear families (characterized by marital fidelity) were exceedingly rare in the early years. Scholars have found a large proportion of illegitimate children in the eighteenth and nineteenth centuries, and only a small percentage of the population was legally married.

This chapter describes the lives of a few residents of the municipality of São Paulo in the late eighteenth and early nineteenth centuries—in as much detail as the documents will allow—to illustrate the way in which illegitimate (disorderly) sexual relationships reinforced the racial hierarchy of the province. It describes illicit sexual relationships, marriages characterized by differences in *qualidade*, and how the racial category of individuals could change in the regional censuses depending on their ownership of property, their marital status, or the sexual relationship that they maintained with an important person. The foundations of this study rest on a wide range of primary source materials: censuses, wills and settlements of estates, parish registers of baptism and marriage, Church processes for marriage and dispensations for consanguinity, the minutes of the municipal council of São Paulo, and documents in the Desembargo do Paço (the Portuguese high court that, among other things, legitimized illegitimate children).

The documents portray a colonial São Paulo where patriarchs exercised great power over women, particularly in sexual matters. The power of these patriarchs was based not only on their gender but also on their race and wealth. Yet the picture is not entirely one-sided. Colonial women made choices, too, and in some cases appear to have used their wealth and status to exert power over men. As a consequence, gender intersected with race, economic wealth, and social class, compounded by the almost absolute power that owners had over slaves.

Although much information will emerge about the lives of several individuals and their families, the main character in this tale is Captain José Antonio da Silva, commander of the militia in the rural Paulista neighborhood of Santana during the last quarter of the eighteenth century.[1] He and his wife were childless, but he had numerous illicit sexual relationships and fathered several illegitimate children. In the documents concerning the settlement of his estate, it is clear that the captain and his wife had given a small farm within their property to Gertrudes Pires, who was the mother of his eight illegitimate children.[2]

At the time there were actually two José Antonio da Silvas in São Paulo. Santana's militia captain was born in Lisbon around 1742, the legitimate son of Adrião da Silva and his wife, Joséfa Thereza, and was always known only by his name, José Antonio da Silva.[3] The other, a man almost ten years younger, was born in São Paulo and was always called José Antonio da Silva, Paulista (a resident of the city and province of São Paulo). The registration for José Antonio da Silva, Paulista's marriage indicates that he had been a foundling, baptized in 1751 and raised by Anna da Silva Pacheco. Following the custom of marriage equality, he also married a foundling.[4] He was described in an ecclesiastical document from 1800 as a businessman.[5] José Antonio da Silva, Paulista, however, was never connected to the neighborhood of Santana, and he appears in none of its censuses.

This is not the case with the Portuguese José Antonio da Silva, who already appeared in the first census of Santana (1765) as a single man, twenty-five years old, and a farmer with considerable capital for the time, 800$000 (800,000 *reis*). In that census there were eighty-three households in the rural parish of Santana, and only 31 percent of them (twenty-six households) declared any capital at all. There was only one household, headed by the widow Maria de Oliveira Furtada, that recorded more in the census than the young José Antonio da Silva; she had 1:659$000. One other single man, Domingos Gomes de Amaral, also declared capital of 800$000. Everybody else had less; the average in Santana was 264$154. This amount was slightly less than the average for the whole city of São Paulo, which was 296$154.[6] Thus, José Antonio da Silva was already a prosperous farmer in Santana in 1765. Where did he obtain this wealth? It seems unlikely that he brought it from Portugal. In that case, he would probably have been a merchant establishing himself in Rio de Janeiro or in some other coastal urban area, not in a rural parish of São Paulo. A more likely answer is that as an even younger man he joined the gold rush in Minas Gerais, Cuiabá, or Mato Grosso, making enough money to settle later as a prosperous farmer in São Paulo.

When he died thirty-two years later in 1797, he and his wife still lived in the rural neighborhood of Santana, although they owned three houses in the city of São Paulo,[7] two of two stories and one of one story. They probably lived in one of the houses whenever they were in the city and rented the other two. In Santana they owned a large agricultural property that included five different houses. The main house included an oratory with images of the Virgin Mary and several saints. Two houses were used to process sugarcane and make cane liquor (*aguardiente*), and the fourth was probably the slave quarters. The house of Gertrudes Pires was listed separately with the small farm surrounding it and a walled orchard. José Antonio and his wife owned cattle, sheep, and twenty-eight slaves. When he died, their estate was worth almost six *contos*, or 6:000$000, which included considerable cash, bars of gold, and bills of credit. He and his wife were undoubtedly the wealthiest family in the neighborhood, and becoming a captain of militia was always related to wealth in colonial Brazil.[8] Santana was not in itself a well-off neighborhood, however, so José Antonio da Silva probably was not one of the richest Paulistas. In addition, the extant documentation does not reveal how much of the money in his estate at the time of his death had been brought to the marriage by the dowry of his wife, doña Clara Maria Ribeira.

Moreover, José Antonio seems to have been a controversial figure, despite his wealth and important position in the militia. One of his duties as captain was to sign the yearly census of the neighborhood, but in the 1783 census an ensign signed in his place. José Antonio was in jail. In all of the thirteen censuses of Santana during this period, this is the only case of someone listed as being in jail at the time of the census. The reason for his incarceration remains unknown. It might have been for some trivial matter, such as not collaborating with a municipal council order that all neighbors contribute to the repair of the Santana bridge or to the construction of the Santana stretch of the road from São Paulo to Goiás. He might even have run afoul of the Church, which also had the power to jail persons. Furthermore, José Antonio died without making a will because two men shot and killed him at his farm. He was clearly a man who had enemies.

On the other hand, there are numerous references to José Antonio da Silva in the eighteenth-century records of São Paulo's municipal council, indicating that he was an important person in the larger community. In 1765, when he was still a young man in his twenties, José Antonio was listed as an *almotacel* (lieutenant). Ten years later he was already a captain and a justice of the peace; he presided over the municipal council of the city of São Paulo. He was clearly a man with power not only in Santana but also in São Paulo.

José Antonio had numerous sexual relationships with women over the years. One early one, mentioned in the judicial process for the settlement of his estate, produced a *filho natural* (illegitimate child), Francisco de Paula da Silva, who filed as an heir. A filho natural was a child of a man and woman who had no canonical impediments to marriage and thus could have married. Francisco's baptismal certificate reveals that while José Antonio da Silva was still unmarried, he became involved with a single woman, Ignacia Franca, the mother of his child and also a resident of Santana. In January 1766, when she was twenty-two or twenty-three and he was around twenty-six, they baptized Francisco together. José Antonio da Silva was named in the parish register as the father, which was unusual. Most baptismal records for illegitimate children gave the mother's name but claimed that the father was unknown. Listing a father's name was dangerous because the Church prosecuted prolonged and scandalous cases of concubinage. Having his name on the baptismal record suggests that José Antonio da Silva and Ignacia were no longer living together and that their sexual relationship had ended. As a result, a prominent person such as José Antonio could openly acknowledge the child.

Seventeenth- and eighteenth-century Paulista society was strongly endogamous; people married only their social equals. Whenever any inequality existed in a relationship, it was usually the wife who was superior to her husband in wealth and status.[9] Any liaison between a man and a woman lower in the social hierarchy, whether because of her race or her lack of property, was always carried on outside of marriage.[10] As a result, despite acknowledging his filho natural, José Antonio probably never intended to marry Ignacia Franca because she was not his social equal according to the criteria of the time. In fact, Ignacia was listed in the 1765 census of Santana as living with her parents, Francisco Franco and his wife, Joanna de Aguiar, and three brothers. Her father declared no capital whatsoever to the census taker, and his race is noted as *bastardo*, the term used in São Paulo to denote persons with a mixture of Indian and European blood. In two subsequent censuses (1778, 1783) her father was called a bastardo, but in two other ones (1779, 1780) he was called a *pardo* (dark-skinned). Pardo was a term used then mostly for people with a mixture of white and black blood, but it was applied sometimes to individuals with any racial mixture, even to Indians. In any case, her father was not considered white. According to the standards of the day, Ignacia was inferior to José Antonio both in race and in wealth and was therefore not a suitable match for him.

The census of 1778 listed José Antonio da Silva as thirty-seven years old and already married to thirty-five-year-old doña Clara Maria Ribeira. She had not been a resident of Santana since she did not appear in the censuses of 1765 or 1768. A much later census in 1802 indicated her birthplace as Rio de Janeiro. The parish record of their wedding is missing, however, making it impossible to know exactly when it took place. She undoubtedly must have brought the customary property to the marriage with her dowry, or it is unlikely that José Antonio would have married her. She was probably also viewed as white, because none of the censuses listing the couple records her race as different from her husband's. Nonetheless, in the 1798 census, after her husband died, she is listed as "Clara Maria parda *viúva* [widow]."[11] Once again, however, in the 1802 census, after her remarriage, she was again classified as white.

In the settlement of José Antonio's estate, the documents indicate that doña Clara Maria Ribeira did not know how to sign her name. Illiteracy was not uncommon for propertied women in eighteenth-century São Paulo, even though many of the wealthier Paulista wives and daughters had learned to read and write. Doña Clara Maria may also have been older than her husband. In the first two censuses she is shown as two years younger than her husband (1778, 1779), but in the next one she is listed as a year older; in the next two censuses she is recorded as from one to four years younger. In the three censuses in the nineties (1795, 1796, 1797) she is shown as five or six years older. Given that she was probably older than her husband, illiterate, and had possible traces of Indian or African blood, it is all the more likely that she brought a substantial contribution of property, slaves, or cash to the marriage.

The next sexual partner of José Antonio da Silva was Gertrudes Pires. He was already married when he started his relationship with her by the time of the 1778 census. Gertrudes was listed there as the daughter of a white man, Salvador Pires Monteiro, and his *bastarda* wife, Anna de Oliveira, both residents of Santana. Gertrudes was considerably younger than Ignacia Franca, only seven by the census of 1765. According to the data, she lived with her parents up through the census of January 1779 but was no longer listed with them in 1780; neither was she listed in José Antonio's household in that year. Three years later, however, in the 1783 census, Gertrudes, twenty-four years old, and her son, Damazio, appeared in José Antonio's household as white *agregados*, a census classification that means a related or unrelated person who also lives in the household of a nuclear family, though not necessarily in the same house. The fact that Damazio was Gertrudes's child was not spelled out in the census.

In the 1787 listing, Damazio and his younger sister and brother, who were born in the interim, were characterized as foundlings. Eight years later, in the census of 1795, Gertrudes and her children were again categorized as agregados without listing the relationship between the mother and her children. In the following year's census, 1796, Gertrudes was called an agregada, but her children were considered foundlings, as they also were in the 1797 census, which did not even record their mother's name. For some reason, no census taker identified the children as belonging to Gertrudes, despite the fact that in other households, a census classification exists to identify the children of agregadas even if they did not live in the same house. The details of the relationship between José Antonio da Silva and his mistress Gertrudes Pires are thereby obscured. Moreover, the baptismal records of these children gave their mother's name but listed the father as unknown.[12]

The settlement of José Antonio da Silva's estate mentions that he also had two mulatto daughters with two of his slave women. His widow made a long declaration that those young women, Maria and Thomazia, were agregadas and should not be counted as slaves. Previous censuses corroborate that their father considered them free—while they are listed as slaves through 1780, they are recorded as agregadas pardas from 1783. Despite doña Clara Maria's protestations, however, in the 1802 census, after she had remarried, Maria and Thomazia were listed as two of the couple's sixteen slaves and the only mulattos that she and her new husband owned. It is not clear whether or not they had been legally manumitted in the 1780s. Their roles may not have changed in the household, thus making it easy to list them as slaves again in 1802. In the 1807 census, Clara Maria had died and her husband had remarried; Maria and Thomazia were not among his slaves. Perhaps Clara Maria formally manumitted them in her will, or else they may have passed to her heirs as slaves.

José Antonio always carried on his extramarital relationships with women who were inferior to him by class or race: his two slaves, who probably had little say in the matter; Ignacia Franca, who was probably of mixed Indian and white ancestry and whose family had no capital; and, finally, Gertrudes Pires, from a somewhat "better" family, since her father was listed as white but had no capital. The disorderly sexual life of José Antonio da Silva reinforced these women's lowly social status in the hierarchical society of São Paulo.

Did these women benefit in any way from these relationships? In all likelihood, they did, and the higher their original position, the more they benefited. The two slaves secured freedom for their children. Ignacia profited from her son's inheritance, and after she finally married, she was listed (and apparently viewed) as white in the census. Gertrudes gained the status of an agregada in José Antonio's household and in later censuses was recorded as white, even after his death. In all likelihood she was probably seen as white by the larger society. She also acquired the farm and house. In addition, Luzia, one of the slaves listed in the 1797 census as José Antonio's, appears as the property of Gertrudes in the 1798 census, together with her five children, suggesting that Luzia was also a gift. Finally, the lives of doña Clara Maria, Ignacia, and Gertrudes demonstrate that women with property in colonial Brazil could easily marry; all three of them remarried much younger men after José Antonio died.

Doña Clara Maria appears in the 1798 census, the year after her husband's death, living with a young married couple who were agregados of her household and owning sixteen slaves, her share of slaves in the community property. Four years later, in 1802, census takers recorded that she had married Francisco Xavier de Moraes, who was only twenty-nine years old. Her age is listed as sixty-two, but she was undoubtedly even older. The records indicate that they had married only eleven months after José Antonio's death. Francisco Xavier's birth certificate put his age at only twenty-three when they wed.[13] By the 1807 census doña Clara Maria had died, and her husband had remarried a woman in her twenties. By this time he held only seven slaves, his share of the community property that he had owned with Clara Maria. He had, in effect, bartered himself in exchange for the prospect of acquiring property, which later permitted him to marry a younger woman with few or no assets (since she appears not to have brought any slaves into the marriage).

Gertrudes Pires also wed a younger man, although the difference in their ages was not so great. The 1798 census recorded her as living alone with her eight children (the eldest was seventeen years old) and six slaves (Luzia and her five children). Gertrudes's offspring could not inherit from their father for they were adulterine illegitimate children. By the 1802 census, Gertrudes, who was then forty-two, had married Reginaldo Damazio da Silva, age thirty-three, and they lived with her children and nine slaves. The parish register indicates that they had married in 1800. Reginaldo apparently owned three adult slaves, which added to their joint property. Nonetheless, neither Reginaldo nor Gertrudes appears in later censuses of Santana; they must have moved away. Her eldest son, Damazio Antonio da Silva, married and continued to live in Santana, perhaps on the property originally given to Gertrudes.[14] He also married well because he and his wife were listed in the 1807 census as owning six slaves; by 1825 that number had increased to nine.

The documents for the settlement of José Antonio da Silva's estate are unclear about whether Francisco de Paula da Silva, his natural son, actually received his inheritance. The will of José Antonio's father indicates that he had a brother in Lisbon who was a collateral heir. After Francisco filed as an heir, the judge who carried out the division of the estate had the part belonging to the deceased auctioned and deposited in the Juizo dos Auzentes (court dealing with intestate goods), probably reserved for the brother in Lisbon. Francisco, however, placed an embargo on the proceeds to keep them from going abroad.

It is possible that he did inherit since there is every indication that Francisco prospered over the course of his lifetime. He first lived with his mother and grandfather until the grandfather died and then continued living with his mother. In all of this time, the family owned no slaves. In the 1798 census, however, less than a year after his father died, Francisco had acquired an adult male slave. The inheritance that he would have received from his father amounted to over two contos, and one slave was worth much less than that amount. Nevertheless, it is possible that Francisco, like many other rural Paulistas of that period, had not owned the land that he worked. He may have invested his inheritance in land, cattle, and one slave (that census reported no property except slaves). He did prosper thereafter; by 1802 he and his mother owned four slaves, produced and sold aguardiente, and kept fifteen horses and six pigs. By 1807, when Francisco was forty years old, these assets had increased substantially. By 1816, however, census takers recorded that he was no longer in Santana. In all likelihood he had died, because the slaves recorded as living in his mother's household were the same ones recorded as part of their joint household. In fact, she probably had inherited them from her deceased son.

Ignacia Franca had become the head of her own household by 1787 and, like her father, was sometimes labeled in the census either as a bastarda or a parda. Moreover, by the 1790s, census takers consistently reported her age as less than it really was. In 1807 they recorded it as fifty-nine when in reality she was sixty-four. By the 1816 census, when her son no longer lived in the household, Ignacia had married Manoel Barboza Bueno, a white man from Minas Gerais. Manoel's age was given as thirty-two and hers as fifty-nine when she was actually seventy-three! In the 1825 census she again appears as Manoel Barboza's wife; his age was listed as forty-two and hers as sixty-nine, even though she must have been eighty-one. In addition, after her marriage she was always labeled white in the census.

Such marriages between older women and younger men run counter to the received wisdom that younger women marry older men for their money. In colonial Brazil, however, the reverse also happened. Men needed capital to establish themselves independently of their parents since there were few other ways to earn a good living. For their part, older women often needed a man to manage their assets, thus allowing male and female needs to coincide in some cases. It seems likely, however, that public opinion frowned on such marriages. The records in the parish register, for example, show that both doña Clara Maria Ribeira's second marriage and that of Gertrudes Pires required a special dispensation from the Church. Gertrudes and her future husband petitioned for the dispensation because "they wish to marry as quickly as possible for urgent reasons."[15] The fact that both weddings were carried out virtually in secret indicates some level of societal disapproval for the marriage of an older woman to a younger man.

Despite the illegitimate and disorderly relationship of both Ignacia Franca and Gertrudes Pires with José Antonio da Silva, both women improved their qualidade, gaining financial assets and being viewed as white. Flaunting Church notions of social order clearly advanced their wealth and social status, perhaps indicating that some women may have made a calculated choice to enter into a sexual liaison outside of wedlock.[16] Slave women, however, could not make such decisions. Although some slaves who had a sexual relationship with their masters were given clothes or preferential treatment, most slave women could only hope to benefit by the manumission of their children or even of themselves. Not all masters freed their slave children or mistresses, but when they did so, it was a wonderful gift. In a few exceptional cases, the children of slaves and their masters were legitimized, even becoming their father's heir. In a few rare cases the slave herself was manumitted and later married her master. Such cases usually occurred in regions where there were few white women, and they brought an unusual sense of order to the disorder of concubinage between masters and slaves.

The life of José Antonio da Silva and his intimate relationships with women demonstrate the tensions between colonial ideas about order and disorder and the realities of life in eighteenth-century Brazil. In his marriage, José Antonio conformed to the precepts of the Church as well as to society's requirement that he marry someone who was his equal in wealth and status. His extramarital liaisons clearly flaunted the moral order of the Church, but because his dalliances were with women considered his inferiors in property and race, they still reinforced the hierarchical racial and class order. In these relationships, men drew power not only from their gender (in a patriarchal society) but also because they were the women's superiors in class and race or, in the most extreme cases, because the female was a slave. Within this social system a woman entering into an extramarital relationship could, with luck, improve her own and her children's material circumstances and even her *qualidade*.

QUESTIONS FOR DISCUSSION

1. Many scholars now believe that race is a social construct. Do the facts reported in this chapter confirm or disprove that theory?
2. In what ways was the marriage of the captain and his wife different from other marriages you have known? To what circumstances do you attribute these differences?
3. Have you known or heard of present-day marriages or relationships in which economic interest is a factor? In what ways are they the same or different from the examples in this chapter?
4. This chapter has demonstrated that in eighteenth-century São Paulo, people did not always live up to the accepted social norms or mores. Can you think of other times or places, including the present, when this has also been true? Why does this happen?
5. Using the data provided by this chapter, discuss what factors influenced a man's or woman's possibilities in life in São Paulo.

NOTES

1. Maria Beatriz Nizza da Silva, "Filhos ilegítimos no Brasil colonial," in *Sociedade Brasileira de Pesquisa Histórica, Anais da XV Reunião* (Curitiba: SPBH, 1996).
2. Arquivo do Estado de São Paulo (hereafter AESP), Inventários Não Publicados (hereafter INP), José Antonio da Silva, 1797, No. de ordem 569 c. 92.
3. I have calculated his approximate date of birth using his age as reported in the censuses of Santana for 1765, 1768, 1778, 1779, 1780, 1783, 1787, 1795, 1796, and 1797 in AESP, Maços de População, Bairro de Santana.
4. Arquivo da Cúria Metropolitana de São Paulo (hereafter ACMSP), Processos de Casamento da Sé, José Antonio da Silva, 6-57-2227.
5. ACMSP, Processos de Casamento, Reginaldo Damazo da Silva, 7-1-2511.
6. Alice P. Canabrava, "Uma economia de decadência: Os níveis de riqueza na capitania de São Paulo, 1765–1767," *Revista Brasileira de Economia* 26, no. 4 (October–December 1972): 101, 103.
7. AESP, INP, No. de ordem 569, c. 92.
8. Elizabeth Kuznesof, "Clans, the Militia, and Territorial Government: The Articulation of Kinship with Polity in Eighteenth-Century São Paulo," in David J. Robinson, ed., *Social Fabric and Spatial Structure in Colonial Latin America* (Syracuse: Microfilms International, 1979).
9. Muriel Nazzari, *Disappearance of the Dowry: Women, Families, and Social Change in São Paulo, Brazil (1600–1900)* (Stanford: Stanford University Press, 1991), ch. 3 and conclusion.
10. Muriel Nazzari, "Concubinage in Colonial Brazil: The Inequalities of Class, Race, and Gender," *Journal of Family History* 21, no. 2 (April 1996).
11. This was a census in which many people were classified as pardos, but it is clearly the same Clara Maria because her age is correct and she is listed as owning sixteen slaves, which corresponds to half of the number she owned with her husband.

12. See ACMSP, Registro de Casamentos, 7-31-2815, for the marriage of Damazio Antonio da Silva in 1803, which includes a copy of his baptismal certificate of 1780.

13. ACMSP, Livro de Casamentos da Sé, 1798, Francisco Xavier de Moraes, Clara Maria Ribeira.

14. ACMSP, Livro de Casamentos da Sé, 1803, Damazio Antonio da Silva, Rita Maria do Espirito Santo.

15. ACMSP, Processos de Casamento, 1800, 7-1-2511, Reginaldo Damazo da Silva, Gertrudes Pires do Nascimento; ACMSP, Livros de Casamento da Sé, 1798, Francisco Xavier de Moraes, Clara Maria Ribeira.

16. Robert McCaa, "Marriageways in Mexico and Spain, 1500–1900," in *Continuity and Change* 9, no. 1 (1994): 11–43.

SUGGESTED READINGS

Further information on marriage and concubinage in colonial Latin America can be found in Asuncion Lavrin, ed., *Sexuality and Marriage in Colonial Latin America* (Lincoln: University of Nebraska Press, 1989), and Lyman L. Johnson and Sonya Lipsett-Rivera, *The Faces of Honor: Sex, Shame, and Violence in Colonial Latin America* (Albuquerque: University of New Mexico Press, 1998).

An extensive study of race and class in marriage and concubinage is Verena Martínez-Alier, *Marriage, Class, and Colour in Nineteenth-Century Cuba: A Study of Racial Attitudes and Sexual Values in a Slave Society* (London: Cambridge University Press, 1974). Another study that considers race and class for a colonial Mexican town is Robert McCaa, "*Calidad*, Class, and Marriage in Colonial Mexico: The Case of Parral, 1788–1790," *Hispanic American Historical Review* 64 (1984): 477–502. Information on the interaction of race with gender in Brazilian concubinage is in Muriel Nazzari, "Concubinage in Colonial Brazil: The Inequalities of Race, Class, and Gender," *Journal of Family History* 21, no. 2 (April 1996): 107–24.

For the infrequency of marriage in colonial Brazil, see Donald Ramos, "Marriage and the Family in Colonial Vila Rica," *Hispanic American Historical Review* 55, no. 2 (May 1975): 200–225. For statistics on Brazilian illegitimacy, see Elizabeth Kuznesof, "Sexual Politics, Race and Bastard-Bearing in Nineteenth-century Brazil: A Question of Culture or Power?" *Journal of Family History* 16, no. 3 (1991): 241–60.

FIFTEEN

Juan Barbarín

The 1795 French Conspiracy in Buenos Aires

Lyman L. Johnson

In the late eighteenth century three great revolutions (in English North America, France, and Haiti) erupted, producing sweeping changes in the prevailing political, social, and economic order in the Atlantic world. Inspired by Enlightenment thinkers who heralded the use of reason to solve the problems of humankind, political leaders in English North America resisted efforts by the British Parliament to raise taxes and tighten political controls, ultimately culminating in a successful revolt against the mother country (1776–1783). Many of the documents promulgated by the English colonists to justify their rebellion, such as the Declaration of Independence, asserted that sovereignty resided with the people rather than with some divinely ordained monarch. After their final victory, the rebels formed the world's first large-scale democratic republic.

Although the American Revolution produced novel political changes, it did not seriously disrupt the colonial social hierarchies, leaving the old ones largely intact. In fact, the Constitution of 1787 maintained the institution of slavery. In contrast, the French Revolution of 1789 produced lasting political and social changes, as King Louis XVI, Queen Marie Antoinette, and a large number of aristocrats and commoners lost their lives in the so-called Reign of Terror engineered by radical leaders such as Maximilian Robespierre. The revolution in Haiti beginning in 1791 also resulted in sweeping social and economic changes, as slaves on the rich sugar-producing island took power and established the hemisphere's second republic, this time run by the former slaves themselves. For elites in Europe and the Americas, traditional views about social hierarchies, economic power, and religion seemed on the verge of collapsing into disorder and chaos.

The three great Atlantic revolutions had a tremendous impact in the American colonies of Spain and Portugal, where people of different social ranks reacted with everything from enthusiasm to abhorrence. Many Creole elites, members of the middle classes, the racially mixed plebeian groups, and Amerindians had chafed under the negative consequences of Bourbon political, fiscal, religious, military, and social innovations. Old colonial centers such as Lima had lost their economic primacy, but discontent simmered even in burgeoning political and commercial centers favored by the reforms, such as Buenos Aires. The crown had opened direct commerce between Spain and the port city and had also made it the capital of the new Viceroyalty of the Río de la Plata in 1776. Nevertheless, higher taxes, tighter commercial controls, and the influx of peninsular Spaniards, who dominated the viceregal bureaucracy and reaped large profits from the trade within the empire, bred resentment among many residents of the city, called porteños. *At the same time, many discontented porteños feared the consequences of revolutionary change. Independence might end loathsome Spanish policies, but it also could bring political chaos and social upheaval, especially among the growing slave population of Buenos Aires. Nevertheless, news of the revolutions in the United States, France, and Haiti provoked lively debates in the port city in the 1790s.*

By 1795 rumors of an impending slave revolt, perhaps led by radical elements of the city's French minority, swept through Buenos Aires and created a tense, highly charged atmosphere. Nevertheless, rumors of insolent behavior by slaves, secret nighttime meetings by Frenchmen, and stockpiled weapons and ammunition were difficult to substantiate. When subversive posters with only the word "Liberty" mysteriously appeared in the city, however, Viceroy Nicolás de Arredondo decided to mount an investigation. The man he chose to head the inquiry, Martín de Alzaga, was a dour, self-important member of the city council who harbored no sympathy for foreigners or revolutionaries. Alzaga's investigation soon focused on members of the French community, especially a prosperous merchant in the city, Juan Barbarín. Witnesses testified that Barbarín served as a sponsor for a black religious sodality, had Afro-Argentines visiting his house, and maintained a close and affectionate relationship with his own slave, Manuel. Barbarín allegedly even defended Robespierre and the bloody revolution in his native France. Alzaga, a staunch defender of traditional social hierarchies of the colony, considered Barbarín's behavior odious, subversive, and even revolutionary. He had the merchant jailed, along with his slave. Although later evidence apparently cleared Barbarín of complicity in any conspiracy, the merchant remained in jail and suffered financial ruin. Barbarín was later exiled to Spain, but his later life remains a mystery. In the end, Barbarín became a scapegoat for a society fearful of revolution; his belief in liberty, equality, and fraternity—the motto of the French Revolution—was his undoing.

It was midmorning, and already the narrow streets of Buenos Aires were oppressed by the damp heat of the Southern Hemisphere's summer. Juan Barbarín walked deliberately toward his shop. His slow progress was monitored by the nervous glances of his neighbors. Barbarín's eyes sought some sign of friendly regard in the familiar faces along his route. In place of the greetings that had punctuated his morning walk only weeks earlier, he was now met with silence and fear. As he crossed the broad plaza and walked past the city's unfinished cathedral, Barbarín felt exposed and vulnerable. Suspicion lay like a heavy cloak on his shoulders. Moving carefully to avoid the horse and ox dung that littered the plaza, he struggled to find a solution to the problems that weighed him down. Whom could he turn to? Whom could he trust?

In January 1795, Buenos Aires was on edge. Throughout this sprawling port city, residents of all classes and conditions talked about the great events that were shaking the foundations of the Atlantic world. Ships from the newly independent United States had begun to arrive in Buenos Aires, and Spanish authorities suspected that a handful of fiercely republican Yankee sailors had circulated the Declaration of Independence in the city. But revolutionary events in France and Saint Domingue (now called Haiti) seemed to threaten the city even more directly than did American republicanism.

In France the guillotine had taken the life of both the unfortunate Louis XVI and his queen. Thousands of priests and nobles had shared their king's terrible destiny. More troubling still to the deeply Catholic residents of Buenos Aires (called porteños) was the news that revolutionaries had dared to attack the Church itself. With the execution of Louis XVI in 1793, Spain and other European powers had been drawn inexorably into war with the revolutionary government of Paris. The political violence that had torn France apart for four years now spread across the face of Europe. News arriving in Buenos Aires in late 1794 indicated that Spain's war with France was going badly. Although there was little chance that Buenos Aires would be threatened directly by French forces, commerce, the lifeblood of this port city, was disrupted, and the prices of imported goods seemed to rise every day.

The urban poor of Buenos Aires, however, were more immediately concerned with the rising price of bread than with the cost of imported cloth. After a formal investigation, city officials revealed that a powerful group of local speculators and bakers had manipulated the effects of a poor harvest by hoarding grain, causing bread prices to rise to punishing heights. Although arrests had been made and illegal grain supplies seized, the price of bread had not fallen. As anger mounted, it was widely repeated in the streets and markets that these predatory culprits were foreigners. Some, it was said, were French. Self-interest and wartime xenophobia combined to produce a volatile political climate where the differences between distant French revolutionaries and local French residents (mostly royalists) were soon obscured.

For most porteños the most terrifying news came not from France but from Haiti, France's rich sugar colony in the Caribbean. Haiti was as notorious for the cruelty experienced by its black slaves as it was for the great wealth of its largely absentee landowners. As revolutionaries in France discussed granting political rights to free blacks and the possible abolition of slavery itself, Haiti's slaves had risen in rebellion against the colonial authorities in 1791. The plantation system had collapsed under the revolutionary onslaught, and the slaves had taken terrible revenge on their exploiters. Violence in Haiti would continue for more than a decade, leading to the creation of the Western Hemisphere's second independent republic. But in Buenos Aires and in other slaveholding colonies, public attention was narrowly focused on the violent elimination of the slave-owning class rather than on the significant political achievements of Haiti's former slaves.

In Buenos Aires, popular opinion linked these two events in a seamless political narrative. It was thought that the irreligious and democratic violence of France had inevitably led to Haiti's slave rebellion and race war. In the coffee shops, neighborhood taverns, and markets of Buenos Aires, men and women expressed their belief that regicide and assaults on the Church could only lead to social and political chaos and the overturning of racial hierarchy. When kings and priests were under attack, the authority of masters over their slaves was necessarily insecure. The fact that Spain was at war with revolutionary France made these distant events more threatening.

Buenos Aires was not a plantation economy, but it was an important destination for the African slave trade in the 1790s. By 1795 it had become the primary slave port for all of Spain's South American colonies. In earlier decades the city had imported slaves from the Portuguese colony of Brazil, then sending many of them to other colonial cities in the interior. With the city's dynamic economic growth in the 1780s, a small number of merchants from Buenos Aires directly entered the African slave trade. During the war with France, other members of the Buenos Aires commercial community purchased licenses as privateers, using their vessels to attack French slave ships off the African coast and bringing captured slave cargoes to Buenos Aires. The combined effect of an expanded legal slave trade with African ports and the wartime seizure of French slave cargoes more than doubled the city's slave population in less than a decade.

Thousands of the slaves who arrived in Buenos Aires from Africa and Brazil were subsequently sent to the mining centers of Bolivia or across the Andes to Chile, where prices for blacks were higher. But despite this secondary trade with other parts of the Spanish empire, the slave population of Buenos Aires had surpassed ten thousand (some 20 percent of the population) in 1795. Many of the city's artisan crafts were completely dependent on the labor of slaves and black freemen. The urban elite and most of the petty merchants, master artisans, and government officials who made up the middle classes all owned slaves as well. Slaves also played an important role in both agriculture and ranching across the region. Even the farms and ranches owned by the Catholic Church's convents and nunneries in surrounding rural areas were completely dependent on the forced labor of slaves. It was the growth of this racially and culturally distinct servile class that fed the fears that would overtake Juan Barbarín.

Popular fears had mounted when anonymous handwritten *pasquines* (pasquinades or lampoons) attacking the local authorities were pasted up around the city's central plaza. Pasquines had long been a part of Spanish colonial political life, and officials often found it difficult to identify authors and prosecute them. In the most common forms, pasquines attacked officials or other prominent residents in insulting terms for private scandals or unpopular political decisions. Despite the anger that these scurrilous or sometimes humorous posters produced among those targeted, they were grudgingly tolerated in most cases. In fact, many of those whose reputations were injured took their revenge through this same vehicle. Pasquines were, in effect, political and social siege weapons skillfully used by both the powerful and the weak. They were almost always handwritten and were seldom produced in multiple copies, the authors relying on word of mouth to multiply the effects of their insults or charges. Pasquines were almost always placed on the walls of public places, although it was not unknown for a pasquine to be thrown through the open window of a private dwelling.

The events that would sweep Juan Barbarín out of his normal routines began in 1795 with a series of inflammatory pasquines that warned of a planned insurrection and condemned Viceroy Nicolás de Arredondo for his failure to protect the public. The anonymous authors claimed that a vast conspiracy of unnamed foreigners sought to incite a slave rebellion. In the end, it was the appearance of a single word that spread fear and outrage to the center of colonial political authority. On the walls of buildings in the vicinity of the central plaza appeared tiny slips of paper broadcasting the era's revolutionary ideology reduced to a single word, *"LIBERTAD"* (liberty). The publication of this perceived incitement to revolution was soon followed by a new round of pasquines excoriating the government for its inactivity and complicity in the face of an insurrectionary threat.

Authorities in Spain and in Buenos Aires had desperately tried to seal off Spain and its colonies from the seductive ideology of "liberty" as celebrated by France's revolutionaries. Efforts to ban the published works of controversial Enlightenment authors had had only limited success. French social and political critics such as Jean-Jacques Rousseau and

Voltaire were universally banned in the Spanish colonies before the French Revolution, but their works and those of other banned authors circulated clandestinely in Buenos Aires. Similarly, republican political tracts from the newly independent United States of America were denied circulation in the Spanish Empire, but copies of the Declaration of Independence and the Constitution also filtered through the often-careless scrutiny of Spanish customs officials. With the beginnings of the French Revolution, however, Spanish officials took greater care to prevent the entrance of any publications that attacked either the monarchy or the Church. These efforts culminated in 1790 with an order to forbid all publications "that contain forms of malignant and false information."

Customs officials now began to examine more carefully the printed materials carried on American and other neutral ships calling in Buenos Aires and Montevideo, the viceroyalty's busiest ports. Any work that contained the word "liberty" or attacked the monarchy or religion was routinely confiscated. As these restrictions took hold, everyone in the colony realized how dangerous it was to have subversive materials. Still, it was an open secret that publications sympathetic to the French Revolution were in circulation among the small circle of educated men and women in Buenos Aires. Although the number of banned books and periodicals was small and the number of readers limited, the impact of these publications was much broader since each reader tended to distill and disseminate these controversial ideas in conversations with friends and associates.

Despite these small pockets of enthusiasm for liberty and secularism, Buenos Aires remained a deeply conservative city. Most porteños, both Spanish immigrants and the native-born Creoles, reacted with horror to the events in France and Haiti. Even the largely illiterate urban underclass, which received its news informally through networks of sailors and ships' passengers, viscerally reacted to attacks on Church and king. Religious belief—indeed, religious ritual—and faith in the essential justice of the distant Spanish king were the essential props of the colonial order. Days were centered on the Catholic Mass, and months and years were organized around public celebrations of saints' days and the births, coronations, and deaths of members of the royal family.

In Buenos Aires there was no public enthusiasm for imitating the revolutions of France or Haiti. Yet one small group of residents refused to accept uncritically the strident criticism of the French Revolution. These were members of the city's small French community and their friends and associates found among other foreign residents. This population was tied together through business dealings or through informal occasions when its members met for meals and shared news from Europe. As this group fell under increased suspicion during the war with France, Juan Barbarín, among others, found that every conversation conducted in public carried the risk that a careless remark might be passed on to colonial authorities. In the superheated political climate of 1795, public opinion was in no mood to distinguish between the nostalgic reminiscence of a French merchant or baker for his homeland and the most incendiary speech made by the most radical Jacobin in Paris.

As news from Haiti circulated in late 1794, many local slave owners reported a growing insolence among their black servants. With the new year, anger and fear had overcome reasoned discourse in Buenos Aires. Distant events had been transformed into local threats by a rising tide of secondhand information and rumor. As popular opinion focused on the perceived threat of insurrection, frustration with the apparent inactivity of Spanish colonial authorities mounted with every passing day. Unable to ignore these fears any longer, Viceroy Arredondo issued a statement in January that acknowledged reports of a conspiracy and notified the public that an official inquiry would be undertaken.

Viceroy Arredondo selected Martín de Alzaga, *alcalde ordinario* (magistrate) of the *cabildo* (city council), to head the investigation. The selection of Alzaga would prove to be a fateful decision. His powerful personality and deep prejudices gave the inquiry a relentless antiforeign character. Born in the Basque region of northern Spain, Alzaga immigrated to Buenos Aires as a young man and apprenticed with a local merchant involved in trade with Spain. Now in business for himself, Alzaga operated within the comfortable confines of the monopoly trade system. He was notoriously unsympathetic toward local merchants who profited from the liberalized commercial arrangements occasioned by the war with France or from contraband. A modestly successful businessman connected by kinship and commercial dealings to some of the wealthiest merchant families in Buenos Aires, Alzaga was among the most influential members of the cabildo. Although most found him difficult and overbearing, he had held numerous local offices in Buenos Aires. Humorless and self-important, he seemed to remember every insult and snub. His patriotism was reinforced by a passion for order and hierarchy. Once convinced of a threat to public order, Alzaga proved merciless in his efforts to track down and punish treason.

Although rumors of conspiracy churned through Buenos Aires, direct evidence was scarce. Where were these plebeian revolutionaries? Where was the local equivalent of the popular anger that had carried the Paris mob to Versailles? When announcing the inquiry, Viceroy Arredondo noted that he had received reports of unidentified individuals purchasing large quantities of powder and shot, but he had provided no real evidence of subversive acts. Alzaga knew that he was appointed in large measure to calm public fears and moved swiftly and energetically to give the appearance of purposeful action. In the dim light of proliferating fear, it was inevitable that his attention would quickly focus on the city's French immigrants. His logic was irrefutable. Was there any other segment of the city's population more likely to promote the dangerous ideal of liberty or attempt to ignite the rebelliousness of the slaves?

Alzaga first attempted to locate the authors of the pasquines, especially the writer of those inscribed with "liberty." His agents fanned out to interview everyone with a story to tell. A priest who lived near the cathedral came forward to testify that he had seen the pasquines scattered late at night by men disguised by broad hats and capes. Unfortunately, he could not identify them. Scores of other residents eagerly came forward to offer hearsay, advice, and, sometimes, evidence. Alzaga, typically, was interested in it all. Priests seem to have been particularly eager to talk to investigators but provided few concrete leads. Father Ramón Yrazabal testified that his colleague Father Manuel Aparicio had seen conspirators placing seditious posters near the Church of Santo Domingo. Questioned soon thereafter by Alzaga, Father Manuel admitted that he had no first-hand knowledge but had merely passed on a story told to him by one of his parishioners, doña Teresa Arellano. When Alzaga tracked down doña Teresa, she testified that she had also heard this tale secondhand from her friend, doña Tadea Rivera. After two days of hard work, the story gave out, one of many dead ends chased down by Alzaga.

Despite the obvious frustrations that followed each of these false starts, there was an unbroken thread that seemed to run through the fabric of testimony, and it was this fragile thread of coherence that kept Alzaga moving forward through the clutter of hearsay and rumor. From various corners of the city, informants reported an observed forwardness and assertiveness in the city's previously passive slave population. Juan Angel Freire, for example, reported that his mother's slave, Pasquala, had defiantly announced that she would soon be "dressed in the finest garments" and would "no longer have to take orders." In separate testimony, Father Angel López claimed to have been physically threatened by a mulatto slave whom he overheard arguing about the French Revolution in front of a tavern near where pasquines with the word "liberty" had been earlier discovered. Slaves themselves seemed equally eager to pass on information about a growing restiveness. Most typically they complained of "commotions" that were unsettling the slave community. The middle-aged slave Antonio, among others, informed the alcalde that while attending an illegal African dance held at the shop of a free black shoemaker, he had overheard two young slaves talk about a planned uprising. Other slaves reported fights and disturbances generated by disagreements over these insurrectionary plans. Alzaga redoubled his efforts.

Although unreliable at best, the first wave of testimony focused the attention of investigators on the urban neighborhood where the city's French residents were concentrated. Alzaga moved swiftly to interrogate the members of this small community. The first two French residents to fall into the alcalde's net were Juan Antonio Grimau, a baker, and the merchant Juan Barbarín. Grimau, a French immigrant, was incriminated by the testimony of his employee, the free black laborer Domingo Sandoval, who provided Alzaga with a convincing story filled with rich details. According to this employee, Grimau had thrown two books written in French into his bakery's oven after hearing news of the investigation. Alzaga then thoroughly questioned all the other employees of Grimau's bakery. He discovered one witness who claimed that after throwing the books on the fire, the baker had placed his chair in front of the oven so that he could watch while the flames consumed them. Another witness, who admitted that he could not read either Spanish or French, claimed that "Voltar" (Voltaire) wrote one of the books consigned to the flames. Alzaga had heard enough; he arrested Grimau and compiled a comprehensive list of all the prisoner's associates and friends for further investigation.

Although Juan Barbarín knew Grimau only casually, he would soon become entangled in the investigation. Pedro Muñoz, who lived near both Grimau and Barbarín, reported to the alcalde that he had overheard a heated discussion of the events in France in the barbershop of a Spanish immigrant, "Fulano Carreto," in November 1794. Since *fulano* is a Spanish word meaning "unknown person" (in English, John Doe), this use by Muñoz suggests that he was more familiar with the barbershop than with the barber, whose name was actually Juan Martín Carretero. Although Muñoz lived nearby, he was neither a client nor an acquaintance of the barber. Nevertheless, Muñoz claimed to have heard the loud argument in detail and offered the investigators what he claimed were direct quotes. As discussion of the war led to a series of angry denunciations of the French, one of the customers in the shop, the thirty-eight-year-old French merchant Juan Barbarín, strongly objected. According to Muñoz, Barbarín spoke provocatively, proclaiming that the French people "had good reasons to imprison and execute Louis XVI." Alone in defending the French and apparently provoked beyond endurance, Barbarín went on to suggest that "the Spanish people might have good reasons to imitate the French."

Upon hearing Barbarín's intemperate statement, one of the other visitors to the barbershop, Baltasar García, attempted to strike the Frenchman with a chair. When thwarted, he threw the chair at Barbarín's nearby shop. Cooler heads soon intervened, preventing bloodshed. The testimony of Muñoz went on to suggest to the authorities that Barbarín had potentially subversive associations, thus placing his apparently spontaneous defense of regicide in a darker political context. Muñoz told Alzaga that Barbarín "maintained a *tertulio*" (a gathering to discuss politics and literature) in his home frequented by French immigrants and other foreigners. For Alzaga, the missing elements of formal conspiracy that had eluded him as he tracked down the rumors and dead ends now seemed visible. According to this eager witness, Barbarín had not only endorsed regicide but had also held subversive meetings at his house. He had even "purchased gazettes with news of France" and then shared these periodicals freely with others. More intriguing still to Alzaga, Muñoz concluded his testimony by testifying that many of Barbarín's neighbors had remarked on the merchant's intimacy with members of the slave community—an intimacy he had maintained during his nearly ten-year residence in Buenos Aires.

The barber provided corroborating testimony that helped concentrate the alcalde's attention on Barbarín. Carretero asserted that before the war, Barbarín had claimed to be from Valencia in Spain and that all his friends had been Spaniards. After news of Spain's war with France became known in Buenos Aires, Barbarín had dramatically changed his patterns and habits, seeking the friendship of other French residents and asserting his French origins. Other witnesses claimed that Barbarín now ignored the Spaniards with whom he had previously socialized. Carretero noted that among these new acquaintances, Barbarín now spent a great deal of time with the young French immigrant Pablo Mayllos y Marcana. Barbarín's every action was now subject to intense scrutiny.

A resident of Barbarín's neighborhood, José de la Riva, offered evidence that further corroborated the damaging testimony of Muñoz. Riva stated that he had heard Barbarín praise Robespierre as "capable of making himself the owner of the world by his abilities." Riva claimed that he had challenged this remarkable belief by asking, "What did this capacity consist of given the atrocities, the abandonment of religion, and the murder of the king?" Barbarín, according to Riva, answered by saying "that if Robespierre had caused deaths he must have had a motive to do so."

Alzaga moved quickly to confirm the testimonies of Muñoz, Carretero, and Riva. Other witnesses to the argument in the barbershop were easily found, and their testimonies matched the rough outline provided in earlier interrogations. The alcalde and his assistants now sought to interview Barbarín's neighbors and business associates. Many of those questioned spoke respectfully of the suspect and noted his honesty and good habits. Some informants, however, wondered about his public interactions with the city's slave community. Barbarín, called Juan Pablo Capdepont or Capdepón when he arrived in Buenos Aires, had drawn the attention of many neighbors and customers by allowing slaves to visit him in his home and by treating his own slave, Manuel, with surprising affection and generosity.

News of the alcalde's intense inquiry into the affairs of the merchant attracted a new wave of testimony. A sergeant of the local garrison informed Alzaga that on numerous occasions he had witnessed Barbarín and his slave walking along the riverfront during the hours of siesta, a part of the day when nearly all the city's residents sought relief from the heat indoors. For this informant, the discreet timing of these walks and the pair's apparent disregard for the local siesta custom appeared suspicious. What could have been the subject of these secretive conversations between master and slave? Once asked, the question seemed to produce its own answer.

By the time Alzaga questioned Barbarín directly, the Frenchman was shaken to his core. When asked to explain his apparent intimacy with the slave community, Barbarín testified that he had served as treasurer of the black religious organization, the Archicofradía de San Benito, until recently, when he had decided to resign. Why had he resigned? Barbarín claimed that his barber had warned him that rumors had linked his service to this black brotherhood to the feared slave uprising. He had resigned, therefore, to allay suspicion. He went on to remind Alzaga that his service with the group was not remarkable. Many other men of substantial means had served in similar capacities with segregated organizations of slaves and free blacks in Buenos Aires.

Barbarín's statement was undeniably true. It was the custom throughout the Spanish Empire to require that white officials be appointed to supervise the fiscal affairs and the public behavior of elected black officers of black lay brotherhoods and guilds. White officers were also placed in command of segregated black militia units. San Benito in Buenos Aires was only one of many black organizations where white officials supervised the members. Like other brotherhoods, it had negotiated with a local parish church to place an altar devoted to San Benito and provide a location for meetings and religious observances. Members paid dues and collected alms in the city's streets to help pay for other members' burial costs, including special masses for the souls of the deceased. These funds were also used to finance the celebrations associated with San Benito's feast day. Why, Barbarín wondered, was his civic service a cause of concern?

According to testimony gathered from his neighbors and associates, Barbarín's welcoming behavior toward the blacks whom he supervised pushed the limits expected of a man of property in such a role. Members of Barbarín's class universally kept all slaves and free blacks at a distance. A number of witnesses stated that Barbarín had even allowed members of the brotherhood to enter his home when they delivered alms solicited in the city's streets and markets. Although no one had thought it necessary to report these visits to authorities earlier and no one had raised objections to Barbarín, this behavior appeared more ominous, even dangerous, in retrospect, once the fear of a slave uprising had spread and Alzaga had begun to interrogate the Frenchman's neighbors. That someone of Barbarín's class and status encouraged this type of casual association with slaves seemed dangerously egalitarian to Alzaga. For him, and for most propertied porteños, black freemen and slaves could never be accepted as guests in the home of a "decent" person. Any intimacy with slaves in an era when revolutionary events in Haiti dominated porteño conversation seemed inherently subversive.

The unusual familiarity that Barbarín maintained with members of the San Benito brotherhood led inevitably to questions about his apparently warm relationship with his own slave, Manuel. Informants from the neighborhood suggested to Alzaga that the Frenchman treated his slave "with great demonstrations of affection and love." The neighbors corroborated the earlier testimony of the patrol sergeant who had observed the master and slave taking walks along the banks of the Rio de la Plata. They also told Alzaga that Barbarín seemed to treat the slave more like a friend than a servant. One informant commented in detail on the intimacy and affection that characterized their conversations. Another reported that Manuel had boasted that his owner had recently promised him his freedom. What, Alzaga wondered, was expected by Barbarín in return? Could the promise of freedom have been used to recruit Manuel into the conspiracy?

In the eyes of the alcalde, Barbarín's decision to hire the young immigrant Pablo Mayllos to teach Manuel to read and write was perhaps the most suspicious and damning aspect of this unusual and complex relationship between a slave and his master. It only took a few days for Alzaga to discover the background and habits of Manuel's twenty-eight-year-old tutor. After arriving in Buenos Aires, Mayllos had struggled to support himself as a private tutor and "letter writer." In addition to the income he received from a small number of students, Mayllos had set up a small table in the central plaza near the cabildo, where he wrote letters for clients found among the city's largely illiterate urban underclass. For a small fee he might compose letters to distant kin or to employers or public authorities in other cities. Mayllos earned very little from these tasks. He took his meager meals at taverns and shared a rented room with another single man, Fermín Sotes. Rather too eagerly, Sotes volunteered to Alzaga that Mayllos often returned to the room very late at night. Another acquaintance noted that Mayllos was "more inclined to diversions than to work."

A French immigrant who knew of the merchant's desire to locate a tutor for Manuel had introduced the nearly destitute Mayllos to Barbarín. The young man eagerly forfeited his unpredictable earnings as a letter writer to accept Barbarín's generous wage of four pesos per month. As this relationship deepened, Mayllos had stayed at times in Barbarín's home as a guest and entered into the merchant's social circle. Almost from the moment that Mayllos was brought to the attention of the investigators, they wondered if he could be the author of the revolutionary pasquines that had been distributed throughout the city. Alzaga noted in a report that Mayllos's hand seemed very similar to the hand that had written "liberty."

Barbarín's warm relations with Manuel seemed to suggest a quiet challenge to what Alzaga held to be an essential prop of the colonial social order: the power of master over slave. The alcalde took the Frenchman's highly unusual decision to provide Manuel with a tutor to be a political act. The deeply conservative Alzaga saw the bloody excesses of the French and Haitian Revolutions as predictable outcomes that inevitably followed intellectual assaults on religion and monarchy and, more recently, on the hierarchy of master and slave. The bloodshed, property destruction, and sacrilege unleashed by both revolutions had their roots, for him, in the era's secularizing passions and in the dangerous erosion of what he took to be a divinely inspired order. The too-familiar mixing of white and black, of slave and free in Barbarín's house as well as Barbarín's desire to educate his slave suggested a dangerous lack of respect for this God-given order as well as a willful negligence of proprieties.

As Alzaga's interest in him grew, Barbarín became the distracted and nervous man introduced at the beginning of this chapter. Repeated visits by Alzaga and his underlings to Barbarín's shop and home had provoked fears and doubts among neighbors and customers. Afraid of drawing the alcalde's attention or, alternatively, suspicious that Barbarín was in fact involved in some terrible conspiracy, once-friendly neighbors and associates now avoided him, choosing to look the other way as he passed by in the street and ignoring his greetings. Only a small circle of other French immigrants and a handful of close friends continued their social contacts with him. As the investigation increased in intensity, even these loyal associates grew increasingly nervous when they met Barbarín in public. Isolated and fearful, Barbarín now avoided his old friends because he was concerned that any meeting or contact with his fellow countrymen might appear to confirm the alcalde's xenophobic suspicions.

Having thoroughly interviewed most of Barbarín's associates, Alzaga finally turned his attention to the slave. Under questioning, Manuel freely admitted that he and his master had occasionally taken walks together. While he was treated "with love and dressed well" by his master, he insisted that this treatment and the shared moments of leisure during the siesta or early evening were completely innocent. He claimed that his master never talked about the revolutions in France or Haiti. Asked if Barbarín had promised him his freedom, Manuel stated that he had in fact been promised his freedom. However, Manuel understood that his freedom would only be granted if Barbarín returned to Spain or died in Buenos Aires. Alzaga then asked Manuel about his tutor. Why had his master paid Mayllos to teach him to read and write? Manuel replied that his master wanted his help in managing the shop's accounts. If he learned to read and write, then Barbarín would be free to leave the shop when business demanded. What, the alcalde inquired, was Manuel reading? Manuel replied that he generally only read accounts and letters relative to his master's business, but that Barbarín was willing to "read any book" to him to advance his instruction. Despite the explanations offered by Barbarín and Manuel, Alzaga clearly thought this relationship revealed

dangerous egalitarian leanings. The Frenchman's willingness to compromise the expected hierarchy of master and slave was by itself a political
provocation.

Having heard enough, Alzaga ordered the arrest of Juan Barbarín. For
good measure, Barbarín's literate slave, Manuel, was arrested as well. A
month later, Mayllos joined them in jail. With characteristic thorough-
ness, Alzaga then ordered the residences and shops of all those arrested
to be searched and their goods seized. It was disappointing to Alzaga
that despite rumors that conspirators were collecting arms and muni-
tions, a search of Barbarín's home and shop had discovered neither.

Conditions in the Buenos Aires jail were notoriously dreadful. The
cells were filthy and infested with pests. The jail's other prisoners were
common delinquents or worse. When in the months preceding this inquiry officials had discovered that some prisoners were near starvation,
the city fathers had responded with characteristic humanitarianism by
having a barred window installed in the jail's street wall to allow prisoners to beg food from pedestrians passing by. Although Barbarín was able
to pay for food for himself and Manuel, he was increasingly desperate
and frightened. Fortunately for him, Alzaga's investigation was now di-
verted by surprising new testimony.

As Barbarín and Manuel languished in jail, don Miguel García de
Bustamonte provided Alzaga with a promising new lead. He testified
that a slave owned by one of his neighbors had been heard to say that the
city's slaves planned to rise on Good Friday. José, placed by his master as
a cook for the caulkers who worked in the Spanish naval yard, had
threatened his work mates with the prospect of a slave insurrection during a lunchtime argument. José later tried to pass off his angry threats as
a joke but provided more information when his master threatened him
with a shotgun. Under pressure, José admitted that he had been recruited
to join a conspiracy by "a man whose name I don't know and whose
occupation I don't know, but who was dressed decently." After questioning the slave closely, Alzaga was able to identify the alleged insurrectionary recruiter as José Díaz, an apparently impoverished free black migrant
from the interior who managed to earn a precarious living running a
livery stable.

With this new conspirator in his sights, Alzaga and his agents abandoned their inquiry into the affairs of Barbarín. The alcalde turned instead to Díaz's wife, neighbors, and drinking companions. Many of these
volunteered that Díaz had talked freely about a slave conspiracy. Some of
his neighbors even claimed to have heard him say that the city's French
residents would soon lead a slave uprising. During one drinking bout in
a neighborhood tavern, Díaz stated that local French residents had offered the slaves freedom if the rebellion succeeded. Confirming Alzaga's
worst fears, witnesses related that Díaz had told them that slaves were
being urged to murder their masters while they slept. They were then to

take the arms and money they had seized and join the French insurrectionists who planned to storm the city's fortifications on Good Friday. Some said that Díaz had openly boasted that six thousand men waited in the interior provinces of Corrientes, Santa Fé, and Paraguay to join the rebellion once it had begun in Buenos Aires. Díaz was arrested and joined Barbarín and the others in jail.

Alzaga now began to hand over his evidence to the *audiencia* (royal court). After a preliminary examination, the chief prosecutor announced his intention to seek the execution of all the traitors. This tidy and expeditious conclusion of the investigation was soon swept aside by the appearance of a completely new conspiratorial trail. Among the scores of free blacks and slaves interviewed by Alzaga, there were very few who offered him anything other than rumor and hearsay. During one of the alcalde's visits to the foreign-owned bakeries and artisan shops spread around the city's central marketplace and nearby smaller plazas, however, a remarkable new witness had been identified — Juan Pedro, the slave of the French baker Juan Luis Dumont (or Dumonte). The testimony of this remarkable figure pushed the investigation forward in a new direction.

Juan Pedro offered detailed testimony that for the first time seemed to reveal a conspiracy large enough and well organized enough to actually threaten the colonial government. According to Juan Pedro, his master Dumont held meetings in his house that drew together many of the city's French residents. He drove home the subversive nature of these meetings with a telling anecdote. In December 1794 a particularly boisterous meeting where the conspirators had toasted "liberty" was abruptly ended when the group's lookout brought word that a patrol of soldiers was nearby. Apparently fearing discovery, Dumont extinguished the lights and his guests dispersed. As remembered by this helpful slave, Dumont and his friends then relocated their meetings to a farm in the nearby countryside where a number of Frenchmen resided. Safely isolated from the city's armed patrols, Juan Pedro claimed that the conspirators' meeting had become larger and more animated. Convinced unambiguously of this threat, Alzaga moved quickly and arrested Dumont and all those who had frequented his home.

There were now more than twenty "conspirators" in the jail along with Barbarín, Mayllos, and Manuel. Alzaga went to the judges of the audiencia to gain permission to question two of the prisoners under torture. These two, he assured the judges, were key to revealing the conspiracy in full. He selected the black freeman, José Díaz, who had talked openly of an uprising, and the watchmaker Santiago Antonini, one of the immigrants arrested on the testimony of Dumont's slave. In Antonini's room, Alzaga's agents had found one of the incriminating pasquines celebrating the word "liberty." Days later, Barbarín and the other prisoners listened to the screams of the two prisoners tortured in the room above their cells. When these torments failed to produce new information about the conspiracy, Alzaga decided to torture the unfortunate Antonini a second time. Again, Barbarín and the other prisoners heard Antonini beg for mercy and scream out in pain as steel pins were driven beneath his fingernails. Despite this agony, Antonini offered Alzaga no new leads, no information on clandestine stores of arms, and no identification of the conspiracy's leadership. Desperate to bring the case to trial, Alzaga now requested permission to torture the other prisoners.

The judges of the audiencia immediately refused this request. This refusal signaled the audiencia's growing reservations about the alcalde's investigation. Thwarted by the royal court, Alzaga was forced to respond to the formal arguments offered by lawyers appointed to defend the prisoners. Although each lawyer adopted a unique strategy to deal with the evidence against his client, the combined weight of these individual attacks swept away much of Alzaga's theory of a treasonous conspiracy organized by the French. The audiencia moved slowly, however. Most of the prisoners, including Barbarín, continued to languish in prison for eight more months before the royal court made a final decision. Even then, its decision left the prisoners' fate unresolved. Convinced by the arguments of the defense lawyers, the judges did not find any foreign prisoner guilty of any crime. There was simply no clear evidence of conspiracy. As one lawyer put it, "Where is this conspiracy that threatens to ruin everyone? Who are the directors of the bloody enterprise? Some poor bakers and a watchmaker."

Neither did the judges exonerate the defendants as demanded by the defense attorneys, however. Instead, the judges decided to send Barbarín and nearly all the other arrested immigrants to Spain without formal sentence. This decision to condemn the defendants to unofficial exile passed the buck to higher judicial authorities in Spain. Unlike the foreign-born prisoners, the intemperate and perhaps mentally ill José Díaz, the only free black prisoner, was condemned to suffer ten years of exile in the desolate Malvinas Islands in the South Atlantic. The royal court seemed to say that there was no convincing evidence of conspiracy or treason, but that finding the defendants innocent was both too dangerous during wartime and too offensive to the powerful Martín de Alzaga, who had led the investigation and ordered the arrests.

This clumsy decision may have been a reaction to the public scandal caused by a wave of bitter denunciations issued by one of the defense lawyers who had ridiculed Alzaga and his agents. Instead of focusing on the case against the prisoners, the court and the new viceroy, Pedro Melo de Portugal, felt compelled to defend Alzaga's reputation and, by extension, Spanish justice. This highly irregular decision acknowledged that Alzaga's long investigation had produced no convincing evidence of conspiracy. Nevertheless, Barbarín and the others would suffer severe punishment. The combination of long months of incarceration in Buenos

Aires and then exile to Spain effectively ruined most of them financially and broke the health of many. The two victims of torture never fully recovered, and the surviving evidence suggests that José Díaz died a prisoner in the Malvinas. Barbarín, who had run a profitable business before his arrest, was forced to inform the royal court from his cell that his customers had stopped paying their debts to him, thus endangering his business and draining his resources.

It is not known what happened to Barbarín after his forced exile to Spain. In August 1796 the French ambassador to Madrid wrote a formal protest to Spanish authorities over the continued incarceration of Barbarín, now called Jean Cap-de-pon, and other French citizens, despite the end of the war. The ambassador's letter imitated the angry language of the defense attorneys in Buenos Aires, excoriating Alzaga and suggesting that he had profited personally from the seizure of Barbarín's goods. There is no evidence that this strong protest led to the immediate release of Juan Barbarín and the others, but a reply to the French ambassador sent by Spanish authorities five months later claimed that there were no longer any French prisoners in the realm.

Was Juan Barbarín a party to a conspiracy? The evidence suggests his innocence. Despite an intense investigation that included a search of Barbarín's residence and shop, Alzaga was unable to discover a single compromising document or any store of weapons. After interviewing hundreds of often-eager neighbors and associates, he was also unable to link Barbarín with either José Díaz, who had drunkenly boasted of his involvement in a planned rebellion, or Dumont's circle, who had too often and too publicly toasted "liberty" and talked favorably of revolutionary France. In fact, there is no evidence that either Díaz or any member of the Dumont group was involved in an active conspiracy or had pursued any serious political objective. There is some evidence, however, that Mayllos, hired by Barbarín to educate the slave Manuel, was indeed the author of at least some of the pasquines. Barbarín and the others were at times indiscreet and even foolish when provoked by Spanish patriots or excited by news from France. But the xenophobic tide caused by war transformed their intemperate remarks and their habit of socializing together into a threat. There is no doubt that the violent events in France and Haiti had helped to fashion the political paranoia that fed Alzaga's investigation and led inevitably to the incarcerations and tortures.

Looking back on these events from our era, we find ourselves drawn to Juan Barbarín. He appears to be a particularly sympathetic figure, a man who embodied much of the transformative idealism of the time. He read widely and sympathized with the ideals of the French Revolution. He looked at its excesses and at its most important political symbol, Robespierre, and still saw the liberating potential of new ideas. This idealism quietly worked in his private life as well. He saw his slave Manuel as a fully human being, enjoyed his company, and planned for his future as a free man. Even in his routine responsibilities as an officer of the black brotherhood of San Benito, Barbarín recognized the humanity and dignity of its members and allowed them to enter his home as peers. Alzaga took these small acts of compassion and generosity as revolutionary. Perhaps they were. In the century that was ready to dawn, the cumulative opinion of thousands of men and women who, like Juan Barbarín, embraced the idea of "liberty" would lead to the independence of Spanish America, the end of the African slave trade, and the abolition of slavery.

QUESTIONS FOR DISCUSSION

1. Why did revolutionary events in France and Haiti create a climate of fear in Buenos Aires?
2. Were there general similarities in the testimony provided by informants to Alzaga? What were the common themes?
3. What do we know about the institution of slavery in Buenos Aires as a result of the role played by slaves in this inquiry?
4. Even though there was little evidence that Juan Barbarín was an active conspirator against Spanish authorities, was the judge Martín de Alzaga correct in thinking that Barbarín was a dangerous man?

SOURCES

Research for this chapter was conducted in Buenos Aires, Argentina, and in Seville, Spain. The records of the legal proceedings in Buenos Aires are primarily found in three lengthy legajos found in the Archivo General de la Nación. See Criminales, Legajo 39, Expediente 14; Tribunales, Legajo 60, Expediente 6; and Interior, Legajo 38, Expediente 1. The Archivo General de Indias in Seville yielded information on the biographies of the prisoners and on the diplomatic efforts undertaken to liberate Barbarín and the others.

SUGGESTED READINGS

For intellectual life in the era of the French Revolution, see Jonathan Israel, *Radical Enlightenment, Philosophy, and the Making of Modernity, 1650–1750* (Oxford, 2001). François Furet, *Interpreting the French Revolution* (New York, 1981), breaks with earlier interpretations that emphasized class and ideology. Georges Lefebvre, *The Coming of the French Revolution*, trans. R. R. Palmer (New York, 1947), presents the classic class-based analysis. See also two newer works, Michael Keith Baker, *Inventing* the French Revolution: Essays on French Political Culture in the Eighteenth Century* (New York, 1990), and Timothy Tackett, *Becoming a Revolutionary: The Deputies of the French National Assembly and the Emergence of a Revolutionary Culture* (Princeton, 1996). Lynn Hunt, *The Family Romance of the French Revolution* (Berkeley, 1992), examines the gender content of revolutionary politics.

The Haitian Revolution has received less extensive coverage than the revolutions in America and France. C. L. R. James, *The Black Jacobins*, 2nd ed. (New York, 1963), is the classic study. Anna J. Cooper, *Slavery and the French Revolutionists, 1788–1805* (Lewiston, NY, 1988), also provides an overview of this important topic. See also Carolyn E. Fick, *The Making of Haiti: The Saint Domingue Revolution from Below* (Knoxville, 1990), and David Barry Gaspar and David Patrick Geggus, eds., *A Turbulent Time: The French Revolution and the Greater Caribbean* (Bloomington, 1997).

For the independence era in Spanish America, see John Lynch, *The Spanish American Revolutions, 1808–1826*, 2nd ed. (New York, 1986), and Jay Kinsbruner, *Independence in Spanish America* (Albuquerque, 1994).

SIXTEEN

Agustín Agualongo and the Royalist Cause in the Wars of Independence

Marcela Echeverri

Inhabitants of the faithful City of Pasto: You have seen and painfully experienced your people's devastation; you have suffered the strongest yoke of the greatest of all tyrannical intruders, Bolívar. It is time for us, faithful Pastusos, to unite our courageous hearts in the defense of Religion, the King, and our Fatherland, because if we stop defending our most sacred rights we will again fall into the hands of the enemies of the Church and Humanity. —Estanislao Merchancano and Agustín Agualongo, June 1823

Pasto is the southern gate, and if we don't have it, we will always be cut off, therefore we need that passage to be clear, without a single enemy in its way. . . . The worst of it is that . . . we have a force of more than 3,000 souls against us—souls made of unbending steel. Since the conquest, no other people has demonstrated more tenacity than they. . . . It's been proven we cannot win over [those wicked ones] and for that reason it is essential to destroy them to their very core. —Simón Bolívar to Colombian Vice President Santander, July 21, 1823

Spain and her empire became embroiled in the wars of the French Revolution by the 1790s, which culminated when the French armies of Napoléon Bonaparte invaded the Iberian Peninsula in 1807. The French occupiers forced the abdication of Spain's King Charles IV and coerced the heir to the throne, Ferdinand, into renouncing his rights to succeed his father on May 6, 1808. The French invaders then placed Joseph Bonaparte, the brother of Napoléon, on the Spanish throne. Many in Spain and the empire saw Joseph as a usurper, and a profound constitutional crisis emerged. A growing number of citizens in the Spanish Empire believed that without a legitimate monarch on the throne, sovereignty returned to the people. Consequently, local groups in Spain and the Indies began

289

establishing a series of governing committees (juntas) in major cities throughout the empire. These juntas were opposed by representatives of the Spanish colonial bureaucracy, who believed that the existing royal governments should rule until the French left Spain. As a result, the political authority of most regional juntas in the Indies was limited, and forming stable alternative governments proved a daunting task. Over time, local Spanish authorities crushed many of these provisional governments in the Indies, while most of the others fell to the armies sent by Ferdinand VII to restore his absolute rule following his restoration to the throne in 1814.

The French invasion of the Iberian Peninsula set in motion a series of political events that would ultimately culminate in the independence of the Viceroyalty of New Granada by 1821. The first autonomous junta in New Granada formed in Quito in 1809, but Spanish authorities in Bogotá and Lima sent troops that suppressed it just a few months later. Creole groups in Caracas created their own junta in 1810, followed by autonomy movements in Cartagena, Cali, Pamplona, Socorro, and most significantly Bogotá, which supplanted the government of Viceroy Antonio Amar y Borbón on July 20, 1810. In December 1810, the junta of Bogotá convoked a congress of representatives from every province in the viceroyalty, but only six delegates attended, and even they failed to agree on the form of a new government in northern South America. While the rebels squabbled, loyalist groups counterattacked in Popayán, Pasto, and Santa Marta, recruiting large numbers of indigenous people with promises of lower taxes and African slaves with assurances of freedom. These loyalist forces eventually carved out territory along the Caribbean coast, in Pasto and Popayán (in the Andean-Pacific region of New Granada), and in the Magdalena River Valley. By then, Ferdinand had returned to the throne and dispatched sizable numbers of Spanish troops to quell any unrest, and by 1816 most of the region had been pacified. The rebel forces under Simón Bolívar did not rally again until 1819, when dissatisfaction with Spanish repression had reawakened opposition to the colonial regime. Bolívar's victories at Boyacá (1819) and Carabobo (1821) and his lieutenant Antonio José de Sucre's defeat of the loyalists at Pichincha (1822) won the independence of New Granada, which became the core of the new republic of Gran Colombia.

One of the more controversial figures to emerge in the turbulent years of the independence era was a mestizo *loyalist leader in the Pasto region, Agustín Agualongo. Colombian nationalist historians have traditionally portrayed Agualongo as a rude, uneducated Indian who represented a fanatical and remote region of the Colombian frontier. These historians present the* Pastusos *as an ignorant, misguided populace who opposed the progressive, liberal Bolivarian republic that formed after independence. Agualongo's successes in southern Colombia provided disturbing evidence to these nationalists about the strength of loyalist sentiment in the region, demonstrating that independence from Spain was hardly inevitable. Moreover, the Pasto region was no isolated backwater, but rather a strategic food-producing region, supplying the gold mines of the Pacific littoral. Pasto also occupied a pivotal geographic position, at the crossroads be-*

tween the highlands surrounding the viceregal capital of Bogotá and the Audiencia of Quito to the south.

When word of the creation of the Quito junta in 1809 reached southern Colombia, Popayán's governor, Miguel Tacón, enlarged the loyalist forces by recruiting large numbers of Amerindians with promises of lower tribute payments; he also recruited slaves by offering freedom to any who fought against the rebel forces from Quito. Tacón's polices upset local miners and landowners, who feared the loss of laborers, and they also dismayed regional indigenous leaders resentful of their declining power over local ethnic groups, who left traditional towns and villages to fight in the royalist army. Among those who flocked to the loyalist banner was a young mestizo painter, Agustín Agualongo, who proved his valor and military savvy in a number of the early battles against insurgent forces, first from Quito and later from other regions of Colombia. Agualongo became a prominent loyalist military and later political leader in southern Colombia, resisting insurgent armies and, after independence, the military forces of Gran Colombia, until he was finally captured and executed on July 10, 1824. Although Agualongo and the royalist forces ultimately suffered defeat, the tenacity of their struggle against the republican forces indicates the political agenda of subaltern groups, who fought for a more inclusive nation that would protect their lands and safeguard their political rights.

Over the past two centuries, Colombian nationalist historians and politicians have viewed the city and region of Pasto, located in the southwest Andean frontier with Ecuador, as disloyal and irrevocably set apart from the rest of the country. This stems in large part from Pasto's stubborn loyalty to the Spanish crown during the independence wars. Pasto's royalism helped make the war in the northern Andes one of the most bitter and long-lasting phases of the independence struggle, as the majority of Pasto's population engaged in a brave but ultimately futile struggle against the diverse insurgent armies that secured Colombia's independence between 1809 and 1824. Even after the Colombian Republic was proclaimed in Pasto, following the defeat of the Spanish army in Bomboná on April 7, 1822, local people still confronted the new republican authorities and posed a serious challenge to the nascent republic. Multiethnic guerrilla forces that had fought in earlier local royalist militias not only threatened the stability of Simón Bolívar's dream of an independent republic of New Granada, they also jeopardized his plans to defeat Spain in the heartland of Spain's South American empire, Peru and Upper Peru. As Bolívar marched southward, he needed to make sure that the rear of his army remained clear of enemies and under the control of his government. But people in Pasto seemed indomitable; their obstinate resistance became a major strategic concern for the Bolivarian army, and the region became a graveyard for all too many of his troops. A major leader in this stubborn struggle of the royalists against Bolívar and his army was the mestizo general Agustín Agualongo.

ROYALISM, AGUSTÍN AGUALONGO, AND THE INDEPENDENCE ERA

Royalism is a contested subject among historians seeking to understand and explain the meaning of the independence wars and the creation of Latin American nations.[1] Colombian nationalist historians of the nineteenth century characterized Pasto's loyalty to Spain as a critical sign of the region's fanaticism and backwardness. In the nationalistic historical narrative of the period, these concepts became inscribed as an indisputable fact; yet the independence movement that emerged triumphant in South America after almost twenty years of bloody military conflicts had originally been characterized as an "insurgency," battling against a legitimate, sovereign Spain. Once the independence movement attained superior military strength, however, the independence project and its republican ideals gained territorial and ideological legitimacy. It was then that these historians and republican politicians transformed the royalists into agitators (*facciosos*), insurgents, and rebels. The standard for loyalty was no longer the king but the nation and the republic of Colombia. Along with losing its legitimacy, royalism was also stripped of its historical importance because the dominant, nationalist metanarrative of the nation would not tolerate any alternative visions of the independence period, roundly condemning those who defended the Spanish colonial state.

As a result, Pasto's greatest independence hero, the royalist Agustín Agualongo, became an antihero in Colombian official independence histories, beginning in the nineteenth century. Yet is it possible to tell an alternative story of Agualongo without viewing him as a stereotypical villain, as nationalist historians have attempted to present him? Given the shortage of documents left by royalist insurgents such as Agualongo, any alternative interpretation of his life and times must depend on a careful reinterpretation of the same documentary evidence (most often created by his enemies) used by earlier scholars to undermine Agualongo and the royalist movement that he led until 1824. Although historians have generally presented a very negative portrayal of royalists in the independence era, there has been an ongoing debate about Agualongo's role in Colombian history over the past two hundred years between local historians writing in Pasto (who do not accept this negative portrait of Agualongo) and nationalist historians who created the narrative that vilifies all royalists. The first historian of the Colombian Republic, José Manuel Restrepo, established an authoritative narrative of the era that portrayed Agualongo and all people from Pasto (or Pastusos) as vile fanatics. Restrepo was a powerful political figure in his lifetime, having served as Bolívar's minister of the interior. Moreover, as an eyewitness of events of the independence era, his opinions had nearly unimpeachable credibility.

Restrepo's account condemned Agualongo as an "ignorant Indian," and his negative portrayal influenced many later historical representations of the royalist warlord, or *caudillo*. This portrayal implied that Agualongo's ethnicity and ignorance led him to fight for the king for nearly fifteen years, repeatedly turning his back on the liberating, progressive promise of the new republic.[2] On the other hand, by describing and labeling him as Indian, Restrepo highlighted Agualongo's lack of judgment by relying on the widespread, racist belief that all Indians were rude, ignorant, and incapable of making rational political judgments. Although indigenous people clearly understood Hispanic law, participated actively in the colonial economy, and understood political events of the day, many Colombian elites clung to the belief that Indians were clearly inferior to people of Spanish descent. Therefore, by calling Agualongo — the symbol of southwestern royalism par excellence — an ignorant Indian, Restrepo explained away the caudillo's support for royalism as reflecting the Indian people's inherent poor judgment, excusing Agualongo for his obviously "delusional" opposition to the independence cause. In presenting this negative, racist portrayal, Restrepo set the tone for the complete dismissal of royalism as a legitimate political and ideological position during the period.

But was Agualongo really an Indian? Based on documentation suggesting that Agualongo was not an Indian but rather a mestizo (of mixed white and Indian ancestry), historians in the twentieth century have challenged Restrepo's negative, racist portrayal of the royalist caudillo. Indeed, his birth certificate provides evidence that Agustín Agualongo Sisneros was born in the city of Pasto of mestizo parents.[3] But in spite of that "fact," stories that echoed Restrepo's account prevailed and even multiplied in the twentieth century. The first manual of history used for educating high-school students in Colombia, for example, was published by Jesús María Henao and Gerardo Arrubla in 1910. In their influential work, Henao and Arrubla described Agualongo as an "astute and brave Indian" but labeled royalists as "fanatics."[4] Other works used Agualongo's surname to brand him as a mere Indian, who had worked serving a wealthy family in Pasto. According to this account, the caudillo's name, "Agualongo," was formed from the repeated calls that his masters made to Agustín to bring them water (*agua* in Spanish). The word *longo* was (and still is) used to refer to Indians, so his last name would have been the result of the command "*Agua, longo!*" or "Indian, bring the water!" This very creative explanation presents the stereotypical image of Indians as servile.[5] Indeed, that assumption underlies Restrepo's characterization of royalism; it was a movement of Indians, who were ultimately manipulated into blindly following royalist leaders at the expense of their "real" best interests.

Restrepo probably also called Agualongo an Indian because the indigenous people were the largest segment of the population in southwest

New Granada, and the royalist army in Pasto and Popayán (the capital of the province) was largely composed of Indians. As a result, although historians have proved that Agualongo was a mestizo and not an Indian, his connection to the royalist cause in the area led people to associate him with the ethnic majority in the region. The Indian population was not, however, the only racial group that made up his army. The Afro-descendants from the town of Patía, north of Pasto, also supported the Spanish cause during the years 1822–1824. Indeed, when Agualongo led the royalist resistance to Bolívar, the *patianos* (men from Patía, a town of free blacks that evolved from a *palenque* or maroon community) formed a significant part of his army, making the royalist movement multiethnic. In fact, Agualongo's last battle, which he lost to Tomás Cipriano de Mosquera, was in Barbacoas, an important gold-mining region in New Granada's south Pacific littoral, where enslaved blacks had mobilized in support of the king's cause between 1810 and 1820 during the independence struggles.

Agustín Agualongo's life (1780–1824) coincided with the late colonial period in New Granada and the entire span of Colombia's long, bitter independence wars. Agualongo lived through the last twenty years of the reformist policies of the Bourbon regime and internal crisis of the monarchy prompted by the Napoleonic invasion of Spain in 1807. When Ferdinand VII replaced his father as king of Spain in 1808, Pastusos such as Agualongo must have understood the political implications of the instability that had enveloped Spain. And in 1809 this sense of instability was compounded when Napoléon Bonaparte forced the abdication of Ferdinand and placed his brother Joseph on the Spanish throne. In those unstable days the city of Pasto demonstrated its support for the Spanish crown and the colonial government as churches across the province celebrated masses to plead for King Ferdinand's well-being. In many areas, however, the conflict raised a serious constitutional crisis. With the king in French captivity, where did sovereignty rest, with the people of America or with the colonial bureaucracy centered in Bogotá? In Quito, local Creole elites answered this question by forming an autonomous junta, or council, that refused to accept Joseph Bonaparte as king, deposed the colonial regime in the city, and claimed to govern in the name of the Spanish monarch, Ferdinand. Quito's major neighboring cities did not approve of its junta, which was also strongly opposed by Viceroy of Peru Fernando de Abascal y Sousa, who sent armed forces from Lima to Cuenca, Guayaquil, and Popayán to stamp out the *Quiteño* government. Nonetheless, in the years when the Spanish king remained under house arrest in France, a series of regional juntas had emerged in the Indies that rejected French imperial aggression and sought to rule in the name of Ferdinand. This trend only accelerated after leadership of the Spanish resistance fell to a group of political liberals in Cádiz, who favored constitutional checks on the monarchy and a representative assembly for Spain and its empire. New Granada, Cartagena, Santa Fe, and Cali formed an alliance that led the first efforts at republican nation building. Agualongo took up arms in 1811 as a volunteer in the royalist militia organized in Popayán, however, to stop any planned invasions from the Creole-led juntas in Cali and Santa Fe. From that moment on, Agualongo was at the center of an unprecedented political and military process, as forces loyal to the Spanish king opposed the autonomous juntas and later the more radical movements for independence, which ultimately achieved its final victory in Colombia with the defeat of Agualongo in 1824.

The royalist movement led by Agualongo demonstrates the depth of the monarchical values held by so many Spanish Americans in the early nineteenth century. The largely untold story of this royalist cause demonstrates that independence was hardly inevitable, forcing historians to question the tendentious portrayal of Spanish colonialism so broadly disseminated by nationalist scholars in Colombia and Latin America. The multiethnic royalist alliances found in Pasto were not unique but had parallels in Coro, Cuenca, Piura, and Cuzco, proving that royalism was a powerful political force in the independence era. Moreover, royalism's multiethnic appeal suggests that the conflict at the heart of the age of revolution in Latin America had complex social and ideological undertones. The story of Agualongo's effort to defend Pasto's place within the Spanish monarchy also hints at the divided and often contradictory political visions within Spanish American national projects in the nineteenth century.

REGIONAL DIMENSIONS OF PASTO'S ROYALIST MOVEMENT

In an attempt to make sense of the unwavering royalism of its inhabitants during the independence wars, Colombian nationalist historians portrayed the Andean city of Pasto as an isolated backwater. Isolation and backwardness were used to explain why the Pastusos rejected the revolutionary processes sweeping across New Granada and the wider Atlantic world at the turn of the nineteenth century. After all, to the south of Pasto in 1809 Quito formed one of the earliest juntas seeking autonomy to prevent the risk of a Napoleonic invasion of Spanish America. Cartagena on the Caribbean coast as well as the cities of Antioquia, Cali, Casanare, Mariquita, Neiva, Pamplona, and Santa Fe (the viceroyalty's capital) had all turned to experiments in local rule by 1810. Pasto, on the other hand, played a fundamental role in the repression of those efforts toward self-rule, instead defending the king's absolute authority to govern. Underlying the positions of both "patriots" and "royalists" were competing visions of the future. The centrifugal tendency that led many cities and towns to claim autonomy was followed by various attempts to dominate smaller or weaker neighbors, inaugurating a period of internal strife and near civil war that Colombian historians have called *La Patria Boba* or "Foolish Fatherland."

The tension that emerged in the southwest between Quito and Pasto resulted from Pasto's resistance against falling under the control of its longtime rival, the now revolutionary Quito. Pasto was hardly an economic backwater, and its royalism certainly did not constitute backwardness. Indeed, Quiteño elites wanted to control Pasto and its surrounding Indian towns precisely because Pasto occupied such a strategic place in the regional economy, supplying foodstuffs to the local gold mines of the Pacific littoral. This lowland gold-mining zone was humid and covered by thick foliage, making food cultivation almost impossible. In addition, Africans slave laborers worked exclusively on gold extraction, not on performing agricultural tasks. Therefore, food production in the Andean region around Pasto developed close commercial ties with the thriving gold economy in the Pacific mines, and indigenous people from the highlands performed a vital role in that productive chain, transporting goods between the two regions. These men, called *cargueros*, assured that products flowed continually between the Andean towns and the Pacific lowlands, a job that gave indigenous men the income needed to pay their tribute (Indian head tax) even in times of agrarian crisis.

Pasto also occupied a strategic political location, at the crossroads of two of the major administrative centers in New Granada, the *audiencia* (high court) in the viceregal capital of Santa Fe and the Audiencia of Quito. This position gave people in Pasto (as well as Popayán) greater political flexibility because they could appeal to either of the two centers to defend their interests, playing off one court against the other. The city of Pasto's position as a royalist stronghold throughout the monarchical crisis also allowed the city to gain political status over its rival, insurgent Quito, as a reward for its loyalty to the crown.[6]

Although royalist Pasto faced formidable foes among the rebellious forces centered in Santa Fe, the city also counted on the support of a powerful royalist confederation, particularly in the southern viceregal capital of Lima. Royalism was not merely the result of isolation and backwardness in regional Pasto; rather, the city formed part of a large alliance of towns and cities that remained loyal to the Spanish crown, centered in Lima. Moreover, royalism was hardly a static political movement in the years following the collapse of the Spanish monarchy but instead involved a multiplicity of political and social forces within the royalist regions, favoring numerous different political projects and ideological visions. Therefore, after stripping away the political rhetoric of Colombia's nationalist historians, it is possible to recognize the vitality of monarchical identities and institutions, as royalists forged cross-regional alliances based on a traditional loyalty to King Ferdinand and his right to rule as an absolute monarch. For a soldier like Agualongo, who took up arms in defense of religion and the king, Lima's firm grip on the Viceroyalty of Peru amid growing political turbulence in New Granada and Rio de la Plata seemed a good reason to believe that royalist forces throughout South America would help Pasto achieve victory over the insurgent traitors in New Granada.

AGUALONGO AND THE ROYALIST ARMY

Around the time of Agualongo's birth during the late eighteenth century, a primary goal of the Spanish Bourbon government was to enhance colonial defenses in response to threats by her enemies—primarily Great Britain and later France—against Spain's overseas empire. These military threats became ever more serious as the century progressed. The crown's defense project also gained momentum as rebelliousness increased among the colonial populations, particularly during the 1780s.[7] The Bourbon military reforms aimed to strengthen fixed fortifications in strategic commercial centers and to recruit militias drawn from the colonial population. The military reforms reached New Granada in the 1770s, but in the southwest, a stubborn aristocracy opposed them, fearing that access to military privileges would provide social mobility for the lower classes and threaten traditional social hierarchies. In spite of this aristocratic opposition, however, colonial authorities still established militias, which played a major role in initial confrontations over the monarchical crisis beginning in 1808.

Following the creation of the Quito junta in 1809, the entire population of Pasto was alerted about the threat of invasion from the south. Popayán's governor, Miguel Tacón, moved fast to enlarge the local militias for the defense of the region, seeking to mobilize people from all classes willing to defend the province from the expected Quiteño attack. From that moment, Popayán's bishop, Salvador Jiménez de Enciso, also issued proclamations to be read during Mass and hung in the churches, reminding urban and rural people across the province about renewing their vows of loyalty to defend the crown. For urban dwellers in Pasto such as Agustín Agualongo and the people living in the rural areas (especially those south of the city, in closer proximity to Quito), this unprecedented situation raised many questions about their immediate future. In the minds of many, an invasion from "revolutionary" Quito became associated with the threat of a French invasion; many locals saw Quiteños as traitors who favored the hated enemies of the monarchy, the French. Governor Tacón also sought help from Viceroy Abascal of Peru, a strong royalist, who was equally committed to crushing the growing rebellion in Quito. At the same time, Santa Fe's viceroy, Amar y Borbón, was too far away and too preoccupied with a potential revolt in his region to provide support for the southern provinces of New Granada. Popayán and Pasto had to rely on Abascal in dealing with any invasion from Quito.

These extraordinary circumstances led to a transformation in the relationship of the government with indigenous people and slaves. Governor Tacón had to increase his military forces urgently, so the governor quickly made overtures to the indigenous and enslaved populations in Popayán Province, seeking to mobilize them in support of the king. Tacón desperately needed to prevent the Quiteño insurgents from recruiting among slaves and in regional indigenous communities, which he believed would be easy targets of insurgent "seduction." In this critical moment, Tacón sought to establish a strong alliance with the Indian communities surrounding Pasto, and he negotiated lowering tribute payments to guarantee their support. In addition, the governor attracted the enslaved populations that lived in the Pacific lowlands to the royalist cause by promising them freedom if they remained loyal and served in the royal army. Although Tacón's decision was consistent with earlier imperial policies to arm people of indigenous or African descent for strategic reasons, it was a source of deep concern among Popayán's slave owners. Their discontent and distrust of the governor's actions fueled a growing confrontation between local elites and the governor. At the same time, however, the indigenous communities surrounding Pasto found Tacón's overtures compelling, inaugurating a new phase in the politics of the Indian communities, which became strongly royalist. Similarly, communities of enslaved Africans saw in royalism an opportunity to better their condition, and many eagerly proclaimed their fidelity to the king.

Although Quito's first junta was defeated by the forces of Popayán, Cuenca, and Guayaquil, Quiteños launched a second attempt in 1811 to organize an autonomous government. Once more Tacón instituted emergency measures in the province of Popayán, calling for volunteers to join his army from the indigenous, slave, and *casta* (mixed-race) populations. In response to the governor's call, Agustín Agualongo enrolled as a soldier in Pasto, appearing for the first time in the military records of these turbulent years.[8] At the time he was a painter by profession, but aside from information about his occupation, Agualongo left no personal records, making it hard to know exactly why he enlisted in the army. Perhaps the unstable political situation in the provinces surrounding Pasto convinced him to join the king's army, or perhaps he feared a "foreign" invasion from Quito. Aside from the renewed threat of a Quiteño invasion, the viceregal government in Santa Fe had fallen to a revolutionary junta in 1810, and the viceroyalty was in political disarray. Moreover, just north of Popayán, the city of Cali had taken the path of insurgency and joined Santa Fe in creating a federal government among the key cities in New Granada. Although insurgents occupied Popayán at times, Tacón continued his close alliance with Peru, and he transferred his royalist forces to Pasto. The governor also established an alliance with a free-black guerrilla force from Patía, which functioned independently but also in the name of the king. Thus, after joining the army Agualongo fought side by side with peasants from Pasto, with freed slaves from the mines and haciendas of nearby Popayán, with the independent forces of the mulatto men from Patía, and with local Indians led to battle by their ethnic leaders or caciques. The royal militia that Agualongo joined, aided by the natural frontier around the Juanambú River, became famous as the most dangerous and invincible royalist army, which later blocked even the army of the great Simón Bolívar from taking the strategic southwestern region.

During the first decade of the independence wars, Agualongo's world was rapidly changing, giving him the opportunity to demonstrate his dogged loyalty to the crown against the insurgencies that had developed in so many provinces of Spanish South America. Agualongo's first major battle in 1811 was against the invaders from Quito, which the royalists won decisively. That same year he participated in a royalist victory over the republican invaders from Cali, which allowed the king's forces to regain control of the provincial capital, Popayán. As a result, Agualongo fought in two consecutive royalist military victories, gaining important military experience and confidence that the royalist cause would prevail. His exemplary performances in these battles also earned Agualongo an impeccable reputation as a warrior and a leader of men, which guaranteed his rapid promotion in the royalist army.

As a sergeant, Agualongo formed part of the Spanish army organized in 1813 by the royalist president of Quito, Toribio Montes, and led by Juan Sámano, a commander recently arrived from Spain. This was the army that fought against Antonio Nariño, a representative from the government of Cundinamarca (with its capital in Santa Fe) and a prominent figure among New Granada's enlightened elite. He had gained international fame for having translated and published *The Rights of Man* into Spanish in the 1790s. Nariño also headed the first unified republican government in New Granada, which ultimately failed in part because of the centrifugal forces of the provincial governments that formed it. Agualongo's participation in the confrontation against Nariño was apparently one of the early turning points in his military and political life. Not only did the young sergeant Agualongo prove his valor and military abilities, he probably learned about the fragility of the republican cause. Indeed, Agualongo perceived the royalist army's decisive victory as a sign that Nariño's republican project was doomed to failure.

Later Agualongo moved south, from Pasto to Ibarra and Cuenca, where he played a role in other significant victories in the defense of the royalist cause. With the defeat of Napoléon in Europe and the return of the popular King Ferdinand VII to the throne in 1814, royalist forces could claim a great moral victory, which inspired confidence and boosted their morale. The king launched a campaign of "reconquest" to quell insurgent factions in New Granada, sending ten thousand men to the region in 1815. During his time in Cuenca, Agualongo surely knew of the formation of a new independence coalition, led by the Venezuelan Simón Bolívar, but in those optimist times after the return of Ferdinand to the throne, he could not have imagined that these insurgent forces would ever claim the final victory in Pasto and Peru.

INDIAN COMMUNITIES AND ROYALIST POLITICS

The city of Pasto was an important administrative center governing more than thirty surrounding Indian towns, and these indigenous communities had a significant impact on the regional political economy. Pasto and its Indian communities were the product of a long effort at settling the indigenous peoples into Spanish-style towns or *pueblos* in the Andes, initiated in the sixteenth century by the Viceroy of Peru, Francisco de Toledo (1569–1581). Although this plan of settlement largely failed with some indigenous people in the Amazon and in the Pacific littoral, especially north in the Chocó, Pasto indigenous communities represented the success of the Spanish imperial project. Indigenous communities in Pasto, descendants of three pre-Hispanic ethnic groups (Pasto, Quillacinga, and Abad), were settled into discrete communities ruled by local caciques. These ethnic authorities had the responsibility to collect tribute from the communities, which they paid to local Spanish magistrates. Indigenous communities were at the center of the political process during the independence wars, but native structures of authority were weakened because royalism offered all Indian commoners the opportunity for political mobilization, whether or not their caciques supported the crown.

Although between 1809 and 1822 Pasto almost continuously remained under royalist power, things had certainly changed. Government was now connected with Quito and Lima to the south, and over the years military figures became central to the structure of power. From Spain, a group of liberals favoring constitutional government led the resistance against the French invaders, and their decision to write a constitution for Spain and its territories overseas in 1812 promised sweeping political changes within the empire. The liberal constitution proclaimed in 1812 was sent to all the provinces in the Americas where royalists remained in power. Among its many provisions, the liberal constitution of 1812 gave full citizenship to Indians in the Americas. It also gave indigenous people voting rights and abolished tribute, transforming their status significantly. For local caciques in Pasto, however, these new reforms were most unwelcome because much of their power and communal authority was based on their legal prerogative to collect tribute. Ultimately, Indians' participation in the royalist army was also an element that disrupted customary structures of authority, and the decade saw increasing conflicts within the communities between commoners and their traditional ethnic leaders.

As a result of these disruptive political changes, numerous confrontations arose between the caciques and the commoners of the Indian towns in Pasto. Caciques feared that their power was waning, so they contested the official tax assessments of the government, which had reduced the amount of tribute that Indians should pay. In doing so, they were going against the interests of the Indian commoners, who demanded lower tribute quotas, which they saw as their just reward for serving in the military for the king. Around 1816 this conflict escalated as the Indian commoners found an ally in the *protector de naturales*, Juan Diaz Gallardo, who was the legal advocate appointed by the Spanish crown to defend Indians in court. The caciques, however, decided to use all their power to win the battle against the Indian commoners, whom they saw as rebelling against their ethnic leaders' authority. The caciques took the case to the audiencia in Quito (now back in royalist hands), where they pleaded for Gallardo's removal. The changing political situation in Spain emboldened the caciques, who acted after the return of King Ferdinand VII to the throne. The king was determined to undo any liberal policies inscribed in the constitution of 1812 that had been instituted in his absence. Although Ferdinand continued to favor rewarding his loyal vassals, including the Indians, the audiencia saw Gallardo as a dangerous troublemaker because of his sympathies for liberal policies favoring the indigenous people. Hence, he was removed, and in his place the audiencia named the head of the local militias in Pasto, Ramón Medina.

Five years later, in 1822, Colonel Agualongo now headed the rebel government that took over Pasto, challenging the Bolivarian regime imposed after the battle of Bombená, and he again appointed Ramón Medina as protector. Medina represented the interests of the Indian elite, which resented the transformations brought by the war and the liberal reforms stemming from the constitution of 1812. Most likely, however, Agualongo, Medina, and the caciques who supported them had a communitarian vision of "Indianness," which hoped to maintain the rights of indigenous people to own their communal land and to have a semiautonomous government. Indeed, after independence, Bolívar proclaimed the new legal framework for his republic, emphasizing private ownership of land and the end of Indian communal holdings. Thus deprived of the lands, the indigenous communities lost their basis for economic prosperity, and they faced a dark future. While some indigenous groups in Colombia embraced citizenship, perceiving opportunities in the liberal proposition to divide and sell their communal lands, the communities of Pasto remained committed to defending their rights to own land as a corporate community.

But the political conflicts over land ownership between the republican government sponsored by Bolívar and the Pastuso indigenous communities formed part of a long battle to defeat all royalist groups in Pasto. Bolívar remained intransigent in his desire to reduce Pasto to loyalty, and as president of Colombia, he had no patience for royalists in the southwest. Bolívar cared little about Indian claims to their traditional communal landholdings. Instead, he remained committed to extinguishing the Pastuso royalist peril. As a result, his response to the antirepublican revolts of 1822 and 1823 was to have Pasto burned and sacked. Either Pastusos were deported to fight the war in Peru, or many were simply killed without a trial. Despite the paucity of documentation about the royalist government that returned to power in Pasto after 1822, a few proclamations authored by Estanislao Merchancano (head of the civil government in Pasto) and Agualongo (military chief) called Bolívar a tyrant and denounced the government of Colombia as an intruder.[9]

Although elites in Pasto accepted the terms of the capitulation that resulted from the defeat of the Spanish army in 1822, the majority of the local population supported Agualongo and Merchancano's project to go on fighting for the royalist cause. Despite the odds, they continued to harbor hopes for a royalist victory in Peru in order to maintain the Pasto-Quito-Lima passageway under royalist control.[10] Given the long history of royalism in the Andean-Pacific region, Agualongo's goal seems to have been to expand his control over the Pacific littoral, where slaves from the gold mines continued to be potential allies of the royalist cause. Even with help from the locals, however, Agualongo was caught and taken to Popayán, where the republican forces summarily shot him on July 13, 1824.

Agualongo's struggle represents the vitality of monarchic values during the independence era. He devoted two decades to defending the king's cause and the full restoration of monarchic rule in the Spanish Empire. The independence wars shaped his life profoundly; an important part of his identity became tied to the military effort against the traitors to religion and his king, and every success in battle, combined with the rewards of a hard-won glory, contributed to his unswerving belief in a victory in the defense of his fatherland's autonomy. Indeed, the royalist bulwark in Pasto resulted from the firm conviction of the common folk, slaves, free blacks, mestizos, and Indians that the monarchical government offered a better life for people of all social classes and ethnicities. The brutal means through which the republic imposed its rule in Pasto and its hinterland are a reminder of the social conflicts that plagued the early history of Colombia and the challenges of postcolonial nation building. Although the royalists were defeated and forcibly pacified, the tenacity of their struggle is testimony to their willingness to defend their alternative vision of the nation, a vision where race relations would be more fluid and equal than anything the Bolivarian republic later offered. One significant legacy of the royalist movement in the Colombian southwest is the persistence of Indian communities that defied the state's individualistic model of governance.

QUESTIONS FOR DISCUSSION

1. Why was Agustín Agualongo a royalist?
2. How has Colombian historiography represented Agualongo's ethnic identity, and why is that important?
3. Why did Agualongo's movement attract indigenous people and mestizos as well as free and enslaved blacks?
4. What were the imperial and local dimensions of Pasto's royalism?
5. When did royalists lose the war in the Colombian southwest, and what does this tell us about Colombian national political history?

NOTES

1. Michel-Rolph Trouillot, *Silencing the Past: Power and the Production of History* (Boston: Beacon Press, 1995), 49.
2. José Manuel Restrepo, *Historia de la revolución de la República de Colombia en la América meridional*, vol. 5 (1827; Bogotá: Editorial Bedout, 1969), 89.
3. Sergio Elías Ortiz, *Agustín Agualongo y su Tiempo* (Bogota: Editorial ABC, 1958), 14; Emiliano Díaz del Castillo, *El Caudillo. Semblanza de Agualongo* (Pasto: Tipografía y Fotograbado Javier, 1983), 5–6.
4. Jesús María Henao and Gerardo Arrubla, *Historia de Colombia para la enseñanza secundaria*, vol. 2 (1910; Bogota: Librería Colombiana, 1920), 410.
5. Ortiz, *Agustín Agualongo*, 14; Alberto Miramón, *Hombres del tiempo heróico* (Bogotá: Empresa Nacional de Publicaciones, 1956), 92.
6. Ortiz, *Agustín Agualongo*, 99; "Representación del Cabildo de Pasto a Don Pablo Morillo" (Pasto, October 13, 1816), in Gustavo Guerrero, *Documentos históricos de los hechos ocurridos en Pasto en la guerra de independencia* (Pasto: Imprenta del Departamento, 1912), 136–42.
7. New Granada was particularly hard hit by the Comunero Rebellion in 1780; see John Leddy Phelan, *The People and the King: The Comunero Revolution in Colombia, 1781* (Madison: University of Wisconsin Press, 1978).
8. Díaz del Castillo, *El Caudillo*, 6.
9. Cristóbal de Gangotena y Jijón, *Documentos referentes a la campana de Ibarra con la narración histórica de la campaña de Pasto* (Quito: Talleres tipográficos nacionales, 1923), 6.
10. Archivo General de la Nación (Colombia), Bogotá, *Secretaría de Guerra y Marina* 43, f. 681.

SUGGESTIONS FOR FURTHER READING

As can be seen in the endnotes, most of the works about Agualongo currently available are in Spanish. Aside from the monographs by Sergio Elías Ortíz and Emiliano Díaz del Castillo, two recent important contributions to the study of Pastuso royalism are Jairo Gutiérrez's *Los indios de Pasto contra la República* (Bogotá: Instituto Colombiano de Antropología e Historia, 2007) and Marcela Echeverri, "Popular Royalists, Empire, and Politics in Southwestern New Granada, 1809–1819," *Hispanic American Historical Review* 91, no. 2 (2011): 237–69.

For more on late colonial New Granada, see Anthony McFarlane's *Colombia before Independence: Economy, Society, and Politics under Bourbon Rule* (Cambridge: Cambridge University Press, 2002) and Allan Kuethe's *Military Reform and Society in New Granada, 1773–1808* (Gainesville: University Presses of Florida, 1978). On the Colombian independence wars, see Margarita Garrido's *Reclamos y Representaciones: Variaciones sobre la política en el Nuevo Reino de Granada, 1770–1815* (Bogotá: Banco de la República, 1993) and Rebecca Earle's *Spain and the Independence of Colombia* (Exeter: University of Exeter Press, 2000). Also of interest is Steinar Saether's "Independence and the Redefinition of Indianness around Santa Marta, Colombia, 1750–1850," *Journal of Latin American Studies* 37 (2005): 55–80, which focuses on the Caribbean provinces of Santa Marta and Riohacha, the other region with widespread popular royalism in New Granada. An excellent comparative example of an indigenous monarchist rebellion in post-Bolivarian Peru is Cecilia Méndez's *The Plebeian Republic: The Huanta Rebellion and the Making of the Peruvian State, 1820–1850* (Durham: Duke University Press, 2005). See Peter Blanchard's *Under the Flags of Freedom: Slave Soldiers & the Wars of Independence in Spanish South America* (Pittsburgh: Pittsburgh University Press, 2008) for more on the participation of enslaved Afro-descendants in the independence wars across South America. And on popular politics in early republican Colombia, see James Sanders's *Contentious Republicans: Popular Politics, Race, and Class in Nineteenth-Century Colombia* (Durham: Duke University Press, 2004).

SEVENTEEN

Angela Batallas

A Fight for Freedom in Guayaquil

Camilla Townsend

The city of Quito formed one of the first ruling juntas *in 1809, following the forced abdications of Spain's Charles IV and Prince Ferdinand. The head of this new government was Juan Pío de Montufar (Marqués de Selva Alegre), scion of a distinguished noble family, and members of this relatively conservative junta initially sought to rule only until the restoration of the monarchy. Dissension among them and their failure to garner widespread support in other regions of the* audiencia *district led to the junta's collapse a mere three months later. When royalist troops occupying the city feared a popular uprising in 1810, however, the soldiers brutally executed most of the rebel leaders in their jail cells. Popular outrage at this massacre contributed to the formation of another provisional government in 1810. This junta ruled for two years, until a royalist army under the command of the newly appointed audiencia president, Toribio Montes, forced them from power and reestablished royal authority.*

The defeat of these provisional governments in Quito discouraged any new Creole autonomy movements anywhere in the audiencia district (what is today Ecuador) until discontent in the port city of Guayaquil led coastal elites to rise up and form the so-called Republic of Guayas, which proclaimed independence for the city and its hinterland. The new regime embraced many prevailing liberal sentiments, which were reflected in its proclamations and legislation. Two laws, for example, prohibited any future residents of the region from being enslaved and also ended the importation of slaves into the republic. Moreover, as of July 21, 1821, all children born to slaves were declared free on their eighteenth birthday. Some legislators even pushed for a decree freeing all of the republic's slaves.

Support for the liberal republic did not extend beyond the coast, however, and formal independence for the entire audiencia district of Quito did not come until the northern insurgent armies of Simón Bolívar's lieutenant, Antonio José de Sucre, won the Battle of Pichincha in 1822. After this victory, Bolívar set up his headquarters in Guayaquil, where he met with the leader of the southern rebel armies, José de San Martín. After that fateful meeting in Guayaquil, San Martín resigned his command, effectively placing all of the major independence forces under Bolívar.

At this crucial juncture of the independence movements in South America, the young slave woman Angela Batallas demanded and received an audience with Bolívar the Liberator. She told an all-too-familiar story. A young slave, she had fallen into a relationship with her owner, Ildefonso Coronel, after he had promised her freedom in return for sexual intimacy. Coronel was in some ways an idealistic and liberal young merchant who gave generously of his time and money to support the independence effort. He also shared his ideas about liberty and freedom with his slave mistress. Problems in the relationship began when Angela became pregnant and later gave birth to a baby girl. Coronel and his family feared that his fathering a child with a slave woman would result in a public scandal and impugn his honor. Nevertheless, Coronel acknowledged the infant as his own on the baptismal certificate, making her legally free, and also sent a regular allowance for his mistress and child.

Angela Batallas, however, wanted more—the freedom that Coronel had promised. This determined young woman filed a legal complaint, secured the services of a lawyer, gathered witnesses, and made an eloquent case. For his part, Ildefonso Coronel (who, in the meantime, had taken a new mistress and also had become engaged to an eligible young woman from a leading Guayaquil family) denied having any sexual relationship with Angela. While pressing her case in court, Angela decided to meet with Bolívar and seek his intervention. Afterward, the Liberator wrote a letter to the court supporting her cause, and the determined young slave woman finally secured her freedom.

In March 1823, Angela Batallas, a slave, demanded to see Simón Bolívar, known as the Liberator, who was leading the war for independence against Spain. The young woman had not chosen the best of moments from the general's perspective. He was camped in the military barracks of the Ecuadorian city of Guayaquil as he tried to organize a southern campaign to expel the royalists remaining in Peru. "A large number of troops is not being sent because it is impossible," he agonized. "I have no ships, no provisions, and no troops here. We have already spent a hundred thousand pesos and we are just beginning the enterprise. In order to send the next 3,000 [men] God knows what we shall have to do."[1] Angela Batallas, however, the legal property of a wealthy merchant in the city, would not be dissuaded and insisted that he make time for her. Her dark hair curled around her face in the steamy heat of the rainy season; her skirts were spattered with the mud of the road, for slaves traveled on foot, not on horseback. Whatever the sentries may have thought, given the general's reputation as a ladies' man, this woman had come there neither to engage in any kind of sexual relations with the Liberator nor to accuse him of being the father of her child. Instead, she had come to make a plea and a statement: she wanted her freedom. She believed that justice and the politics of the Liberator were on her side, and she demanded that he hear her out.[2]

There were numerous tensions embedded in the scene that Angela Batallas was about to make. In the hierarchy of the colonial world that Bolívar and Batallas both knew well, he was at the top and she was at the very bottom. The son of a wealthy sugar planter, he was educated in Europe and was now a military general. As a female slave, many would have said that she had even less power than an indigenous peon. Batallas was expected to be docile in her role—grateful to both her master and the general for sharing with her their civilization and religion, for planning the economy that provided her with food, and for protecting her in a world they assumed she could not understand. Yet both Bolívar and Batallas had experienced the different realities of the dynamic between slave owners and the enslaved. Real people of all colors and classes interacted with each other every day. Masters regularly abused their power even by the standards of their own era, and slaves asserted themselves whenever and wherever they could, in a long continuum of possibilities ranging from completing a task more slowly than a master desired to outright rebellion. Furthermore, Spanish law issued by the crown had always allowed slaves some legal rights vis-à-vis their masters: they could, for example, testify in court and keep their own gardens and retain the proceeds. In an urban environment, the enslaved were especially knowledgeable about their rights and active in defending them because most households consisted not only of masters and slaves but also of free black and *mestizo* (mixed European and Amerindian) servants with widely varying life experiences.

The present moment brought a new twist on the old theme. In the early years of the nineteenth century, many of the gentlemen of the Enlightenment who believed that the colonies should be free of control by Spain also considered the possibility that slaves should be free of their masters. Bolívar himself had complex thoughts on this subject. But true to their notion of the natural social hierarchy, all such liberal gentlemen assumed that the slaves would eventually be released by enlightened champions. The reality, however, as Angela Batallas was shortly to remind the general, was that the slaves themselves in many cases took an active interest in politics. They could listen to stories of current events and speak their minds; they could also adroitly turn events to their own advantage.[3] Despite the whites' expectations to the contrary, the enslaved blacks were not waiting passively for their patriotically minded masters to turn their attention to the slavery question.

In the story that Batallas recounted to Bolívar in the Guayaquil barracks, both the traditional and the then-current social tensions surrounding the realities of slavery were exquisitely illustrated. On one hand, she presented the age-old narrative of a man of the master class selecting the mistress of his choice from among his human chattel and then leaving her to face the consequences; on the other hand, that man was forced to learn that control over the woman he thought to dominate was actually impossible. On another level, the drama unfolded at the exact eye of the hurricane of the independence movement. While battles raged around them, the patriot-master who considered himself enlightened on the issue of slavery (among others) was himself effectively attacked by a woman slave, and even Bolívar the Liberator was chastened.

It is difficult to learn about the slaves' part in the dynamic interactions with their owners or to catch glimpses of their political views. They were discouraged even from speaking and certainly were not taught to write or leave diaries. Depending on their own political perspectives, historians have often assumed increasing radicalism or conservatism on the part of the enslaved during the late colonial era and struggle for independence. Neither view is illogical. It is true, for example, that slaves were busy washing floors and plucking chickens and might easily have felt some impatience with their young masters' heady talk of independence, believing that nothing would ever really change for them. On the other hand, the enslaved heard news of uprisings up and down the continent from sailors, many of them black, and from priests sympathetic to their cause; they might have perceived that a new day was coming if they seized their opportunities. Actual evidence as to their views is thin; the best comes from court cases brought by slaves suing for freedom at this time. Such testimony must be used with caution because it comes to us filtered through the Spanish legal apparatus and can hardly be seen as a direct transcription of a slave's first thoughts.

Angela Batallas was one of the many who brought suit against their masters, and it is her case that will be explored here. Indeed, she went to see the Liberator specifically to gain his support. Due to the nature of the court proceedings, the historian can hear only snippets of her own voice, which might be meaningless to the modern ear if quoted out of context or considered from only one angle. For that reason, an effort is made to describe in some depth what was going on in the world in which she made her utterances. The disjunction between her experiences and the political conversations of the day struck her forcibly.

SLAVERY AND GUAYAQUIL

In July 1822 the two great patriot generals, Simón Bolívar and José de San Martín, met for the first time in the city of Guayaquil. Over the course of ten years, Bolívar had successfully fought his way south and westward from his native Venezuela, while San Martín had crossed the Andes from Argentina into Chile and then made his way northward. Now the two men organized the final campaign against the royalists still left in Peru. Yet despite these momentous events in their own backyard, daily life for the region's ordinary folk in many ways remained unaltered. Change came especially slowly to the countryside surrounding the city. Near the ocean's shore the province of Guayas was dry and sandy: Indians dove for pearls and for the shells used to make purple dye, but there was little vegetation. Not far inland, however, around a network of creeks and rivers, the land turned lush and green, rising gently to peak ultimately in the Andes Mountains.

Plantains, rice, and other food crops grew well in the littoral, making agriculture important. African slaves traditionally worked on the larger plantations. Over the course of the last generation, however, landowners had turned increasingly to hired help. Migrant workers had been coming down from the highlands in large numbers in flight from the depression in their weaving industry, caused by an influx of British textiles under recent government trade reforms. And planters had learned that cacao, which was used for making chocolate and was growing in importance as a cash crop, did not require year-round attention. It was often more cost effective to hire temporary laborers than to buy slaves. The plantation owners could sell superfluous bondsmen to passing traders or send them to Guayaquil to work for wages as domestic servants, artisans' assistants, or laborers.

In the pre-independence era, slaves thus constituted about 8 percent of the population of the city of Guayaquil, which was home to roughly twenty thousand people. The proportion was higher, however, in the town center, on the bank of the Río Guayas where the wealthy lived. Even after the war, on the most fashionable blocks, 24 percent of the residents were enslaved, but toward the outskirts of the city, only 4 percent were held in bondage. Life experiences varied considerably for the slaves in the different sections of town. In the most elegant area, one out of every four people was enslaved, and in this sense they could not have felt isolated. Yet they were a people apart within their own neighbor-hood—darker than the majority and of a clearly lower status. Courtroom evidence indicates that white neighbors knew to whom they belonged, for example, but did not necessarily know their names. On the other hand, further inland from the wealthy riverwalk lived a greater number of people of color, of both Indian and African descent, and most of these, although relatively poor, were not enslaved. The bondsmen among them were not necessarily marked as slaves in their daily workaday lives, and their neighbors probably knew their names. Yet for them, life was filled with its own trials; a slave here was usually the sole servant of his or her owner and thus carried a heavy workload. Such slaves were aware that they comprised by far the largest share of their masters' wealth. One white man who died in 1823 left 600 pesos' worth of property, of which 550 came from the value of his slave and her two children.[4]

Besides working almost ceaselessly, enslaved women also had to endure unwanted sexual advances and then live with the repercussions. Their vulnerability to sexual overtures on the part of a series of owners and sometimes other men in the household is demonstrated not only by the high incidence of sexually transmitted diseases among them but also, more tellingly, by the high incidence of the discovery of such diseases by their masters, who often then sued the sellers of the female slaves.[5]

In 1820, two years before the arrival of the famous generals, the province of Guayas had declared itself independent, and the few Spanish soldiers in the area, unable to obtain reinforcements, put up only token resistance. The change in local government may not have made dramatic changes in most people's lives, but from that moment it was clear that in this part of the world, at least, the patriot cause was in the ascendance. The passing battalions of freedmen fighting in the armies of Colombia and Venezuela told their stories. Men who enrolled in the republican army in exchange for freedom had reason to believe that they would be on the winning side. Some joined the army only to desert later; their women might help them hide. A documented rise in the number of runaways indicates that some took advantage of the atmosphere of chaos caused by the militarization to flee.

In the current political climate, a popular language of "liberty" and "independence" reigned. Thus, there arose among enthusiastic white patriots a certain degree of discomfort with slavery. Did people fighting "tyranny" have the right to tyrannize others? Here the elites could not create a simple dichotomy between white and black as their rebellious North American counterparts had done not long ago, for in this southern world people came in a more varied range of colors and shades, and free and slave were not always visually distinguishable. Only two months before Angela Batallas visited the Liberator, the public defender who had represented slaves in their legal cases under the colonial regime was pleased to remind the court that it was the Spaniards who had introduced slavery into the New World. He spoke of the "unhappy people . . . whose liberty was snatched away so barbarously by the Spanish."[6] Throughout South America, white enthusiasts for liberty were susceptible to this kind of argument. They remained concerned about protecting their property and their privileged position in the social hierarchy, but at the same time they proudly defined themselves as the creators of a new and more just world.

In the heady days of republican triumph, the young radicals who governed the independent Republic of Guayas from 1820 to 1822 passed two new laws that directly impacted the slaves: the latter were not themselves freed, but it was made impossible for future Guayaquileños to be enslaved. Further importation of slaves in Republican territory was pro-hibited—current prices were frozen to prevent speculation—and, as of July 1821, all children born to slaves henceforth were to be freed on their eighteenth birthday. Later a manumission fund was established of mo-nies collected through a small tax on inheritances and deposits made by participating slaves who were hoping to buy their freedom with the aid of the fund. There was even talk of a possible "decree of liberty." Many slaves did not waste time waiting to see if such a decree would ever be issued. Instead they set about working in their off hours and depositing weekly sums in the manumission fund. In record numbers they argued with or sued their owners to lower the prices for self-purchase. If liberty was within their grasp, they would reach for it.[7]

THE SUIT OF ANGELA BATALLAS

Angela's childhood remains unknown, even the exact year of her birth, although it was certainly not long after 1800. This utter blank in her story is all too typical. Slave children, except in their occasional church-re-corded baptisms, do not exist in the written record of the period. They may appear in the margins of portraits of their masters or as unnamed messengers referred to indirectly in letters, but that is all. Angela Batallas appears in the historical record for the first time only at the moment when her life intersected with that of a leading proponent of the patriot cause. She was still a very young woman when Ildefonso Coronel noticed her and decided to buy her from her old master. It was November 1821, and Guayaquil was in a storm of excitement. The armies of the indepen-dence wars were on the move, and the new gradualist emancipatory laws had just been passed. Twenty-seven-year-old Coronel was a wealthy young man actively involved in the patriot movement that was brewing in elite homes like his own, where young people's clubs met to read the works of men such as Thomas Jefferson and Abbé Raynal. Although he had been born in the mountain town of Cuenca to a plantation-owning family, he had lived in this city with his widowed mother since the age of sixteen and was accepted there as a leading citizen. Coronel was a mer-chant-trader, and he hoped that his city's new freedom from Spanish control would allow him to negotiate profitably with British business-men. He would soon forge a solid relationship with the firm of Gibbs, Crawley & Co. In the meantime, he gave generously of his time and resources for "the cause," so his name appeared with some frequency in the city's new paper, *El Patriota de Guayaquil*.

Ildefonso paid 350 pesos for Angela, slightly higher than the average price of 325 pesos for a young woman. What her former owner thought we do not know: perhaps he was one of the many who were eager to sell at this time, fearing a general emancipation edict from the new government. Ildefonso did not rape Angela. In fact, he was kind to her. Over the course of the next two months, he did not make direct sexual overtures. When he saw her, he talked to her. They may have spoken about the dramatic current events that everyone was discussing and that influenced them both directly, although in different ways. On the day he approached her to initiate a sexual relationship, he did not threaten her, nor did he promise her the usual pretty clothes or offer her the carrot then most popular—a lowered self-purchase price. Instead, Ildefonso promised Angela her liberty. In the glory of the new republic that he and his peers were creating, he told her that his love for her would set her free.

In those early months of 1822, Angela apparently was happy, or at least she complained to no one. Her circumstances were not unenviable. She was living in an exciting time. The world around her was unshackling itself, and so was she. A wealthy and powerful man had told her that he loved her. He set her up in a little house by a bridge over a stream that cut into the city from the river, and he came to visit her there, in what she felt was her own home. (He lived with his mother in a fine house on the riverwalk.) Angela later claimed that Coronel treated her as an equal in their private dealings. Master or not, it was the only way he could treat her if he wanted to continue to see genuine joy in her face when he went to her. When she presented herself to the court, she knew how to write her name beautifully, ending her signature with a distinctive flourish. Although this did not prove that she actually knew how to read, even signing her name was more than many free deponents knew how to do. Probably Ildefonso had taught her, or if not, then she had come to him with an unusual degree of sophistication. In either case, it seems likely that they were enjoying together the great days of 1821 and 1822, when the elites of Guayaquil governed their world themselves for the first time, when slavery met the beginning of its end, and when Bolívar purposefully wended his way toward their suddenly important city and then arrived with pomp and met with San Martín.

There were, however, problems. Angela became pregnant almost immediately. At first this did not seem to distress Ildefonso, but eventually he became very upset. It became clear to him that the choices he was making were more complicated than he had thought. He simply could not keep his position in society and at the same time have Angela as the equivalent of a wife or even recognize their child. The radical patriots had not intended this kind of change. He tried to persuade Angela to go to his family's plantation near Cuenca for the birth in order to keep the child a secret. She refused to go and indeed may have threatened to make the issue public if he attempted to force her, for he did not insist. There in the city, with the help of a free black midwife, Angela gave birth to a daughter, María del Carmen. Ildefonso handed the midwife a note to take to the priest for baptism, indicating that the child was his. He did not mention the slave status of the mother, so the child was implicitly free now rather than having to wait for her eighteenth birthday, according to the recent law. He did not continue to visit often, but he sent a servant every week with an allowance for the baby's support.

Either late in the pregnancy or right after the birth, Ildefonso chose to distance himself by beginning a relationship with another woman. This time he tried to avoid complications. Melchora Sánchez was free, and she would not press him for marriage or even support: she was already married. She knew about Angela and María del Carmen and was angry that Ildefonso continued to visit them. At the same time, Ildefonso's mother complained bitterly about his scandalous relationship with a slave. She was probably concerned that it would be difficult to arrange a good marriage for him while he was engaged in such an affair. The young man conceived a plan that would satisfy both his mother and Melchora: he moved Angela to the house of his mistress so that the latter could supervise her movements, and he told his mother that he had sold the slave. Then he chose to make himself scarce and went to Lima on a business trip.

While Ildefonso was away, Melchora taunted Angela that she really was to be sold. Angela struck her. She later recounted the incident to her lawyer, apparently without any embarrassment and perhaps even with pride, patiently explaining why Melchora was particularly angry with her. More important, it was after this turn of events that Angela decided to sue for her freedom. She paid the money necessary for the official paper and the cost of a scribe—she could have earned it doing laundry or other chores—and she dictated her complaint. She signed it herself and presented it at the Casa de Gobierno.

The next day she appeared again as she had been told to do, this time with her evidence. She had the baptismal certificate and a list of five women who could serve as witnesses, including the midwife, the servant who had brought the weekly allowance, and the respectable free woman who had served as the child's godmother. Angela must have been beloved by her friends—or else they loathed Ildefonso—for they risked his wrath to testify for her. The servant actually worked in his mother's household, yet she spoke up as bluntly as the others. Perhaps her age gave her confidence—she was nearly fifty—and certainly she had been charmed by the baby.

Ildefonso denied everything, but Angela clearly had other supporters as well, for she then found a lawyer to present her case. Whether she had saved some money, or he volunteered his time, or friends helped to secure him is not clear. Later the judge, who was also the governor, ruled that as a slave she was entitled to free representation by the public defender. She would need his services, for Ildefonso went to great lengths to account for the misinterpretation that he claimed all the witnesses were maliciously promoting. He clearly felt a great need to do this and in fact seems to have made a definite decision as to the form he wanted his life to take. By now he must have been courting Mercedes Mateus, a young girl of about sixteen years from one of Guayaquil's leading families, whom he married in February 1824.[8] Coronel argued that the child in question was not his but rather that of a free black man who had befriended Angela. Or perhaps, he said, it had actually been sired by the lawyer, because a slave woman clearly could not have paid him in cash and likely paid with sex. If that were the case, she had probably been his lover for a long time.

It is small wonder that Ildefonso wanted to discredit the lawyer, for with that same lawyer, Angela had presented the most eloquent version of her case. In their statement, the two tied the rhetoric of independence and liberal democracy to Angela's situation as a slave and a woman. They argued that one could not free the colony without freeing all the people. They began by approaching the case from a woman's perspective, arguing that a patriot such as Coronel who had declared himself free of colonial shackles could not become intimate with a person who was unfree. He had become one with her, through intercourse and through their child. Therefore she, too, must be free: "The union of two people of opposite sex renders them one, for from this act regularly results issue: *et erum duo in carne una*. And is it possible to believe, using good judgment, that Ildefonso Coronel, when he proposed such a union to me, wanted half his body to be free, the other half enslaved, subject to servitude, sale and other hatefulness, which some disgraced people cling to as relics of the feudal system that has enveloped us for nearly three centuries?"

The united bodies of the one couple in many ways symbolized the larger body politic: for the whole to be free, all its parts would have to be liberated. In case they had not yet made their point, Angela and the attorney went on to say specifically that a government promoting itself as republican and demanding popular loyalty on those grounds was going to have to side with liberty in order to retain its internal logic and widespread support. In European thinking there had, of course, been tension between the principle of slavery and the principle of republicanism since the first appearance of the latter. The lawyer, the judge, and probably Ildefonso were familiar with attempts at reconciliation between the two ideas going back as far as Aristotle and Plato. But the Enlightenment era that had culminated in the independence movement had poked holes in the traditional logic. In Angela's voice, she and her lawyer were confident that this new government would not accept her enslavement: "I do not believe that this tribunal will justify it, nor that meritorious members of a Republic that, full of philanthropic and liberal sentiments, has given all necessary proofs of liberalism, employing their arms and heroically risking their lives to liberate us from the Spanish Yoke, would want to promise to keep me in servitude, even against the promise that Coronel made to me the first time he united himself with me."

The language of the presentation is clearly filled with the expressions of the lawyer, Rufino Mora. Whether Angela Batallas could read or not we will never know, but she certainly could not quote Latin. It might be tempting to conclude that a well-educated abolitionist and patriot simply used Angela's pathetic story to make his own points in a public forum. A closer examination of the case, however, indicates that such a conclusion would not be fair. The evidence suggests that Angela herself was actively involved in the construction of the discourse.

At the heart of the argument presented are two ideas: first, that the joining of the bodies is socially significant, and second, that the patriots are not defending their honor in a consistent manner. Both of these ideas were Angela's. They may have occurred independently to her lawyer, or they may have been in common parlance. The relevant fact here is that she did not owe the ideas to him. She expressed them on her own in her dictated complaint and also verbally in court in a transcribed deposition before Ildefonso denied the charges and before she hired a lawyer. (Ildefonso's charge that she had probably been sexually involved with the lawyer for many months was ignored by the court and still seems dismissable now.) Before the lawyer took over the presentation of the case, Angela talked graphically and without any Latin about the importance of the union of bodies. She emphasized the resulting child who was literally the embodiment of both parents. Of Ildefonso she said: "He is trying to torment a slave woman with whom he has united his blood." Instead of simply referring to her pregnancy, the midwife quoted her as speaking of "the child of his that she carried in her belly."

The idea of the patriots losing their honor through inconsistency may have loomed even larger for Angela than did the concept of the joining of two bodies. The focus of her argument lay in the fact that Ildefonso, a good patriot, had "promised" her liberty. She repeated several times that she had responded to his advances in the first place only because he had given her his word. Once, in her oral testimony, she lost her temper, forgot her social station in relation to those around her, and spoke sarcastically: "Coronel tried to send me to Cuenca to give birth, for the ridiculous reason of not losing his honor—which he values so highly."

Angela touched on a sore point here. Honor had always been a subject of concern to those descended from the Spanish *hidalgos* (noblemen), but it had taken on new resonance in the independence era. The patriots' language was full of references to it. Indeed, they were risking their property and their very lives for their honor: as they saw it, they were asserting their manliness and independence to fight on the side of justice and to defend a savagely abused land and people. They were self-declared heroes. And heroes do not break promises, nor are they hypocrites. Angela implied that if Guayaquil's elite wanted to govern as heroes in a free land, there was only one course open to them.

There is other, less direct evidence that Angela had a hand in forming the argument of Rufino Mora's legal brief. First, she obviously had a strong personality and was unlikely to let herself be pushed aside by a man whom she had herself hired or at least agreed to work with. Second, in the next deposition, the one prepared by the assigned public defender, over whom she would have had no control, the arguments are dry in tone as well as being substantively different. Rather than follow the political lines of argument she had set in her earlier oral testimony, as did Rufino Mora, the new lawyer concentrated instead on a legal technicality: the baptismal certificate proved that Coronel had treated Angela as if she were free and that he had recognized the child as his own. Finally, Rufino Mora wrote erratically, sometimes using flowery rhetoric and foreign words and sometimes speaking like anyone on the street. There are times when he apparently quoted Angela directly. Before launching into one of the polished speeches cited earlier, he wrote the following convoluted— almost chatty and conversational—sentence: "The baptismal certificate is convincing that he considered me free, and that is why he did not mention the character of my servitude, which Coronel certainly had not forgotten about, rather he had already promised me my freedom."

It was certainly Angela Batallas alone who chose to visit Bolívar. Anyone could have thought of it; she did it. Two months after meeting with San Martín, the Liberator had left to tour the highlands, traveling to Cuenca and Quito. He was away when most of the case unfolded, during which time Angela was lodged by the court with a temporary master who volunteered to buy her from Coronel in a lease-like arrangement while the case was being settled. Not long after Bolívar returned to Guayaquil to prepare for the Peruvian campaign, Angela went to see him. No one recorded their conversation, but shortly afterward Bolívar ordered his assistant to write to the court of Guayaquil. He did not try to protect her master's name, despite his high station. "The slave woman Angela Batallas has presented herself to His Excellency the Liberator, complaining of her former master Ildefonso Coronel. His Excellency orders me to recommend to you justice for this unhappy slave."

The note was effective: the public defender who received it submitted it that same day to the court, where it became part of the permanent record. Even though Ildefonso responded that there was no new proof of wrongdoing on his part, the public defender for the first time felt strong enough to say that it did not matter if some of the witnesses were slaves speaking without their owners' permission, or even if Angela was immoral and the child was actually another man's. The point was that Ildefonso's note to the priest for the baptismal certificate proved that he had promised freedom to the woman: the "integrity" of the new government demanded that Coronel be forced to pay the temporary master for her freedom so that she might be released. The usually dry-toned public defender went so far as to say that Coronel was a "miserable man without principles."

It is possible to interpret Angela's visit to Bolívar not as a political statement or even a savvy effort to intervene in a judicial process stacked against her, but simply as the traditional act of a supplicant appearing before a lord. For generations, the powerless had dreamed of bypassing their overseers to speak to the master or of bypassing their masters to speak to the king. There is something different in this instance, however. Bolívar was hardly a king. He was not ultimately all-powerful in Angela's world: he was the head of one army, still fighting another, not necessarily victorious, and certainly moving on, probably never to return. She knew that he could not simply free her. It is more likely that she saw him as a great and articulate spokesman for ideas she believed in, as someone who would be able to convince others where she had failed. The evidence suggests that Angela Batallas did not visit the Liberator merely to beg a favor, but rather to ask him to publicly side with her on an issue of sweeping importance. In so doing, she forced the slaveholding landowner and patriot, Ildefonso Coronel, to reckon with her in a way that he had never intended.

The importance of Angela Batallas lies in the fact that she not only heard everything that was going on around her, thought about it, analyzed it, and perceived the master class with her own eyes, but that she also spoke out about the issues. Despite their best efforts and their wishful assumptions, owners could not keep their slaves from reacting to events. It had to have happened on a daily basis in the colonial era: it took on new significance in the independence era. When political chasms loomed visibly among the elites at the dawn of the nineteenth century and political debate became commonplace, owners could not prevent slaves from participating in their own way. Angela Batallas, like other slaves, used her knowledge of republicanism to further her own case, and she vocalized connections between her own plight and the plight of others who were unfree. Once the enslaved had done that, nothing in the former colonial kingdom could ever be the same again. Now they were engaging in more than psychological struggles with individual owners: they were taking sides in a political battle.

QUESTIONS FOR DISCUSSION

1. Without knowing this case, what might our traditional assumptions be concerning an enslaved woman's reasons for seeking out Simón Bolívar?
2. After familiarizing yourself with this case, what do you personally believe were Angela Batallas's reasons for seeking the encounter with the famous general?

3. What clues to the political consciousness of the enslaved do we have, other than court transcripts?
4. What might Ildefonso Coronel have been thinking when he initiated a sexual relationship with one of his slaves?
5. Why was Ildefonso Coronel unable to control Angela Batallas, even though he had legal power over her as her owner?

NOTES

An earlier version of this article originally appeared in *Colonial Latin American Review* 7, no. 1 (1998): 105–28.

1. Harold A. Bierk, ed., *Selected Writings of Bolívar* (New York: Colonial Press, 1951), 359.

2. Archivo Histórico del Guayas, Guayaquil (henceforth AHG), document 698, "Angela Batallas contra su amo, sobre su libertad" (1823). All quotations from the Batallas case come from this document.

3. For example, see Peter Blanchard's chapter in the first edition of this volume for a discussion of slaves who joined the royalist army to escape their bondage.

4. Archivo de la Biblioteca Municipal de Guayaquil, vol. 136, Padrones of 1832. AHG document 608, "Inventarios de los bienes quedados por la muerte de Pedro Gonzales" (1823).

5. The *Cuaderno de Conciliaciones* for 1822–1823 (AHG document 1546) contains more cases of this kind than of any other type.

6. AHG document 1546 (1822).

7. Camilla Townsend, "En Busca de la Libertad: Los esfuerzos de los esclavos guayaquileños por garantizar su independencia despues de la Independencia," *Procesos: Revista Ecuatoriana de Historia* 4 (1999): 73–86.

8. Over the course of the next twenty-eight years, Mercedes went on to bear eighteen children, a number of whom died young. Pedro Robles Chambers, "Genealogía de los Mateus," *Contribución para el estudio de la sociedad colonial de Guayaquil* (Guayaquil: Imprenta de la Reforma, 1938).

SUGGESTED READINGS

Information on Angela Batallas is confined to the records of the Archivo Histórico del Guayas in Guayaquil. However, her life can be compared with that of another female slave: *María Chiquinquirá Díaz, una esclava del siglo XVIII: Acerca de las identidades de amo y esclavo en el puerto colonial de Guayaquil*, by María Eugenia Chaves (Guayaquil, 1998). More information on Batallas's master is available in Guillermo Arosemena, "Los Coronel: Grandes comerciantes guayaquileños del siglo XIX," *Revista Ecuatoriana de Historia Económica* 12 (1995): 91–147. A journal kept by a foreign visitor to Guayaquil during the exact period of this narrative makes interesting reading: Basil Hall's *Extracts from a Journal Written on the Coasts of Chili, Peru and Mexico* (Edinburgh, 1824). To place these events in the context of larger changes in the nation, see Kenneth Andrien, *The Kingdom of Quito, 1690–1830: The State and Regional Development* (Cambridge, MA, 1995). For more on the historical struggles between masters and slaves in the area, see David Chandler, "Slave over Master in Colonial Colombia and Ecuador," *The Americas* 38 (1982): 315–26. For the larger Afro-Latino experience, see Herbert Klein, *African Slavery in Latin America and the Caribbean* (New York, 1986). For the theoretical debate on slaves' assertion of power while in their relatively weak position, start with Orlando Patterson, *Slavery and Social Death: A Comparative Story* (Cambridge, MA, 1982) and the more recent collection of essays edited by Stephen Palmié, *Slave Cultures and the Cultures of Slavery* (Knoxville, TN, 1996). For the tensions between slavery and freedom born at the end of the colonial era, see the classic by David Brion Davis, *The Problem of Slavery in the Age of Revolution, 1770–1823* (Ithaca, NY, 1975).

Index

Abascal y Sousa, Fernando de, 294, 297
Abreu Funari, Pedro Paulo de, 147n5
abuse, sexual, 27, 141
Account of the Things in Yucatán
  (Landa), 25, 30n13
Acosta, José de, 184
Acuña, Angelina de, 56
Acuña, Juana de, 50, 56
Acuña, Juan de, 48, 49, 50, 51, 54, 56, 59
Acuña, Mariana de, 56
Acuña, Pedro de (don), 81, 87, 94n5
Africans, 2; slaves, 3, 10, 13, 133, 309.
  See also Amerindians
agriculture, 137, 138, 309
agro-pastoral enterprises, 4
Agualongo, Agustín, 219, 289; with
  enlistment in army, 298; ethnicity
  of, 293; historical portrayal, 290,
  292–293; as "ignorant Indian", 293;
  with Indian communities and
  royalist politics, 300–302; military
  legacy of, 291, 299; in political
  context, 294; with regional
  dimensions of Pasto's royalist
  movement, 295–296; with royalism
  and independence era, 292–295;
  with royalist army, 294, 297–299
aguardiente (white rum), 240, 241, 250,
  260, 265
Aguiar, Joanna de, 262
Alberro, Solange, 212n19
albinos, 4
Albornoz, Cristóbal de, 182–184, 185
Alva, Bartolomé de, 120
Álvares Cabral, Pedro, 8, 63
Alvares Caramurú, Diogo, 65, 74n2
Álvarez, Arturo, 169n19
Alzaga, Martín de, 285; with evidence,
  283; with French Conspiracy
  investigation, 270, 275–277, 278,

278–279, 280, 280–281, 282; with lack
  of conspiracy proof, 284; with
  torture, 283, 284
Amar, Antonio, 233
Amaral, Domingos Gomes de, 260
Amar y Borbón, Antonio, 290, 297
American Revolution, 269
Amerindians: in Brazil, 4; epidemic
  diseases, 3, 7, 16, 33, 36, 77;
  prohibited transport to Europe, 79;
  with legal separation of races, 3;
  Roman Catholic Church and
  conversion of, 2, 3, 8, 97, 199; in
  social hierarchy, 1
Anama, Ana (doña), 51
ancestors: cults, 41; land claims with
  occupation by, 58, 59
Andeans, 11; Aymara language, 44n2,
  60n1; evangelizing of, 184–187;
  migration, 56, 187; with literacy for
  elites, 187, 188, 189; with Quipu
  system of communication, 173; with
  Quipu translated into alphabetic
  script, 173; transition to Spanish
  values from, 43; Yarovilca dynasty,
  193
Andes: in historical context, 33–34,
  101–102; with Incas and gender
  inequality in historical context,
  47–48; literary awakening in, 174;
  property ownership customs in,
  56–58; Spanish distinctions for
  indigenous peoples in, 180, 182
Angasnapon, Francisco (don), 38
Angasnapon, Pedro (don), 38
Antonini, Santiago, 283, 284
Aparicio, Manuel, 276
apprenticeship, artistic, 192, 193
Apurimac, map of, 183
Arataca (Chief), 65, 66, 69

Archicofradía de San Benito, 279, 280, 286
architecture, of Iberian towns, 2
Arellano, Teresa (doña), 276
Argüello, Bernardo de, 79
Aricoma, Diego (don), 54
Aristotle, 314
army, royalist, 294, 297–299, 305, 318n3
Arredondo, Nicolás, 270, 273, 275
Arrubla, Gerardo, 293
artisan production, 4
Atahualpa, 37
Augustinians, 41
auto-da-fé (public punishment), 24, 25
autoeroticism, 119
Avila, Francisco de, 174
Ayacucho, map of, 183
Ayarza, Antonio Nicanor, 222, 223, 228, 231–232, 233, 234, 235
Ayarza, Josef Ponciano, 222, 223, 227–228, 229, 230–231, 232, 233, 234, 235
Ayarza, Pedro Crisólogo, 222, 223, 228, 231–232, 233, 234, 235
Ayarza, Pedro de, 218; first petition, 1795-1797, and, 226–231; fourth petition, 1807, and, 234; with lives changed by whiteness, 235; military service of, 226; passing and, 222; with reasons for purchasing whiteness, 223; second petition, 1799-1803, and, 231–232; supporters of, 226–227, 228; third petition, 1804-1806, and, 233; with whiteness purchased for self and sons, 223, 225, 226, 234, 235
Aztec empire, 7

Báez, Francisco, 79, 81, 82, 83, 85, 86, 88
banking systems, absence of, 55
Barbarín, Juan, 219, 270; with Archicofradía de San Benito, 279, 280; conspiracy and testimony against, 277–279; with cultural context of Buenos Aires, 271–276; imprisonment of, 282, 284; innocence of, 285; investigation of, 279–281, 282; with slave-master relationship, 270, 278, 280, 281–282,

285, 286; supporters of, 285; with turn in investigation, 282–284; with unofficial exile, 270, 284, 285
Barboza Bueno, Manoel, 265
Basques, Leonor (doña), 113
Batallas, Angela, 219; Bolívar's meeting with, 306–308, 317; with fight for freedom, 306; with slavery in Guayaquil, 308–310; suit of, 311–317
Bautista, Juan, 42
beasts, colonialists as predatory, 177, 179
Bejarano, Lorenso María, 233
Bellini, Ligia, 130n6
Bernal, Alonso, 121
Betancourt, Gregorio (don), 251
Bezerra, Antônio Jácome, 142
blood, purity of, 2, 3, 78, 92, 204
Bolívar, Simón, 219, 289, 290, 291, 299, 301, 306; with Batallas case, 306–308, 317; military legacy of, 308, 309
Bolivia: Audiencia of Charcas, 47, 48; Inca empire, 35; Lake Titicaca, 151; La Plata, 47, 48, 51, 53, 53, 58, 58; mining centers, 56, 57, 101, 117, 155, 165
Bonaparte, Joseph, 218, 234, 289, 294
Bonaparte, Napoléon, 216, 218, 289, 294, 299
books: banned, 68, 274; burning of, 24, 30n11, 277; with European book culture, 175
Borla de los Santos, Francisco (don), 230
Bran, María, 113
Brazil: Amerindian groups in, 4; economy in, 98; gold in, 257, 258; map, viceroyalty of, 10; mature colonial order in, 97–98; population, 257, 258; Portuguese settlement of, 8, 216; sugar economy in, 133, 216. *See also* Portugal; São Paulo, Brazil
brazilwood, 4, 8, 63
bribes, 78, 82
Brides of Christ, 111
Brito Freire, Francisco de, 138
bruja (sorcerer), 206
brujería, 206. *See also* witchcraft

Buenos Aires: cultural context,
271–276; with slaves and unrest,
275–276; slave trade in, 272, 273
Bustamonte, Miguel García de (don),
282
Butler, Judith, 157

Cabello Balboa, Miguel, 184
Cabezas, Tiburcio (don), 251
Cacica, 104
Cacicazgo (chieftancy), 51, 53, 54
Cacique principal (paramount lord),
37, 38, 42, 47, 48, 49, 56, 58, 60n1, 180
Caciques (indigenous lords), 34, 35, 38,
48, 298, 300, 301
Calidad (social rank), 200, 258
Cajamarca: census of, 39–41, 40;
Franciscans with religious changes
in, 41; kuraka's responsibilities in,
38, 39–41. *See also* Caruarayco,
Melchior
Camacho, Juan, 89
Cámara of the Indies, 221–222, 224, 225
Cano, Isabel de, 105
Capdepont, Juan Pablo, 278
Caribbean. *See* Spanish Caribbean
Carmen, María del, 312–313
Carmen, Virgin of, 103, 106, 110, 113
Caro, Rodrigo, 83, 85
Caro Baroja, Julio, 212n19
Carretero, Juan Martín, 277, 278
Carrilho, Fernão, 142, 143
Carua, Juana (doña), 56
Caruarayco, Luis, 42
Caruarayco, Melchior (don), 11; with
Andes in historical context, 33–34;
with Cajamarca census, 39–41, 40;
family lineage of, 36–37; with
Franciscans and religious changes,
41; last will and testament of, 38–39;
with leadership challenged, 41–42;
responsibilities as kuraka, 38, 39–41;
with Spanish influence on kurakas,
34–36; successor to, 42; with
transition from Andean to Spanish
values, 43
Caruatongo (son of Chuptongo), 37, 41
Carvalho e Melo, Sebastião José de, 216

Casa de la Contratación, 79, 88, 89, 90,
91, 92
Casas, Bartolomé de las, 94n3
caste, 78, 79, 81, 93, 222
Castilla, Francisco de, 82, 83, 86
castizo, 4
Castro, Justo (don), 248
Catalina: with allegations of sexual
services, 82; with colonial ideas of
caste and gender, 78, 79; documents
with "true" identity of, 89, 92;
judgment for, 88; questions about
true identity of, 92–93; testimony
against, 79–80, 81–82, 82–83, 85;
testimony in favor of, 83–85, 86–87,
91
Catequil (deity), 41
Caxal, Juan, 90
Cédula de Gracias al Sacar, 218, 221,
222
census, 264; of Cajamarca, 39–41, 40;
with pardos, 267n11; Quito, 241;
Silva, José Antonio da, and, 260,
262, 263; whiteness and, 263, 265
Chachapoyas, 187, 189
Charles II (King of Spain), 215
Charles III (King of Spain), 215
Charles IV (King of Spain), 218, 223,
289, 305
Chi, Ah Kulel (father), 15, 16, 16, 25, 26
Chi, Gaspar Antonio (son), 11;
Christian education for, 18, 18–19;
dawn (1530-1535), 15; descriptions
of, 19, 21; family tree, 21, 22; on
father's murder, 16, 25; Franciscans
and, 14, 17, 18, 21, 23; Landa's
influence on, 19–20, 21, 23, 24, 25;
languages spoken by, 19, 21; life in
context, 14; maturity (1561-1578),
21–25; name change for, 17; on
Otzmal massacre, 16, 26; political
influences on, 23; with royal
questionnaires, 16, 21, 26; senior
years (1578-1610), 26–28; as
translator, 11, 14, 19, 25, 26, 27,
27–28; twilight (1610), 28–29; youth
(1536-1560), 16–21; with Yucután in
historical context, 13–14
chicha (maize beer), 39, 50

children: illegitimate, 53, 54, 218, 221, 222, 244, 259, 261, 262, 263–264, 266, 306, 312–313; legitimate, 60n12; with marriage choices controlled, 221; in Palmares settlement, 139; with schools for sons of nobles, 18; slave, 311; slaves and freedom for, 305–306, 312–313, 315; women and rearing of, 47
Chinchon, Conde de (Viceroy), 42
Chinori Guarachi, Martín (don), 51
Chocoboto, María (doña), 52
Christ. *See* Jesus Christ
Christianity, 2; mixed with traditional beliefs, 3; schools, 18, 18–19
Chuplingón, Alonso, 37, 41–42
Chuptongo (son of Concacax), 37, 43
Chuquichambi, Hernando, 50
churches, monastic, 18, 20
Cisneros, Jiménez de, 94n3
Ciudad Rodrigo, Pedro de, 23
Clare of Assisi, 105–106
cloth, 239, 245, 246
Cobo, Bernabé, 104
Colombia, 289–291. *See also* Pasto, Colombia
colonialism, "space in between", 175
colonialists, as predatory beasts, 177, 179
Columbus, Christopher, 7
communal laws, 55–56
communitarian economies, 136–138
community property, 50, 51–52. *See also* Itquilla, Domingo; Sisa, Isabel
Comunero Revolt, 216
Concacax (Guzmango Capac), 37
Concepción, Francisco de la, 105
concubinage, marriage and, 257–266
confessions: with confessional manual, 119–121; Ludeña's, 91; Ruiz's, 121–122, 122–124, 125, 126–127, 129; Vega's, 209
conspiracy: allegations of, 277–279; investigation, 279–281, 282–284; lack of evidence for, 284; torture for, 283, 284, 285
convents, for women, 104–107, 119. *See also* Jesús, Ursula de; Ruiz, Agustina
conversions. *See* religious conversions

Copenhagen, 194, 196
Córdova y Salinas, Diego de, 105
Coronel, Ildefonso, 306, 311–314, 315, 316–317
Corral, Francisco del (don), 80, 81
Corregidor de indios, 7, 33, 37, 42, 49, 189, 191
Corro, Miguel Alvares del (don), 248
Cortés, Hernán, 7, 15
Cosatongo (Guzmango Capac), 37
Council of Trent, 120, 156
Couto, Frei Loreto de, 145
Covarrubias, Sebastían de, 169n17
Cristo, Catalina de, 105
Cristo, Juana de, 105
Cruz, Francisca de la, 113
Cuenca, Gregorio González de, 40–41
Cueva, Louis de la (don), 85
cults, ancestor, 41
culture, 1, 175; hegemony, 4, 5; in Palmares settlement, 138–139
cupping, 204

d'Almeida, Paula, 68
dark skinned. *See* pardo
da Silva, Adrião, 259
da Silva, Damazio Antonio, 265
da Silva, Francisco de Paula, 261, 265
da Silva, José Antonio, 218, 219; census information on, 262, 263; as controversial figure, 261; cultural context and, 257, 258, 258–259, 261, 262; family background of, 259; illegitimate children of, 259, 261, 262, 263–264, 266; legacy of, 260, 264; legitimate heirs of, 265; marriage of, 262; as military man, 259, 261; with settlement of estate, 263, 265; sexual liaisons of, 258, 259, 261, 262, 262–264, 266, 267
Delgado, Juan, 79, 80, 86
deliverance, from purgatory, 113
demandadores, 154–155, 156, 165. *See also* Ocaña, Diego de
de Silva, Nicolás, 81
desire, forms of, 121, 126
devil, 124, 125, 199, 208
diaries, 103, 110, 114n1. *See also* Jesús, Ursula de

Dias, Diogo, 68
Díaz, José, 282, 283, 284, 285
Díaz, Maria, 81, 82
Diaz del Castillo, Bernal, 2
diets, in communitarian economies, 137
diseases, 35, 144, 193; epidemics and, 3, 17, 36, 241; humors and, 204; indigenous populations decimated by European, 3, 17, 36; sexually transmitted, 310
domestic violence, 51
"don": as birthright, 2; as self-proclaimed title, 3, 48, 58; *See also specific dons*
"doña", 2; *See also specific doñas*
donada (religious servant), 101–102, 104, 107–108, 108–109, 111–113. *See also* Jesús, Ursula de
Donoso, Mariano (don), 249, 250
dreams, 35
Duarte, Ana, 84
dueño de indio (high ethnic lord), 44n2
Dumont, Juan Luis, 283, 285
Durán, Madroñal, 169n19

earthquakes, 101, 104, 241
Echevarria, Manuel Antonio de, 234
economies: in Brazil, 98, 133, 216; communitarian, 136–138; expansion of colonial, 4; in Quito, 239–240; sugar, 4, 8, 133, 216; with textile mills, 239
Ecuador. *See* Guayaquil, Ecuador; Quito, Ecuador
education: with Franciscan schools in Yucatán, 18, 18–19; Spain and requirements for higher, 2
Enciso, Salvador Jiménez de, 297
encomenderos (conquistadors holding encomienda grants), 7, 16, 19, 26, 34, 40, 88, 242
encomienda, 7, 13, 33, 37
Enlightenment, 269, 314
Enríquez, Diego, 84, 85
entrepreneurship, as reason to settle New World, 1, 2, 3, 4
epidemics, 241; indigenous populations decimated by

European, 3, 17, 36. *See also* diseases
Esau (son of Isaac), 163, 169n16
Espinosa y Albares, Lorenzo Corbacho de (don), 226–227
Esquivel, Rafaela de (doña), 107, 111
Esteva-Fabregat, Claudio, 94n1
ethnicity: of Agualongo, 293; with healing ability, 204; with Quito's ethnic makeup, 242; undocumented, 241. *See also* whiteness
Europe: goods from, 249; indigenous populations decimated by disease from, 3, 17, 36; *See also specific countries*
evil, 199, 200, 206, 209
exile, 86, 88, 141, 174, 191, 203, 209, 270, 284, 285
Ezpeleta, José de, 229

families: background of da Silva, José Antonio, 259; of Chi, Gaspar Antonio, 21, 22; history of Loza, Victorina, 241, 242; with lineage of Caruarayco, Melchior, 36–37; in Palmares settlement, 137, 139, 142; polyandrous, 139; of Zumbi of Palmares, 142
Ferdinand VII (King of Spain), 2, 218, 289, 290, 294, 296, 299, 301, 305
Fernández Farias, Antonio, 87
Fernández Jaramillo, Juan, 79, 82, 83, 86, 86–87
Ferrera, Alonso, 87
filho natural (illegitimate child), 261. *See also* children
"Foolish Fatherland", 296
forastero (migrant), 56, 180, 187, 189
Forster, E. M., 5
Franca, Ignacia, 258, 261, 262, 263, 264, 265, 266
France, 297; French Revolution and, 269, 270, 274, 276, 280, 289–290; Iberian Peninsual invaded by, 290
Franciscans, 11; with Cajamarca and religious changes, 41; Chi, Gaspar Antonio, and influence of, 14, 17, 18, 21, 23; with punishment of Maya for idolatry, 23–25; schools in Yucatán

run by, 18, 18–19
Franco, Francisco, 262
freedom: censorship of "liberty" and, 274, 276, 283; with Guayaquil's independence, 310; independence with royalism and, 292–295; from slavery, 107, 266, 305–306, 312–313, 315. *See also* Batallas, Angela
free will, 109
Freitas, Décio, 136, 137, 148n10, 148n11
French Conspiracy. *See* Barbarín, Juan
French Revolution, 269, 270, 274, 276, 280, 289–290
friars. *See* Ocaña, Diego de; priests
Furtada, Maria de Oliveira, 260

Galen, 204
Gallardo, Juan Diaz, 301
gananciales (community property), 51
Ganga Zumba (Chief), 134, 139–140, 141, 142–143, 143–144
García, Baltasar, 277
Garcia Sambrano, Juan, 200, 201, 203, 205–206
Garcilán, Lucas, 81
Garibaldi, Alonso de, 121–122, 124
gender, colonial ideas of caste and, 78, 79
gender inequality: in Andes with Inca, 47–48; with inheritance laws, 47–48
genealogy, inheritance laws and, 53
gifts: slaves as, 264; spiritual, 102, 109, 110–111, 112
gods, hierarchy of indigenous, 47
gold, 35, 40, 296; in Brazil, 257, 258; as reason for settling in New World, 2, 3, 4; regional markets based on, 4
Gómez, Cristóbal, 80
González, Luis, 81
governments: Guaman Poma with Philip III and good, 193, 193, 194, 195; junta, 218, 290, 291, 294, 295, 297, 298, 305; slaves, indigenous people and relationship with, 298
Gramsci, Antonio, 4
Grimau, Juan Antonio, 276–277
Groot, Pedro (don), 228
Guadalupe. *See* Our Lady of Guadalupe; Virgin of Guadalupe

Guaman Poma de Ayala, Felipe, 39, 99; Albornoz and approval of, 184; ancestral background of, 177, 180; on Andean elite and importance of literacy, 187, 188, 189; artistic apprenticeship of, 192, 193; criminal accusations against, 191; with *El Primer nueva corónica y buen gobierno*, 174, 175, 175–177, 176, 178, 179, 193, 194, 194, 195, 196; with evolving social role and identity, 175, 180, 182; as Indio ladino in eyes of Spanish, 182; as interpreter and witness with land proceedings, 187; with kin's claims to land, 187, 189–191; literary evolution of, 174; with litigation and legal defeat, 187–192; on missionary guidance and reform, 184; on policies of Toledo's administration, 186–187; punishment for, 191, 192; self-proclaimed title of, 180, 182, 191; with service to church and state, 182–187; writing to expose injustice, 192–193
Guayaquil, Ecuador: independence for, 310; slave population of, 309; slavery and, 308–310
Guayas, Republic of, 305, 310
Guayna Capac, 35, 37
Gutiérrez, Magdalena, 56
Gutiérrez, Ysabel, 84, 85
Guzmango Capac, 37

Haiti, slave uprisings and revolution in, 272, 275, 280
Hamamani, Domingo (don), 52, 53, 54
head taxes, 3, 8
healers: in colonial Mexico, 202–206; ethnicity and, 204; influence of, 203, 205–206; physicians and role of, 201, 203–204. *See also* Vega, Ana de
heaven: purgatory and, 109; visions of, 113. *See also* purgatory
hegemony, cultural, 4, 5
heirs: legitimate, 265; wills, kinship and, 52, 53–55, 57–58. *See also* children; wills, last
hell, 109, 110. *See also* purgatory

Hemming, John, 74n2
Henao, Jesús María, 293
hereditary rights, wills and, 47, 58, 59
Hernández Portocarrero, Martín, 88
Herrera, Beatriz de, 17
Herrera Chi, Gaspar Antonio de. *See* Chi, Gaspar Antonio
hierarchy: of natural order, 5; social, 1, 2, 4, 203
Hieronymites, 154–155, 160, 169n7. *See also* Ocaña, Diego de
Hippocrates, 204
history: daily life influenced by, 1, 5; family, 241, 242; rewritten with Spanish conquests, 173
Holy Office of the Inquisition, 11, 73n1; with Amerindians and conversion, 3; information gleaned from documents of, 202, 209; manual of, 206; Mexican Inquisition and, 117–118, 121–122, 122–124, 125, 126–127, 129, 199–209; mystical practices in Lima condemned by, 104; Portuguese Inquisition, 64, 68–72, 71, 74n6, 74n7; purity of faith and, 3; Spanish Inquisition, 67, 68. *See also* Roman Catholic Church
homosexuality, 141, 148n11
honorific titles: with altered rank, status or heritage, 221; as birthright, 2; purchased, 218, 228, 232; self-proclaimed, 3, 48, 58, 180, 182, 191, 225
Huamanga, Peru, map of, 190
Huanca, Catalina, 104
Huascar, 37
Huayna Capac, 189
humors, 204
husbands, with rights to manage wife's capital, 244, 245, 246

Iberian Peninsula: French invasion of, 290; New World and ties to, 1–3; religion in, 2; social hierarchy in, 2. *See also* Portugal; Spain
idolatry: extirpation of, 182–184, 185; Maya punished for practice of, 23–25; torture for practice of, 23–24
illegitimate child. *See* filho natural

images, holy. *See* Ocaña, Diego de; Virgin of Guadalupe
Inca empire (Tawantinsuyu), 7, 47, 186; fall of, 35; with gender inequality in historical context, 47–48
Inconfidencia Mineira, 216
Indians: Agualong as "ignorant", 293; lobo beget from torna atrás and, 4; with royalist politics in Pasto, 300–302; slaves and sugar, 63–64, 65, 66, 73; with Spaniard beget mestizo, 4
Indies. *See* Spanish Indies
indigenous peoples: with colonialism and "space in between", 175; epidemic disease from Europe and decimation of, 3, 17, 36; government's relationships with slaves and, 298; languages of, 173–174, 175, 177; leaders of, 11; resistance of, 99; with Spain's legal code, 11; Spanish distinctions for, 180, 182; taxes levied against, 3, 7. *See also* Amerindians; *specific indigenous peoples*
Indio ladino, 182
indulgences, purgatory and, 110
inequality: cultural, 4; gender, 47–48; resistance to, 5
inheritance laws: based on genealogy, 53; gender inequality with, 47–48. *See also* Itquilla, Domingo; Sisa, Isabel
inks, tattoo, 70
Inquisition. *See* Holy Office of the Inquisition
intercession, purgatory and, 110
investments, land, 250, 251
Isaac (father of Esau and Jacob), 169n16
Isabel (Queen of Spain), 2
Isidore (saint), 52
Islam, 2
Itquilla, Alonso (don), 53, 54
Itquilla, Diego (don), 53, 54
Itquilla, Domingo (don), 11; with communal law, 55; hereditary rights and, 47, 58; illegitimate children of, 53, 54; kinship and heirs of, 52, 53–55; last will and testament of, 47,

51–55, 56, 57–58; property ownership and, 57–58; with will contested by wife, 56, 58

Jacob (son of Isaac), 169n16
Jaga, 135
James (saint), 177, 178
Jauli, Domingo, 191
Jefferson, Thomas, 311
Jesuits, 66, 67, 68–69, 104, 136, 184
Jesús, Ursula de, 98; background of, 102; with cloistered convent life, 105–107; diary of, 103, 110, 114n1; as donada, 101–102, 104, 107–108, 108–109, 111–113; early childhood of, 103; with freedom from slavery, 107; influence of, 113; with race and racism in religious life, 111–113; spirits petitioning help from, 102, 109–110; spiritual gifts of, 102, 109, 110–111, 112; spiritual renaissance and, 104; spiritual renewal for, 106–107; with visions about heaven, 113; with visions of Christ, 111, 112, 112–113; with visions of purgatory, 109–111, 113
Jesus Christ: Brides of Christ and, 111; visions of, 102, 109, 111, 112, 112–113, 119, 124, 125, 127
Jews, 2, 3, 67, 68, 69, 199
João VI (King of Portugal), 216
Juáres de Illanez, Pedro, 38
Judaism, 2, 68, 69. See also Jews
judgments. See legal judgments
juntas (governing committees). See governments

kinship: with claims to land, 187, 189–191; last wills, heirs and, 52, 53–55, 57–58
Konetzke, Richard, 236n5, 236n8
kurakas (traditional leaders), 33, 186; Cajamarca and responsibilities of, 38, 39–41; changing role of, 35, 36; divine powers and, 33; last will and testament of, 38–39; lineage of, 34; old-style, 42. See also Caruarayco, Melchior

labor force, purchase of, 251
ladino (Hispanicized, cultured), 19, 21, 182
land: ancestral occupation and claims to, 58, 59; Guaman Poma, kin and claims to, 187, 189–191; with Guaman Poma as witness to land proceedings, 187; investments, 250, 251; as open resource, 39; as reason for settling in New World, 2, 3; textile mills and, 239
Landa, Diego de, 14, 19, 30n13; Chi, Gaspar Antonio, and influence of, 19–20, 21, 23, 24, 25; death of, 23, 26; with religious persecution of Maya, 24–25; return to Spain, 25; rivalry with Toral, 21, 23, 24, 25
languages, 135; indigenous, 173–174, 175, 177; learned in schools, 19; Maya, 20, 21; in Palmares settlement, 138–139; speaking in tongues, 69. See also Quipu
Lavrin, Asunción, 130n2
laws. See legislation
lawsuits, 244, 245, 248, 250, 252, 253
leaders, 11, 305. See also kurakas; Zumbi of Palmares
legal judgments, 88
legal trials. See Catalina; Itquilla, Domingo; Ludeña, Francisco de; Ruiz, Agustina; Sisa, Isabel
legislation: communal laws, 55–56; indigenous people with, 11; inheritance laws, 47–48, 53; New World and sumptuary, 3; patriarchy supported by Spanish, 50–51; Spain and sumptuary, 2
legitimation, edict of, 218, 221, 222, 224, 225
Levia, Damián, 84
Lewis, Laura, 212n21
"liberty," censorship of, 274, 276, 283
lies, under oath, 94n7
life: history influencing daily, 1, 5; social tensions influencing daily, 1
life, cloistered: Jesús with convent and, 105–107; race and racism in, 111–113; for religious servants and slaves, 102, 104, 106, 107–108,

111–113

Lima, Peru: in historical context, 101–102; population growth, 105; religious buildings in, 101; religious population of, 104; Roman Catholic Church and evangelizing in, 184–187; Third Church Council in, 184

limpieza de sangre (purity of blood), 2, 203

literacy: importance of, 59, 187, 188, 189; Peru with alphabetic, 175; for slaves, 280, 281–282, 285

literature, 175; with books banned, 68, 274; with books burned, 24, 30n11, 277; with literary awakening in Andes, 174

lobo, 4

Lopes, Manuel, 142

López, Angel, 276

López de Aguila, Juan, 89

López de Cogolludo, Diego, 17, 19, 30n14

Lorenzo Navarro, Diego, 90

Losar, Diego del, 161, 162, 163, 169n14

los Rios, Gerónima de, 103

Louis XVI (King of France), 269, 271, 277

Lovell, W. George, 94n7, 95n8

loyalty, 292. *See also* royalism

Loza, Manuel (don), 241

Loza, Victorina, 218, 240; business partners of, 248; business transactions of, 248–250, 251; as emerging merchant, 244; family history, 241, 242; with joint legal affairs, 246; land investments of, 250, 251; last will of, 253; with lawsuits, 244, 245, 248, 250, 252, 253; legacy of, 253, 254; life in Quito, 240–241, 242, 242–243, 244; marriages of, 244, 245–248, 251–253; private life of, 251–253; with purchased labor force, 251; trade routes of, 247

Lucas de la Peña, Fernando, 240, 244–245

Ludeña, Francisco de: with bribery attempt, 82; with colonial ideas of caste and gender, 78, 79; confession of, 91; defense of, 83–85, 86–87; documents with Catalina's "true" identity and, 89, 92; judgment for and appeal against, 88; with prosecution witnesses discredited, 86–87; re-arrest and new charges against, 88, 90; release of, 91–92; return to Spain, 88; testimony against, 79–82, 83, 85

Ludeña Valdes, Mateo de, 89

Madrid, Spain, 194, 196

Mairena, Anton de, 80, 85

Mairena, Catalina de, 91, 92, 93. *See also* Catalina

Malcaden, Pablo (don), 42

Maldonado, Melchor (don), 89, 90

mamelucos (mixed-blood offspring), 63, 64, 65, 66, 68, 69, 72, 73, 74n5, 145

mandoncillos (lesser lords), 38, 39

mandones, 39

manuals: confessional, 119–121; Inquisitor's, 206

manufacturing, 4

maps: Apurimac, 183; Ayacucho, 183; Brazil, 10; New Spain, 9; Peru, 10, 181, 183, 190, 217

marcavoc (possessor of people), 44n2

Marie Antoinette (Queen of France), 269, 271

Mariscal, López de, 169n19

Marqués de Selva Alegre. *See* Montufar, Juan Pío de

marriage: concubinage and, 257–266; of da Silva, José Antonio, 262; with equals, 261; of Loza, Victorina, 244, 245–248, 251–253; Roman Catholic views on, 258; Royal Pragmatic on, 221, 222; women and benefits for, 246

Martínez de Murgia, Juan, 91

Mary. *See* Virgin Mary

massacres: at Otzmal, 16, 16, 17, 17, 26; of rebel leaders, 305

masters. *See* slaves

masturbation, 119–120, 121, 123

Mata, Juan de, 38

Mateus, Mercedes, 314

Maya, 7, 23; with burning of books and literature, 24, 30n11; conquest of, 13–14; diseases and decimation of, 17; idolatry and punishment of, 23–25; language, 20, 21; Roman Catholic Church and influence on, 14; social class and, 13; Xiu clan, 11, 14, 16

Mayllos y Marcana, Pablo, 278, 280, 281–282, 283, 285

mayordomo (sSteward), 38, 155

Medina, Ramón, 301

Melgarejo, Luisa de, 103, 104, 110

Melo, Antônio, 134, 141, 142, 148n11

Melo, Pedro, 134, 141, 142, 148n11, 216

Melo de Portugal, Pedro, 284

men: as descended from gods, 47; as merchants, 246; monasteries for, 104, 154; multiple spouses for, 44n1; in Palmares settlement, 136, 137; with right to manage wife's capital, 244, 245, 246; with tribute service, 40–41; women dominated by, 5, 51. *See also* gender inequality

Mendoza, Juana de, 89

Meneque, María, 121–122, 124

Merchancano, Estanislao, 289, 302

merchants: class, 242–243; disparity between men and women, 246; textile mills and, 239, 245, 246; women, 243–244, 246; with woolens exchanged for European goods, 249. *See also* Loza, Victorina

Mesa, Francisco de, 90, 91

mestizaje (racial mixture of European and Indian), 78

mestizo, 4, 78

Mexia, Andrés, 27

Mexia, Jordana (doña), 40

Mexican Inquisition: manual of, 206; in Peru and New Spain, 117–118, 121–122, 122–124, 125, 126–127, 129; religious persecution by, 199; with Ruiz's confession, 121–122, 122–124, 125, 126–127, 129; Satan and stance of, 199; with Vega and witchcraft, 200–209

Mexico, colonial: healers in, 202–206; witchcraft in, 201–202, 210

Mexico City, as political and economic hub, 117

miracles, 161. *See also* visions

mita (cyclical corvée), 57, 186

mitimaes (fixed residence), 40, 180

mitmaq (Inca settlers of newly conquered lands), 177, 180, 186, 189

mocambos (fugitive slave settlements), 133, 135, 148n10

monasteries, for men, 104, 154. *See also* Ocaña, Diego de

monastic institutions, population in, 104

money-lending, 55

Montejo, Francisco de, 13, 15, 16, 17, 18

Montejo Xiu, Francisco de, 18, 25

Montes, Toribio, 299, 305

Montoro, Andrés de, 124

Montufar, Juan Pío de (Marqués de Selva Alegre), 305

Moors, 2, 3, 86, 87

Mora, Rufino, 315, 316

Morales, Ana de, 200, 201, 201–202, 205–206, 207, 209

morisco, 4, 78

Mosquera, José María (don), 245, 248

Mott, Luiz, 148n11

mulatto, 4, 212n21

Muñoz, Pedro, 277, 278, 278

Murúa, Martín de, 192–193

Muslims, 2, 3

mystics, 104, 212n19. *See also* Jesús, Ursula de

Nachi Cocom, 16, 25, 27

Nahuatl, 19, 21, 25, 120, 129

Napoléon (Invasion of Iberian peninsula), 216, 218, 234, 289, 294, 295, 299

Nariño, Antonio, 299

Native Americans, 203, 212n21

native-borns. *See* originarios

natural disasters, 101, 104, 241

natural order, hierarchy of, 5

nature, 34

Navarro, Diego Lorenzo, 90

Negros, 4

Nesado, Anton, 81

New Christians, 67, 69

New Granada, 215, 239, 290
New Spain: map, viceroyalty of, 9;
  Mexican Inquisition in, 117–118,
  121–122, 122–124, 125, 126–127, 129;
  viceroys in, 7
New World: beginnings and colonial
  social order, 7–11; Iberian Peninsula
  and ties to, 1–3; map, viceroyalty of
  New Spain, 9; reasons for settling
  in, 1, 2, 3, 4; social hierarchy in, 1, 4;
  sumptuary legislation in, 3
Ninalingón, Sebastián, 42
Nobre, Domingos Fernandes
  (Tomacauna), 11; confession of,
  70–71; denounced by wife, 69;
  idolatry accusations against, 68,
  69–70; with Portuguese Inquisition,
  64, 68–72, 71; with Santidade sect,
  64, 68–70, 71; sentence of, 71–72; as
  slaver, 64, 64–65, 66; with tattoos,
  64, 70
nuns, 104, 110–111

oaths, lies under, 94n7
Obregón, Antonio de, 89, 91
Ocaña, Diego de, 99, 165–167, 168n3,
  169n8; as demandadores, 154–155,
  156; early life and entrance into
  monastery, 154; with incident in
  Saña, 158–160; influence of, 152–153;
  messages in sermons, 159; miracles
  and, 161; on mission dangers, 160;
  with mission to Peru, 154–157, 158;
  with original image of Our Lady of
  Guadalupe, 156; with rival image of
  Our Lady of Guadalupe, 158; self-
  perception with spiritual mission,
  159, 160; temptation of, 160–164,
  165; with vow of poverty, 161–164;
  writing through challenges, 157, 158
Oliveira, Anna de, 263
Olmedo, Martín de, 53
omens, 35
Oré, Luis Jerónimo de, 184
originarios (native-born members of
  Andean settlements), 180
Otzmal massacre, 16; memorial shield,
  17; repercussions, 16, 17; report on,
  16, 26

Our Lady of Guadalupe, 50, 156, 158,
  166

pachacuti (inversion of world), 36
Pacheco, Anna da Silva, 259
Padilla, Simón de, 81, 86
Palmares settlement: assault on,
  145–146; children in, 139;
  communitarian economy in,
  136–138; culture and society in,
  138–139; families in, 137, 139, 142;
  formation of, 136, 140; influence of,
  135, 147; language in, 138–139; men
  in, 136, 137; peace accords and, 143,
  144; political system in, 140, 141,
  142, 144; pottery, 147n5; religion in,
  140; terrain in, 135, 136; women in,
  136, 137, 139; Zumbi of, 99, 134,
  141–143, 142, 143–146. *See also*
  Zumbi of Palmares
parcialidades, 38, 40
pardo (dark skinned), 262, 267n11
Parejo, Bartolomé, 201, 205
pasquines (hand-written political
  lampoons), 273, 276, 280, 283
passing, 222, 222. *See also* Ayarza,
  Pedro de; whiteness
Pasto, Colombia: Bolívar on, 289; as
  loyal to Spain, 289, 291; in political
  context, 291; Quito and tensions
  with, 296; royalist movement and
  regional dimensions of, 295–296;
  royalist politics and Indian
  communities in, 300–302; as
  strategic geographic location, 290,
  291, 296; as strategic political
  location, 296. *See also* Agualongo,
  Agustín
patriarchy, Spanish law's support of,
  50–51
pax colonial, in Yucután, 20
peace accords, in Palmares settlement,
  143, 144
Pedro (Prince of Portugal), 216, 218
Pedro, Juan, 283
Peña, Fernando Lucas de la (don), 240,
  244, 245, 246–248
persecution, religious: of Jews, 2, 3,
  199; of Maya, 24–25; by Mexican

Inquisition, 199
Peru: with alphabetic literacy and European book culture, 175; with Andes in historical context, 33–34; Chachapoyas as ethnic group in, 187, 189; legislation with civil status of native population, 175; map, departments of Ayacucho and Apurimac, 183; map, viceroyalty of, 10, 217; map of, 181; Mexican Inquisition in, 117–118, 121–122, 122–124, 125, 126–127, 129; Ocaña and mission to, 154–157, 158; Roman Catholic Church in, 151–152, 153; viceroys in, 7. *See also* Huamanga, Peru; Lima, Peru; Saña, Peru
peyote, 212n19
Philip II (King of Spain), 67, 89, 119, 154, 168n4
Philip III (King of Spain), 174, 192, 193, 193, 194, 195
Philip V (King of Spain), 215
philters (magic potions), 206
physicians: Greek, 204; healers and role of, 201, 203–204; lack of licensed, 203, 204
Pires, Gertrudes, 258, 259, 260, 262–263, 264, 265, 266
Pires Monteiro, Salvador, 263
Pius V (pope), 67
Pizarro, Francisco, 7, 37
Plato, 314
political posters. *See* pasquines
politics, 1; Chi, Gaspar Antonio and, 23; in Palmares settlement, 140, 141, 142, 144
Polo, Cristóbal, 225
polygyny, 41, 45
Pombol, Marquis of (Sebastião José de Carvalho e Melo). *See* Carvalho e Melo, Sebastião José
Ponciano, Josef, 222–223, 227, 228, 229, 231, 232, 233, 234, 236n12
populations: Brazil, 257, 258; Cajamarca, 40; growth in Lima, 105; Lima's religious, 104; mocambos, 148n10; in monastic institutions, 104; Quito, 241; São Paulo, 258;

slaves in Guayaquil, 309
Porras, Martín de, 105, 112, 115n14
porteños, 270, 271, 272, 274, 279
Portugal, 1; Brazil's settlement by, 8, 216; in historical context, 63–64; Roman Catholic Church's political influence in, 2; social hierarchy in, 2; sugar economy in, 133
Portuguese Inquisition, 64, 68–72, 71, 74n6, 74n7. *See also* Holy Office of the Inquisition
Posada, Martín de, 152, 154, 158
potions, magic, 206
pottery, in Palmares, 147n5
poverty, vow of, 161–164
powers: kurakas and divine, 33; nature and divine, 34; witchcraft and mystical, 212n19
Prica, Juan (don), 52
priests, 27, 104, 128, 276; Ocaña with wealthy, 161–164; women and confessional questions from, 120

El Primer nueva corónica y buen gobierno (Guaman Poma), 174; with colonialists as predatory beasts, 177, 179; frontispiece, 176; with history rewritten of Spanish conquests, 177; with indigenous populations, colonialism and "space in between", 175; influence of, 175, 175–177, 193, 194, 196; inspiration for, 193; St. James, 177, 178; in Madrid and Copenhagen, 194, 196; with Philip III and good government, 193, 194, 195

probanza de mérito, 28
procurador (solicitor), 87
property ownership: based on inheritance and genealogy, 53; community, 50, 51–52; customs in Andes, 56–58; Spain and, 49; wills and, 57–58. *See also* Itquilla, Domingo; Sisa, Isabel
Protomedicato Real, 204, 212n31
Public Lives, Private Secrets, 225, 236n8
public punishment. *See* auto-da-fé
Puglar, Inés de, 103

punishments: for Guaman Poma, 191, 192; Maya idolatry and Franciscan, 23–25; public, 24, 25; Ruiz's sentence and, 126, 128–129; Vega's, 209

purgatory: deliverance from, 113; with indulgences purchased, 110; intercession for souls in, 110; religious dignitaries in, 110–111; time spent in, 109; visions of, 109–111, 113

purity, of blood. *See* limpieza de sangre

questionnaire, royal, 16, 21, 26

Quijada, Diego de, 24

Quilombo (film), 134

quilombos (fugitive slave settlements), 133, 135

Quipu, 173

Quito, Ecuador, 294, 297, 298; census, 241; economic evolution in, 240; ethnic makeup of, 242; juntas in, 305; life in, 240–241, 242, 242–243, 244; merchant class in, 242–243; natural disasters in, 241; Pasto and tensions with, 296; riots in, 241; textile mills in, 239. *See also* Loza, Victorina

race: mixtures, 4; passing and, 222; religious life with racism and, 111–113; Spanish Indies and legal separation of, 3–4. *See also* whiteness

racial hierarchy, 208, 259, 272

Ramalho, João, 65, 74n2

Ramírez, Bernardo, 230

Rappaport, Joanne, 59

Raynal, Abbé, 311

rebel leaders, massacre of, 305

Rebellion of the Barios (Quito, 1765), 215, 240, 255

rebellions, 5, 216, 240

Recôncavo, 64, 68, 69, 70, 71

Reconquista, 2, 3

Red Gold: The Conquest of the Brazilian Indians (Hemming), 74n2

Reducciones, 3, 43, 57, 186, 187

religions: with Christianity mixed with traditional beliefs, 3; Franciscans in Cajamarca with changes in, 41; in

Iberian Peninsula, 2; in Palmares settlement, 140; persecution of, 2, 3; as reason for settling in New World, 1; with religious buildings in Lima, Peru, 101; *See also specific religions*

religious conversions: of Amerindians to Roman Catholic Church, 2, 3, 8; Jews and forced, 2, 3, 199

Restrepo, José Manuel, 292–293

revolts: slave, 270, 272; violence and, 5, 216

revolutions, 270, 289. *See also* American Revolution; French Revolution

Rey, Josef (don), 228

Ribeira, Clara Maria (doña), 258, 260, 262, 263, 264, 266, 267n11

The Rights of Man (Sámano), 299

Río de la Plata, 215

riots, 28, 241

Riva, José de la, 278

Robespierre, Maximilian, 269, 270, 278, 285

Rocha Cardoso, Brás da, 141

Rodríguez, Bartolomé, 85

Rodríguez, Catalina, 80, 85

Rodríguez, María, 86, 87

Rodríguez Sierra, Diego, 91

Roman Catholic Church: Amerindians and conversion to, 2, 3, 8, 97, 199; Augustinians in, 41; confessional manual and, 119–121; with evangelizing of Andeans, 184–187; Franciscans in, 11, 14, 17, 18, 18, 18–19, 21, 23, 23–25, 41; free will and, 109; Holy Office of the Inquisition and, 3, 64, 67, 68, 68–72, 71, 74n6, 74n7, 104, 117–118, 121–122, 122–124, 125, 126–127, 129, 199–209; influence of, 1, 7; Jesuits in, 66, 67, 68–69, 104, 136, 184; Jews and conversion to, 2, 3, 199; Maya and influence of, 14; Muslims and conversion to, 3; in Peru, 151–152, 153; Portugal and political influence of, 2; with purgatory, 109–111, 113; with responsibility to slaves, 114n10; sexual abuse in, 27; sexual transgressions and, 119–121; Spain and political influence of, 2, 3; with

Third Church Council in Lima, 184; views on marriage, 258
Rose of Lima (saint), 102, 104, 113, 118, 126
Rousseau, Jean-Jacques, 273
Roxas, Gómez de, 80
royalism: independence era and, 292–295; Indian communities and politics of, 300–302; with movement in Pasto, 295–296; with royalist army, 294, 297–299
Royal Library of Denmark, 194
Royal Pragmatic on Marriages, 221, 222
royal questionnaires, 16, 21, 26
Ruiz, Agustina, 98; assessing case of, 125–128; denounced, 119, 121, 122; historical background of, 118; Mexican inquisition and confession of, 121–122, 122–124, 125, 126–127, 129; mystical experiences with Jesus and, 125–126, 127; mystical experiences with Virgin Mary and, 125, 127; with punishment and sentence, 126, 128–129; with sexual transgressions and Roman Catholic Church, 119–121; trial of, 121–124, 125, 126–127, 129; visions of, 125–127

Salazar, Diego de, 42
Salem, Massachusetts, 200
sales tax, 240, 241
Sámano, Juan, 299
Sambrano, Francisco, 99, 200, 201, 201–202, 203, 205–206, 207–209, 212n31
Sambrano, María, 200, 203, 205, 207, 209
Saña, Peru, 158–160
Sánchez, Melchora, 313
Sánchez, Pedro, 80
Sánchez de Aguilar, Pedro, 19, 20, 21
Sánchez de la Flor, Francisco Xavier, 218, 240, 245, 251–253
Sánchez Solano, Diego, 121, 122, 127
San Francisco, Agustina de, 105
San Joseph, Estephanía de, 105
San Martín, José de, 306, 308, 309, 312, 316

Santa Cruz Pachacuti Yamqui Salcamaygua, Juan de, 174
Santander, Francisco de Paula, 289
Santidade sect, 64, 68–70, 71
Santillana, Pedro de, 21
Santo Tomás, Manuel de, 118–119, 122
São Paulo, Brazil, 257, 258. *See also* da Silva, José Antonio
Satan, 199
schools: languages learned in, 19; for sons of nobles, 18; Yucatán and Franciscan, 18, 18–19
Sequera, Juan de, 81, 82, 86, 87
sertão (wilderness interior), 63, 64, 66, 68, 72
servants, religious, 101–102, 104, 107–108, 108–109, 111–113
Seven Years' War, 215
sexual abuse, 27, 141
sexual advances, slaves enduring, 310
sexuality, priestly, 128
sexual liaisons, benefits of, 264, 312
sexually transmitted diseases, 310
Silva, José Antonio da, 218, 258; extramarital affairs, 258, 259, 261, 262, 263, 266; illegitimate children of, 258, 261, 262, 263; wife of. *See* Ribeira, Clara Maria (doña)
Silva, José Antonio da (Paulista), 259, 260
Silva, Reginaldo Damazio da, 264
silver, 35, 38; as reason for settling in New World, 2, 3, 4; regional markets based on, 4
Sisa, Isabel (doña), 11; communal laws and, 55–56; with gender inequality and inheritance laws, 47–48; with gender inequality in historical context, 47–48; hereditary rights and, 47, 58, 59; husband's will contested by, 56, 58; with kinship and heirs, 52; last will and testament of, 48–49, 49–51, 52, 55–56, 59; personal belongings of, 50, 59; property ownership and, 57–58; with property ownership customs in Andes, 56–58; Spanish colonies, last wills and, 49; with Spanish law's support for patriarchy, 50–51

slavers, 64, 64–65, 66, 72. *See also*
Nobre, Domingos Fernandes
slavery: freedom from, 107, 266,
305–306, 312–313, 315; Guayaquil
and, 308–310; whites and
discomfort with, 310
slaves, 44n2; African, 3, 10, 13, 72, 133,
309; children, 311; with conspiracy
to revolt, 282, 283; freedom for
children of, 305–306, 312–313, 315;
fugitive, 133–134; as gifts, 264;
government's relationships with
indigenous peoples and, 298; in
Haiti, 272, 280; last wills and, 253;
literacy for, 280, 281–282, 285;
population in Guayaquil, 309;
religious servants and, 102, 104, 106,
107–108, 111–113; revolts, 270, 272;
Roman Catholic Church and
responsibility to, 114n10; sexual
advances endured by, 310; sexual
liaisons with, 264, 266; with slave-
master relationship, 270, 278, 280,
281–282, 285, 286, 311–317; sugar
and Indian, 63–64, 65, 66, 73; with
sumptuary laws, 3; trade, 63–64,
272, 273; unrest, 275–276; value of,
310, 311. *See also* Batallas, Angela;
Palmares settlement
smoking, of tobacco, 69
Soares, Antônio, 146
social hierarchy: in Iberian Peninsula,
2; in New World, 1, 4; Spanish
ideals of, 203
social status: passing and, 222; as
reason for settling in New World, 1,
2, 3
Society of Jesus. *See* Jesuits
Solsol, Baltasar, 189
sorcerer (bruja), 206
Soria, Alejandra, 169n19
Sota, Juan, 191
Sotes, Fermín, 280
South America, 215, 216
space, in between: colonial and
indigenous, 175. *See also* purgatory
Spain: castizo beget from mestizo and
woman from, 4; with distinctions
for indigenous peoples, 180, 182;
with ethnicity and healing ability,
204; French Revolution and,
289–290; higher education
requirements in, 2; honorific titles
in, 2; with ideals of social hierarchy,
203; indigenous people and legal
code of, 11; Jews expelled from, 2, 3;
kurakas and influence of, 34–36;
Ludeña's return to, 88; mulatto
beget from Negro and woman from,
4; Pasto, Colombia, as loyal to, 289,
291; property ownership and, 49;
Roman Catholic Church's political
influence in, 2, 3; with Royal
Pragmatic on Marriages, 221, 222;
social hierarchy in, 2; sumptuary
legislation in, 2; trade with South
America and, 215, 216; with
transition from Spanish to Andean
values, 43. *See also* Madrid, Spain;
New Spain
Spaniards: albino beget from morisco
woman and, 4; Castizo woman and
Spaniard beget, 4; mestizo beget
from Indian and, 4; morisco beget
from mulatto woman and, 4; torna
atrás beget from albino woman and,
4
Spanish Caribbean, 77–78
Spanish Indies: legal separation of
races in, 3–4; mature colonial order
in, 97; Roman Catholic Church and
conversions in, 97
Spanish Inquisition, 67, 68
spirits, petitioning for help, 102,
109–110
Suárez, Magdalena, 252
Suárez, Pedro, 92
Suárez de Poago, Licentiate Melchior,
80, 87–88, 94n4
Sucre, Antonio José de, 290, 306
sugar: African slaves and, 72;
economy, 4, 8, 133, 216; Indian
slaves and, 63–64, 65, 66, 73
sumptuary legislation: in New World,
3; in Spain, 2

Tacón, Miguel, 291, 297–298
Taki Unquy, 184

Talavera, Gabriel de, 154–155
tattoos, 64, 66, 70
Tawantinsuyu, 33; expansion and
    influence on, 47. *See also* Inca empire
taxes, 33, 34; head, 3, 8; indigenous
    peoples and, 3, 7; sales, 240, 241
terrain, in Palmares settlement, 135,
    136
testaments, last. *See* wills, last
testimony, 208; against Catalina, 79–80,
    81–82, 82–83, 85; of Catalina, 80, 91;
    in favor of Catalina, 83–85, 86–87,
    91; against Ludeña, 79–82, 83, 85
textile mills, 239, 245, 246
titles. *See* honorific titles
Toledo, Francisco de (don), 57, 175,
    180, 186, 186–187, 300
Tomacauna. *See* Nobre, Domingos
    Fernandes
tongues, speaking in, 69
Toral, Francisco, 14, 21, 23, 24, 25
torna atrás, 4
Torres, Tomás Andrés, 226
Torres y Portugal, Fernando de, 189
torture: for conspiracy, 283, 284, 285;
    Jesus Christ and perpetual, 102; for
    practice of idolatry, 23–24
Tozzer, Alfred, 30n14
trade: in communitarian economies,
    138; fairs, 8; routes, 247; slave,
    63–64, 272, 273; with Spain and
    South America, 215, 216; woolens
    for European goods, 249
translators. *See* Chi, Gaspar Antonio
treaties, 20–21, 27, 30n15
Trexler, Richard C, 94n6
tribute, 40–41, 55
Trinidad, Catalina de la, 121
Tupa, Hernando (don), 56
Túpac Amaru, 5, 186, 216
Túpac Inca Yupanqui, 37
Túpac Katari, 216

ugliness, 208, 212n35
UNESCO Memory of the World
    Register, 175
Uz, Fernando, 28

Valdes, Gerónimo de, 81, 82, 86

Valdes, Leonor de (doña), 89
Vargas, Leonor de, 212n35
Vásquez, Diego, 59
Vásquez Albán, Tomasa (dona), 241
Vecino (citizen), 53, 81, 82, 89, 241
Vega, Ana de, 99; accusations against,
    202, 207–208; confession of, 209;
    from healer to witch, 206–209;
    imprisonment of, 202; influence of,
    201–202, 203–204, 205–206;
    Inquisition documents about, 202,
    209; with patient's diagnosis, 200,
    201, 205; punishment for, 209; with
    source of healing materials, 212n21;
    with unlicensed status, 204, 212n31;
    with witchcraft and Mexican
    Inquisition, 200–209
Vega, El Inca Garcilaso de la, 174
Velho, Domingos Jorge, 145, 146
Venezuela, 83, 233, 299, 309, 310
Veracruz, 7, 117
Verdugo, Melchior, 37, 40
viceroyalties: map of Brazil, 10; map of
    New Spain, 9; map of Peru, 10, 217
Vieira de Melo, Bernardo, 145
Villacis, Catalina de, 89, 92, 93. *See also*
    Catalina
Villalpando, Luis de, 18

de Villaorellana (marquis), 251

Villavicencio y Guerrero, Vicente
    Isidro (don), 248–249, 249–250
violence: domestic, 51; revolts and, 5,
    216
Virgin Mary, 125, 127. *See also* Our
    Lady of Guadalupe
Virgin of Guadalupe, 152, 153, 169n7
visions: of heaven, 113; of Jesus Christ,
    102, 109, 111, 112, 112–113, 119, 124,
    125, 127; of purgatory, 109–111, 113;
    Ruiz's, 125–127
visita (inspection), 111, 182, 215
visita general (general inspection), 57
volcanic eruptions, 241
Voltaire, 274, 277

weapons, 138, 144, 146, 270, 285. *See
    also* pasquines

whiteness, 225, 226, 262; Cámara of Indies and, 221–222, 225; with census classification, 263, 265; passing and, 222, 222; price paid for, 224; purchased, 223, 234, 235; with race and status altered by Spanish monarchs, 223–225; reasons for purchasing, 223. *See also* Ayarza, Pedro de

whites, slavery and discomfort of, 310

will, free, 109

wills, last: communal laws and, 55–56; contesting of, 56, 58; hereditary rights with, 47, 58, 59; with kinship and heirs, 52, 53–55, 57–58; kuraka's, 38–39; Loza, Victorina, 253; personal belongings and, 50, 59; property ownership and, 57–58; Spanish colonies and last, 49; uses, 49

witchcraft: brujeria, 206; in colonial Mexico, 201–202, 210; Mexican Inquisition, Vega and, 200–209; mulattos and, 212n21; mystical powers of, 212n19; in Salem, 200; signs of, 201, 202

wives, husbands' right to manage capital of, 244, 245, 246

women: albino beget from Spaniard and morisco, 4; with benefits of sexual liaisons, 264, 312; as Brides of Christ, 111; castizo beget from mestizo and Spanish, 4; with confessional questions from priests, 120; convents for, 104–107, 119; as descended from goddesses, 47; with husband's right to manage capital of wife, 244, 245, 246; marriage benefits for, 246; men dominating, 5, 51; merchants, 243–244, 246;

morisco beget from Spaniard and mulatto, 4; mulatto beget from Negro and Spanish, 4; as multiple spouses for men, 44n1; in Palmares settlement, 136, 137, 139; with rearing of children, 47; sexual advances endured by slaves, 310; Spaniard beget from Spaniard and Castizo, 4; torna atrás beget from Spaniard and albino, 4. *See also* gender inequality

woolens, 249

Xavier de Ezterripa, Francisco (don), 228

Xavier de Moraes, Fancisco, 264

Xiu, Ix Kukil, 15, 21

Xiu clan, 11, 14, 16. *See also* Maya

Xulcapoma, Cristóbal (don), 41

Xulcapoma, Sancho (don), 41

Yanaconas (Andeans in service of Europeans), 180, 191

Yrazabal, Ramón, 276

Yucatán: Franciscan schools in, 18, 18–19; historical context, 13–14; monastic church in, 18, 20; riots in, 28; royal questionnaire on, 16, 21, 26. *See also* Chi, Gaspar Antonio

Zuazo Casasola, Jerónimo de, 94n5

Zublián, Diego (don), 38

Zumbi of Palmares, 99; as chief, 134, 143–146; childhood of, 134, 141; death of, 134; family of, 142; homosexuality and, 141, 148n11; influence of, 134; as refugee, 141; as resistance leader, 142–143, 143–146. *See also* Palmares settlement

About the Editor and Contributors

Kenneth J. Andrien is Edmund J. and Louise W. Kahn Chair at Southern Methodist University. He is the author of *Crisis and Decline: The Viceroyalty of Peru in the Seventeenth Century* (1985); *The Kingdom of Quito, 1690–1830: The State and Regional Development* (1995); and *Andean Worlds: Indigenous History, Culture, and Consciousness under Spanish Rule, 1532–1825* (2001). He has also coedited (with Rolena Adorno) *Transatlantic Encounters: Europeans and Andeans in the Sixteenth Century* (1991) and (with Lyman Johnson) *The Political Economy of Spanish America in the Age of Revolution, 1750–1850* (1994). He is also the author (along with Allan J. Kuethe) of *The Spanish Atlantic World in the Eighteenth Century: War and the Bourbon Reforms, 1714–1796* (forthcoming from Cambridge University Press). Professor Andrien has published numerous scholarly articles in *Past and Present, Hispanic American Historical Review, The Americas, Journal of Latin American Studies, Colonial Latin American Review*, and various books, encyclopedias, and research guides.

Rolena Adorno is Sterling Professor of Spanish and chair of the Department of Spanish and Portuguese at Yale University. She has published on a wide range of subjects in colonial textual studies, including *Colonial Latin American Literature: A Very Short Introduction* (2011); *The Polemics of Possession in Spanish American Narrative* (2007), which won the Katherine Singer Kovacs Prize from the Modern Language Association; *Guaman Poma: Writing and Resistance in Colonial Peru* (1986; rev. ed., 2000); and *Guaman Poma and His Illustrated Chronicle from Colonial Peru/Guaman Poma y su crónica ilustrada del Perú colonial* (2001). She coauthored, with Patrick Charles Pautz, *Álvar Núñez Cabeza de Vaca: His Account, His Life, and the Expedition of Pánfilo de Narváez*, 3 vols. (1999) and coedited, with Kenneth J. Andrien, *Transatlantic Encounters: Europeans and Andeans in the Sixteenth Century* (1991). She is the scholarly editor of the digital edition of *Nueva corónica y buen gobierno* at the Royal Library of Denmark (2001) (http://www.kb.dk/permalink/2006/poma/info/en/frontpage.htm).

Christiana Borchart de Moreno received her doctorate in social and economic history at the University of Bonn and later took up permanent residence in Quito, Ecuador, where she has held numerous research and academic posts. After publishing her first book on merchants in late colonial Mexico, *Los mercaderes y el capitalismo en México (1759–1778)* (1984), she turned her attention to Ecuadorian history. She has published a wide range of seminal articles in the field of socioeconomic history of the Audiencia of Quito, and a collection of her articles has appeared in book form: *La Audiencia de Quito: Aspectos económicos y sociales (siglos XVI–XVIII)* (1998). Her most recent books are: *El corregimiento de Otavalo: Territorio, población, y producción textil (1535–1808)* and *Retos de la vida. Mujeres quiteñas entre el Antiguo Régimen y la Independencia.* She has also worked on Alexander von Humboldt and his contacts in the Audiencia of Quito.

Joan Bristol is associate professor of history at George Mason University. She is author of *Christians, Blasphemers and Witches: Afro-Mexican Ritual Practice in the Seventeenth Century* (2007) and has published articles in the *Boletín General de la Nación* (Mexico) and the *Journal of Colonialism and Colonial History* as well as in several edited volumes, including *Black Mexico* (2009) and *Gender and Religion in the Atlantic World* (2009).

Noble David Cook is professor of history at Florida International University. His early work concerned demographic history, culminating in his seminal book, *Demographic Collapse: Indian Peru, 1520–1620* (1981). Since that time, he has explored a wide range of topics in colonial Spanish American social history, including his widely read study (coauthored with Alexandra Parma Cook), *Good Faith and Truthful Ignorance: A Case of Transatlantic Bigamy* (1991) and his edited and translated edition (with Alexandra Parma Cook) of Pedro de Cieza de León, *The Discovery and Conquest of Peru* (1998). His more recent books are *Born to Die: Disease and New World Conquest, 1492–1650* (1998), (coauthored with Alexandra Parma Cook) *People of the Volcano: Andean Counterpoint in the Colca Valley of Peru* (2007), and (coauthored with Alexandra Parma Cook) *The Plague Files: Crisis Management in Sixteenth-Century Seville* (2012).

Marcela Echeverri received her doctorate from New York University and is assistant professor of Latin American history and MacMillan Research Fellow at Yale University. She has written about the history of anthropology in Colombia and the history and historiography of royalism in Spanish America. Her most recent articles are "'Enraged to the Limit of Despair': Infanticide and Slave Judicial Strategies in Barbacoas, 1789–1798," published in *Slavery & Abolition* 30, no. 3 (2009): 403–26, and "Popular Royalists, Empire, and Politics in Southwestern New Granada, 1809–1819," published in the *Hispanic American Historical Review* 91, no. 2 (2011): 237–69. She is currently completing the manuscript of a book that examines the participation of Indians and slaves in the royalist forces that rose in the defense of the colonial order in southwestern New Granada during the crisis of the Spanish monarchy between 1808 and 1820.

Lyman L. Johnson is professor emeritus of history at the University of North Carolina at Charlotte as well as a leading authority on the social and economic history of Argentina in the colonial and early republican periods. He has written numerous articles and is the coauthor (with Mark A. Burkholder) of *Colonial Latin America* (2001). He has also edited (with Enrique Tandeter) *Essays on the Price History of Eighteenth-Century Latin America* (1990); *The Problem of Order in Changing Societies: Essays on Crime and Policing in Argentina and Uruguay* (1990); (with Kenneth J. Andrien) *The Political Economy of Spanish America in the Age of Revolution, 1750–1850* (1994); and (with Sonya Lipsett-Rivera) *The Faces of Honor: Sex, Shame, and Violence in Colonial Latin America* (1999). He is also the author of *Workshop of Revolution: Plebeian Buenos Aires and the Atlantic World, 1776–1810* (2011).

Mary Karasch is professor emerita of history at Oakland University in Rochester, Michigan. She is a noted authority on slavery in Brazil and received her doctorate at the University of Wisconsin. Professor Karasch has written numerous articles in her field and is the author of a seminal book on Brazilian slavery, *Slave Life in Rio de Janeiro* (1987).

Alida C. Metcalf holds the Harris Masterson Jr. chair in history at Rice University in Houston, Texas. She received her BA from Smith College in 1976 and her PhD in 1983 from the University of Texas at Austin, where she studied with Richard Graham. A specialist in Brazilian history, she is the author of *The Return of Hans Staden: A Go-between in the Atlantic World* with Eve M. Duffy (2012), *Go-betweens and the Colonization of Brazil: 1500–1600*, which was awarded the Roberto Reis BRASA Book Award in 2006, and *Family and Frontier in Colonial Brazil: Santana de Parnaíba, 1580–1822* (1992), which was awarded the Harvey Johnson Book Award in 1993 and Honorable Mention for the Bolton Prize in 1994. Her current research focuses on representations of Brazil on sixteenth-century maps and the social and architectural history of Rio de Janeiro (with Farès el Dahdah).

Kenneth Mills is professor of history and chair of the Department of History at the University of Toronto. He has published numerous articles and essays, most recently "Religion in the Early Modern World" in *The Oxford Handbook of the Atlantic World, 1450–1850*, ed. Nicholas Canny and Philip Morgan *Oxford Handbook Series* (Oxford: Oxford University Press, 2011), 433–48, and "The Naturalization of Andean Christianities," in *Cambridge History of Christianity, Volume 6: Reform and Expansion 1500–1660*, ed. R. Po-chia Hsia (Cambridge and New York: Cambridge University Press, 2007), 508–39, and has coedited a popular sourcebook of primary texts and images (with William B. Taylor and Sandra Lauderdale Graham), *Colonial Latin America: A Documentary History* (1998). Professor

Mills is also the author of *Idolatry and Its Enemies: Colonial Andean Religion and Extirpation, 1640–1750* (1997). He is currently writing a book about Ocaña's journey, and forthcoming from the University of Toronto Press is the multiauthor, multidisciplinary *Lexicon of the Hispanic Baroque: Technologies of Transatlantic Transfer and Transformation* (with Evonne Levy).

Muriel S. Nazzari is associate professor emeritus at Indiana University in Bloomington. She received her doctorate at Yale University and over the course of her career has produced several pioneering articles on race and gender in colonial Brazil. Professor Nazzari is the author of *The Disappearance of the Dowry: Women, Families, and Social Change in São Paulo, Brazil (1600–1900)* (1991).

Ana María Presta is professor of history at the University of Buenos Aires and also holds a research appointment from CONICET, at the Instituto Emilio Ravignani in Buenos Aires, Argentina. She is the author of *Encomienda, Familia y Negocios en Charcas Colonial. Los Encomenderos de La Plata, 1550–1600* (2000) and editor of *Espacio, Etnías, Frontera. Atenuaciones Políticas en el Sur del Tawantinsuyu* (1995) and the forthcoming *Qaraqara-Charca. Reflexiones a tres años después*. She has also published in *Runa, Andes, Memoria Americana, Anuario del IEHS, Población y Sociedad, Revista Andina, Histórica, Allpanchis, Historia y Cultura, Anuario del ABNB, Revista de Indias, Revista de Estudios Extremeños, Nuevo Mundo Mundos Nuevos, Colonial Latin American Review*, and *The Hispanic American Historical Review*, and in edited volumes dealing with ethnicity, gender, family, and Charcas's early colonial society.

Susan E. Ramírez holds the Neville G. Penrose chair in history at Texas Christian University and is a leading authority on Andean colonial history. Her early work concerned the growth of Spanish landed estates in northern Peru, which culminated in the publication of *Provincial Patriarchs: Land Tenure and the Economics of Power in Colonial Peru* (1986). She then turned her attention to the study of Peru's indigenous peoples in the sixteenth century, with the publication of numerous articles and her prize-winning book, *The World Upside Down: Cross-Cultural Contact and Conflict in Sixteenth-Century Peru* (1996). More recently, she summarized her broadened interest on the wider Inca empire in the book *To Feed and Be Fed: The Cosmological Bases of Authority and Identity in the Andes* (2005).

Matthew Restall is Edwin Erle Sparks Professor of Latin American History at Pennsylvania State University. His pioneering analysis of Maya-language documentation enabled him to offer new insights into the internal workings of indigenous communities in colonial Yucatán—work that contributed to the development of the New Philology movement in Mexican studies, founded by his graduate-school mentor, James Lockhart.

Professor Restall has also been at the forefront of the development of another historiographical school of scholarship, the New Conquest History, which has used new archival research and an emphasis on indigenous protagonists—like Gaspar Antonio Chi—to revise dramatically our understanding of the Spanish conquests in the Americas. Since 1995 he has published sixteen books and numerous articles and essays on the Spanish Conquest, Maya history, and the African experience in the Spanish colonies. These include *The Maya World: Yucatec Culture and Society, 1550–1850* (1997), *Maya Conquistador* (1998), *Seven Myths of the Spanish Conquest* (2003), *Invading Guatemala: Spanish, Nahua, and Maya Accounts of the Conquest Wars* (with Florine Asselbergs, 2007), *The Black Middle: Africans, Mayas, and Spaniards in Colonial Yucatán* (2009), *2012 and the End of the World: The Western Roots of the Maya Apocalypse* (with Amara Solari, 2011), and *The Conquistadors* (with Felipe Fernández-Armesto, 2011).

Zeb Tortorici is assistant professor in the Department of Spanish and Portuguese at New York University. His work centers on the intersections of sexuality, desire, colonialism, and the body in Latin America between the sixteenth and early nineteenth centuries. He has published articles in *Ethnohistory*, the *Journal of the History of Sexuality*, *History Compass*, *e-misférica*, and in the edited volumes *Death and Dying in Colonial Spanish America* and *Queer Youth Cultures*. With Martha Few, he recently coedited *Centering Animals in Latin American History* (2013), and he is currently coediting a special issue of *Radical History Review* on the topic of "queering archives." He previously held positions as visiting assistant professor in the Department of History at Tulane University and as ACLS New Faculty Fellow in the Department of History at Stanford University.

Camilla Townsend received her doctorate from Rutgers University and is professor of history at Rutgers, the State University of New Jersey. She has produced several articles as well as written a book comparing social and economic life in two distinct cities, *A Tale of Two Cities: Race and Economic Culture in Early Republican North and South America: Baltimore, Maryland, and Guayaquil, Ecuador* (2000). She is also the author of *American Indian History: A Documentary Reader* (Oxford, 2009), *Malintzin's Choices: An Indian Woman in the Conquest of Mexico* (2006), and *Pocahontas and the Powhatan Dilemma* (2004).

Ann Twinam is professor of history at the University of Texas at Austin and a noted authority on colonial Spanish America. Her first book, *Miners, Merchants, and Farmers in Colonial Colombia* (1982), provided a pathbreaking socioeconomic history of the Bourbon reforms in Medellín, Colombia. She has explored questions of gender, sexuality, and honor in a wide range of published articles and in her prize-winning recent book, *Public Lives, Private Secrets: Gender, Honor, Sexuality, and Illegitimacy in*

Colonial Spanish America (1999). Professor Twinam has published a pamphlet for the American Historical Association titled *Women and Gender in Colonial Latin America* (2007). She is finishing a monograph on the Gracias al Sacar titled "Erasing These American Defects: Pardos, Mulatos, and the Purchase of Whiteness in the Spanish Indies," under contract with Stanford University Press.

Nancy E. van Deusen is professor of history at Queen's University, Kingston, Ontario. A well-known specialist on female religious in seventeenth-century Peru, she has published numerous articles and a book, *Between the Sacred and the Worldly: Recogimiento in Colonial Lima* (2001), as well as a critical edition of writings about the mystical experiences of Ursula de Jesús, *The Souls of Purgatory: The Spiritual Diary of a Seventeenth-Century Afro-Peruvian Mystic* (2004).